ROCKY MOUNTAIN
GARDENER'S HANDBOOK

First published in 2012 by Cool Springs Press, an imprint of the Quayside Publishing Group, 400 First Avenue North, Suite 300, Minneapolis, MN 55401, USA.

The information in this book is true and complete to the best of our knowledge. All recommendations are made without any guarantee on the part of the author or Publisher, who also disclaims any liability incurred in connection with the use of this data or specific details.

We recognize, further, that some words, model names, and designations mentioned herein are the property of the trademark holder. We use them for identification purposes only. This is not an official publication.

Cool Springs Press titles are also available at discounts in bulk quantity for industrial or sales-promotional use. For details write to Cool Springs Press, 400 First Avenue North, Suite 300, Minneapolis, MN 55401, USA.

To find out more about our books, visit us online at www.coolspringspress.com.

Library of Congress Cataloging-in-Publication Data

Cretti, John L.

Rocky Mountains gardener's handbook: all you need to know to plan, plant, & maintain a Rocky Mountain garden / John Cretti, Mary Ann Newcomer.

p. cm.

Includes bibliographical references and index.

ISBN 978-1-59186-540-7

1. Landscape plants--Rocky Mountains Region. 2. Landscape gardening--Rocky Mountains Region. 3. Gardening--Rocky Mountains Region. I. Newcomer, Mary Ann. II. Title. III. Title: All you need to know to plan, plant, and maintain a Rocky Mountain garden.

SB407.C78 2012

715.09792'2--dc23

2011023106

President/CEO: Ken Fund

Group Publisher: Bryan Trandem

Publisher: Ray Wolf

Associate Publisher: Mark Johanson

Design Manager: Brad Springer

Design and Page Layout: S. E. Anderson

Printed in China

10 9 8 7 6 5 4 3 2 1

ROCKY MOUNTAIN
GARDENER'S HANDBOOK

MARY ANN NEWCOMER AND JOHN CRETTI

COOL
SPRINGS
PRESS

Growing Successful Gardeners™

MINNEAPOLIS, MINNESOTA

ACKNOWLEDGMENTS

I am grateful for the support, shared experiences and knowledge of the following:

Liz Ball, Bob Polomski, Michael Dirr, Kelly Grummons, Eleanor Welshon, Jo Kendzerski, Candace Stuart, Patt Dorsey, Don Schlup, Panayoti Kelaidis, Whitney Cranshaw, Barbara Hyde, Jerome Pfeifer, Cece Droll, Shirley Marken, the late Herb Gundell and George Kelly, Jim Feucht, Brent and Becky Heath, Felder Rushing, Karen Panter, "Mick" Paulino, Nancy Styler, Steve and Patty Imber, David Winger, Brian Gueck, the Menough brothers, Dee Lovisone, Nancy Perry, and all the gardeners who have crossed my path over the years. May your gardens grow and prosper!

Thanks to the staff of Cool Springs Press, my publisher, and the late Roger Waynik, Hank McBride, Billie Brownell, Ramona Wilkes, Mary Buckner for the encouragement and help through the journey.

Above all, give thanks to the Master Gardener of all time, our Lord and Savior, who invites us to grow in His earthly garden, rest as He stills the turbulent waters of our lives, and trust in Him as he leads us through our continuing journey.

To my family, for their simplicity of living and inspiring me to garden by following the wisdom of Nature.

—John Cretti

Thanks to the folks who got me here.

To D, my rock, forever and a day. To Nanc: my lifetime, lifeline, partyline, sublime, sound-of-mind friend. Friend isn't a big enough word. To Ruth Ann, whose wisdom and smart alleck-y attitude go hand in hand. To Bobby, my number one coach in all things moving forward.

To Susan Appleget Hurst who guided me to GWA; Debra Prinzing who holds my hand along the way; Lorene who's always got my back; and David Perry who constantly dares me to get out the crayons.

To Dave who keeps my glass full. Rod and John and Don who taught me everything I know about gardening and then some; the rest I learned from Ann DeBolt, Roger Rosentreter, and Debbie Cook. To Liz, Rita, G, Judy and Kerry, Karl, and Jayme. For my buddy in garden crimes: Jeff. Of course, thanks to the Plurkettes. Hugs to Lorene, Nan and Scott who nudge and humor me so much of the time.

To my beloved grandmother Catherine D. Norton and granddad, John M. Norton, you gave me my first place to garden.

My editors, Billie Brownell and Kathy Franz have guided me through this project and I thank them for their support and kindness. What a year it was!

And my eternal devotion is declared, now and forever, to the Timbuktu Typing Pool and Secret Sisters of Botany.

The new *Rocky Mountain Gardener's Handbook* is built on the good words and hard work of several folks. It relies heavily on several previously published Cool Springs books. I want to thank Bob and Cheryl Moore-Gough for the excellent section on vegetable gardening in the Rocky Mountains. Lynn Mill's and Dick Post's expertise was essential for gardening in Nevada. The section on sustainable gardening and the environment originally appeared in Joe Lamp'l's *The Green Gardener's Guide*. Thanks Joe. But by far the biggest thank you is for John Cretti. His books on gardening in the Intermountain West make up the backbone of this book and for that I am grateful.

—Mary Ann Newcomer

CONTENTS

WELCOME TO GARDENING

in the Rocky Mountain States

Gardeners, fresh and seasoned, are to be commended for getting their hands dirty. We garden for many reasons. Some gardeners hope not only to beautify their homes but to increase their property values with more curb appeal. For others, it's all about growing the latest, newest, biggest, and prettiest. There are some for whom gardening is about improving health and fitness by growing their own food and getting some exercise in the process. For many, gardening is about making their world a more beautiful place and spending some time with nature.

We love our part of the world for its stunning natural beauty. But majesty and grandeur go hand-in-hand with Basin and Range topography: high altitudes and hot deserts, lean and mean soils, serious water issues, and heavy population of various grazing creatures, with and without spines. Then there's our crazy-makin' weather: rain, no rain, hail the size of golf balls, and temperature extremes that can drive a gardener to distraction. Gardening here is not for the faint of heart, and there's certainly no room for sissies.

Never fear, you are in good company. Many great gardeners went before us: not just our parents and grandparents but our great-grandparents and their ancestors, who were pioneers and homesteaders across the Intermountain West. These people survived and flourished here, feeding themselves and their families from their gardens and orchards with nary a watt of air conditioning or pressurized irrigation. These hardy souls grew great gardens without the technology we rely upon to help lift the heavy load.

Rocky Mountain Gardener's Handbook was created to give you a hand up. Plants were chosen for their reliability, adaptability, and beauty. While there are hundreds of plants available to the home gardener, we couldn't include them all. I hope you are encouraged to grow the ones in the book and adventure beyond these pages on your own.

The states included in the *RMGH* include Idaho, Montana, Wyoming, Utah, Colorado, and Nevada—almost 600,000 square miles. The information will be relevant for gardeners in eastern Washington and Oregon as well. A look at the map of the region shows southern Nevada's climate more closely aligned with the garden regions of the Desert Southwest. For that reason, palms, agaves, and succulents were not included. In many instances, you will be advised to check with your County Extension Office for best local practices in your town. A helpful list of regional resources is included on page 244.

To the determined gardener in the Rocky Mountains, keep this thought in mind from Henry Mitchell, *The Essential Earthman*:

> There are no green thumbs or black thumbs. There are only gardeners and non-gardeners. Gardeners are the ones who ruin after ruin get on with the high defiance of nature herself, creating in the very face of her chaos and tornado, the bower of roses and the pride of irises. It sounds very well to garden a "natural way." You may see the natural way in any desert, any swamp, any leech-filled laurel hell. Defiance on the other hand, is what makes gardeners.

Now, go ahead and dig in.

USDA COLD HARDINESS ZONES

Cold-hardiness zone designations were developed by the United States Department of Agriculture (USDA). They are based on the minimum average temperatures all over the country. Each variation of 10 degrees Fahrenheit represents a different zone, indicated by colored bands on a zone map. Because perennial plants, whose roots survive winter, vary in their tolerance for cold, it is important to choose those plants that are suitable for the zone for your region of the Rockies. Consult this map to learn in which zone you live. Most of the plants in this book will perform well throughout the region. Though a plant may grow (and grow well) in zones other than its recommended cold-hardiness zone, it is best to select plants labeled for your zone, or warmer.

In this book, the zone notation means the plant is hardy down to the stated zone. However, these zones are only guidelines and not hard and fast rules limiting what you can or cannot grow. Each landscape includes mini-zones (called microclimates) that no zone map can indicate. Microclimates vary from the surrounding area due to topography, exposure to wind, heat, and sun, drainage, soil texture, and other factors. These differences in microclimates may affect zone ratings by as much as two hardiness zones. The important thing to remember is that no zone system is perfect and it should only be used as a guide. Experiment by growing different plants and have fun in your gardening endeavors.

SUN PREFERENCES

Full sun is six hours or more of direct sun per day. Part sun is four to six hours of direct sun, preferably in the morning with protection from hot afternoon sun. Part shade is two to four hours of direct sun per day, primarily in the morning, or all day bright indirect light. Shade means all indirect light or dappled shade.

FULL SUN	☼
PART SUN	☼
PART SHADE	☼
SHADE	☀

COLORADO, IDAHO, MONTANA, NORTHERN NEVADA, UTAH, AND WYOMING COLD HARDINESS ZONES

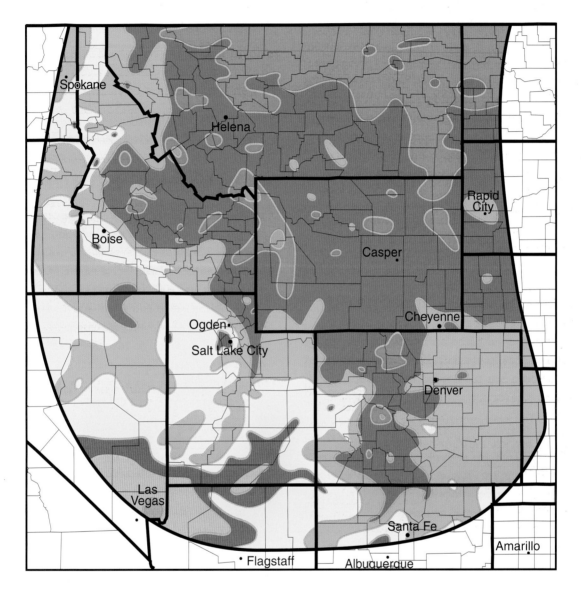

ZONE	Average Annual Min. Temperature (°F)	ZONE	Average Annual Min. Temperature (°F)	ZONE	Average Annual Min. Temperature (°F)
2	-40 to -50	5	-10 to -20	8	20 to 10
3	-30 to -40	6	0 to -10	9	30 to 20
4	-20 to -30	7	10 to 0	10	40 to 30

ANNUALS
for the Rocky Mountain States

Annuals have been part of gardening for thousands of years. The Chinese created flower gardens, and China is believed to be where the chrysanthemum originated. In Babylon, Persia, Egypt, and Greece, annuals were featured in the homes of the wealthy. Flowers were not valued in the Middle Ages, but interest re-emerged because plants could be valuable for food, medicine, and other practical purposes. Later, biological expeditions were organized to seek out new and rare flowers. During this period, flowers were introduced into Europe from Brazil, Mexico, Australia, Japan, China, and the United States. This led to the crossing of new and interesting varieties.

Annuals by definition are plants that complete their life cycles within a year and then die. In nature, the life cycle begins at the start of the growing season when the seed germinates. Marigolds, petunias, and zinnias are just some examples. Annuals grow long enough to produce flowers followed by seeds for the next generation. Generally speaking, annuals mean color!

GARDENERS WITHOUT GARDENS

Annuals lend themselves to container gardening as well. Hanging baskets of annual flowers spilling over the sides add beauty and a new dimension to patios, decks, and to downtown streetscapes. The choice of containers is limitless. As home lots have become progressively smaller and buildings take priority over open spaces, many people don't have access to a full-fledged garden. But we still have window ledges, front steps, balconies, and backyards. This presents a new challenge—to become gardeners without gardens. Growing annuals in containers is an innovative way to go. We now have compact annuals, which are ideal for containers. Garden centers stock easy-to-handle soil and pottery that blends with the plant to produce a rather pleasing effect. Almost every style of gardening that can be expressed in a full-size garden can be replicated in a container garden.

THE UNIQUENESS OF ANNUALS

Annuals can be hardy, half-hardy, or tender. These terms indicate the temperature ranges that various

BEGONIA

annual seeds need in order to germinate (or sprout) and grow successfully, and the plant's ability to endure freezing or subfreezing temperatures after sprouting. These two separate criteria account for the seeming paradox of some annuals, such as the sunflower, whose seeds survive outdoors in regions of subfreezing winters but germinate after the last frost and produce tender plants. In this case, the seed is hardy but the plants themselves are not. Plant hardiness terms identify the two most important dates to know: the last expected frost in spring and the first anticipated frost in fall.

Some annuals are more tender than others. In this case, wait to plant until temperatures consistently exceed 45°F. These tender annuals are noted in the book by the following icon: 45°

Annuals are specialists at producing seeds. They invest their energy in making as many seeds as possible during the growing season and then die, often from exhaustion. They bloom more quickly, more freely, and longer than any other types of plants. An important task to remember is to remove the spent flowers (called "deadheading"). This will increase and extend the flowering for the whole season. Petunias, for example, really respond to this. The result will be lots of flowers

COSMOS

right up until the first killing frost in fall. A complete fertilizer added according to directions for weekly use will reward you with exceptional blooms, especially for those annuals in containers and those on drip irrigation systems.

And don't forget wildflowers! They add an exciting dimension to gardens. We all know how dramatic they are in the desert; they can also have a dramatic effect in your yard. But to duplicate a desert environment, be sure to stay away from planting everything in straight rows.

UNSELFISH ANNUALS

Annual flowers unselfishly give continuous color all summer long. Because of their brilliance, annuals instantly transform a drab landscape into a refreshing scene. They represent a good starting point for the first-time gardener. You can easily correct any mistake made with annuals, and they are so versatile!

Annuals provide an opportunity to grow huge plants (think sunflowers), to produce pleasant or weird color combinations, to grow edible flowers for the dinner table, or to provide an array for cut-flower arrangements.

Because annuals can form a basic component of any landscape design, they are often overlooked in the planning process—but they shouldn't be, as they offer so much color and variety to any garden.

CLEOME

ALYSSUM
Lobularia maritima

Why It's Special—Sweet alyssum is prized for its wonderful fragrance and dainty blossoms. One of the easiest of garden annuals to grow, alyssum is showy in containers, flowerbeds, or as an edging plant. It's especially charming when allowed to spread in gravel pathways. 'Clear Crystals' is a mix of lavender, purple, and white with extra- large blossoms. 'Allure Bronze' is difficult to find, but the dusty pink/ apricot color is a nice addition to plantings.

How to Plant & Grow—Direct seed into the garden after the danger of frost has passed. Plants may be purchased in 6 packs or cell packs and planted 9 to 12 inches apart.

Care & Problems—Alyssum appreciates good drainage, and can go without water for short periods of time after it has become established. It has no problems to speak of.

Color(s): White, purple, rose, cream, lavender, and pink

Peak Season: Late spring until the first hard frost

Mature Size (H x W): 3 to 9 in. x 12 to 16 in.

Water Needs: Moderate to low

BACOPA
Sutera cordata

Why It's Special—Bacopa is a very popular trailing plant for container gardens, especially hanging baskets and window boxes. It also makes a nicely matted ground cover as an edging for flowerbeds. Its long stems are covered with blossoms all season.

How to Plant & Grow—Plant in late spring after the danger of frost has passed. Bacopa is happy in full sun or part shade. Space plants 8 to 10 inches apart. It will benefit from a slow-release fertilizer. Place plants at the edge of a container so the plants can trail over the sides.

Care & Problems—Do not allow bacopa to dry out. Water deeply and on a regular schedule. Aphids may pose a problem. Apply insecticidal soap according to the instructions, or spray with a garden hose to knock the insects from the plant.

Color(s): White, pink, and lavender blue

Peak Season: Early summer until the first hard frost

Mature Size (H x W): 4 to 8 in. x 12 to 24 in.

Water Needs: Moderate

BAT-FACED CUPHEA
Cuphea spp.

Why It's Special—Bat-faced cuphea gets its name from the unique bat-like appearance of the blossoms. The pink or red petals of the blossoms are the "ears" and the dark throat resembles a bat's face. Little white tips on the blossom resemble eyes. It's a very heavy bloomer with a nicely mounded shape and adds pizzazz to beds, borders, window boxes, and all containers.

How to Plant & Grow—Plant in late spring after the danger of frost has passed. It prefers sunny exposures with well-drained soil. Space plants 8 to 12 inches apart. It benefits from a slow-release fertilizer.

Care & Problems—Allow the soil surface to dry out between deep waterings. The plants do not like wet soil. There are possible issues with whiteflies and aphids. Use insecticidal soap to control (but read instructions *carefully*).

Color(s): Red, pink, and orange with purple and white accents

Peak Season: Early summer until the first hard frost

Mature Size (H x W): 12 to 24 in. x 12 to 24 in.

Water Needs: Low once established

BIDENS
Bidens ferulifolia

Why It's Special—Also called Mexican gold, bidens put on a sunny show in the hottest part of the summer. Its wispy foliage and trailing habit make this an excellent spiller for container combinations and a lush filler for hanging baskets. 'Pirate's Treasure' is a newer variety, sporting masses of double, deep yellow blossoms. 'Pirate's Pearl' is the first white variety to reach the market. 'Lemon Star' is a new bicolor.

How to Plant & Grow—Plant in late spring after the danger of frost has passed in full or part sun. Space plants 12 inches apart. Plants will appreciate an application of a granular, slow-release fertilizer when they're planted.

Care & Problems—Bidens have regular water requirements. Just be sure to let the top of the soil dry out between deep, regular watering. There are no pests to speak of.

Color(s): Bright yellow, deep yellow, lemon yellow, bicolors, and white

Peak Season: Early summer until the first hard frost

Mature Size (H x W): 10 to 12 in. x 12 to 24 in.

Water Needs: Regular

CALENDULA
Calendula officinalis

Why It's Special—Also known as pot marigold, organically grown calendula flower petals can be used as colorful additions to green salads. Pot marigolds make a vibrant hedging plant for the vegetable garden. The orange blossoms really stand out when planted with purple eggplants, dark kales, and plants with blue blossoms. A mix of calendula varieties in a large container with red and green lettuces, spring onion sets, and baby bok choi will make an edible "patio salad bowl."

How to Plant & Grow—Direct sow seeds in the garden in late spring in a sunny spot. Thin to 12 inches apart when plants have their second full set of leaves. Removing spent flowers (called "deadheading") will encourage continuing bloom. In very hot regions, pot marigold benefits from some afternoon shade. Most varieties gently reseed.

Care & Problems—You may allow soil to dry out between waterings. Calendula has no problems.

Color(s): Bright yellow, lemon, orange, apricot, and pale pink

Peak Season: Early summer until the first hard frost

Mature Size (H x W): 6 to 18 in. x 12 in.

Water Needs: Low

COLEUS
Solenostemon scutellarioides

Why It's Special—Coleus is not just for grandma's garden anymore. This striking foliage plant is perfect for container gardens. Coleus leaves are variegated, ruffled, wavy, or smooth, and many have deeply scalloped edges. A most desirable choice for container combinations, coleus can be paired with hot orange or fuchsia-colored blossoms or with soft pastel blossoms for a cooler look. The new sun coleus varieties (particularly the red ones) are able to withstand more sun than the older varieties.

How to Plant & Grow—Set out plants after the last frost. Pinch flower buds to encourage branching and lush foliage development. An application of slow-release fertilizer will keep them strong throughout the season.

Care & Problems—Coleus loves moist, well-drained soil. It's a plant that's relatively free of pests and diseases, but can be munched on by earwigs and slugs. Use deterrents like diatomaceous earth and homemade traps. Earwigs are easily trapped between sheets of moistened newspaper set at the base of the plants.

Color(s): The range of foliage colors is vast. You will find color combinations of green, red, pink, chartreuse, burgundy, plum, pumpkin, white, rose, maroon, yellow, cream, and bronze.

Peak Season: Leaves all summer long (it's not grown for blooms)

Mature Size (H x W): 12 to 24 in. x 24 to 36 in.

Water Needs: Moderate

COSMOS
Cosmos bipinnatus and *C. sulphureus*

Why It's Special—A cottage garden favorite for decades, cosmos are one of the easiest annuals to grow. They come in a wide range of colors, and some varieties, such as 'Seashells Mix', have intriguing tubular petal formations, handsome feathery foliage, and daisylike heads that wave in the breeze. Scattered throughout a flower border or in large drifts, these heat lovers are a delightful "must have" for the summer garden.

How to Plant & Grow—Plant seeds in late spring as soon as the soil has warmed. Cosmos loves well-drained, fertile soil. Thin and transplant to 18 inches apart. When the plants reach 18 to 24 inches tall, pinch back the main stem to encourage bushier growth.

Care & Problems—Cosmos will appreciate a good, deep, occasional watering. Cosmos flowers are subject to earwig damage. Set out traps made from sheets of moistened newspaper sheets or deter with diatomaceous earth.

Color(s): White, rose, pink, orange, yellow, lavender pink, deep red, wine red, peach, soft yellow, and bicolor

Peak Season: Midsummer to the first frost

Mature Size (H x W): 2 to 6 ft. x 2 ft.

Water Needs: Low

DUSTY MILLER
Senecio cineraria

Why It's Special—Dusty miller is a handsome foliage plant for the summer garden, and it "cools down" the bold colors in the flower garden. Dusty miller tolerates heat and performs well as a water-thrifty annual. The genus name *Senecio* comes from the Latin for "old man"; the name refers to the thick mat of white whiskers covering the leaves. It looks especially handsome with purple- or blue-flowering plants or pink geraniums. Dusty miller is also available in various foliage shapes. It makes a very good edging or border plant.

How to Plant & Grow—Plant in late spring after the danger of frost has passed. Dusty miller enjoys sunny exposure with well-drained soil. Space plants 6 to 12 inches apart. Pinch back leaf tips to encourage bushier growth.

Care & Problems—Once established, dusty miller is quite drought tolerant. In fact, it will rot if the soil is too wet. The plants are virtually free of insects and diseases.

Color(s): Silver

Peak Season: Summer (grown for foliage only)

Mature Size (H x W): 6 to 15 in. x 12 in.

Water Needs: Low

FAN FLOWER
Scaveola spp.

Why It's Special—The unusual, fan-shaped flowers and trailing habit make this a noteworthy plant for hanging baskets, container gardens, and window boxes. Fan flower can take the heat of our hot dry climates. It is exceptionally low maintenance, requiring no deadheading and only a regular drink of water. Look for 'Whirlwind Blue'—actually lavender-blue—or 'Spring Secret' and 'New Wonder' for soft blue flowers.

How to Plant & Grow—Scaveola likes fertile, lightweight, well-drained soil (not heavy clay). It works well with white and pastel flowers and lime green- or gray-foliage plants. The interesting shape of the flowers stands out when used with petunias and million bells. It's a tender annual, so plant in late spring after the danger of frost has passed.

Care & Problems—There are no problems associated with fan flowers, which makes them an exceptional choice for today's busy gardeners.

Color(s): White, blue, and lavender

Peak Season: Early summer until first hard frost

Mature Size (H x W): 9 to 18 in. x 12 to 24 in.

Water Needs: Moderate

FLOWERING KALE

Brassica oleracea (Acephala Group)

Why It's Special—Flowering kale and ornamental cabbage are prized for their highly ornamental leafy rosettes in deep, rich colors. Flowering kale develops a looser head with fringed leaves, whereas flowering cabbage develops a tighter head with smooth-edged leaves. It definitely prefers cool temperatures, making it a great end of summer through early winter plant.

How to Plant & Grow—Flowering kale is especially effective when planted as a single color in groups of five or more. Plant single colors to outline beds of other cool-tolerant plants such as pansies and calendulas in spring; plant with mums in the fall. Use in containers (including hollowed out pumpkins and large squash) for accents and late-season color.

Care & Problems—Allow the soil surface to dry out between waterings. Flowering kale is not especially susceptible to pests or diseases. Just remove the occasional unsightly or old leaf through the growing season.

Color(s): White, cream, purple, maroon, and variegated

Peak Season: Late summer through early winter

Mature Size (H x W): 10 to 18 in. x 18 to 24 in.

Water Needs: Moderate

FLOWERING TOBACCO

Nicotiana spp.

Why It's Special—The incredible old-fashioned 'Only the Lonely' is a towering 5-foot-tall plant with intensely fragrant, white, trumpet-shaped flowers. The new hybrids, Perfume series and Sensation Mix, have been scaled down for smaller gardens. They come in luscious colors and are especially fragrant at night.

How to Plant & Grow—Flowering tobacco likes good, light, well-drained soil. It works well paired with other white and pastel flowers, and lime green or gray foliage plants. Lime green *N. langsdorfii* looks handsome planted next to a bronze ninebark or purple smokebush. All varieties will appreciate some afternoon shade, especially in very hot areas.

Care & Problems—Flowering tobacco is a plant that needs regular watering. The tall varieties may need staking.

Color(s): Deep red, white, lime green, and pink

Peak Season: All summer

Mature Size (H x W): 9 to 18 in. x 6 to 9 in. for short varieties. 24 in. x 5 ft. ('Only the Lonely')

Water Needs: Regular

FOUR O'CLOCKS

Mirabilis jalapa

Why It's Special—A sentimental cottage garden favorite, the gaily colored, trumpet-shaped flowers open in the late afternoon, but only on dry, uncloudy days. Very easy to grow and care for, four o'clocks are loved by hummingbirds and pollinating moths, and many forms are fragrant. It reseeds freely but seedlings are easy to remove and transplant.

How to Plant & Grow—Plant in late spring after the danger of frost has passed. Four o'clocks need sunny exposure with well-drained soil. Space plants 18 to 24 inches apart. Trim plants to encourage fullness and more blooms. **Note:** *All parts of this plant are toxic. It is not for use where children or pets can reach them.*

Care & Problems—Water deeply once a week. Plants may require staking. Grasshoppers can be a problem; handpick them or use diatomaceous earth as a deterrent.

Color(s): Yellow, rose, white, red, magenta, striped and marbled

Peak Season: Early summer until first hard frost

Mature Size (H x W): 18 to 24 in. x 24 in.

Water Needs: Low

GERANIUM

Pelargonium hybrids

☼

Why It's Special—Geraniums offer bright, cheerful color for summer gardens and containers. Use them in containers, flowerbeds, and window boxes. Ivy geranium (*Pelargonium peltatum*) with its trailing stems is an excellent choice for hanging baskets.

How to Plant & Grow—Plant in late spring after the danger of frost has passed where they will get plenty of sun. Space 12 to 15 inches apart. Remove faded flowers to encourage more blooms. Apply an organic, slow-release plant food.

Care & Problems—Allow the surface of the soil to dry out between deep watering. Geraniums are susceptible to budworms; the tiny caterpillars tunnel into the developing buds. Buds that don't open, flowers with chewed or missing petals, and small holes in foliage leaves are indicators of budworms. Treat the plants early in the season with a dusting of *Bacillus thuringiensis*; follow label directions.

Color(s): Red, purple, pink, orange, white, fuchsia, salmon, and burgundy

Peak Season: Early summer until the first hard frost

Mature Size (H x W): 12 to 24 in. x 12 to 24 in.

Water Needs: Moderate

HYBRID ANGEL WING BEGONIA

Begonia spp. 'Dragon Wing'

☼ 45°

Why It's Special—An excellent annual for shady areas, the shiny green leaves and drooping scarlet flowers will brighten containers and hanging baskets. The plant will mound 15–18 in. tall and will have a nonstop show of blooms from May until October.

How to Plant & Grow—Hybrid angel wing begonias are purchased as potted plants. They love a moderately moist soil and would appreciate any humidity you can provide for them. Plant in fast-draining soil, and feed regularly with an organic, well-balanced plant food.

Care & Problems—Keep the plants well groomed, removing any debris like spent blossoms or dried leaves.

Color(s): Purple, maroon, pink, silver, gold, white, green, striped, swirled, and so forth

Peak Season: Late spring until the first hard frost

Mature Size (H x W): 18 in. x 6 to 18 in.

Water Needs: Moderate to high

IMPATIENS

Impatiens walleriana

☼ ☼ 45°

Why It's Special—These brightly colored annuals dress up a shady garden, container, or window box. Older varieties are well adapted to shade; newer varieties will tolerate some sun. Single plants can grow into a flower-covered mound. They are exceptionally nice in mass plantings and light-filtered woodland settings. New Guinea varieties have variegated foliage.

How to Plant & Grow—Plant in late spring after the danger of frost has passed, in well-drained soil. Space plants 10 to 12 inches apart. Remove faded flowers to encourage more blooms.

Care & Problems—Do not let impatiens dry out. They need well-drained soil that remains consistently moist, but not wet. Slugs, snails, and earwigs can be a problem. Sprinkle used coffee grounds around the plants or use a commercial deterrent (bait) or homemade traps. Read and follow label instructions.

Color(s): Red, pink, orange, white, fuchsia, salmon, lavender, yellows, apricot, and bicolor

Peak Season: Early summer until first hard frost

Mature Size (H x W): 12 to 18 in. x 12 to 18 in.

Water Needs: High

LANTANA
Lantana camara

☀ 45°

Why It's Special—Lantana is a rugged annual; it is very drought tolerant with the ability to handle the heat in the high deserts of the Intermountain West. Also called shrub verbena, the tiny blossoms are clustered together, sometimes in several shades of the same color within the same cluster. It makes an eye-catching display when trailing over the side of a container or window box.

How to Plant & Grow—Purchase small plants as soon as the danger of frost has passed. Plant them near the edge of your container. A slow-release fertilizer will keep it blooming all season.

Care & Problems—*Lantana camara* is not bothered by insects. When the leaves are crushed or bruised, some find the fragrance unpleasant. Be mindful of this when planting it near a busy area of the garden.

Color(s): White, orange, yellow, red, apricot, and multicolor

Peak Season: Early summer until the first hard frost

Mature Size (H x W): 18 in. x 3 ft.

Water Needs: Low

LARKSPUR
Consolida ambigua

☀ ☀

Why It's Special—Known to some as the "annual delphinium," larkspur has many single flowers along the stem in spike formation, generally in very rich shades of blue. Grow it in a sunny border and be sure to plant enough for cutting. Once they are well established in the garden, this vivid flower is more tolerant of dry soil.

How to Plant & Grow—Sow seeds as soon as the ground is workable. They may be broadcast sown, which means tossing seed into the garden and lightly covering with soil. This will result in a very soft, random type of planting. Thin to 12 inches apart. **Note:** *All parts of this plant are toxic. It is not for use where children or pets can reach them.*

Care & Problems—Slugs and snails may be problematic with larkspur. If so, sprinkle coffee grounds or a commercial bait over the area to repel them. Larkspur will reseed; to keep it in check, pull seedlings when they're small.

Color(s): Deep blue, other shades of blue, white, and pink

Peak Season: Early summer

Mature Size (H x W): 18 to 36 in. x 12 in.

Water Needs: Moderate

LOVE-IN-A-MIST
Nigella damascena

☀ ☀

Why It's Special—Love-in-a-mist is an old-fashioned favorite. Its romantic name refers to the pastel blossoms that hover above soft, green, fernlike foliage. The most beautiful forms of this annual are those with clear sky blue or delphinium blue blossoms. The horned seedpods give this plant another common name, devil-in-a-bush. Love-in-a-mist's inflated seedpods, with their maroon stripes, are quite attractive and can be used, either fresh or dried, in floral arrangements.

How to Plant & Grow—It can be planted in early spring and tolerates cool temperatures. It's best sown from seed directly in the garden. Thin seedlings 6 to 8 inches apart. Use love-in-a-mist in the perennial garden to fill open spots, or let it self-sow in the vegetable and herb garden for accents. Used in a rose garden, this annual's flowers and fernlike foliage accent the roses.

Care & Problems—Love-in-a-mist has regular water needs but is somewhat drought tolerant. It doesn't have any pest or disease problems.

Color(s): Blue, rose, and white

Peak Season: Early summer

Mature Size (H x W): 12 to 18 in. x 6 to 8 in.

Water Needs: Regular

MARIGOLD
Tagetes spp.

Why It's Special—Easy to grow, vibrant marigolds stand out like bright lights in the annual flowerbed. The French marigold with fernlike foliage grows 6 to 14 inches tall. Flowers may be single, double, or crested. Marigolds offer brilliant color for mass plantings.

How to Plant & Grow—Seeds germinate in seven to ten days, depending on soil temperature. Set out transplants after the danger of frost has passed. Marigolds prefer warm weather and full sun, but tolerate some light shade. Depending on the type, space marigolds 6 to 15 inches apart.

Care & Problems—Water once or twice a week but don't get water on the flowers, or you will shorten their lives. Deadhead (remove) faded flowers often to stimulate more blooms and to keep the plants tidy. During hot weather watch for spider mites, which cause the foliage to turn silvery gray. Hose down foliage to discourage these pests.

Color(s): Bright yellow, gold, orange, lemon yellow, pale cream, and blends

Peak Season: Early summer to frost

Mature Size (H x W): 6 to 36 in. x 6 to 18 in.

Water Needs: Moderate

MILLION BELLS
Calibrachoa spp.

Why It's Special—A nonstop bloomer, this is a *must-have* annual for the summer garden. Resembling small petunias, million bells love full sun, can take a little shade, and are trouble free. They come in a riot of colors and look fantastic in hanging baskets or trailing over containers; they combine beautifully with spiky plants or any of the sweet potato vines.

How to Plant & Grow—Plant in late spring after the danger of frost has passed, in well-drained soil. Space plants 10 to 12 inches apart. Remove faded flowers to encourage more blooms. They will appreciate an application of slow-release plant food.

Care & Problems—Do not let million bells dry out. They need well-drained soil that remains consistently moist, but not wet. Slugs, snails, and earwigs can be a problem. Sprinkle used coffee grounds around the plants or use a commercial deterrent (bait) or homemade traps. Read and follow label instructions.

Color(s): Red, pink, orange, white, hot pink, yellow, lavender, dark blue, and light blue

Peak Season: Early summer until the first hard frost

Mature Size (H x W): 12 to 30 in. x 12 to 18 in.

Water Needs: High

MOSS ROSE
Portulaca grandiflora

Why It's Special—Moss rose is able to survive and bloom in the most inhospitable places—dry, parched, poor soils in full sun. The bright, satiny flowers bloom profusely on succulent, reddish stems. Flowers are 1 to 2 inches in single or double forms.

How to Plant & Grow—Plant after the danger of frost has passed, with a sunny exposure in well-drained soil. Space plants 6 to 9 inches apart. Remove faded flowers to encourage more blooms. Moss rose is quick to establish, sprawling and trailing along the ground. The creeping stems hug the ground, making it an excellent ground cover.

Care & Problems—Water soil only as it becomes dry; do *not* overwater. Moss rose can withstand drought conditions, but will maintain vigorous growth with regular supplemental watering. Moss rose has no pest or disease problems.

Color(s): Red, yellow, scarlet, magenta, pink, orange, and white

Peak Season: Early summer until the first hard frost

Mature Size (H x W): 4 to 6 in. x 6 to 10 in.

Water Needs: Low

21

NASTURTIUM
Tropaeolum majus

☀ ◐

Why It's Special—Nasturtiums have been grown for centuries and are still in favor today. 'Empress of India', dating from the Victorian era, is a deep vermillion red with nicely contrasting blue-green foliage. They come in mounding or trailing varieties, with green, blue-green, or variegated foliage and can be very showy in hanging baskets. The blossoms are a wonderful addition to a salad (if grown organically).

How to Plant & Grow—After your last frost date, nasturtiums can be directly seeded into flowerbeds or containers. Plant them 8 to 12 inches apart in good, loose soil. In very hot areas, afternoon shade is a must.

Care & Problems—Water thoroughly every few days. Occasionally there may be aphids and slugs; a strong water spray will remove the aphids. Coffee grounds sprinkled at the base of plants will discourage slugs.

Color(s): Deep red, orange, salmon, cream, yellow, and bicolor

Peak Season: Summer

Mature Size (H x W): 6 to 12 in. (tall or trailing) x 6 to 9 in. wide

Water Needs: Moderate

PANSY
Viola x wittrockiana

◐

Why It's Special—These old-fashioned flowers perform with gusto in spring and fall. Fall-planted pansies continue to flower through November and poke their faces out of melting snow in winter. Johnny-jump-ups (*Viola tricolor*) are a welcome sight in the garden with their charming purple, yellow, and white faces.

How to Plant & Grow—Pansies are best treated as annuals; they begin to lose their vitality by the second year. They like a little shade. Exposure to the afternoon sun dries the plants out quickly. Pansies do best in cool weather. Space plants 6 to 9 inches apart in groupings of three or more. In autumn, plant them over newly planted bulbs.

Care & Problems—Pansies perform best in uniformly moist soils. If slugs or snails become an issue, sprinkle used coffee grounds around plants. Earwigs love the foliage and blooms. Set out homemade traps or deter with diatomaceous earth. Removing faded flowers encourages more blooms.

Color(s): Blue, purple, white, splotched, orange, mahogany, multicolor and violet.

Peak Season: Early summer until the first hard frost

Mature Size (H x W): 6 to 9 in. x 6 to 9 in.

Water Needs: Moderate

PENTAS
Pentas lanceolata

☀ ◐ ⬡45°

Why It's Special—Star-shaped clusters of blossoms make this an attractive annual for full to nearly full sun sites. Pentas is sometimes called the "Star of India" because of the small five-petaled, star-shaped blossoms. The 3- to 4-inch flower clusters are held on upright stems above rich green, deeply veined leaves. Pentas is very showy and attracts butterflies and hummingbirds.

How to Plant & Grow—Plant in late spring after the danger of frost has passed, in well-drained soil. Space plants 16 inches apart. Remove faded flowers to encourage more blooms. Don't allow them to dry out. Pentas plants appreciate an application of slow-release, all-season fertilizer, preferably one that is low in nitrogen.

Care & Problems—Slugs and snails can be a problem with pentas. To prevent this, sprinkle used coffee grounds or apply a commercial deterrent according to the label instructions.

Color(s): Red, white, pink, and lilac

Peak Season: Early summer until the first hard frost

Mature Size (H x W): 12 to 24 in. x 12 to 24 in.

Water Needs: Moderate

PERSIAN SHIELD
Strobilanthes spp.

Why It's Special—A stunning foliage plant for the summer garden, the metallic sheen of the purple leaves makes Persian shield a sought-after companion plant for showy container groupings. It's especially handsome grown with other purple plants or plants with hot pink or silver coloring. Consider a trailing silver dichondra and hot pink impatiens for companion planting. Persian shield occasionally shows a pale purple bloom.

How to Plant & Grow—Plant in late spring after the danger of frost has passed, in rich, well-drained soil. Space plants 16 inches apart. Pinch the tips of the branches to encourage fullness. In high heat areas, the plants will perform the best, and the foliage will color up handsomely in partly shady sites.

Care & Problems—Persian shield needs regular, deep watering although you can allow the surface of soil to dry out between waterings. It doesn't have any problems.

Color(s): Iridescent pink and purple

Peak Season: A foliage plant, lushest in the summer

Mature Size (H x W): 1 to 3 ft. x 1 to 3 ft.

Water Needs: High

PETUNIA
Petunia x *hybrida*

Why It's Special—Many varieties of petunias exist and range from ground cover types to giant, mounded plants. They may have double blossoms; smooth, clear blossoms; deeply-veined blossoms; or pinwheel-striped blossoms.

How to Plant & Grow—Petunias are best set out as small plants. Do *not* put them out until all danger of frost is past. Some varieties need deadheading but most of the newer ones do not. Use a time-release, granular fertilizer to feed them all summer.

Care & Problems—Regular, deep watering is a must, especially when temperatures reach 90 degrees Fahrenheit. Ground cover varieties need water more often. Some years budworms may pose a problem. Plants can be dusted with Bt (*Bacillus thuringiensis*) or DE (diatomaceous earth). Apply according to package instructions.

Color(s): Red, terra cotta, pink, white, yellow, purple, almost black with lime green, magenta, striped, and veined

Peak Season: Early summer until the first hard frost

Mature Size (H x W): 4 to 24 in. x 12 to 60 in. (trailing)

Water Needs: Moderate to high

SALVIA
Salvia spp.

Why It's Special—*Salvia splendens* is a popular bedding and container plant for summer. Reliable newer varieties include 'Sizzler' and 'Salsa'. Another type of annual, *Salvia guarantica*, is much taller and works well in larger gardens. 'Black and Blue' is very showy with deep blue flowers, black stems, and bright, almost lime green foliage.

How to Plant & Grow—Purchase and plant annual salvias when all danger of frost is past. The *S. splendens* types work well in mass border plantings. The taller pineapple sage or 'Black and Blue' can be used as border accents or dramatic centerpieces in large containers.

Care & Problems—All varieties are widely adaptable and can tolerate some dryness. Aphids may be a problem for salvia. A quick, hard shower of water from the hose nozzle will wash them off.

Color(s): Red, pink, white, purple, blue, and apricot

Peak Season: Early summer until the first hard frost

Mature Size (H x W): 12 in. to 18 in. x 12 in. to 36 in.

Water Needs: Low to moderate

SNAPDRAGON
Antirrhinum majus

☼

Why It's Special—Snapdragons, also called "snaps," are cottage garden favorites and especially fun for small children, whose little fingertips can fit into the "dragon's" mouth of the blossoms. Choose tall varieties for the back of the border and shorter varieties for containers and the front of the border.

How to Plant & Grow—Plant in late spring after the danger of frost has passed; snaps need a sunny exposure with well-drained soil. Space plants 6 to 9 inches apart. When they are 4 to 6 inches tall, pinch out the tips to encourage bushy growth. Deadhead regularly and stake if necessary. They appreciate an application of slow-release, all-season fertilizer.

Care & Problems—Snapdragons prefer well-drained soil. Avoid overhead watering. 'Dulcinea's Heart' is somewhat drought tolerant. Rust can be a problem, so look for rust-resistant varieties. Earwigs will munch on the flowers. Set traps in the garden made from sheets of moistened newspaper.

Color(s): White, yellow, pink, red, orange, peach, maroon, purple, and bicolor

Peak Season: Early summer until the first hard frost; they will languish in hot areas

Mature Size (H x W): 6 to 12 in. x 12 to 36 in.

Water Needs: Moderate

SPIDER FLOWER
Cleome hassleriana

☼ ◐

Why It's Special—Spider flowers are exotic in appearance, yet easy to grow, tall with elegant, unusual, wispy blossoms. They will bloom all summer, and may gently reseed. Great for the back of the border or with ornamental grasses, they are heat, drought, and humidity tolerant. Some people find the fragrance unpleasant, so keep this in mind when choosing a place for spider flower in the garden. Look for the newer varieties 'Sparkler Blush' and 'Violet Queen'.

How to Plant & Grow—Plant in late spring after the danger of frost has passed, either by direct sowing or placing seedlings out 18 to 24 inches apart. Plants will do well in sandy or any well-drained soil.

Care & Problems—Spider flower seedlings need evenly moist soil to become established, then *Cleome* is drought tolerant. There are no problems.

Color(s): White, pink, purple, and rose

Peak Season: Early summer until the first hard frost

Mature Size (H x W): 12 to 18 in. x 3 to 5 ft.

Water Needs: Low

SUNFLOWER
Helianthus annuus

☼

Why It's Special—The sunflower is a North American native annual. Showy cultivars that suit the home landscape include the short 'Teddy Bear' (1 foot tall) to the 'Russian Giant' (10 feet or taller). Some are hybridized to be pollenless, making them desirable for cutting.

How to Plant & Grow—Sunflowers are easy to grow; sow seeds directly in the garden in May. They prefer full sun and well-drained soil that has been amended with compost. Sustain them throughout the growing season by adding a slow-release, organic plant food. Thin seedlings as suggested on the seed packet. To harvest the seed heads, cut the flowers off and hang them in a cool garage or shed to dry.

Care & Problems—Birds and squirrels will want the seeds. Before they ripen, cover the seed heads with gauze or cheesecloth to thwart them.

Color(s): Lemon yellow, deep yellow, gold, mahogany, creamy white, and bicolors

Peak Season: Early summer until the first hard frost

Mature Size (H x W): 2 to 12 ft. x 1 to 3 ft.

Water Needs: Low

WAX BEGONIA

Begonia semperflorens-cultorum hybrids

Why It's Special—Wax begonia is a favorite plant for mass plantings at the edges of beds and borders. The flowers of the wax leaf begonia are colorful and showy. Glossy leaves, ranging from bright green to bronze, provide nice textural contrast in container combinations. Wax begonia pairs nicely with any of the impatiens varieties and sweet alyssum.

How to Plant & Grow—Plant in late spring after the danger of frost has passed in full or part shade. Space plants 8 to 10 inches apart. Plants benefit from a slow-release fertilizer.

Care & Problems—Do not allow wax begonias to dry out. Water deeply and on a regular schedule. Begonias are very easy to grow, but slugs or snails sometimes trouble them. Scatter used coffee grounds around the base of the plants or treat with a commercial bait or trap, following label directions.

Color(s): Red, pink, or white, single or double blossom

Peak Season: Early summer until the first hard frost

Mature Size (H x W): 4 to 8 in. x 12 to 18 in.

Water Needs: Moderate

ZINNIA

Zinnia elegans

Why It's Special—True to their Mexican origin, these rugged and durable annuals are perfect for a water-thrifty flower garden. Zinnias make wonderful cut flowers. Butterflies, bees, and hummingbirds also love them. Their bright showy blossoms come in various colors and forms. Dahlia-flowered types sport wide petals that form a rounded bloom up to 6 inches across. Cactus-flowered types, with blooms up to 6 inches, have quilled, ruffled petals.

How to Plant & Grow—Plant in mid- to late-spring after frost danger has passed. They germinate in seven to ten days. Set young transplants in the garden after the soil has warmed from mid- to late May. Zinnias do best in full sun and well-drained soils.

Care & Problems—Zinnias thrive in hot, dry summers, but require weekly watering for profuse flowering. Persistant wet foliage may cause serious leaf and stem disease. Carefully plan your water schedule.

Color(s): Red, orange, yellow, pink, lavender, white, lime green, and striped

Peak Season: Early summer until the first hard frost

Mature Size (H x W): 6 in. to 3 ft. x 1 to 2 ft.

Water Needs: Low to moderate

JANUARY

- Create your planting plans. Sketch out your bed designs and select containers.

- Research the latest plant varieties and know where to find them.

- Care for wintered-over indoor plants by watering and fertilizing if necessary.

- Start seedlings for early spring annuals. They will need plenty of light.

FEBRUARY

- Attend flower and garden shows to hone up on the latest trends, new designs, and planting ideas.

- Order seeds and plants now. New and popular varieties go fast, so be prepared.

- Repot those annuals brought in from the outdoors last fall. Select and pot the strongest cuttings. Fertilize at half strength with every other watering.

MARCH

- Don't hurry to plant outdoors. Soil needs plenty of time to warm up and dry out.

- Prepare planting beds. Clean out leftover annuals and apply a slow-release fertilizer when the soil is workable.

- Repot seedlings as they outgrow their original containers.

- Groom your newly potted annuals by pinching back new growth to prevent legginess and to promote fullness.

APRIL

- Prepare containers for planting; use fresh planting soil if possible. For large containers, mix aged compost, potting soil, and slow-release fertilizer in the top 6 to 8 inches of planting mix.

- Weeds are starting to grow enthusiastically, so stay ahead of them.

- Put plant-starts outdoors during the days and nights to begin the hardening-off process. Monitor outside temperatures and move the plants in if freezing temperatures are predicted.

- Weather can be considerably dry and warm. Monitor planting beds for moisture.

- Deadhead established potted annuals and prune leggy plants lightly.

MAY

- Time to plant outdoors. Keep an eye on wild temperature fluctuations; plants may need to be covered.

- Deadhead flowering annuals to prolong blooming.

- Before planting, make certain soil in beds is moist. Slowly apply 1 to 1½ inches of water.

- Mulch beds after planting, topping with 2 inches of mulch.

- Continue aggressive weed removal. This month they can take over the garden.

- Attend garden tours for new ideas: plant combinations, fresh designs, new cultivars.

JUNE

- Another big weed patrol month—keep after them!

- Fill in the spaces left by early spring plants with fresh annuals.

- Thin, deadhead, and fertilize container annuals. Annuals are heavy feeders and watering container plantings rapidly leaches out nutrients.

- Stake taller plants as needed.

- Continue light pruning of annuals to keep them shapely.

JULY

- Vacationers must arrange container watering. Assemble containers in partial shade for convenience and protection.

- Start seeds of fall annuals.

- Thin plants as needed in beds and containers.

- Control pests. Best to hose off plants every few days or use insecticidal soap.

- Don't use high-nitrogen fertilizers that promote leafy growth. This can stress plants in hot weather.

AUGUST

- Evaluate the performance of various plants through the summer heat. Plan modifications for next year, making notes in a garden journal on the calendar.

- Replenish mulch. Apply 2 inches deep but keep away from the plant stems.

- Replace spent plants with fall annuals: mums, ornamental kales, and cabbages.

- Keep beds and containers free of dead blooms, dead leaves, and other spent plant material for a tidy appearance.

SEPTEMBER

- In cooler zones, it's time to move annuals (and tropicals) indoors if you plan to overwinter them. Some will be fine in a heated garage.

- Examine these plants and containers, wiping them down if possible to discourage stowaway pests from coming indoors.

- Keep a record of how plants fared and which survived the first light frosts.

- Watering needs are diminished, but September can still be warm and dry. Monitor moisture content in containers and beds.

- Remove dead or weak plants from containers and beds.

OCTOBER

- Time to take cuttings of annuals you intend to use as houseplants.

- Note the killing frost date in your journal or on your calendar.

- Continue watering as needed.

- Monitor for pests on plants brought indoors. Wash pests off with water and treat with an insecticidal soap.

NOVEMBER

- Remove and discard all dead annuals from containers and planting beds.

- Empty and clean small and midsized containers. They should be scrubbed and sterilized with a diluted bleach solution.

- Study gardening books to help you revise and improve your annual plantings for next season.

- Groom and water indoor annuals. Do not fertilize until they show signs of new growth.

- Decorate outdoor containers with a variety of dry grasses, colorful branches, live boughs, ornamental corn, and dried gourds.

DECEMBER

- Go skiing.

- Drop hints to friends and family about cool gardening and gift ideas!

- Finish cleaning beds and amend soil with raked leaves and compost.

- Check plants that were brought indoors for moisture.

- Start imagining and planning the next growing season.

IMPATIENS

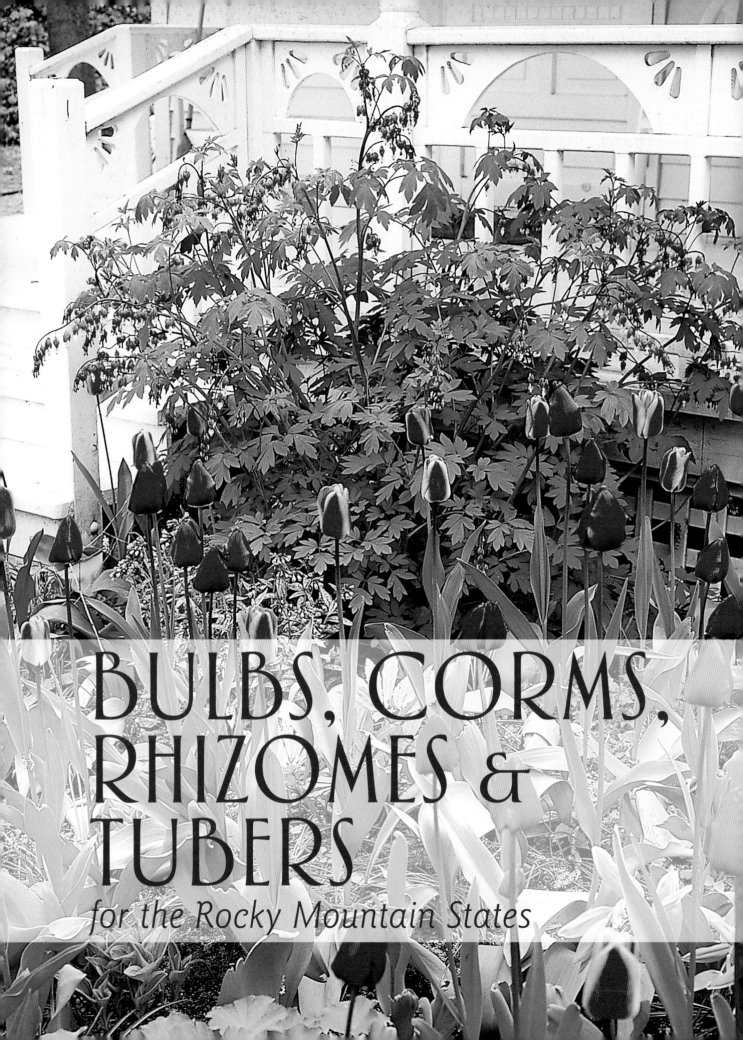

BULBS, CORMS, RHIZOMES & TUBERS

for the Rocky Mountain States

I have chosen a broad definition of the word *bulb* to include plants that form swollen, underground storage roots or stems that allow them to survive through the cold and dry periods of the growing seasons. This includes bulbs, corms, tubers, and rhizomes.

Technically, a bulb is made of swollen, fleshy bases of leaves. Other storage structures are formed by different parts of the plant. A crocus's corm is a swollen stem base. Some irises have both bulbs and tuberous roots; others have rhizomes and fleshy storage roots. Dahlias are swollen storage tubers with buds that arise at the tip of the tuber.

You can have crocuses peeking through melting snow in February, patches of golden daffodils in March, and radiant tulips and hyacinths in April. These are just a few of the fall-planted bulbs that cast their magic spell in spring.

WHAT TO LOOK FOR

When purchasing bulbs locally, select plump, firm, blemish-free bulbs. Many varieties have skins like onions, in that their skins are partially or completely removed. This will not affect their quality as long as the bulb has solid integrity and is free of soft spots. If you find that you cannot plant bulbs within a day or two after making your purchase, store them in a cool (40 to 50 degrees Fahrenheit), dry location in mesh bags or ventilated containers.

WHEN TO PLANT

To plant your pretty visions of spring, you must start this fall. In our Rocky Mountain region, spring-flowering bulbs are planted in late September through November. Soil temperatures have begun to cool down, and the embryonic flower inside the bulb requires a cold period in order to mature for successful spring blooms. Once planted, bulbs must develop a strong, healthy root system before the ground freezes.

WHERE TO PLANT

Spring-flowering bulbs are among the most versatile perennials when planted properly. They can be interplanted with herbaceous perennial flowers, around shrub borders, along pathways, in separate flowerbeds, and naturalized in lawns. Some favorite plantings include crocus, muscari, daffodils, and selected types of tulips in casual drifts around the landscape and along garden pathways. This is a technique we term *naturalizing* since the plants appear as though placed by Nature's hand.

Most spring-flowering bulbs perform best with morning sun and afternoon shade. Flowers will last much longer in such a setting, but you must provide protection from drying winds, which often scorch flower petals.

The early-blooming bulbs, including snowdrops (*Galanthus*) and winter aconite (*Eranthis*), will do beautifully beneath trees and shrubs whose canopy of shade does not unfurl until after blossoms fade.

WELL-DRAINED SOIL IS THE KEY

All spring-flowering bulbs will grow best in well-drained soils. This is especially important to ensure bulb longevity. If you've ever planted bulbs only to find they've lasted for just one season, you're not alone. Poorly drained, water-logged soils may be the culprit. Be aware, too, of how much water your bulbs will get during the summer. Some, like *Eremurus*, or foxtail lily, like to stay bone dry. A good part of your garden may be drought-tolerant plants, but do not overwater; your bulbs will last for years.

To prepare the soil, loosen the area with a heavy-duty rototiller or shovel; dig down to a depth of 8 to 10 inches. If your soil is predominantly clay, it is important to mix in a combination of compost and sphagnum peat moss to improve drainage and encourage healthy root development. Add organic bulb fertilizer as recommended on the label. These specialty bulb fertilizers are generally high in phosphorus, which is the middle number in a fertilizer formula.

HOW TO PLANT

The bulb-planting charts shown in national marketing campaigns that promote fall bulb planting are for well-drained soils, which are not typical of our region. Most bulbs will do best and survive the longest in sandy or clay loam. In heavy, clay-textured soils, plant bulbs 1 to 2 inches more shallow than recommended. Soils with high clay content can be amended with perlite or scoria (crushed volcanic rock) at a rate of 25 percent by volume for improved soil texture and proper aeration.

Many gardeners like to dig individual holes for each bulb with a bulb planter, but the spring bloom is much more effective when bulbs are planted in a group or mass planting. Never plant in rows like soldiers in formation.

To plant in groups, remove enough soil to accommodate all bulbs going into a given area. Fertilizer and compost can be easily applied at the bottom of the excavated bed and incorporated a bit deeper where the roots will grow. After the bulbs are in place, cover them with approximately half of the amended, excavated soil, and lightly scatter additional bulb fertilizer on top. Remember to amend the backfill soil with compost (25 to 30 percent by volume) before shoveling it onto the planted bulbs. Finish filling the bulb bed with remaining soil and water the area thoroughly. A clever trick for marking the bulbs' location is to use a disposable wooden chopstick or popsicle stick on which you have written the name of the bulb.

Consider planting bulbs with ornamental grasses. As the foliage dies back on the bulbs, it will be hidden by the new spring growth of the ornamental grasses.

Since we often lack adequate natural precipitation in our region during the fall, it is important to water new bulb beds periodically throughout the season to ensure good root growth. Check the soil with a hand trowel. If it is beginning to dry out, water as necessary before the soil freezes solid. Fall and early winter watering may be necessary every three to four weeks, depending upon the flowerbed's exposure.

After the first hard frosts, apply a layer of organic mulch to the bulb bed. Two to three inches of shredded cedar mulch, aspen mulch, dried grass clippings (those not treated with herbicides), or shredded leaves will help to retain moisture, reduce weed growth, and prevent soil heaving.

WHICH END IS UP?

Bulbs should be planted with root end downward and growing end upward. It isn't always easy to tell which is which. Most bulbs, on close inspection, reveal a few root remnants or nubs to help guide you. The growing point is often already formed and apparent. Bulbs such as tulips and hyacinths have a pointed end, which is planted up, and a flattened basal plate, which goes down. When in doubt, lay the bulb on its side.

Some rhizomes or tubers like *Anemone blanda* show very little hint of either growth points or roots. Fortunately, these little bulbs will adjust in nearly any position, so simply scatter them.

TENDER BULBS

Bulbs that are not winter-hardy in our region are unable to survive the freezing temperatures. These include dahlias, gladiolus, begonias, cannas, calla lilies, and caladiums. Most are planted in the spring after the danger of frost has passed. Plant gladiolus corms when daffodils are blooming; they will not grow through the surface until the danger of frost is over. Stagger planting every two weeks for a continuous bloom over the summer months.

Get a head start on the flowering season by starting indoor summer-flowering bulbs in pots. Plant them in commercial potting mixture in containers that have drainage. You can plant dahlia bulbs in 1-gallon black, plastic pots and set them in a warm, sunny spot. Water dahlia pots just once, at the time they are planted, and not again until the first leaves appear. Too much water and too little sun will cause them to rot. When the danger of frost has passed, started plants can be set in the garden. Be sure to have stakes or other plant supports ready. Plant the bulbs, tubers, corms, or rhizomes at the depth indicated on the label or from their profile in this book.

CARE OF TENDER BULBS FOR WINTER

Tender bulbs must be removed from the garden soon after the first hard frost. Carefully lift plants, roots and all, with a heavy spading fork. Cut back tops to within a couple of inches of the crown. Shake off

A mass planting of spring bulbs like these irises provides an elegant pathway.

excess soil, and bring clumps into the garage or patio to dry. After they have dried, separate clumps, and store them in a cool, dry place over the winter. You can use plastic foam coolers that are filled with peat moss. They will help protect bulbs from frost and retain natural moisture so they won't shrivel.

Check stored bulbs monthly over the winter to make sure they are not rotting or shriveling. If they get too dry, lightly sprinkle them to provide some moisture, but don't overwater.

DEALING WITH PESTS

To keep rodents, including meadow mice, voles, pocket gophers, squirrels and chipmunks, from devouring bulbs, plant your bulbs in homemade wire baskets. They are easy to make using ½-inch mesh hardware cloth; this size allows stems and roots to grow properly. Cut a 6- to 8-inch strip of any length and make a circle. Then cut a bottom piece, and wire it to the cylinder-formed basket. Dig the planting holes at the proper depths for the specific bulbs, place the basket in the hole, set the bulbs in, and cover with amended soil. Finish by laying a piece of wire mesh directly onto the wire basket, and then add more backfill soil.

TIP

Certain tulip cultivars may last only 1 to 2 years in the garden. Do your research to determine longevity of the cultivar before purchasing and planting tulips.

AUTUMN CROCUS
Colchicum autumnale spp.

Why It's Special—Beautiful, colorful flowers brighten the late-season garden. Autumn crocus has several blooms on each naked stem. Foliage appears alone, in spring or early summer. Single, double, and fringe forms are available. The saffron crocus opens to reveal bright red stigmas, which is the spice saffron. They are great in the ground or in patio pots.

How to Plant & Grow—Check planting depth and distance for each variety. *Colchicum* species can vary in color, depending on planting location. They can also bloom without being planted in soil. Saffron crocus should be planted twelve bulbs per square foot and to the front of the border where their amazing stigmas can be seen.

Care & Problems—Good drainage is essential to prevent rotting. Since the foliage dies all the way back, it's a good idea to mark bulbs' locations. **Note:** *Bulbs of either crocus are poisonous if eaten.*

Color(s): White, cream pink, violet, and intense purple

Peak Season: August to September

Mature (H x W): 12 in. x 3 to 12 in.

Water Needs: Low

CAMAS
Camassia spp.

Why It's Special—Noted by the Lewis and Clark expedition, *Camassia quamash* was an important food crop for the Nez Perce Indians of Idaho. Its tall spikes of star-shaped flowers look great when planted *en masse*. Many fine cultivars are available to the home gardener, ranging in color from a deep, clear blue to white.

How to Plant & Grow—All the camas varieties seem to tolerate damp, even clay soils. They do especially well in low, damp, meadow-type settings. Follow planting instructions for each particular variety. Depth and distance will vary.

Care & Problems—In drier areas, such as high desert locales, camas tend to fade away after a few years. They are worth replanting. **Note:** *Some varieties are poisonous.*

Color(s): White, blue, purple, and yellow

Peak Season: May, June, and July, depending on elevation and temperatures

Mature (H x W): 12 to 36 in. x 3 to 6 in.

Water Needs: Low to high

CANNA
Canna spp.

Why It's Special—These stately plants sport torchlike blossoms, often topping boldly colored foliage. 'Pretoria' (also known as 'Bengal Tiger') is an all-round favorite with brilliant orange blooms atop foliage that is green with orange stripes. 'Red King Humbert' has scarlet blooms and large, bronze leaves.

How to Plant & Grow—Cannas need a minimum of four hours of sun per day. In very hot, high desert areas, they will do best with late afternoon shade. Plant rhizomes 12 to 18 inches apart, and cover with 2 inches of soil.

Care & Problems—Cannas do well planted in pots or the ground. Add some composted manure or an organic rose fertilizer to the soil. Removing spent flowers will improve their appearance. They really respond well to generous waterings.

Color(s): Orange, yellow, salmon, red, pink, and bicolor

Peak Season: July through September

Mature (H x W): 3 to 6 ft. x 3 ft.

Water Needs: Moderate to very high

CROCUS

Crocus spp.

☀️

Why It's Special—The first sign of crocus is the first sign of spring! They take up very little space, so tuck a handful here and there in the garden, and always plant three times as many as you think you need. Crocus are small, and you need all the color you can get at the end of a long winter. 'Lady Killer' and *Crocus tommasinianus* 'Ruby Giant' are sensational varieties. The mixed bags of crocus colors are a good idea too.

How to Plant & Grow—Crocus can be tucked anywhere in the garden except in wet, boggy spots. Impressive when planted *en masse*, they are also charming tucked into turf grass. Plant 3 to 6 inches deep, 3 to 4 inches apart, in groups of 20 to 30 bulbs.

Care & Problems—There are virtually no problems with crocus.

Color(s): White, pink, lavender blue, blue, violet, yellow, gold, and bicolor

Peak Season: February to April

Mature (H x W): 4 to 6 in. x 3 to 6 in.

Water Needs: Low

DAFFODIL

Narcissus spp.

☀️ 🌤️

Why It's Special—All daffodils are in the genus *Narcissus*. The names "daffodil" and "narcissus" are interchangeable. Having cleared that up, every garden needs some daffodils. Their sunny trumpets truly herald the arrival of spring.

How to Plant & Grow—Plant daffodil bulbs in fall in moisture-retentive, yet well-drained soil. They tolerate drier conditions in summer. Large trumpet varieties should be planted 6 to 8 inches deep and 4 inches apart. Plant in clusters of seven or more. To naturalize, cast a handful of bulbs randomly across an area and plant them where they fall.

Care & Problems—It is best to leave daffodils undisturbed in the ground. Their foliage should not be tied or braided, as it needs oxygen and sunlight to photosynthesize and feed the bulbs for next year. After four weeks, foliage can be removed. Interplanting hostas, daylilies, and daisies will hide the old daffodil foliage.

Color(s): White, yellow, salmon, and bicolor

Peak Season: Early to late spring

Mature (H x W): 6 to 18 in. x 6 to 8 in.

Water Needs: Low to moderate

DAHLIA

Dahlia spp. and hybrids

☀️ 🌤️

Why It's Special—Dahlias are strong, handsome plants well adapted for the summer garden in the Rockies. Dahlias come in a wide range of flower shapes, plant sizes, and colors, from small, round pompons to giant, dinner-plate blooms. Some have dark bronze foliage.

How to Plant & Grow—Dahlias are not hardy; treat them as annuals or be prepared to lift, dry, and store until the next season. About six weeks before your area's average last frost date, pot up tubers in black, plastic pots in rich soil. Water in just once. Place the pots in sunny area. When new growth appears, water once a week. Transplant into garden or containers.

Care & Problems—A stake inserted when planting tubers will keep you from poking tubers later and provide support for tall plants. Dust for earwigs as needed using diatomaceous earth powder.

Color(s): Every color but blue

Peak Season: Mid- to late summer

Mature (H x W): 1 to 7 ft. x 1 to 2 ft.

Water Needs: Moderate

DOG-TOOTH VIOLET

Erythronium spp.

☀️

Why It's Special—Collected by Lewis and Clark in Idaho, dog-tooth violet is lovely in a woodland garden. The species *E. grandiflorum* has many names: glacier lily, trout lily, avalanche lily, fawn lily, and adder's tongue. Graceful blossoms with recurved (turned back) petals bloom facing downward.

How to Plant & Grow—Please purchase bulbs from a reputable source, and never collect them from wild habitat. Dog-tooth violet will grow in several types of garden settings; try woodland, moist meadow, or shade gardens with rich moist soil. Plant the long, narrow bulbs horizontally; they should be 3 inches deep and 3 inches apart.

Care & Problems—The bulbs are low maintenance. They can be divided every three to four years.

Color(s): White, pink, and yellow

Peak Season: April to May, depending on elevation

Mature (H x W): 6 to 9 in. x 6 to 9 in.

Water Needs: Low to moderate

DWARF IRIS

Iris reticulata

☀️ ☀️

Why It's Special—The earliest iris to flower, these tiny beauties should be included in borders and rock gardens. As with crocus, plant two to three times what you think you need. These bulbs always surprise gardeners with their sudden bloom. 'Harmony', 'J. S. Dijt', and 'Katherine Hodgkin' are readily available, and some varieties are fragrant.

How to Plant & Grow—Dwarf iris bulbs should be planted 2 to 3 inches deep, in groups of five or seven bulbs (or a larger uneven number). Space 3 inches apart, unevenly for a more natural look.

Care & Problems—Clumps can be divided and replanted about four weeks after blooms have faded. Dwarf iris welcome spring rains, then prefer extreme dryness during the rest of the year.

Color(s): White, pale blue, lavender, violet, and yellow

Peak Season: March to April

Mature (H x W): 3 to 6 in. x 3 in.

Water Needs: Very low

ELEPHANT EAR

Colocasia esculenta

☀️

Why It's Special—The giant, purplish-black leaves of 'Black Magic' add instant tropical punch to a summer garden. Also known as taro, it is grown for poi in Hawaii. Plant several of these at the edge of a pond for a jungle effect or a single one as a stunning focal point. You can also plant them in large containers where you can keep them very wet. Even one of these in a large container will add an exotic flair to your garden.

How to Plant & Grow—In hot, sunny gardens, *Colocasia* will need some shade to prevent crispy, scorched leaves. Plant in very rich, water-retentive soil, and don't let it dry out.

Care & Problems—Elephant ear has no serious problems. To carry over from year to year, dig up after the first frost and overwinter in a cool, dry place. Do not allow tubers to freeze.

Color(s): Purple-black or green foliage

Peak Season: Summer to fall

Mature (H x W): 3 to 6 ft. x 3 to 6 ft.

Water Needs: High

GLADIOLUS
Gladiolus spp.

☼ ☀

Why It's Special—The Latin word *gladius* means "little sword," and glads were an integral part of Roman culture. They are reputed to have been the floral emblem of gladiators, and gladioli paintings can be found at the site of the ancient city of Pompeii. For a great effect and vertical accents in the garden, plant clusters of a single color. *Gladiolus byzantinus* are winter hardy and considerably smaller; they are definitely worth growing.

How to Plant & Grow—If you are planting the tender annual varieties, stake at planting time. The stakes will be hidden by the foliage. Plant one-half inch corms 1 inch deep, plant 1-inch corms 4 inches deep, and larger corms should be planted 6 inches deep.

Care & Problems—Keep soil evenly moist. If tiny thrips attack foliage, dust foliage with diatomaceous earth or use an insecticidal soap, always following label directions.

Color(s): Every color except true blue

Peak Season: June through August

Mature (H x W): 1 to 5 ft. x 6 in.

Water Needs: Moderate

GLORY-OF-THE-SNOW
Chionodoxa luciliae

☼ ☀

Why It's Special—The sky blue blossoms of *Chionodoxa* are a cheerful sight in early spring, and as befits their name, the flowers often get caught in a spring snow. The star-shaped, 1-inch-wide flowers number ten or more per stem and grow over handsome grassy foliage. Each flower has a starry white center and faces skyward. Bold plantings of fifty to one hundred bulbs produce the best displays.

How to Plant & Grow—Plant glory-of-the-snow in the fall in a sunny location, though it will tolerate shade from emerging foliage of deciduous trees. Plant 3 to 4 inches deep and 3 inches apart in well-drained soil. When planting large masses, incorporate an organic 5-10-5 fertilizer and water in thoroughly.

Care & Problems—During extended dry periods in the fall and winter, water where the bulbs were planted.

Color(s): Blue, white, and pink

Peak Season: Early spring

Mature (H x W): 4 to 5 in. x 4 in.

Water Needs: Moderate

GRAPE HYACINTH
Muscari spp.

☼ ☀

Why It's Special—*Muscari*, or grape hyacinth as it's commonly known, is strong, dependable, and an excellent choice for naturalizing in swales of blue in a woodland setting. Some people don't care for the excessive, strappy foliage; it is green and falls in tufts around garden. The charming little flowers are clusters of tiny bells in the form of an inverted grape cluster. Don't overlook special cultivars: 'Valerie Finnis', icy, pale blue; 'Album', a clear white; *M. latifolium*, a lovely bicolor of light and dark blue; and *M. macrocarpum*, an unusual dark blue and yellow bicolor.

How to Plant & Grow—Plant 4 inches deep and 2 to 5 inches apart, not too perfectly spaced; you want the plants to look natural. Plant these and forget them. They're pretty planted under a white, pink, or yellow blooming spring shrub.

Care & Problems—There are seldom any pests or problems.

Color(s): White, blue, violet, yellow, and bicolors

Peak Season: Early spring

Mature (H x W): 4 to 8 in. x 3 in.

Water Needs: Low

LILY

Lilium spp. and hybrids

Why It's Special—Lilies are an incredible group of plants and flowers with entire books devoted to them. Heavenly fragrance, stunning trumpet flowers, and speckled faces are a few reasons to plant lilies.

How to Plant & Grow—Lilies can be planted in full sun. Madonna lilies need 1 inch of soil cover; others need 4 to 6 inches of soil. The larger the bulb, the deeper the hole. Good drainage is necessary and can be accomplished by planting on a slope, in a raised bed, or in a container. Dig a generous hole with space for roots to spread. Lilies look great in groups of three, five, seven, and so forth. Water in after planting.

Care & Problems—If possible, stake the lilies when you plant so you'll know where they are and avoid poking them later. Mulch with leaves for winter protection.

Color(s): Every color but blue or true black

Peak Season: Early to late summer

Mature (H x W): 18 in. to 8 ft. x 12 to 36 in.

Water Needs: Moderate

ORNAMENTAL ONION

Allium spp.

Why It's Special—*Allium* species make a perfect exclamation point in the garden. Their distinctive lollipop shape makes people smile. Their easy-going nature should encourage you to plant several varieties. 'Purple Sensation' is an outstanding performer.

How to Plant & Grow—Bulbs should be planted three times as deep as the width of the bulb, so a 1-inch diameter bulb should be 3 inches deep. Consider the size of the bloom when spacing the bulbs. The jumbo species *A. christophii* should be planted one per square foot. Over-lapping and random spacing looks best.

Care & Problems—Ornamental onions aren't fussy about the soil they are in, as long as it is well drained. The foliage can look ratty early on, so plant *Allium* species among other perennials and grasses to cover the plant's base.

Color(s): Blue, purple, and yellow

Peak Season: May and June

Mature (H x W): 8 to 42 in. x 20 in.

Water Needs: Low

SIBERIAN SQUILL

Scilla siberica

Why It's Special—Dainty blue flowers droop toward the ground, making lovely spots of color against strappy dark green foliage. A welcome early-spring bloomer. *Scilla* will naturalize easily and comes back reliably year after year. This is a great bulb for the front of the border and sprinkled throughout rock gardens.

How to Plant & Grow—Plant *en masse* under shrubs and trees, in large sweeps on hillsides, or in woodlands. Siberian squill can also be planted in a lawn. It's very handsome planted with early daffodils or tulips. Plant 3 inches deep.

Care & Problems—Siberian squill loves good drainage. It is trouble free, which makes it a great choice for first-time gardeners.

Color(s): Blue

Peak Season: April

Mature (H x W): 5 to 8 in. x 3 to 6 in.

Water Needs: Moderate

SICILIAN HONEY LILY

Nectaroscordum siculum var. bulgaricum

Why It's Special—The unique dangling flower clusters are cream, tinged with a maroon stripe and a hint of lime green. The little blossoms face downward until they are finished, and tan-colored seed heads reverse their direction and face upward. A majestic bulb, the flowers hang from 2- to 3-foot stems. This would look pretty planted with a red or pink peony in late spring.

How to Plant & Grow—A member of the *Allium* family, the Sicilian honey lily can be planted in part shade or sun. It needs excellent drainage. Plant four or five per square foot, 4 inches deep. Clusters of odd numbers make an impressive display.

Care & Problems—Because it's a member of the onion family, these bulbs are not bothered by squirrels or mice.

Color(s): Cream with maroon and lime green

Peak Season: May, June, July, depending on elevation and temperatures

Mature (H x W): 12 to 36 in. x 3 to 6 in.

Water Needs: Low

SNOWDROPS

Galanthus nivalis

Why It's Special—With their drooping white blossoms, snowdrops are a sure sign of spring. Some of the varieties have green markings or dots on the white blossoms. They grow very well under deciduous trees and are especially beautiful planted in large clumps or drifts. Since they prefer cool climates, snowdrops are happy in Rocky Mountain gardens. Collecting snowdrop varieties is all the rage in some gardening circles.

How to Plant & Grow—Plant 4 inches deep and the same distance apart. Snowdrops prefer a dry summer, so planting under leafy trees is a plus. A nice top dressing of compost will encourage naturalization.

Care & Problems—Snowdrops have no known serious insects or diseases. If transplanting, do so after the foliage has started to yellow. Do not allow the bulbs to dry out in the process.

Color(s): White

Peak Season: February and March

Mature (H x W): 6 to 9 in. x 4 to 6 in.

Water Needs: Moderate

SPANISH BLUEBELLS

Hyacinthoides hispanica

Why It's Special—Versatile and long-lasting Spanish bluebells put on quite a show in late spring. Once they are established, they will grow into large showy clumps. A great bulb for dry shade, bluebells are good for cutting and have a nice, soft fragrance. All bluebells are not blue; pink, white, and mixes of all three colors are available.

How to Plant & Grow—Plant 4 inches deep and roughly 3 to 4 inches apart. Give them a couple of thorough soakings in the fall when planting. Be sure the soil is well draining, as too much water will cause the bulbs to rot.

Care & Problems—Spanish bluebells have no known problems.

Color(s): White, pink, and blue

Peak Season: May and June

Mature (H x W): 16 in. x 4 to 6 in.

Water Needs: Low

TULIP
Tulipa spp. and hybrids

Why It's Special—It's hard to do tulips justice in a few paragraphs. Their glory has brought emperors to their knees. Tulips shout "Spring!" in every language and come in a wide range of colors, heights, types, forms, and differing bloom times. Tall, stately Darwin hybrids have good cold tolerance. They, and the short species, are the longest-lived varieties.

How to Plant & Grow—Plant in full sun to part shade, in well-drained, compost-enriched soil. Plant larger bulbs 6 to 8 inches deep with pointed tips up. In colder areas, plant 8 to 10 inches deep. Cover with prepared soil; water in thoroughly.

Care & Problems—Tulips like regular watering during their growing season. As foliage fades, the soil can be left on the dry side. Apply bulb fertilizer over planting areas in early spring and autumn. Remove seed heads before they ripen.

Color(s): All colors but true blue and black

Peak Season: March, April, and May

Mature (H x W): 4 to 28 in. x 10 to 12 in.

Water Needs: Moderate

WINDFLOWER
Anemone blanda

Why It's Special—Windflowers are a welcome sight in the spring garden. Their happy, daisylike flowers are short in stature but beautiful in bold drifts. 'Charmer' is rosy pink and looks especially pretty under cream-colored daffodils.

How to Plant & Grow—Plant in the fall in groups of thirty or more. Windflower does best in moist, well-drained soils, in sunny or partly shady locations. Plant 2 to 3 inches deep and 4 to 6 inches apart. Add compost, grit, or sand to clay soil to improve drainage.

Care & Problems—In the coldest areas, windflower planting will benefit from a good layer of mulch (cedar shavings, pine needles, or leaves). Soak bulbs overnight before planting.

Color(s): Pink, blues, lavender, and white

Peak Season: Early to mid-spring

Mature (H x W): 3 to 12 in. x 3 to 4 in.

Water Needs: Regular

JANUARY

- This is a good time to select summer-flowering bulbs, corms, rhizomes, and tubers for the garden season ahead. Study up on available types by reading your garden catalogues or the book *Bulb*, by Anna Pavord.

- Design bulb plantings on paper, noting how many of them you will need. Dahlia tubers are small when you buy them, but the plants can be as tall as 5 to 6 feet. Plan accordingly.

- If you planted bulbs in containers for forcing, don't forget to bring them out into a sunny spot.

- Outdoors, if there is a prolonged period of warm weather without rain or snow, water bulb beds on sunny exposures. Water only if the ground is unfrozen, and water early in the day so it can sink in.

FEBRUARY

- Order your dahlias, cannas, and elephant ear bulbs now for the best selection.

- Pick up some pansies, and plant them near the emerging bulb foliage.

- You may need to give those bulb plantings a good drink of water.

- You may have to put hardware cloth or chicken wire over your bulbs if the squirrels and rodents start nibbling on them.

MARCH

- Spring-blooming bulbs are starting to blossom; have some buckets handy if a heavy snowfall is forecast. You can cover any of the bloomers with the buckets, which will protect them from collapsing under the weight of the snow.

- Plan for continuing bloom from March through May by selecting blubs that bloom at different times. Make a note of this, and put it in your journal.

- Keep an eye on the moisture level of your planting areas, bulbs and otherwise. If you need to water, do so when the ground is not frozen.

APRIL

- Plan to leave the healthy green foliage of the bulbs in place as they finish their bloom cycle. This foliage is needed for next year's blossoms.

- If you haven't already potted up the cannas, dahlias, and caladiums, now is the time to do so.

- Watch for invasions of insect pests in the garden. Aphids can get into the folds of iris leaves and blossoms. You may need to hose them down or apply an insecticidal soap. Always follow the label directions when applying any chemicals to your garden.

CROCUS

MAY

- When the danger of frost is past, set out those tender bulbs. Stake the tall ones as you plant them, being careful not to poke the stake through the tuber.

- Were there bare spots in the spring bulb display? Make a note of it now, and keep it in your garden journal so you know what to buy and plant next fall. Mark your calendar as a reminder as well.

- Keep ahead of the pests and weeds.

JUNE

- Disbud your dahlias. That is, pinch off the two small buds on either side of the main, large bud. This will put all the energy into one premium-sized blossom.

- Snap the seed heads off spent tulips if you haven't already done so. This takes the focus off seed development and pushes the plant's energy into next year's bloom cycle.

JULY

- If the dahlias and glads are going strong, pick some to bring indoors or for sprucing up the backyard picnic table. If you have lots of them, take a couple of bouquets to the soup kitchen in your town.

- Keep disbudding the dahlias and deadheading spent and faded flowers.

- Earwigs are downright gross. Put out traps for them now before they eat the buds of your prize dahlias.

- Keep foliage trimmed and clean. Remove diseased and rotting iris blades, and put them in the trash, not the compost bin.

AUGUST

- During periods of high heat and little rain, check the summer bulbs and keep their moisture even.

- Prepare some garden spots for fall planting of spring-blooming bulbs.

- Cut back the old stems of maturing lilies.

SEPTEMBER

- When at the nursery or garden store, carefully select new bulbs for your planting areas. Pick firm, unblemished specimens. Get them in the ground right away.

- Pot up spring-flowering bulbs and put them in the garage to pull out in the spring. These can go in patio containers for showy displays. Chilling may take sixteen weeks, so plan accordingly.

- When planting hardy bulbs, sprinkle some organic, slow-release fertilizer in with the backfill soil. Do not let the fertilizer touch the bulbs.

OCTOBER

- Keep planting those bulbs. How about some more crocus? Remember that daffodils turn to face the sun, so plant them where you can see them and keep this in mind.

- A hard frost will have done in the dahlias and gladiolas. Now is the time to dig them up and store them in a cool dark place.

- Keep up the note-taking in your garden journal. How was your garden season? What bulbs did you plant? Where? How many?

- Start your holiday *Amaryllis* bulbs so they will be blooming in time for Christmas.

NOVEMBER

- Check those bulbs you put in storage. The dahlias and glads should be inspected so you can put any moldy or rotten ones in the trash.

- Give the potted up spring bulbs a nice drink.

- If you live in an area where meadow mice, field mice, voles, and other creatures are an issue, mulch your bulb beds after the ground freezes. This will deter them from setting up house for the winter in the bulb beds.

DECEMBER

- Go skiing.

- Check the bulbs in storage and in pots. Water the potted bulbs just once this month.

- Deck the halls with amaryllis blossoms and paperwhite narcissus blooms.

EDIBLES: FRUIT, VEGETABLES & HERBS

for the Rocky Mountain States

There's an old saying that goes something like this: a failure to plan is a plan to fail. It may not seem like much, but developing a garden plan will go a long way toward creating a successful vegetable gardening experience. (And in case there is any doubt, success means veggies to eat!) We address vegetables here, because they are planted every year, whereas fruits, berries, and most herbs are perennial and stay in one place. Vegetables are often rotated in the garden.

Begin by scanning the new seed catalogs to see what you might like to plant. Then, ask yourself a few questions, and be brutally honest about the time you have to invest in vegetable gardening, how much financial investment you want to make, and your interests. Remember, you will become a better gardener in time but it's tempting to bite off more than you can chew in the beginning!

HOW BIG IS BIG ENOUGH?

How big of a garden is enough for you? If you're new to gardening (or even if you're not), there is no shame in starting on a scale that's manageable to fit within your life. First, plant only what you like! If you plan to preserve your vegetables, then plant more. A ¼-acre garden (10,000 square feet) will feed a family of five for a year. If you include potatoes, cucurbits, or other space hogs, then you'll need additional space. If your time is limited, then perhaps a garden of 2,500 square feet or even 625 square feet (25 × 25 feet) is a better fit. Some beginning gardeners consider a 10 × 10-foot garden a good size. Perhaps the most commonly sized vegetable garden is 25 × 25 feet. But with a garden this size plant only those vegetables that are the most space-efficient, such as beans, root crops, crucifers (broccoli, cabbage, and so forth), onion and garlic, and the leafy crops such as Swiss chard, lettuce, and spinach. Avoid space-hogs such as pumpkin, squash, potato, and corn. If you must have cucurbits, train them to grow on a trellis, plant the bush type, or plant them at the edges of the garden and let them sprawl onto the lawn.

Once you identify the vegetables you think you want to grow, check the approximate yields per length of row that are included in the profiles of individual vegetables later in the book to help determine the garden size.

VEGETABLE YIELD CHART

A ten foot long row of these vegetables will generally yield:

VEGETABLE	YIELD
Artichoke	5 or 6 buds per plant
Asparagus	3 pounds
Beet	10 pounds roots, 4 pounds greens
Broccoli	7.5 pounds
Brussels sprouts	6 pounds
Cabbage	6 pounds
Carrot	10 pounds
Cauliflower	9 pounds or 6 "curds" (heads)
Collards	7.5 pounds
Corn	2 dozen ears
Cucumber	12 pounds
Eggplant	7.5 pounds
Garlic	40–60 bulbs or heads
Horseradish	3 pounds
Leek	20 plants
Lettuce	5 pounds
Muskmelon	10 melons
Okra	variable
Onion	10 pounds
Parsnip	7 pounds
Pea	2 pounds
Pepper, hot	5–7 pounds
Pepper, sweet	5–7 pounds
Potato	20 pounds
Pumpkin	20 pounds or more
Radish	10 bunches

Continued on following page

Rutabaga	15 pounds
Snap bean	8 pounds bush, 15 pounds pole
Spinach	4 pounds
Squash, summer	20 pounds
Squash, winter	10 pounds or more
Swiss Chard	5 plants
Tomato	15 pounds or more
Turnip	5 pounds
Watermelon	7 pounds or more

LOCATION, LOCATION, LOCATION

Where you plant your garden is more important than *what* you plant in it. If you choose the wrong site it won't matter what you plant. Select a spot that receives full sun for at least eight hours each day. If this is not possible, then pick a site that gets the most sun and plant leafy vegetables.

PLANTS THAT PRODUCE IN LIGHT SHADE*

Beet	Kale	Radish
Cabbage	Leek	Spinach
Carrot	Lettuce	Swiss chard
Green Onion	Mustard	Turnip

(*Light shade can be that cast by buildings, fences, trellises, and tall garden plants.)

The site should be well away from trees and easy to water. A tree's roots can extend at least 1½ times the spread of its branches, and believe us, you don't want to lug a hose any farther than you must. Another consideration is exposure; southern exposure is the warmest and produces the earliest crops. However, soil on a site with southern exposure will dry faster than soil facing other exposures. Warm-season vegetables ripen earlier when planted near the south side of a building or fence. Northern exposures are moister but too cold for a good garden, so never plant within ten feet of the north side of a one-story building. Move the garden even farther away from taller buildings. Western exposures are nearly as warm as southern exposures but plants there may be exposed to strong prevailing winds.

Elevation is of primary importance in the selection of vegetable varieties for your garden. It is nearly impossible for a 110-day corn to ripen fully in a 110-day season, so at higher elevations plant the varieties that require fewer days to maturity. In general, cool-season crops perform best at higher elevations since they generally require shorter growing seasons and fewer days until harvest. Almost all cool-season vegetables are grown for their vegetative parts (leaves, roots, stems, petioles, and immature buds). Cool-season vegetables have smaller root systems and tops than warm-season ones, are frost-hardy, and their seeds germinate at cooler soil temperatures. Their shallow root systems respond to lower levels of nitrogen and phosphorus. Some are biennials, such as cabbage, that are prone to premature seed stalk formation ("bolting") upon exposure to prolonged cool weather. Bolting renders an otherwise edible portion of a vegetable unpalatable. Warm-season vegetables such as tomatoes, peppers, and squash tend to be large plants with large root systems and require a longer season and higher temperatures to mature. They are generally grown for their fruit. Peas are an exception, being a cool-season vegetable grown for its seeds, as is New Zealand spinach, a warm-season vegetable grown for its leaves.

ELEVATION

If you garden below 5,000 feet elevation you can easily grow all of the cool-season and many of the warm-season vegetables that require fewer days to harvest. For example, if you garden just below 5,000 feet you can easily harvest transplanted tomatoes that have less than a 68-day season and corn with less than a 70-day season. At about 6,000 feet you will have to be a bit more selective since you can expect a frost nearly every Memorial Day. Plant only those warm-season vegetables that need very few days to harvest, such as cherry and grape tomatoes and tomatoes of Siberian origins. All will

It's a good idea to use mulch in your herb or vegetable garden to keep the weeds down.

have seasons fewer than sixty-five days. It will be tough to grow cucurbits, eggplant, and okra at this elevation, but it can be done by modifying a garden's microclimate. Above 7,000 feet choose only varieties with absolutely the fewest numbers of days to harvest and strongly consider season extenders to create warmer microclimates. One season extender option is to plant against a south-facing wall with protection from wind. Root vegetables, peas, onions, garlic, shallots, potatoes, leafy vegetables, and the crucifers should perform nicely for you. You will have a tough go getting eggplant, peppers, corn, tomatoes, and the cucurbits to mature. In all cases and especially at higher elevations, encourage rapid growth with a good fertilizer that is high in phosphorus, a

nutrient that encourages strong growth in cool soils. Go easy on the nitrogen, which delays maturity and ripening.

A gentle slope of not more than 1 percent (1 inch drop every 8 feet) provides good air circulation and allows cold air to flow down and away from the garden. If the slope faces south, the soil will warm faster in spring, allowing earlier planting. Buildings and trees located at the bottom of a slope impede airflow and contribute to the formation of a frost pocket. Gardens sited in low areas and affected by frost pockets are more likely to suffer frost damage and their soils may be cold, wet, and poorly drained.

If you are considering planting next spring in an area that is now lawn, kill the grass before you till it under. Cover the area with black polyethylene (plastic) weighted down. Leave the plastic in place for the entire growing season to kill the grass. At the end of summer, turn under the dead grass to add valuable organic matter to your soil.

Most of us cannot choose the best soil type for our garden, and many of us must garden in thin, infertile soils. But if you have a choice, then plant in a sandy or silt loam. These combine both good water-holding capacity with good drainage and are light enough to allow good root penetration. We'll share more about soils later.

SPACE SAVERS

Some of us just don't have the space to plant a large garden, but you can make the most of what you have by using space-saving techniques.

RAISED BEDS

Raised beds are usually about 6 to 9 inches deep with soil held in place by 2 × 8- or 2 × 10-inch lumber. The soil in them is easier to improve with liberal additions of organic matter and can be brought to a fine tilth (lots of good, fluffy particles in the soil) by thorough preparation. Soil in raised beds warms up earlier in spring than soil in a conventional garden, especially if the bed is sloped about 1 to 5 percent to the south.

TRELLISES

Cucurbits and indeterminate tomatoes like to sprawl, but you can train them to run up a trellis to save space. This "vertical cropping" saves lots of space. A trellis can be built with a wooden frame and poultry fencing and set on posts at a 45° angle. Cucurbits will climb up a trellis but you will have to tie tomato stems in place. A trellis made of heavy twine or wire strung between sturdy wooden posts is an excellent way to train tall peas, pole beans, cucumbers, and even tomatoes. The vertical orientation may be a little too much for the vine crops that bear heavier fruit, such as winter squash and pumpkins, so some gardeners make good use of old brassieres, nylon stockings, and onion bags by supporting the fruit in them and tying them to the trellis to take the weight off the fruit stem. It looks odd, but it works.

BROADCAST SOWING

Most of us plant vegetables in rows, but the walkways between the rows take up a lot of space. To save space, consider broadcasting seeds in one row up to 4 feet wide. It will be tougher to weed but you will be able to harvest an abundance of quick-growing crops such as spinach, Swiss chard, leaf lettuce, and radish.

PUTTING YOUR PLAN ON PAPER

You don't have to be a Picasso, but draw your garden plan on paper before the planting season. Include the varieties, crop succession (a new vegetable to follow the one in place), the amount of space you plan to allow for each vegetable, row length and spacing, and the planting dates. Group perennial vegetables, such as rhubarb, horseradish, and asparagus, on one side of the garden so they will be out of the way of the tiller. Plant vegetables that need more growing days, such as parsnip, tomato, melon, and winter squash, on another side of the garden, and short-season crops, such as carrot, radish, and leaf lettuce, on yet another side. Try to group plants that have similar cultural requirements and that are susceptible to the same pests. For example, group the crucifers (cabbage, broccoli, cauliflower, and so forth) together, the root vegetables together, and the cucurbits together. Plant tall plants like corn on the north side of the garden so they won't unduly shade the rest of the garden.

It is a relatively minor consideration, but try to plant in rows running north to south to allow the best distribution of sunlight. Plant corn in small blocks of several rows each, rather than in a few long rows, to permit better pollination and greater yields.

Sow fast-maturing, short-season vegetables such as leaf lettuce and radishes in short rows at two-week intervals. This allows an extended harvest season so that you don't end up with ten bushels of radishes in a single harvest! Consider intercropping; that is, planting fast-maturing vegetables such as radishes and leaf lettuce between rows of long-season ones such as tomatoes and peppers. The radishes utilize the empty space when the tomatoes are small. By the time the tomato plants need the extra space, the radishes will have been harvested.

See the Garden Vegetable Planting Guide in the index for information on basic planning and growing transplants. The table includes days to maturity, planting depth and spacing, projected yields and germination temperatures for 40 common vegetables.

If you follow the simple steps outlined in this chapter to plan before planting your garden, you will be on your way to a rewarding experience!

COOL-SEASON VEGETABLES WITH SPECIAL CONSIDERATIONS

Cool-season vegetables that mature quickly:

Kohlrabi	Mustard	Radish	Turnip
Leaf lettuce	Peas	Spinach	

Cool-season vegetables that do poorly in hot weather; transplant for early ripening or plant for fall harvest:

Butterhead lettuce	Cauliflower
Broccoli	Celeriac
Brussels sprouts	Celery
Cabbage	

Cool-season vegetables requiring a long season:

Beet	Kale	Potato
Carrot	Leek	Salsify
Endive	Onion	Shallot
Garlic	Parsnip	Swiss chard
Horseradish		

WARM-SEASON VEGETABLES WITH SPECIAL CONSIDERATIONS

Warm-season vegetables with shorter seasons that can be directly sown to the garden at lower elevations:

Beet	Okra	Sweet corn
Cucumber	Squash	

Warm-season vegetables with long seasons that should be transplanted to the garden:

Eggplant	Pepper	Watermelon
Muskmelon	Tomato	

Many herbs can be grown successfully in small containers.

APPLE
Malus domestica

Why It's Special—We can start with the apple in the Garden of Eden. It may well have been a pomegranate but the apple story has staying power. And things are "as American as apple pie." An apple a day . . . and Johnny Appleseed.

How to Plant & Grow—Plant small trees in a full sun spot in early spring as soon as the ground can be worked. Bare root, 2-year-old whips should be soaked before planting. Container trees or whips are planted in well-prepared holes with good drainage. Stake at the time of planting. They may be planted in large containers or espaliered (trained) against a warm wall in a narrow space. Some type of supportive structure is necessary to bear the fruit load. Semi-dwarf varieties of apples are the most productive trees adapted to this ornamental way of training. Apple varieties may be self-fertile or require another variety for cross-pollination. Determine this before planting.

Care & Maintenance—Fruit trees are pruned in the early spring. Organic care is recommended. Check with your nearest extension office for best practices for your specific area. Plants need at least 1 inch of water per week, minimum. If the leaves start to curl, water deeply.

Harvest & Best Selections—A taste of the apple, as well as its color, will tell you when it is ready. There are so many apple varieties and everyone has a favorite. Here are some of ours: 'Braeburn', 'Granny Smith', 'Gala', and 'Honey Crisp'.

APRICOT
Prunus armeniaca

Why It's Special—Apricots are considered very special. They are one of the first tree fruits of the season. Their warm honey fragrance is as lovely as their taste. Apricots make a delicious jam for toast. If you are lucky enough to have bushels of them, dry them and keep them for snacking through the winter months.

How to Plant & Grow—Plant small trees in a full sun spot in early spring as soon as the ground can be worked. Place them in the garden away from cold pockets, as they are very susceptible to frost injury of the blossoms. Plant in well-drained light to medium soil, neutral to slightly acid. Most varieties are self-fruitful (meaning they don't need a second tree as a pollinator), but experts suggest planting two varieties close together for best pollination. Apricots need a deep watering once every 7 to 10 days.

Care & Maintenance—Fruit trees are pruned in the early spring. Organic care is recommended. Check with your nearest extension office for spraying and pruning schedules specific to your area.

Harvest & Best Selections—You can usually tell if an apricot is ripe when it gives a bit under the gentle pressure of your thumb. Apricots are generally ripe around July 4th. For the warmer areas of the Rockies, these varieties are recommended: 'Wenatchee', 'Tilton', and 'TomCot'. For the cooler regions, try 'Moongold', 'Sungold', or 'Harcot'.

BLACKBERRY
Rubus spp.

Why It's Special—Blackberries are a luscious summer fruit, fleeting in the market, if you can even find them. If you do, they are costly, and seldom taste as good as you think they should. They are easy to grow at home, they won't have to be transported, and you can eat them right from the vine. If there are any left, you can make some jam, hide it in the pantry, and pull it out in February when you need to be reminded what summer tastes like.

How to Plant & Grow—Plant canes in the spring as soon as the ground can be worked. They need a sunny, well-drained site, but avoid planting them where any members of the nightshade family, such as tomatoes, may have been planted recently. Avoid sandy or clay soils. Erect varieties should be 4–6 feet apart and the rows 8–10 feet apart. Provide sturdy trellising or wire supports strung between sturdy posts. If you are growing only a few plants, train canes in a spiral around the stake.

Care & Maintenance—Keep canes free from weeds and firmly corralled by trellising. Various cultivars need specific pruning. Check with your local extension office for this information. Blackberries need 1 inch of water per week until harvest time in June.

Harvest & Best Selections—Blackberries should be harvested every few days, depending on the weather. 'Cherokee', 'Cheyenne', and 'Triple Crown' are recommended for the Rockies.

BLUEBERRY
Vaccinium spp.

Why It's Special—Blueberries are good and good for you too. Smart food, they are called—good for your brain and your immune system. Blueberries may take some extra work to get settled in the garden, but like all the other fruits in this chapter, nothing beats picking them fresh and popping them in your mouth. The shrubs themselves fit beautifully in the flower garden and mixed border since they turn a brilliant hot pink and red in the autumn.

How to Plant & Grow—Check with your extension agent for a soil test and recommendations on how to best prepare your soil for planting blueberries. They must be planted in soils with a high acidity so amending will be critical. Garden sulfur will need to be added, as well as organic compost. Raised beds are ideal for improved drainage. Plant the berries in full sun with plenty of room for air circulation.

Care & Maintenance—Blueberries need evenly moist soil and will require regular acidifying soil amendments.

Harvest & Best Selections—Berries will detach easily from the stems when ripe. Put a container under a branch and run your hands through the berries. Good varieties for the Rockies: Northblue with Northsky as pollinator; Chandler—world's largest blueberry, Zones 4–7; Blue Ray—good for hot summers, cold winters; Bluecrop, Hardy Blue—Zones 4–8, tolerant of clay soils; Patriot—very hardy to -30 degrees.

CHERRY
Prunus avium

Why It's Special—Cherries are a luscious summer fruit. They dangle like gems from the branches of the tree, beckoning cherry lovers one and all, including the feathered ones. Cherries go in cherries jubilee, cherry pie, cherry preserves, cherry brandy, brandied cherries over pork, and cherry cobbler.

How to Plant & Grow—Dig a hole as deep and two times as wide as the container the tree came in. Cherry trees need a minimum of 8 hours a day of full sun, and well drained soil. The hole must be big enough to allow the roots to spread out nicely. Plant so the graft line is 2 inches above the soil line. After backfilling, gently tamp down the soil to remove any air pockets. Water thoroughly at planting time. Soil should be moist 4 inches below the surface.

Care & Maintenance—Do not overwater. The spraying regimens for insects and diseases vary tremendously, so consult with your local extension agent for the best plan for your cherry trees.

Harvest & Best Selections—Dwarf trees produce in their third year. For cooking, 'Montmorency' is recommended; for sweet table cherries, try 'Bing', 'North Star', 'Lambert', and 'Rainier'.

CURRANT
Ribes spp.

Why It's Special—Currants are not a big ticket item in the local produce section, so the only way to guarantee fresh currants for jams and jellies is to grow them yourself. Yes, you will have to fight the birds for them, but it's worth it.

How to Plant & Grow—Shrubs are available in the nurseries in March. You can order bare-root plants in January, but don't have them shipped until you can get them in the ground, probably March. Plant in well-drained soils. If summer temperatures are generally in excess of 90 degrees, plant on the north side of your house. Enrich the soil with organic matter and mulch established plants with organic compost. Do not apply nitrogen. Plant 1 inch deeper than it came in the nursery pot. Drip irrigation is a plus; set it to water once a week, and thoroughly.

Care & Maintenance—Red currants are generally self-fruitful. Black currants need a second cultivar for fruit production. Currants have few insect issues but the birds love them. Netting may be in order.

Harvest & Best Selections—Fruits generally ripen in late summer. Black currants recommended: 'Consort' and 'Crusader', hardy to Zone 3. Red currants: 'Wilder', 'Red Lake', and 'Hinnomaki', hardy to Zone 4.

GOJI BERRY
Lycium barbarum

Why It's Special—Goji berry, or wolfberry, is a sweet, red-orange berry, eaten fresh but more often dried and used like raisins. The berries are extremely high in antioxidants, full of beta carotene and loaded with other minerals and nutrients. The plants and berries aren't bothered by pest or diseases. While hardy to only -10 degrees Fahrenheit, Gojis are heat- and drought-tolerant and do well in gardens in the Rockies. They are grown commercially in Northern China. The fruits can be used for raisins in granola or baking.

How to Plant & Grow—Goji berry plants are small shrubs, 6–8 feet tall at maturity. They need a sunny spot. They are self-fertile and will begin bearing one to two years after planting. The berries bloom in late spring and will ripen in the late summer or early fall.

Care & Maintenance—The plants and berries aren't bothered by pests. But keep the moisture even until they are well established.

Harvest & Best Selection—Only one variety is available now, 'Crimson Star'. Harvest in late summer or early fall when the fruit is sweet to the taste.

GRAPE
Vitis vinifera spp. *vulgaris*

Why It's Special—Grapes are an excellent edible landscape plant for the home garden. They provide shade, screening, and food. Grapes are available for jelly and juicing, as table fruits, or for winemaking. Vines live fifty to one hundred years, so consider them an investment.

How to Plant & Grow—Choose a sunny, sloping location, especially with a south or southwest slope, as this will be warmer and less prone to frost. Plant vines in rows going north and south. When planting, prune back all but one vigorous cane, and prune that back to two buds. Plant vines where they don't have to compete with lawn or trees.

Care & Problems—Grapes should be trained on a sturdy trellis and pruned carefully each spring. There are several pruning techniques, so please check with your county extension office for diagrams and instructions.

Harvest & Best Selections—For jelly, harvest when the grapes taste ripe. For your table, pick when color and flavor are at their best and before fruit drops from the vine. 'Concord', 'Interlaken', 'Vanessa', 'Valiant,' 'Canadian', 'Suffolk', and 'Glenora' are recommended. If you are interested in making homemade wine, contact your extension office for the best varieties for wine grapes and how to grow and train them.

PEACH AND NECTARINE
Prunus persica

Why It's Special—Peaches and nectarines are the quintessential late summer fruit. Unfortunately, the trees are not dependable in the coldest parts of the Rockies. Because they bloom very early, the flowers are often frost damaged and fail to produce fruit. For gardeners in the warmer region of the Intermountain West, plant these trees and hope for a luscious harvest. Even a few peaches every few years may be worth the effort.

How to Plant & Grow—Nectarines are essentially peaches without the fuzz, so what works for the peach tree will work for the nectarine. They need to be planted in well-drained soil, and if you can find a microclimate where they might be spared an early frost and still get 8 hours of sun, plant there.

Care & Maintenance—Prune after the first full season, carefully removing crossed or damaged branches. There are several pests and diseases that threaten peach trees, but each one needs specific treatment. Consult your local extension expert for advice.

Harvest & Best Selections—Harvest when the color is all yellow for peaches—a slight blush for nectarines—and there is a slight give to the shoulder flesh of the fruit. Fragrance is an indicator of ripeness too. Handle carefully to avoid bruising. Varieties with excellent flavor: 'Reliance', 'Elberta', 'Contender', 'Haven', and 'Polly'.

PEAR
Pyrus communis

Why It's Special—Juicy, fragrant pears are a fruit lovers' delight. Yes, you can grow them, in spite of short seasons and cold climates. Pears are a delicious source of Vitamin C and they "pair" well with cheeses (blue and aged white Cheddar).

How to Plant & Grow—Pear trees need full sun and well-drained soil. Espaliered trees are the solution for the gardens with very little space for a home orchard. "Espalier" means the trees are trained flat against a support or trellis. This method has been used for centuries in small gardens.

Care & Problems—Choose fire- and blight-resistant varieties and late bloomers.

Harvest & Best Selections—Pears are generally picked before they are ripe and need "curing." Harvest just as the color changes from deep green to yellow-green. Keep at 60 degrees to 70 degrees and allow them to ripen for seven to ten days. 'Gourmet' and 'Harvest Queen' are hardy in Zones 3–6; 'Bartlett' in Zones 5–8 ripen in August; 'Comice' in Zones 4–9; and 'Flemish Beauty' in Zones 4–7.

PLUM
Prunus domestica

Why It's Special—Plums are delicious eaten warm and fresh from the tree or made into conserves or a redolent, rich jam. They can be baked in pies and plum claflouti or dried as prunes. The trees are a beautiful ornamental addition to the garden.

How to Plant & Grow—Plum trees, like most plants, love rich, well-drained soil and full sun. European varieties are the hardiest. Stanley is sweet and rich, and though listed as self-fertile, a second European plum will increase yield. Careful pruning is important for fruit production.

Care & Problems—Borers and sawflies can damage plum trees. Great care should be used when treating fruit trees with insecticides. Pheromone (sex attractant) traps may be useful in trapping adult insects. Your local county extension office will have this information (free of charge).

Harvest & Best Selections—Recommended varieties include: 'Hildreth'—midseason, excellent quality, developed in Wyoming; 'Italian Prune' and 'Stanley'—Zones 4–9; and 'Mt. Royal' ripens in August—self-pollinating, Zones 5–9.

RASPBERRY
Rubus idaeus

Why It's Special—Raspberries, oh raspberries! The beautiful ruby jewels of the summer garden. These berries are very fragile, hence their price at the grocery store. They are easy to grow if you aren't overwhelmed by primocanes and floricanes.

How to Plant & Grow—Any well-drained soil is good for raspberries. Different varieties have different pruning needs so be sure to check with your local County Extension Service for the correct techniques for your specific plants. Try planting both summer- and fall-bearing varieties for extended harvests.

Care & Problems—Adequate water is needed for good fruit development. Check the soil 6–9 inches below the surface. Moist and cool is what you want. Water deeply and thoroughly before the ground freezes in late autumn. Hot, dry weather brings spider mites. Wash them off with a burst of water from the hose nozzle.

Harvest & Best Selections—Berries are ripe when they are plump and fully shaped. They should slip easily from the plant. Red varieties include 'Boyne'—early season, very hardy; 'Nova'—midseason, disease resistant; 'Latham'—midseason; and 'Heritage'—fall bearing. A good golden-colored option is the fall-bearing 'Fall Gold'.

RHUBARB
Rheum rhabarbarum

Why It's Special—For pure pucker power and good cooking, rhubarb is your plant. Tough as nails, it can take the bitter cold climate of the Rockies and still produce like a champ. When combined with strawberries, cherries, apples, custard, sugar, and a touch of ginger, it makes a delicious wine or rhurbartini.

How to Plant & Grow—The leaves are high in oxalic acid, and are toxic to people and animals. Grow rhubarb from crowns or starts in well-drained, organic soil. Rhubarb is a heavy feeder and appreciates regular side dressings of aged compost. Water deeply until it is well established.

Care & Problems—Trouble free, a well-sited, well-planted rhubarb crown can produce for decades. You can take cuttings from time to time to increase the number of plants in your garden. Visit www.rhubarbinfo.com for extensive information on rhubarb.

Harvest & Best Selections—Do not harvest the first season, allowing the plant to settle in and develop a good root system. The second year, stalks can be harvested by gently tugging at their base and giving a slight twist. You may also cut them at the bottom. Always leave a few stalks. 'Victoria', 'Macdonald's Crimson', and 'Crimson' are excellent cultivars.

STRAWBERRY
Fragaria spp.

Why It's Special—Strawberry shortcake. A bowl of strawberries for breakfast. Strawberry jam. That's why you grow strawberries. Homegrown strawberries will taste like strawberries are meant to taste. Plant plenty of them—the birds love them as much as we do!

How to Plant & Grow—Plant some of each type to extend your harvest: June bearing, everbearing, and day-neutral. Day-neutral will fruit the first year. They love well-drained soil; raised beds are a big plus. Plant them 9–12 inches apart in all directions.

Care & Problems—Strawberries need good drainage; deeply tilled sandy loam is ideal. Slugs can be a problem with berries that rest on the ground. Growing them in raised beds, woolly pockets, or in strawberry jars keeps them off the ground and away from the slugs. If they will be spreading on the soil, you may need to handpick slugs and snails or use a commercial bait product. Carefully follow the application instructions on the label.

Harvest & Best Selections—Look for these: 'Honeoye' and 'Totem'—especially cold hardy, June bearing; 'Tristar'— day-neutral; 'Fort Laramie' and 'Quinalt'— double cropping everbearing; 'Mara des Bois'—exquisite taste and fragrance, hard to find, late season; and 'Surecrop'— June everbearing.

ARTICHOKE
Cynara scolymus (Scolymus Group)

Why It's Special—Artichokes are exotic looking, fun to eat, and easy to grow. They are a staple of the Mediterranean diet, used in soups, salads, and grilled, steamed, or pickled. In the U.S, they are generally served as an appetizer or first course. To eat the artichoke (once it is cooked), peel the outer leaves off one by one, and bite against the soft end where it was connected to the bud, scraping the flesh from the leaf with either your bottom or top teeth.

How to Plant & Grow—Artichokes must be planted in full sun and given plenty of room. Artichokes may grow to be 3–4 feet tall and 4 feet wide. They do well in Zones 4–9. Transplants will give you a jump on the season. Move them into the garden when soil temperatures reach 60–65 degrees, generally early- to mid-spring.

Care & Maintenance—Removing small lateral buds near the largest bud tends to increase the size of the primary bud. Water well, but don't keep the soil too wet. Good drainage is essential. Aphids may be problematic. Wash off with a strong spray from the hose.

Harvest & Best Selections—Cut to harvest when heads are plump, firm, and the scales are still soft and green, before they start to open. That's about eighty-five to ninety-five days from transplant. Two varieties are easy to find: 'Green Globe' and 'Violetta'.

ASPARAGUS
Asparagus officinalis

Why It's Special—Asparagus is one crop that heralds the arrival of spring. It's a hardy perennial, delicious when prepared so many ways, and beautiful when left to go to seed in the garden. This is one more plant that can be tucked into the flower garden. Its feathery fronds make a perfect backdrop for other perennials.

How to Plant & Grow—Plant asparagus knowing it will stay in place for many years. Prepare the planting spot or trench well. The hole or trench should be 8 inches deep. Place the crown in the hole, and spread the roots out carefully. Cover with an inch or two of soil. Continue to fill the hole as the shoots grow until you have regained the original soil level, allowing the top inch or two of the shoot to remain above the soil line. Water thoroughly as the plants become established.

Care & Maintenance—Keep the weeds out of the asparagus plantings.

Harvest & Best Selections—The old advice was to forgo the first two seasons' harvest. That is no longer the case. You can harvest lightly the first season and a bit more the second. Snap the spears at the soil line when they are a size you want. When the plant is only pushing small thin spears, cease the harvest and allow those small ones to become fronds. Look for the pretty 'Purple Asparagus', and the male varieties, 'Viking' and 'Jersey Centennial'.

BEAN, SNAP
Phaseolus vulgaris

Why It's Special—Fresh green snap beans, slender *haricot verts* (French for fresh bean), steamed a bit, napped with a dash of olive oil and salt and pepper, eaten with the fingers? Oh, yes! Green beans are a good vegetable for freezing for later use. Wash them, blanch for a minute or two in boiling salted water, drain, and freeze in freezer bags.

How to Plant & Grow—Plant seeds in the garden two weeks before last frost in a sunny spot, in well-drained soil. Sow bush beans 2–3 inches apart, pole beans 6 inches apart and 1 inch deep. Beans need an inch of water per week. Be certain pole beans grasp their supports; they twine counterclockwise. Once they are twining, water and weed regularly.

Care & Problems—Do not handle the beans or plants when they are wet to avoid spreading diseases. If holes appear in leaves, you may have leaf bean beetles. Dust with diatomaceous earth. Wash pods thoroughly before eating.

Harvest & Best Selections—Harvest snap beans when they are not quite mature, just before you can see the swelling of the seeds in the pods. This is especially important when the summer weather turns real hot. Snap the bean off just above its cap. Pole bean recommendations are: 'Italian Romano', 'Kentucky Wonder' and 'Tricolor'. Bush bean recommendations include: 'Blue Lake', 'Kentucky Blue', 'Slenderette', and 'Dragon Tongue'.

BEET
Beta vulgaris

Why It's Special—Beets are all the rage again: red beets, golden beets, baby beets, striped beets, and all because someone decided to start roasting them. Oh, sure, they were always there—sweet and sour, pickled and cubed, or julienned on the salad bar—but they are BACK! You can pay quite a bit for a simple beet salad. Of course, it will come with some blue cheese or goat cheese and a couple of candied walnuts. You'll be glad you tried beets again.

How to Plant & Grow—Direct seed one month before last frost, in full sun in rich, loamy soil. Plant 1 inch deep, 2–4 inches apart, 12–30 inches between rows. Beets need 1 inch of water every seven to ten days.

Care & Maintenance—Keep the beet rows free of weeds, and keep them thinned as the crop progresses. You can eat the thinnings as small micro beets or baby beet greens. Beets have few pests. Occasionally, there will be leaf miners on greens but they won't hurt the root.

Harvest & Best Selections—Harvest when the roots are approximately 2 inches in diameter. Greens are harvested at the same time. Here are some recommended varieties for your garden: 'Bull's Blood' for greens, 'Chioggia' (red and white striped), 'Detroit Dark Red', 'Early Wonder', and 'Golden'.

BROCCOLI
Brassica oleracea (Italica Group)

Why It's Special—Eat your broccoli, it's good for you. It's a member of the cruciferous family and is loaded with calcium, Vitamin A, fiber, and potassium. It's a powerful antioxidant.

How to Plant & Grow—Broccoli is best set out as new seedlings. They may be purchased or sown inside several weeks before the last frost date in your area. Plant outside when the soil temperatures reach 40 degrees, in the early spring. Plant in full sun or with a little bit of shade, but not less than 5 hours of sun. Plant in rich, well-drained soil, 12–24 inches apart in rows that are 18–36 inches apart.

Care & Maintenance—Broccoli needs a minimum of 1 inch of water per week. The presence of white butterflies means you have cabbage worms. Use row covers to prevent adult butterflies from laying their eggs.

Harvest & Best Selections—Depending on the variety you planted, broccoli is ready in fifty-five to seventy-eight days. Cut when heads are 3–6 inches in diameter and cut 8–10 inches of the stem. Soak in cool salt water 15 minutes to remove cabbage worms. Look for these varieties: 'Premium Crop', 'Windsor' (heat tolerant), and 'Goliath' (early with many side shoots).

BRUSSELS SPROUTS
Brassica oleracea (Gemmifera Group)

Why It's Special—Brussels sprouts developed from wild cabbage. Legend has it they were first discovered growing in the fields near Brussels, Belgium, in the 1600s. By 1821, they had become wildly popular in Belgium and France. Brussels sprouts are a non-heading cabbage grown for its auxiliary buds. Most gardeners agree that the sprouts we grow ourselves taste superior to the store-bought ones.

How to Plant & Grow—Direct seed or transplant as soon as the soil can be worked. Brussels sprouts are generally set out as transplants in the cooler parts of the Rockies because of the shorter growing season here. Plant in full sun or in a site with a little afternoon shade. Plants should be 18–24 inches apart and the rows 24–40 inches apart. They require regular watering, at least 1 inch per week.

Care & Maintenance—Brussels sprouts tolerate cold better than some crucifers. They can survive temperatures below 20 degrees. Cool temperatures mellow and improve their flavor and help the plant form tight, compact buds.

Harvest & Best Selections—Remove the end bud after the lower sprouts have begun to form. This increases the size of the remaining sprouts. Begin with the lowest leaf; remove it by cutting the leaf stalk at its base, then cut the lowest bud from the stem, continuing up the stem as buds are ready. 'Jade Cross', 'Tasty Nuggets', and 'Oliver' are recommended.

CABBAGE
Brassica oleracea (Capitata Group)

Why It's Special—Cabbage has been eaten for more than three thousand years. Prior to that, it was considered medicinal only. The modern "heading" types were grown in England by 1536. It was introduced into Virginia in 1669. Folks that wouldn't be caught in the same room with cooked cabbage will eat coleslaw without a whimper. Fermented cabbage is what we know as sauerkraut.

How to Plant & Grow—Sow seeds indoors eight weeks before the last frost date, and set out six weeks later. Plant cabbage in full sun or a spot that has a few hours of afternoon shade. Plan for it to mature before the temperatures go above 80 degrees. Space the plants 12–24 inches apart with 24-36 inches between the rows. Direct seed for fall crops when soil temperatures fall below 65 degrees.

Care & Maintenance—Inadequate water will cause the heads to crack; give cabbage at least 1 inch per week. Soaker hoses are preferred. Cabbage worms can be problematic. Use row covers to prevent adult butterflies from laying their eggs. Treat worms with Bt, (*Bacillus thuringiensis*) as the package directs.

Harvest & Best Selections—Cut heads from plants when firm and mature, leaving a few of the wrapper leaves on the head (this helps retain moisture). Good varieties for the Rockies include 'Early Copenhagen Market', 'Stonehead', 'Red Express', and 'Alcosa', a savoy type.

CARROT

Daucus carota var. *sativus*

Why It's Special—Carrots have been cultivated for thousands of years. The roots of early carrots were purple and the yellow-orange color arose as a mutation. The Dutch further developed orange varieties in the 1600s.

How to Plant & Grow—Sow seeds as soon as the soil can be worked. Follow with new plantings every two to three weeks. Plant carrots in full sun, where the soil has been deeply prepared and is free of rocks. Light sandy soil is a plus and will yield straight and smooth carrots. Cover seeds with just ¼ inch of fine soil. When plants appear, thin to one plant every 2 inches.

Care & Maintenance—Weed carefully. You should mound the soil over the green root tops a couple of weeks before harvest to avoid the greening of their "shoulders." Carrots have few pests. Water regularly, and do not let the soil dry out.

Harvest & Best Selections—Carrots mature in fifty-five to seventy days. Harvest when they are 1–1½ inches in diameter at the top of the root. Look for seeds of 'Purple Haze', 'Napoli', and 'Scarlet Nantes'.

CAULIFLOWER

Brassica oleracea (Botrytis Group)

Why It's Special—Cauliflower is a beautiful vegetable, and another one that is loved by some and reviled by others. It is good when it is slightly steamed or blanched, a process that makes it easier for many to digest. There are all kinds of recipes for cauliflower heads: roasted in a hot oven, drizzled with a cheese sauce, stir-fried, or pickled in the famous condiment called Italian giardiniera. Giardiniera is a hot or mild pickle made with cauliflower, celery, olives, peppers, and carrots.

How to Plant & Grow—Cauliflower grows best in cool moist weather. Transplant seedlings in early spring or a minimum of sixty days before first frost. Plant in full sun but be prepared to blanch the "curds" (heads)—protect from sunlight to get a nice white curd. Plants should be 14–24 inches apart in rows 30 inches apart. Rich, organic soil is required for good "curd" development. Cauliflower needs moderate water, at least 1 inch per week.

Care & Maintenance—Try to avoid summer heat by planting in early spring or late summer. Leaves may be placed over forming "curds" to keep them white. Sometimes there are problems with cabbage worms; check your county extension office for assistance.

Harvest & Best Selections—Cut the blanched curd from the stem when it is about 6 inches in diameter. Recommended selections are: 'Early White', 'Snow Crown', 'Graffiti', and 'Veronica' (lime green Romanesco type).

COLLARDS

Brassica oleracae (Acephala Group)

Why It's Special—Collards are a form of non-heading cabbage. They were enjoyed by the Greeks and Romans before a banquet with the thought that they prevented one's mind from being clouded by wine. Like many vegetables, they are biennials grown as annuals and very popular in Southern gardens. They are excellent sautéed with a little chopped onion, some garlic, and of course, some cured pork bits.

How to Plant & Grow—Direct seed or transplant as early as the soil can be worked. Best grown as a spring or fall crop. Plant in full sun or part shade 8 inches apart in rows 18–30 inches apart. Well-prepared, fertile, well-drained soil is standard.

Care & Maintenance—Harvest older, larger leaves, and the bud will continue producing as the stem elongates. After several weeks of harvest, the plant will resemble a tuft of leaves on a tall stalk. If multiple harvests aren't the issue, harvest the entire plant when it is 6–12 inches tall. Cabbage loopers and worms should be handpicked or the plants treated with Bt (*Bacillus thuringiensis*) according to the label instructions.

Harvest & Best Selections—Collards are ready to harvest in about sixty days. 'Champion' and 'Vates' are the most popular varieties.

CORN

Zea mays var. *saccharata*

Why It's Special—Corn is good in so many ways: fresh corn on the cob with butter running down your chin, popcorn, creamed corn, fried corn, tortillas, corn chips, the list goes on. Corn is one of the few native American vegetables. Sweet corn is a mutant of "field corn" or "cow corn" wherein the conversion of sugar to starch is delayed.

How to Plant & Grow—Sow corn directly into the garden when soil temperatures reach 60 degrees. Plant early, mid-season, and late-ripening varieties at the same time. Plant in blocks to aid in pollination. Locate the corn in full sun. When plants are about 5 inches tall, thin to ·10 inches apart. Soil should be well amended with rich, organic compost. Corn will not tolerate drought or flooding. Water deeply and on a regular schedule. If the leaves are tightly rolled, water right away.

Care & Maintenance—Corn ear worms and earwigs might be an issue. As corn pests and diseases vary by region, please consult with your local extension agent for appropriate remedies.

Harvest & Best Selections—Maturity varies widely depending on the varieties you are growing, generally from sixty-three to ninety-one days. Examine the ears twenty days after "silking." After the silks begin to dry, crush a kernel with your finger. If "milk" comes out, it's ready. Favorites are: 'Bodacious', 'Butter and Sugar', 'Early Sunglow', 'Northern Xtra Sweet', 'Silver Queen', 'Sugar Buns', and 'Spring Treat'.

CUCUMBER

Cucumis sativus

Why It's Special—The cucumber may have originated in Southeast Asia at least twelve thousand years ago. It has been grown for its fruit for the last three thousand years and passed from India into Greece and Rome. The Romans raised cucumbers in greenhouses in the winter. DeSoto reported the native people in Florida were growing cucumbers "better than those found in Spain."

How to Plant & Grow—Plant cucumbers as seeds or seedlings when all danger of frost has passed. They need full sun and should be planted 3–4 inches apart in a row or a hill. Thin to 8–12 inches apart with rows 4–6 feet apart. Plant at the edges of the garden so they have room to spread or grow on a trellis. Black plastic mulch increases yields substantially. Cultivate shallowly and often until the plants begin to flower.

Care & Maintenance—Pick the fruit while green and several inches long (slicers) or 2–4 inches long for making pickles. Never let cucumbers ripen on the vine. This is a signal for the plants to stop producing.

Harvest & Best Selections—Cucumbers are ready to harvest approximately sixty days after planting. Keep them picked. Excellent varieties to grow include 'Straight Eight', 'Burpless', 'Pickalot', 'Boston Pickler', and 'Sweet Slice'.

EGGPLANT

Solanum melongena var. *esculentum*

Why It's Special—Eggplant has a long culinary history dating back to at least the fifth century B.C. It may have originated in China, making its way to Spain and the Middle East, Africa, and Brazil before it came to the New World. Unfortunately, as a member of the nightshade family of plants, it was considered poisonous and was avoided by early American settlers. Eggplant is delicious grilled, layered with mozzarella, in the dip baba ganoush, or in eggplant Parmesan.

How to Plant & Grow—Plant transplants into the garden when warm weather arrives and frost is no longer a threat. Plant in full sun in soil that has been amended with organic compost. Eggplants have beautiful lavender flowers and fit nicely into patio containers or tucked into a perennial border. Keep plants well watered as drought stress and cold weather will reduce yields substantially.

Care & Maintenance—Eggplants need little maintenance, once established in the garden. An additional side dressing of plant food every six weeks will promote fruiting. Flea beetles may be a problem but a dusting of diatomaceous earth will reduce their numbers.

Harvest & Best Selections—Harvest when the fruits are glossy and the proper size indicated on the tag/seed packet. 'Black Beauty', 'Ichiban', 'Millionaire', and 'Fairy Tale' are good choices.

GARLIC
Allium spp.

Why It's Special—Full of chemical compounds that are good for the heart and the immune system (noted for its ability to fight infection), it makes sense to grow your own organic garlic. It is easy to grow at home, and it takes just a little bit of space in the vegetable garden or tucked into the perennial border. Yes, tuck edibles into the flowerbeds.

How to Plant & Grow—Plant in the early spring where the spring seasons are long enough; where they are short, garlic performs better as a fall-planted crop to be harvested next summer. Fall planting should be done from September 15 to October 15. Plant where the soil is rich, loose, and in full sun. The bulb is a compound of small cloves, each having two mature leaves and a vegetative bud. Separate cloves before planting, root side (flat side) down, pointy tip up.

Care & Maintenance—Growing garlic in dry soil reduces bulb size. Garlic has few pests.

Harvest & Best Selections—Stiff-neck garlic: when the scape (flowerbud) straightens, the bulbs are ready to harvest. Soft-neck garlic has no woody scape; it is ready for harvest when the bottom leaves have turned brown. Soft-neck recommendations include: 'New York White' and 'Chesnok'. Stiff-neck recommendations: 'German Extra Hardy' and 'Inchelum'.

HORSERADISH
Armoracia rusticana

Why It's Special—Horseradish is a potent root with very little aroma until it is cut open. When it releases its volatile oils, it will make a grown man cry. "Prepared horseradish" is generally a mixture of the grated white root with salt and vinegar. It is sold in the supermarket, but lacks the oomph of the homemade version. Try a little fresh or prepared horseradish in a Bloody Mary. A dab of it with some good ketchup makes a tasty cocktail sauce for steamed shrimp.

How to Plant & Grow—Root cuttings can be transplanted in early spring when soil can be worked. Select fairly straight roots about 10 inches long and nickel thick, and plant them at a 45-degree angle, 4–5 inches deep and 18 inches apart. Position the tops of the roots upward. Plant them in full sun, in fine soil. Horseradish needs low to moderate water.

Care & Maintenance—Dig the roots when the tops have been killed by frost. Remove the tops and cut the longest side roots for planting next year, cutting their tops square but making a slanting cut on their bottoms. Leave in the ground over winter. Dig and set out in the spring. If the leaves are small and discolored and the plants look stunted, they may have rust or mosaic and must be removed from the garden.

Harvest & Best Selections—Harvest anytime after killing frost. 'Maliner Kren' and 'Big Top Western' are good cultivars. **Note:** Always grind horseradish outside or in a well-ventilated area. Trust us.

LEEK
Allium ampeloprasum

Why It's Special—Leeks are the mild-mannered granddaddies of the onion family. They have a subtle onion flavor and have been used for centuries in soups, braised for side dishes, and tucked into meat and vegetable pies. Julia Child introduced American cooks to the famous French dish *Vichyssoise*, a chilled leek and potato soup.

How to Plant & Grow—Leek plants are usually started in hot beds or cold frames and transplanted in early spring. If you're started with seeds, plant ¼ to ½ inch deep. Thin to 6 inches apart. Hill the soil around their bases to blanch the lower portions as they grow through the season, beginning when they are several inches tall.

Care & Maintenance—Water thoroughly every week.

Harvest & Best Selections—Leeks will be ready to harvest in about seventy-five to ninety days. Harvest them when they are at ½ to 1 inch in diameter and have 4 to 6 inches of blanched stem. Some cultivars I recommend include 'King Richard', 'Large American Flag', 'Titan', and 'Giant Musselburgh', which are all excellent disease-resistant cultivars.

LETTUCE
Lactuca sativa

Why It's Special—Lettuce is the stuff of which salads are made. Sadly, over the years, 'Iceberg' developed a bad rap, kind of like the Titanic. 'Iceberg' has some redeeming possibilities: sliced into a wedge and topped with a dollop of chunky blue cheese or ranch dressing, a sprinkling of crispy bacon bits and maybe some chopped tomato—*that* is a salad! Lettuce is the "L" in BLT. Try a grilled romaine salad for a whole new twist on lettuce salads.

How to Plant & Grow—Direct seed after spring nighttime temperatures are above freezing. It does well planted in the fall too. Direct seed in rows or blocks. You can eat the thinnings as you pull them.

Care & Maintenance—Lettuce needs a moderate amount of water. Do not let the soil dry out for more than a day. Bolting is the result of long days, hot temperatures, and drought. Planting in spring and fall will alleviate these issues. Slugs and snails can be a problem; handpick and discard them.

Harvest & Best Selections—Loose-leaf varieties are harvested forty to fifty days after planting. Baby lettuce mixes may be harvested anytime. Butterhead and romaine are ready in fifty-five to seventy days. 'Red Sails' and 'Red Salad Bowl' are two pretty varieties.

MUSKMELON
Cucumis melo (reticulatus)

45°

Why It's Special—Few true cantaloupes are grown in the United States. Rather, you eat a muskmelon with your breakfast, not a cantaloupe. Marketers changed the name because cantaloupe sounds so much better than muskmelon. Okay. Try it with a piece of prosciutto wrapped around it or puréed in a cold soup. Muskmelons, the orange ones in particular, are chock full of beta carotene and good for your immune system.

How to Plant & Grow—Plant after the last frost date in your area. Direct seed in hills or rows, planting them 1 inch deep, and thinning to 18–24 inches apart in the "hill" system. You can have three plants in a 48-inch diameter hill. Water thoroughly once a week or more if the vines start to wilt. Drip irrigation is recommended because it keeps the foliage and fruit from getting wet. Black plastic mulch may increase production. Melons can be trained on a fence or trellis as long as you support the heavy fruits with mesh bags tied to the support system.

Care & Maintenance—Cucumber beetles can be picked by hand. Choose varieties resistant to fusarium wilt and blight.

Harvest & Best Selections—Muskmelons are ripe when the rind changes from green to tan/yellow. The stem should separate easily from the vine. Excellent varieties include 'Charentais', 'Ambrosia', 'Golden Gopher', and 'Harper Hybrid'.

OKRA
Abelmoschus esculentus

Why It's Special—The stuff of gumbos and vegetable horror stories, you either like okra or you don't. Try it prepared in stir-fries or pickled when the texture hasn't been ruined. Grow it for the gorgeous, baby hibiscus-like flowers if for no other reason. Or quickly stir-fry with bacon, tomatoes, and a touch of sugar. The dried seedpods are great for craft projects such as holiday wreaths (this tidbit was offered up by one of those folks who won't eat okra but who still grows it).

How to Plant & Grow—Spineless types are popular; look for Clemson Spineless. Soaking seeds in water at room temperature overnight just before planting speeds germination. Plant when the soil has warmed to 75 degrees. Although okra does do well in short mountain seasons, it thrives between 85 and 95 degrees. Set transplants in the garden but do not disturb their roots.

Care & Problems—When the pods start to form, side dress carefully with an organic 5-10-5 plant food.

Harvest & Best Selections—Cut the pods when they are four to six days old and 2–4 inches long and their color is bright. Recommended selections include 'Clemson Spinless'—fifty-five days, heirloom; 'North and South'—fifty days, tolerates cool weather, very productive; 'Cajun Delight'—forty-nine days, good for northern gardens; and 'Red Burgundy'—fifty-five days, red stems and pods.

ONION
Allium cepa

Why It's Special—"You make us cry without hurting us . . ." wrote the poet Pablo Neruda in his "Ode to an Onion." Few pantries are without these pungent beauties and for very good reasons. The simple, layered onion can elevate the humblest of foods to delicious heights. Onions come in red, yellow, white, green as in spring onions or scallions, flat brown Italian onions known as cipollinis, and small, white pearl onions, just to name a handful. Please grow some.

How to Plant & Grow—Onions are easy to grow and they can be harvested when they are about pencil thick. Onion sets produce a crop three to four weeks earlier and yield more than seeded onions. Plant the sets right-side up about 3 inches apart and cover lightly with soil. Dime-sized sets are perfect.

Care & Problems—Onions must be well watered but excess water results in soft bulbs that store poorly. Stop watering when the onion tops begin to fall over to encourage the plants to "harden up."

Harvest & Best Selections—Pull for drying when the tops fall over. Recommendations are 'Candy'—eighty-five days, mild, sweet; 'Red Burgermaster'—one hundred twelve days, red, excellent quality; 'Stuttgarter'—one hundred two days, long storage life; and 'Ebenezer'—one hundred five days, heirloom, mild, sweet, longkeeping.

PARSNIP
Pastilnaca sativa

Why It's Special—Parsnips are not as well known as they deserve to be but they've been around forever, mentioned as early as the first century and grown on Charlemagne's imperial estates in Europe since the ninth century. Take a long, nice, creamy white parsnip, peel it, cut into ½-inch slices, dress with olive oil, salt, and pepper, and roast at 500 degrees for 10–20 minutes. This way of cooking yields a positively delicious parsnip and is a great reason to grow them.

How to Plant & Grow—Parsnips need nice fine soil, free of stones and hardpan. Direct seed as soon as the soil is tillable, planting ½ inch deep. They take up to three weeks to germinate. Start cultivation ("weeding" by another name) as soon as the foliage appears. Some folks plant each seed in a soil-filled toilet paper tube, and then insert the soil plug with a beginning parsnip right into the garden. The paper tube will disintegrate as the parsnip grows to maturity.

Care & Problems—Tunnels and worms can be headed off by planting a "trap" crop of radishes nearby. Rotate root crops and avoid planting them in the same place for three years.

Harvest & Best Selections—Dig roots as you need them. Recommendations include 'Hollow Crown'—one hundred five days; 'Harris Model'—one hundred twenty days; and 'Javelin'—one hundred ten days.

PEA, GARDEN
Pisum sativum (Garden Pea)
Pisum sativum var. *macrocarpa*
(Edible-podded Pea)

Why It's Special—In the old days, green peas were considered unfit to eat. I don't mean in 1950 when mom cooked the canned peas to within an inch of their salty, mushy little lives. Until a few hundred years ago, only dried peas were eaten. The colonists brought the English pea with them. Now we have garden peas, edible pods, sugar snap peas, and the latest delicacy, pea vine tendrils.

How to Plant & Grow—Plant seeds as soon as the soil temperatures reach 40 degrees. Many folks make a ritual of planting on St. Patrick 's Day. Plant in full sun, rich soil, in a single or double row. Plant seeds 3–4 inches apart, 2 feet between the rows. Twigs and sticks make great free supports for pea vines. When the crop is harvested, compost or throw away the branches and dead vines.

Care & Maintenance—Water peas thoroughly once a week.

Harvest & Best Selections—Harvest by grasping the pods in your hand and snapping them from the stem. Harvest early in the morning or drop freshly harvested peas in ice water to retain sweetness. Snap pea: 'Sugar Ann'. Snow pea or pea pod: 'Oregon Sugar Pod'. Standard green peas include: 'Little Marvel', 'Wanda', and 'Frosty'.

PEPPER, HOT
Capsicum annuum (Conoides Group)

45°

Why It's Special—In 1493, Columbus took peppers across the sea. He reportedly introduced chili peppers to Europe, and their use spread rapidly; the fruits were dried, ground, and used as a substitute for expensive black pepper. Peppers were so valued that jalapeños were bartered and used to pay taxes during the Spanish conquest of Mexico.

How to Plant & Grow—Peppers should be transplanted into warm garden soil after your last hard frost. Soaker hoses are preferred—or a watering can—to keep water off the leaves and fruit. Black plastic mulch will increase the yield of high quality fruit.

Care & Problems—Flower drop can occur when the weather has been too cold or too hot or if the soil is overwatered. It is a very good idea to carefully read the plant tag or seed packet growing instructions.

Harvest & Best Selections—When a pepper has developed the color and size you want, pick it. Wear gloves when harvesting and cooking hot peppers as the oils in their flesh can easily irritate skin. Recommendations include 'Thai Dragon'—seventy-five days, very hot; 'Red Rocket'—sixty-five to eighty-five days, cayenne type, hot; 'Jalapeño'—sixty-five to eighty days, cayenne type, hot; and 'Habañero'—seventy-five to one hundred days, very hot.

PEPPER, SWEET
Capsicum annuum (Grossum Group)

45°

Why It's Special—Sweet peppers add zing, a layer of aroma, and great color to many dishes. Red, yellow, and orange bell peppers have a milder flavor than the green ones, yet most folks think of green peppers when they think of cooking with them. Spend some time investigating the many different pepper varieties available: sweet, hot, and mild.

How to Plant & Grow—Sweet bells should be transplanted outdoors when all danger of frost is over and the soil is warm. Black plastic mulch may improve yields but any organic mulch will keep the soil moist and the weeds at bay.

Care & Problems—Too much water causes the flowers and small fruit to abort. Soaker hoses or drip irrigation works nicely to keep water off the foliage.

Harvest & Best Selections—Harvest by cutting or snapping the stem of the ripe peppers. A green bell pepper is still unripe; if left on the plant, they will ripen to a beautiful red. Recommended selections are 'California Wonder'—seventy-five days, heirloom; 'Gypsy'—sixty-five days, great for stir-frying; and 'Big Bertha'—seventy days, very large fruit.

POTATO, IRISH
Solanum tuberosum

Why It's Special—Entire fortunes are staked on the famous Idaho potato, and it still appears on the Idaho automobile license plates. Nothing beats a wonderful Idaho russet when it comes to bakers or twice-baked potatoes or a greasy, salty, incredible French fry. Grow your own for the freshest, easiest, and tastiest varieties. Potatoes are available in dozens of shapes, sizes, and colors.

How to Plant & Grow—Plant your seed potatoes in soil that has warmed to 45 degrees. Set them 4 inches deep in a trench or a hole and fill it as the plant grows, lightly covering the apex of the plant with soil until it is filled in. Gardeners are also planting spuds in jumbo potato "grow bags" or large perforated pots.

Care & Problems—Plant in dry soil; tubers can easily rot in wet soil. Maintaining even, thorough soil moisture is important. Soaker hoses are a good idea.

Harvest & Best Selections—'Red Norland', 'Red Pontiac', 'Adirondak Blue', 'Kennebek' (white skin) and 'Yukon Gold' do well here. Dig potatoes about two weeks after the vines have started to yellow and die.

PUMPKINS AND WINTER SQUASH
Cucurbita maxima

Why It's Special—A pumpkin was used for Cinderella's carriage, and Halloween wouldn't be hallowed were it not for jack-o-lanterns. And there's the fact that pumpkins and winter squash can be stored and eaten all winter. That's why they are special!

How to Plant & Grow—Winter squash and pumpkins require a long, warm season from eighty to one hundred forty days. Dry, sunny weather is important for good pollination. Plant seeds of bush varieties 2 feet apart in rows 5 feet apart. In the "hill" method, create a raised hill 48 inches in diameter and plant three to five seeds. Thin to two to three plants when they have their first set of leaves.

Care & Problems—Squash bugs can ruin a crop in very little time. Do your best to handpick.

Harvest & Best Selections—Harvest pumpkins and winter squash when they are fully mature (eighty to one hundred forty days after planting) and a deep color. The fruit rinds should be so hard your fingernail cannot puncture them. Harvest before a frost. Cut from the vine leaving a 2-inch piece of stem on the fruit. There are many, many varieties. Here are a few standard types: 'Hubbard', 'Table Ace', 'Butterqueen', 'Lumina,' 'Baby Boo', and 'Big Max'. A beautiful pumpkin—reportedly the model for Cinderella's carriage—is the heirloom named 'Rouge Vif d'Etampes'.

RADISH
Raphanus sativus

Why It's Special—A good many gardeners started gardening with radishes as their very first crop. The first sets of leaves are heart-shaped and appear in seven to ten days. Radishes are good fresh, cooked, and pickled. Spicy Salad green seed mixes include radish seeds. You may see the tiny red radish root when you harvest the greens. They add a kick to any green salad. In France, radishes are served with fresh butter and salt as an appetizer.

How to Plant & Grow—Plant seeds ½ inch deep, aiming for 1 inch apart. Thin to 1 inch when leaves appear. Plant more seeds every seven to ten days for a steady supply. Radishes flourish when temperatures are between 50 and 65 degrees. Plant plenty of seeds; use the thinning in salads or like sprouts on a sandwich. Plant a second crop in late August or the first of September for a second harvest.

Care & Problems—Hot weather and inadequate water will cause the radishes to turn "hot" to the taste. Because they grow quickly and are harvested quickly, they aren't susceptible to many diseases. A row cover will help with flea beetles.

Harvest & Best Selections—Harvest when a "test" radish is pulled and appears to be the perfect size. 'Champion', 'Cherry Balls', 'Daikon Long White', 'Easter Egg', and 'French Breakfast' cultivars do well in the Intermountain West.

RUTABAGA
Brassica napos

Why It's Special—Originally from Scandinavia, rutabagas, also called Swede turnips, are yellow to orange, smooth and high in Vitamin A. They have purple shoulders, as do turnips, but are generally larger and coarser in appearance. Their rich, earthy flavor makes them ideal for cubing, tossing with good olive oil, salt and pepper, and roasting at 500 degrees for 10 to 20 minutes. As with turnips, you may want to cube a rutabaga and add it to boiling potatoes for a little kick to your mashers.

How to Plant & Grow—Plant in fertile soil, ¼–½ inch deep about 4 inches apart. Water well in dry weather. A good crop for planting in July, as rutabagas will be ready in October.

Care & Problems—Rotate crops and where they are planted from year to year. Rutabagas do not compete well with weeds so stay on top of weeding chores. Aphids can be thwarted with a strong spray of water on the leaves or careful application of insecticidal soap. Handpick cabbage worms or treat plants with Bt (*Bacillus thuringiensus*).

Harvest & Best Selections—Harvest (dig) when the bulbs are 3–4 inches in diameter, before the first hard frost. 'American Purple Top' and 'Marian' are recommended.

SPINACH
Spinacia oleracea

Why It's Special—Spinach packs a punch when it comes to vitamins and nutrients. It is simple to grow, and it can be cut in the garden and on the salad plate in a matter of minutes.

How to Plant & Grow—The 1982 edition of the *Victory Garden Cookbook* has it right: prepare the spot for spinach in the fall, so come spring, the seeds can be planted the day the soil thaws. If planted in a wide row, or large container, you can eat the thinning as the crop develops. Cool weather, nice soil, and adequate moisture will result in a healthy crop of spinach. Replant in August.

Care & Problems—If you snip the plants for salads, as they grow to a perfect size, they will regrow for several harvests. Do not get the foliage wet. Leaf miners may be a nuisance. Remove "tunneled" leaves from the garden.

Harvest & Best Selections—'Melody', 'Bloomsdale Long-standing', and 'Tyee' are recommended for Rocky Mountain gardens. Malabar spinach (*Basella alba*) is a heat-loving spinach-like green with beautiful red stems. It grows as a vine and shines in hot weather. Provide netting or some sort of support for it to grow on.

SUMMER SQUASH
Cucurbita pepo

45°

Why It's Special—Who doesn't love squash? Pickled, steamed, made into (zucchini) bread—it's delicious! Summer squash comes in many colors and shapes. Most common are squash that are green, yellow, or white. Squash dimensions can be round, flat (called patty pan), or straight. Zucchini can also be round ('Eight Ball' and 'Cue Ball') or club-shaped.

How to Plant & Grow—Summer squash need only about 40 to 60 days to produce a bumper crop. Dry sunny weather is critical for good pollination, though drought will reduce fruit set. Bush varieties are well behaved in today's smaller gardens. Plant seeds of bush varieties 2 feet apart in rows 5 feet apart. In the hill method, mound up a raised dirt hill 48 inches in diameter and plant 3 to 5 seeds. Thin to 2 to 3 plants when they have their first set of leaves.

Care & Problems—Squash bugs can ruin a crop in very little time. Remove them by hand picking. Do not wet the foliage when watering.

Harvest & Best Selections—Pick squash 2 to 8 days after bloom when the fruit is 4 to 8 inches long, 2 inches in diameter (3 to 4 inches for patty pan), and when the rind is still soft. Zuke varieties include 'Cue Ball', 'Eight Ball', 'Raven', and the heirloom 'Romanesco'. Favorite patty pans include 'Scallopini', 'White Scallop', and the beautiful 'Pattison Striped', which is an heirloom.

SWISS CHARD
Beta vulgaris

Why It's Special—Swiss chard is a lovely edible green, perfect for sautéing whole when the leaves or small bunches are small, or if the plants have grown larger, just chop them coarsely and steam or sauté them a little longer. They can be mixed with other greens, onion, and a bit of bacon if you prefer. The new Bright Lights chard is a double bargain; it looks gorgeous in the ornamental garden and makes a tasty edible when harvested.

How to Plant & Grow—Direct seed or set out transplants as soon as the soil can be worked. Chard does best in full sun with regular watering. Thin seedlings to stand 4 inches apart, and then again at 10 inches, when the plants start to mature.

Care & Maintenance—Spring-planted chard lasts through the summer and into the fall. It responds well to large amounts of organic matter, so amend soil at planting time and side dress again in the summer. To control slugs and snails, use bait, drown, or broadcast diatomaceous earth or spent coffee grounds around the base of the plant.

Harvest & Best Selections—Cut entire plant at the base, or by removing the outer stalks over time about 1–2 inches above the soil line. Try 'Fordhook Giant', 'Virgo', 'Bright Lights', and 'Rhubarb'.

TOMATO
Lycopersicon lycopersicum

 45°

Why It's Special—Tomatoes are the most popular vegetable in the home garden. Whoever who has the first, the biggest, the ugliest, the prettiest, OR the tastiest tomato can claim bragging rights for at least one entire growing season.

How to Plant & Grow—Transplants are the preferred method for starting tomatoes in our unpredictable climate. The soil should be warm and the last frost over. Plant 24 inches apart in good soil. You may plant them deep enough to cover the first set of leaves on the stem; remove them before planting. Soaker hoses are the best way to deliver water to the plants.

Care & Problems—Tomatoes should be supported or staked. Pinch out the side shoots or suckers that develop in the "V" between the main stem and the strong branches. Try to be vigilant about this, as it keeps the plant's energy directed to fruit production. Regular adequate watering is critical. Failure to get the watering right results in blossom end rot and poor fruit production. Nasty hornworms should be removed by hand and disposed of. Use Bt *(Bacillus thuringiensus)* to control hornworms when they are still small.

Harvest & Best Selections—'Early Girl' and 'Celebrity' are top performers. For big slices, try 'Brandywine' the heirloom and 'Beefsteak'. 'Sungold' is a yellow cherry tomato that shines in our heat. Italian varieties are best for sauces and drying.

TURNIP
Brassica rapa

Why It's Special—Turnips have been used for food since prehistoric times. They grow wild in Siberia. Like the rutabaga, potato, and carrot, the turnip is delicious when cubed, tossed with olive oil, salt, and pepper, and roasted at high heat (500 degrees) for 10–20 minutes. Turnips are also delicious pared, sliced, and dressed lightly with some lemon juice and fresh salt and pepper. Add a chopped turnip to boiling potatoes and mash them all together with garlic and butter. Mmmm!

How to Plant & Grow—A fall crop has better flavor, so plant in August, ½ inch deep, 2–6 inches apart. A compost-rich soil will aid in producing a good crop. Fine, well-tilled soil results in nice, round, uniform turnips.

Care & Problems—Flea beetles can be discouraged with a spray of insecticidal soap or by using floating row covers. This will also deter root maggots since the adult flying insects will be kept at bay.

Harvest & Best Selections—Harvest when the roots are 2–3 inches in diameter. Greens can be harvested four to six weeks after planting. Maturity: fifty days for greens and sixty to seventy for roots. Recommended selections are 'Purple Top White Globe', 'Shogoin', and 'Seven Top' (exclusively for greens).

WATERMELON
Citrullus lanatus

 45°

Why It's Special—Ripe, juicy watermelons bring to mind summer fun and picnics. Believed to have originated in Africa, Dr. Livingstone (I presume) discovered fields of wild watermelons. They were also reported by European settlers in North America as being grown in the Illinois River Valley by Native Americans in the 1600s.

How to Plant & Grow—Northern and high elevation gardeners should try the "icebox" types of watermelons. These are small (about 10 pounds) and require only seventy to eighty days to ripen. Water is critical during fruit set and growth. They should be direct seeded in hills 48 inches across or started in peat pots and set out in the pot. They resent transplanting.

Care & Problems—As with so many edibles, a drop or soaker irrigation system is the preferred method of watering. Allow plenty of space to run.

Harvest & Best Selections—The groundspot, or pale spot, on a melon's rind where it has been sitting on the ground will turn from white to yellow as the fruit matures. The tendril opposite the melon will turn brown or black when the melon is ripe. Recommended selections are 'Sugar Baby'—Icebox type, seventy to eighty days; 'Charleston Grey'—heirloom, one hundred thirty days; 'Crimson Sweet'—large, one hundred thirty days; and 'Moon and Stars'—large heirloom, one hundred thirty days.

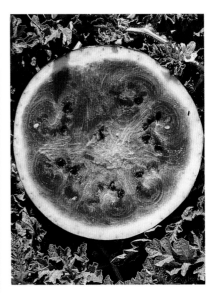

BASIL
Ocimum basilicum

Why It's Special—Basil is the essence of summer and when grown in your garden, it is pungent and perfect. There are many types of basil: cinnamon flavored, Eastern or Holy basil (*B. tenuiflorum*), and the distinctive Thai basil, identified by its reddish purple stems and sharper flavor.

How to Plant & Grow—Plant seeds 12 inches apart in well-drained fertile soil, where it is sunny and warm. Alternatively, set out seedlings after the last hard frost. Water regularly and do not let the soil dry out completely.

Care & Problems—Pinch off flower spikes and branch tips to encourage fullness and increased leaf production. If aphids appear, wash them off with a strong spray of water. You can treat basil with insecticidal soap but *always* wash the leaves well before eating them.

Harvest & Best Selections—Basil is ready to harvest in about 60 days, depending on the variety. 'Purple Leaf', 'Genovese', 'Thai' and 'Spicy Globe' are favorite cultivars.

In the Kitchen with Mary Ann—Add a few torn leaves of basil to an otherwise plain green salad. For a classic summer presentation, *Insalata caprese* can be made in minutes. Arrange fresh garden tomato slices with fresh mozzarella slices. Tuck fresh basil leaves among the tomatoes and cheese. Sprinkle with good olive oil, a dash of balsamic vinegar, sea salt, and fresh-ground pepper.

CHIVES
Allium spp.

Why It's Special—Embarrassingly easy to grow, the mild onion-y flavor of chives is good in deviled eggs, snipped into salads, and is a requirement for baked potatoes with sour cream. Soften a stick of butter, add some chopped chives, mix well, and spread on crisp baguette pieces.

How to Plant & Grow—Sprinkle seeds in moist fertile soil. To encourage new growth, cut back after flowers have developed but before they have gone to seed. Chives are wonderful in a container herb collection.

Care & Problems—Chives are very self-sufficient with just enough water.

Harvest & Best Selections—Chives are often obtained as "passalong" plants or divisions. Garlic chives have flat, blade-like green leaves with white, star-shaped flower clusters 12 inches tall. Regular garden chives, *Allium schoenoprasum*, have purple, globe-shaped flowers atop the stem. The leaves are round and hollow, and it grows 12 inches tall.

In the Kitchen with Mary Ann—Snips of garlic chives or regular chives add a soft onion-y kick to scrambled eggs. To make Four Onion Jam for steaks, sauté one thinly sliced red onion, one sliced leek, several snipped chives, and some chopped green onions in a small amount of olive oil. Sprinkle with salt and pepper. Yummy!

CILANTRO/ CORIANDER
Coriandrum sativum

Why It's Special—Many folks can't abide the taste of cilantro, but for those who like it, growing it at home ensures a fresh supply. It adds that special "something" to many Asian (Thai, Vietnamese) and Mexican foods.

How to Plant & Grow—Best seeded in pots; thin to about 4 inches apart. It does not like to be transplanted. Sow some every ten days for a continuous crop. Broadcast seeds, cover with ¼ inch of soil. Harvest leaves for eating/using in salads. Allow seed heads to ripen if harvesting for seed.

Care & Problems—Seedheads may need support, so as they fill out, stake gently. Take care when cleaning cilantro; let it sit in a bowl of water to let some of the fine debris settle out. Swish and rinse, then wash again.

Harvest & Best Selections—Harvest fresh leaves for eating. They have no flavor when dried. 'Slow Bolt' is widely available in seed form.

In the Kitchen with Mary Ann—Add whole fresh cilantro leaves to tacos, bean and rice dishes, tortilla soup, and Asian stir-fries, just before serving. Coarsely chopped cilantro added to bottled salsa will freshen it right up. To store, wash cilantro thoroughly in cool water, leaving the stems attached. Put in a glass jar with some water, and cover with a plastic bag. Refrigerate.

DILL
Anethum graveolens

Why It's Special—Dill has many uses: It will rob witches of their powers and it may soothe the tummy of a colicky infant. For tea, steep 1 teaspoon dill seed in 1 cup hot water. It goes well with salmon. Dill is, of course, the dill in dill pickles.

How to Plant & Grow—Plant dill in an open seeded bed, and cover the seeds with a fine layer of soil. Thin plants to stand 9–12 inches apart. Plant seeds every couple of weeks to extend the harvest. Flavor is best just as it starts to flower.

Care & Problems—Dill can be very invasive by self-sowing so take care to remove all stalks after harvest.

Harvest & Best Selections—Fifty to seventy-two days after sowing, snip leaves from fresh green plants to use in salads and sauces. Use fresh or dry. Allow seedheads to ripen and turn brown. Shake seeds from the seedhead, allow to dry, and store in a glass jar in a dark cool, dry place. 'Fernleaf' is compact; 'Bouquet' is great for flower arrangements; and 'Tetra' and 'Dukat' are strong flavored and slow to bolt, making them great for pickling.

In the Kitchen with Mary Ann—For a classic pairing with grilled salmon, make a compound butter. Mix one stick of softened butter, add some chopped fresh dill (any amount to your liking), a squeeze of lemon juice, and a little salt. Just before removing the salmon from the grill, put a pat of dill butter on each piece of fish and let it slowly melt.

ENGLISH LAVENDER
Lavandula angustifolia

Why It's Special—Beautiful, intensely aromatic, and drought tolerant, lavender has dozens of uses including being edible. Only *L. angustifolia* varieties should be used for cooking. They are wonderful in cookies and tea. The flowers are beautiful in salads.

How to Plant & Grow—Plant lavender in lean soil in a very hot site. Perfect drainage is the key to overwintering lavender. Shear the plant to the new bud growth; do not cut into the woody stems. Trim back half the foliage the first spring. The second spring, remove the flowers after flowering.

Care & Problems—Too much water will damage the roots and cause lavender to die. *Never* water the leaves, and do not prune into old, gray wood. A gravel mulch will protect the crown.

Harvest & Best Selections—Harvest blossoms and thin skinny branches just before they open, early in the morning on a dry day. 'Hidcote' is the darkest purple of the English lavenders, 'Munstead' is most heat tolerant, and 'Jean Davis' is pastel pink.

In the Kitchen with Mary Ann—Lavender adds a delicious twist to lemonade. Bring 1 cup sugar and 2 quarts water to a boil, stirring to dissolve the sugar; remove from the heat. Immediately add 4 to 5 sprigs of fresh lavender to the pot. When it's cool, add the juice of 4 to 5 fresh lemons. Serve over ice.

FENNEL
Foeniculum vulgare var. *dulce*

Why It's Special—Fennel is a staple in Italian cuisine adding a slight licorice flavor to a dish. It's a food source for migrating swallowtail butterflies and hosts the "good" parasitic garden wasps. *Foeniculum vulgare* var. *dulce* is grown for its edible bulb. You can slice it fresh and toss in salads, steam, sauté, or grill.

How to Plant & Grow—Sow fennel in open soil when all danger of frost has passed. Do not plant near coriander or dill to prevent cross-pollination with them. It's pretty planted as a backdrop to other perennials in the mixed border.

Care & Problems—Too much heat and not enough water will make fennel taste bitter. It also has a tendency to reseed rampantly. Because it has a strong tap root, remove unwanted seedlings while they are small.

Harvest & Best Selections—Bronze fennel is a pretty addition to the garden. Pick leaves as they appear. Use them fresh in salads, sauces, and vinegars. Harvest seeds as they turn from green to brown; dry well and store in a cool, dry place.

In the Kitchen with Mary Ann—For a refreshing green and white salad, thinly slice one fennel bulb, one medium head Romaine lettuce, and two green onions. Add ½ cup shaved fresh Parmesan cheese. Toss with a splash of white vinegar and a little olive oil. Sprinkle with snipped fennel fronds and serve with fresh sea salt and black pepper.

FRENCH TARRAGON
Artemisia dranunculus

Why It's Special—Native to the Caspian Sea area, true tarragon carries with it a bit of ancestry: Henry VIII may have divorced Catherine of Aragon "for her reckless use of tarragon." Used in mustards and with fish, true tarragon is critical to the success of the classic Bernaise sauce. It has a licorice taste. French tarragon is part of the herb blend *fines herbes*. It is the king of herbs in French cooking.

How to Plant & Grow—Grown only from cuttings and division, tarragon has a light anise flavor. It does very well in pots. Too much water is undesirable.

Care & Problems—Divide established plants every other year. Prune back to a few inches above the crown in the early spring and again in the summer to force fullness and fresh growth. Do not let it go to seed.

Harvest & Best Selections—Harvest by snipping fresh leaves and branches during the growing season. Leaves may be dried, but they are not as flavorful as fresh leaves. Russian tarragon is a poor substitute, but often mistaken for the French variety; it is *Artemisia drancuculoides*.

In the Kitchen with Mary Ann— Tarragon combines beautifully with most chicken dishes. Place a couple of sprigs in the cavity of a whole chicken before roasting.

LEMON BALM
Melissia officinalis

Why It's Special—Once upon a time, lemon balm was used to drive away evil spirits, prevent baldness, and cure mad-dog bites. Today it is grown for its fresh, green leaves used in salads and for making a tisane, an herbal tea. A large bouquet will give a room a lovely fresh lemon scent.

How to Plant & Grow—Lemon balm can be invasive. Grow in pots so you can keep an eye on it and keep it from running. As with mint, if it is grown in a pot, check the drainage hole to monitor escaping roots. Prune it back to the ground in the spring, and prune again in the summer before it starts to bloom and go to seed. One plant of lemon balm is usually more than a person needs.

Care & Problems—Lemon balm will not tolerate waterlogged soils. It has no known pests or problems. In fact, it is almost too healthy.

Harvest & Best Selections—Pick leaves fresh before the flowers open. Cut a few sprigs and put in your bathwater as you fill the tub for a refreshing fragrance.

In the Kitchen with Mary Ann— Submerge a handful of fresh small lemon balm leaves (washed) in a pint of boiling water. Let them steep, no more than 5 to 8 minutes. Remove the leaves and serve hot or over ice.

MINT
Mentha spp.

Why It's Special—Mint might be called ubiquitous as a flavoring and rambunctious as a garden plant. But nothing comes close to the refreshing taste and fragrance it adds to iced tea, hot tea, chewing gum, and toothpaste. It is the key flavoring ingredient in Mint Jelly, served with lamb dishes. Steeped in hot water, mint's fragrance is relaxing and soothes colds.

How to Plant & Grow—Mint is best corralled in an ample-sized planting pot. It needs good drainage, but keep an eye on the roots that may try to sneak through the drainage hole in the pot or planter.

Care & Problems—Take care to keep mint in check; it's invasive.

Harvest & Best Selections—Harvest leaves as they grow for fresh salads and adding to tea. Clip leaves before it flowers for drying purposes. Available in many flavors and cultivars: Cinnamon, Orange, Pineapple, Peppermint, Chocolate, and Wintergreen. There are hundreds of varieties and several species available.

In the Kitchen with Mary Ann— When steeping black tea for a hot tea drink or for iced tea, add a handful of washed mint leaves to the hot water as the tea is steeping. Also, a few torn mint leaves added to a salad will punch up the flavor of plain lettuce.

OREGANO
Origanum vulgare

Why It's Special—Oregano loves tomatoes, onions, lamb, and fish. Medicinally, oregano has excellent antiseptic properties. It fits perfectly in our Rocky Mountain setting as the name translates to "joy of the mountain."

How to Plant & Grow—Oregano can be grown from seed or propagated by making divisions of existing plants. A native of the Mediterranean region, it appreciates lean, sharp soils in hot, sunny gardens. Oregano does well with other dry-minded herbs.

Care & Problems—Cut back twice a year—once in early spring to tidy the plant and again after it blooms in late spring or early summer. This will encourage new growth and keep the plant somewhat compact.

Harvest & Best Selections—Harvest leaves before the plant blooms whether drying or using fresh.

In the Kitchen with Mary Ann—Oregano is most flavorful when it's dried. Often used in southern Italian cooking, it is essential for a classic pizza Margherita. Scatter fresh or dried leaves on top of the pizza just before serving. When roasting chicken or lamb, tuck a couple of fresh sprigs of oregano in with the meat before cooking.

PARSLEY
Petroselinum spp.

Why It's Special—Thank heavens the practice of putting a lovely sprig of curly parsley on every restaurant plate has passed. Fresh parsley is superb when it is snipped and added to fresh salads, hot pasta, and salad dressings. Parsley is a handsome plant grown just for its good looks. Italian flat leaf parsley has a more pronounced flavor than the curly variety; it is used extensively in Italian cuisine.

How to Plant & Grow—Parsley is easily grown from seed or purchased as a small plant. Soak seeds in warm water overnight before planting. Cover with $\frac{1}{8}$ inch of soil and keep damp. Do not allow parsley to dry out between watering. In our hottest areas, make sure parsley has some shade in the hottest part of the day.

Care & Problems—If you harvest parsley from the outermost leaves and work your way to the center of the plant, it will continue to push leafy new growth throughout the growing season.

Harvest & Best Selections—Harvest fresh leaves until the plant sends up its seed stalk. Fresh parsley can be washed, blotted with a paper towel, snipped into pieces, and frozen in small bags. *P. crispum* is the curly variety; *P. neopolitana* is the Italian flat-leaf variety.

In the Kitchen with Mary Ann—Coarsely chop large bunches of fresh parsley and add them to any salad for a flavor pick-me-up.

ROSEMARY
Rosmarinus officinalis

Why It's Special—Rosemary's pungent fragrance makes it one of the most beloved herbs in existence. The needle-shaped dark green leaves give off their fragrance when lightly touched. Put a few sprigs on the grill when cooking vegetables or chicken to impart some of the aroma. Tie a bundle of fresh twigs (four or five) together and hang them in the shower. Rosemary pairs beautifully with pork and lamb. It is also the herb of remembrance.

How to Plant & Grow—Hardy in only the driest and warmest parts of the Rockies, it is always worth planting one every year just to have it on hand to cook.

Care & Problems—Hot dry sites with perfect drainage are required for growing rosemary. Too much water anytime is the kiss of death for this plant.

Harvest & Best Selections—Strip the oily leaves from the stems and lay them out to dry. Store in a glass jar in a dark, cool place. Rosemary can be propagated by root cuttings. If shopping for plants, look for the tag to say *Rosmarinus officinalis*. The prostrate rosemary is a beautiful plant but not nearly hardy enough for our region.

In the Kitchen with Mary Ann—For a delicious marinade, mix ¼ cup Dijon mustard, 1 tablespoon soy sauce, ½ cup good olive oil, and some ground black pepper. Strip the leaves from a sprig or two of rosemary and add. Brush this paste on pork chops, roasts or chicken before grilling.

SAGE
Salvia officinalis

Why It's Special—Aromatic, with soft gray-green leaves, this plant has been used medicinally and for cooking for thousands of years. Sage is a beautiful garden plant, and if allowed to flower, it attracts butterflies. Sage is one of the main ingredients in store-bought poultry seasoning. Better to dry and crumble your own for a taste that can't be beat. A few fresh sage leaves under the skin of a turkey or roasting hen will make the house smell incredible.

How to Plant & Grow—Sage loves the alkaline soils of the Intermountain West and in all but the coldest areas, it will winter over nicely. Prune lightly in the spring to remove tattered leaves and to improve the plant's shape. It needs a warm, dry, sunny, well-drained place to thrive.

Care & Problems—Don't crowd sage. Give it room to grow and provide good air circulation. If sage is planted in a perfect, warm microclimate, it may be harvested all winter.

Harvest & Best Selections—Pick fresh leaves anytime. Sage can be snipped, laid out to dry, and stored in glass jars away from heat and light.

In the Kitchen with Mary Ann—Wash and carefully dry a small handful of fresh sage leaves. Melt ½ to 1 stick of butter in a frying pan until it's hot (but not smoking). Add the sage leaves and fry until they're crispy. Remove leaves and drain on a paper towel-lined plate. Garnish pasta or chicken with them—if you don't eat them all first.

THYME
Thymus vulgaris

Why It's Special—Simon and Garfunkel wrote a song about it: "Parsley, Sage, Rosemary and Thyme." Thyme is a classic culinary herb, one most cooks cannot do without. It goes into the French seasoning bouquet garni. It takes up very little space in an herb garden or container. Try several varieties.

How to Plant & Grow—One of the Mediterranean herbs, thyme likes to grow hot, dry, and well drained. Thyme can be seeded, purchased as a plant, or divided in the fall. Keep the soil lean; do not add plant food or compost. Thyme bouquets can be cut and laid out to dry. Store the dried branches in an airtight container; a jar is fine, in a cool dark place.

Care & Problems—In early spring, prune the thyme plant neatly and tightly, removing all debris. It will benefit from a second haircut after it blooms.

Harvest & Best Selections—Snip leaves as needed. *Thymus vulgaris* is the common cooking herb. Dot Well's French is an excellent variety, also for culinary use. English thyme, *T. s. vulgaris*, is a broadleaf culinary selection. Orange thyme, *T. c. fragrantissimus*, is an interesting twist on the culinary varieties; add some of the tiny fresh leaves to a salad.

In the Kitchen with Mary Ann—Fresh sprigs of thyme can be carefully slipped between the skin and meat of chicken before it is roasted. It looks pretty and adds great flavor.

JANUARY

- Start planning your vegetable garden, sketch it on graph paper, really play with it.

- Make your seed lists. The sooner you order, the greater your chances of getting exactly what you want.

- If you grow herbs indoors, pinch back the flowers and give them a good drink.

FEBRUARY

- Collect all your seed starting supplies: planting mix, drainage trays, heat mats, lights (need new bulbs?), and seed trays.

- Start cool-season crops indoors.

- Start herbs indoors now.

- If possible, water seed trays from the bottom to prevent rotting and damping off.

You can enjoy the fruits of your labor long past the gardening season by canning and preserving.

MARCH

- As soon as the soil is workable, prepare the beds for planting. If you are using black plastic to warm the soil, it can go down now.

- Broadcast an organic, granular, slow-release fertilizer over the beds where early crops will be planted.

- Harden off the herbs you started indoors. Set them outside (in bright, indirect light) during the day if the weather is well above freezing.

- Start warm-season vegetables seeds indoors. Do not overwater.

- Label all the seed trays with the variety, date, and days to harvest.

- Plant your peas and potatoes.

APRIL

- If you've planted seedlings out, protect from late frosts by covering with cardboard boxes or row covers.

- Cool-season seeds can be directly planted in the garden now.

- Start the remaining warm-season seedlings indoors, transplant small seedlings into the "next size up" container.

- Make sure the seedlings are getting enough light.

- Prune herbs to encourage lots of fresh new growth.

MAY

- After your last frost date, plant out the tender vegetables which are tomatoes, peppers, eggplants. Watch for frost.

- Direct sow seeds of melons and squash.

- Water new plants on a regular basis; do not use overhead sprinklers. And don't overwater.

- Stay on top of weeds, pulling them as you see them.

- Keep the root crops thinned, making salads of the edible greens from your thinnings.

- Pick off or wash pests off plants. If you must, use an insecticidal soap according to the label instructions.

JUNE

- Harvest crops when they're in their prime; lettuces and other cool-weather greens are ready now.

- Finish mulching the beds and the rows between the plantings. This will keep the weeds at bay, the soil cool, and will aid in moisture retention.

- Pull any plants that have gone to seed, and thin root crops like carrots and parsnips.

- Most crops need at least 1 inch of water a week. Check your irrigation system if you have one. Make sure it is delivering the right amount at the right time.

JULY

- If you are lucky, there will be some apricots ripening at the first of the month.

- Always, always, always pull the weeds and get rid of the bad bugs.

- If you are planning a vacation, ask someone to check on the garden.

- If there are empty spots in the garden, plan to fill them with cool-weather seeds at the end of the month.

- Harvest vegetables at their peak.

- Prune herbs to prevent flowering and to keep the plants lush.

AUGUST

- What's working and what's not? Evaluate the layout and the performance of plants. Make notes in your garden journal.

- Now's a good time to plant the second round of cool-season vegetables.

- Mulch. Water. Weed.

- Take a salt shaker to the garden and enjoy that first ripe tomato on the spot.

- Remove plants that have stopped producing. Put them in the trash, not the compost pile.

- Keep an eye out for squash borers.

SEPTEMBER

- Harvest is in full swing right now; keep harvesting.

- At the end of the month, some of the higher elevations will see their first frosts of the season. Be prepared to protect crops with row covers and cardboard boxes.

- Root crops can be left in the ground until after the first hard frost.

OCTOBER

- The water needs of plants will slow a bit now; adjust the sprinkler system accordingly.

- A fresh crop of lettuces and greens will be ready now.

- Remove the weeds so they don't go to seed.

- You can put a layer of organic compost on the empty beds in the garden. It will break down with the frost and rain.

- Harvest the root crops that are ready.

- Apples will be ready for making sauces and freezing for pies.

- Squash and pumpkin rinds are hardening now.

NOVEMBER

- Start a list in your journal: "What I want to try next year." Make a note of the seeds you want to plant.

- Clean, oil, service, and sharpen garden tools now. Store them in an organized manner. Put away all the seeds and fertilizers. Store them safely away from children and animals.

- Remove the dead annual vines, tomato bushes, and leftover frost bitten vegetables.

- Any fallen leaves can be mower mulched and put on the garden now.

DECEMBER

- Wax those skis.

- Turn the compost pile.

- Make a list of great garden gifts you'd like to give *and* receive.

GROUND COVERS
for the Rocky Mountain States

We tend to forget to use ground covers in our gardens, which is too bad for they add a dimension you just can't get with other plants. They not only cover the soil and form a continuous, low mass of foliage, but they are an undemanding substitute for turfgrass because these plants need little upkeep and they thrive where traditional turfgrass struggles. Loosely gathered under the umbrella term *ground cover*, these include, but are not limited to, low-growing, creeping, or spreading shrubs, vines, perennials, and some annuals. Long a staple of parks, highway rights-of-way, and other public landscapes, ground covers are finding an important place in home landscapes. In addition to handling problem spots and cutting down on lawn maintenance, ground covers provide an exciting design element; their wide range of foliage and flowers can add splashes of color or texture to the garden.

PLUMBAGO

ADVANTAGES OF GROUND COVERS

It's worth examining for a moment why we "cover" the ground in the first place. If you don't plant ground covers, nature will provide them in the form of weeds. Therefore, a leafy cover of your choosing will inhibit weeds, keep the soil cooler, and break the force of a drenching rain. Beneath the surface, roots of ground covers will hold the soil against erosion and allow for better water penetration. In the dry parts of the interior West, ground covers can reduce the amount of dust coming into the house.

Trees can cause two problems for lawns: shade and competition for roots. One or the other can make growing grass difficult; the two together permit a skimpy lawn at best. A number of tough ground covers perform better than a lawn under trees. Steep slopes in a lawn area can also make it difficult to establish and maintain a lawn, where ground covers will do fine. Some home landscapes have areas that are just not large enough for a lawn. For instance, if an area is too small for a lawn mower, think of a patch of ground cover as a throw rug. Some ground covers can also easily flow around boulders and between steppingstones.

Those narrow strips of soil between a curb and a fence, a fence and a wall, or a driveway and a sidewalk are well suited to the use of restrained ground covers. Ground covers are particularly important in these narrow areas as a means of reducing the same amount of weekly maintenance as needed for lawns. In large areas not subject to foot traffic, you might also consider masses of low-growing shrubs as a ground cover because they will cover large blocks of space with flowers and foliage instead of bare ground.

GOOD FOR THE ENVIRONMENT

The wide range of color and texture found in the foliage and flowers of ground covers can be deployed in the landscape—much as a painter uses color on a canvas—to create bands, drifts, or large pools of color. Foliage color, because it can persist through much or all of the year, creates permanent effects.

As attractive as ground covers can be, there is also a strong economic consideration: the savings in resources and labor. Nowhere is this savings more visible than in the use of water. The lawn is by far the thirstiest customer in the home landscape, the greediest in its use of fertilizers, and the most demanding of attention. The dry West, which has for decades faced the problem of a rapidly growing population and a scanty water supply, can appreciate how water-conserving ground cover plants offer a unique alternative to lawns. Plus, ground covers do not need weekly mowing.

Select plants adapted to your site and to your growing conditions; once they are established, they will usually take care of themselves, with perhaps an annual grooming and occasional damage repair.

Ground covers are the near-perfect, "green"-living, often colorful solution to dry shade, erosion, weed control, saving water, and weekly maintenance.

BEARBERRY
Arctostaphylos uva-ursi

Why It's Special—This evergreen ground cover offers year-round interest and is an excellent choice for poor soils. Its showy flowers, colorful berries, and lovely fall color make this plant attractive all year long to birds and humans. Also called kinnikinnick, bearberry stabilizes hillsides and slopes. It is an excellent choice to plant beneath pines and spruce. Light pink flowers in spring are followed by small, red berries in fall. Bearberry is drought tolerant once established, and works well in rock gardens.

How to Plant & Grow—Plant bearberry in late spring after danger of frost has passed. Sun or part-shade exposure with well-drained soil is best. However, these woody creepers tolerate sandy, dry, or acidic conditions equally well. Space 5 feet apart.

Care & Problems—Do not fertilize. Bearberry can be susceptible to cankers, wilts, sooty mold, and black mildew.

Hardiness: Zones 3 to 6

Color(s): White to pale pink

Peak Season: Summer

Mature Size (H x W): ½ to 12 in. x 36 to 72 in.

Water Needs: Low to moderate

BRASS BUTTONS
Leptinella squalida

Why It's Special—This tiny evergreen ground cover is prized for its fernlike foliage, which tolerates light foot traffic. It spreads prolifically through rhizomes, forming a dense cover. Flowers and fruit are insignificant; the tiny button flowers are a sharp yellow. The cultivar 'Platt's Black' has attractive, bronzy black foliage. The more sun it gets, the darker the foliage becomes. It is a good choice for planting along pathways and between stones on patios.

How to Plant & Grow—Brass buttons are easily grown in medium moisture. It can replace turf in low-traffic areas and prefers loamy, acidic soil. Propagate these spreaders by dividing in the spring or fall. *Leptinella squalida* can be lifted, cut into sections, and replanted at the same depth as it was originally growing. Space 12 inches apart.

Care & Problems—Do not allow brass buttons to dry out. Verticillium wilt, aphids, and mites can be occasional problems.

Hardiness: Zones 4 to 10

Color(s): Yellow-gold

Peak Season: Summer

Mature Size (H x W): 3 in. x 12 in.

Water Needs: Moderate

BUGLEWEED
Ajuga reptans

Why It's Special—Bugleweed, or ajuga, is a mat-forming, colorful ground cover, great for shaded areas. Dark green, spoon-shaped leaves take on a purplish blue effect as weather cools. In late spring, plants send up 6-inch blue flower spikes. 'Black Scallop" has dark purple leaves that contrast with bright blue flower spikes in spring; it looks terrific under a red Japanese maple or near forest grass. The very showy 'Burgundy Glow' features reddish foliage marbled green and white.

How to Plant & Grow—*Ajuga* propagates itself by aboveground runners; add plenty of organic matter to the soil for new roots that emerge from nodes to thicken mat. An old-fashioned bobby pin or macramé pin will hold new starts in place until they take root. Space plants 6 to 12 inches apart.

Care & Problems—Bugleweed has few known problems.

Hardiness: Zones 3 to 8

Color(s): Pale blue flower spikes; dark purple/bronze, mottled pink/green, and green foliage

Peak Season: Spring to early summer

Mature Size (H x W): 3 in. x 12 to 18 in.

Water Needs: Low

75

CREEPING JENNY

Lysimachia nummularia

Why It's Special—The bright lime green leaves of creeping Jenny look terrific trailing over a rock wall in the garden or covering the ground under small shrubs. Also called moneywort, in the perfect, moderately moist position, creeping Jenny can be rampant, but in most of the drier parts of the interior West, that is generally not an issue. 'Aurea' is a good one.

How to Plant & Grow—Plant in an area where creeping Jenny will get some sun, but not the hottest sun of the day. Too much intense sun and heat will cause it to turn yellow and brown around the edges. The plant will root itself along the runners wherever a root node contacts the soil.

Care & Problems—Water new plants once a week. In hot dry areas, regular watering is important. There are very few problems with creeping Jenny.

Hardiness: Zones 3 to 8

Color(s): Chartreuse foliage; yellow flowers

Peak Season: May to June

Mature Size (H x W): 1 to 2 in. x as permitted

Water Needs: Moderate

CREEPING THYME

Thymus serpyllum, and *praecox* 'Coccineus'

Why It's Special—Tough, drought tolerant, with aromatic dark green leaves and masses of tiny magenta flowers, creeping red thyme is an exceptional ground cover. It is a nice alternative to turf grasses and can withstand moderate foot traffic. Thymus pseudolanuginosus, woolly thyme, is excellent for flagstone paths.

How to Plant & Grow—Plant out small plants about 8–12 inches apart. Water regularly until it takes hold. Creeping red thyme makes a fantastic backdrop for the darker sedums (Matrona, Purple Emperor) or for the clear red Knock Out roses (Red Razz). You may also like Pink Chintz thyme, a soft pink variety of creeping thyme or woolly thyme with fuzzy gray green leaves.

Care & Problems—It is not necessary, but some gardeners like to give their creeping thyme a "clean up" hair cut after its big bloom, sometime in midsummer. Too much water and heavy soil will cause thyme to rot.

Hardiness: Zones 4 to 10

Color(s): Reddish purple

Peak Season: Late spring, summer

Mature Size (H x W): 3 in. x 12 to 24 in.

Water Needs: Low

DEADNETTLE

Lamium maculatum

Why It's Special—This small, perennial ground cover is loved for its handsome foliage in a variety of green and silver patterns, which brighten dark garden spots. The foliage is also why it's called spotted deadnettle. 'Hermann's Pride' is eye-catching in containers or hanging baskets. It serves well as ground cover under trees and shrubs, on shaded slopes, and in bulb gardens.

How to Plant & Grow—Plant 12 to 18 inches apart, anytime from spring through fall. It grows quickly to fill open areas, readily rooting at leaf joints to form a tidy ground cover. Water weekly to help plants establish. Once well established, *Lamium* tolerates dry shade.

Care & Problems—Even moisture with good drainage is important. Shear back after flowering to keep compact and neat. Divide in spring or early summer by lifting sections and separating plants. Replant, keeping new divisions moist until they are established. There are no serious pests or diseases.

Hardiness: Zone 3 to 7

Color(s): White, pink, and rose-pink

Peak Season: Spring through summer

Mature Size (H x W): 6 to 8 in. × 12 to 36 in.

Water Needs: Moderate

ENGLISH IVY

Hedera helix

Why It's Special—This evergreen, woody perennial is prized for its deep green, glossy leaves, which spread or cling to the ground and other surfaces. It is very fast-growing and makes an ideal façade for walls and trellises. A thick ground cover and lawn alternative, English ivy is extremely easy to grow and tolerates a variety of conditions. It also provides evergreen winter interest.

How to Plant & Grow—Propagate ivy by cuttings. Birds, attracted to ivy's dark berries, may ingest and disperse the seed. It spreads rapidly where stems touch the soil, and is best grown in part shade to full shade, but tolerates full sun. Ivy prefers rich soils, but it may thrive in poor loams and is drought-tolerant once it is well established.

Care & Problems—Mites can be prolific. Be wary of potential damage from ivy growing directly on buildings; it may penetrate flimsy exterior walls and damage surfaces it clings to.

Hardiness: Zones 4 to 9

Color(s): White

Peak Season: Fall

Mature Size (H x W): 75 ft. x 100 ft.

Water Needs: Low to moderate

HARDY ICE PLANT

Delosperma spp.

Why It's Special—Hardy ice plant 'Table Mountain' is a wonderful hot-spot ground cover with single, fuchsia blooms. The succulent foliage is deep green and shiny. Dry, sandy, hot spots make this ice plant happy. *Delosperma nubiginum* is a yellow ice plant with the same fine attributes.

How to Plant & Grow—Ice plant requires little to no care. It performs well and looks great as a ground cover in a rock garden or in front of a perennial border. This hardy plant works very well planted with a "spiky," contrasting perennial coming up through it, especially hummingbird mint 'Ava,' or a hot pink or purple penstemon. The fluffy, silver foliage of *Artemisia* 'Powis Castle' or 'Valerie Finnis' would also pair nicely.

Care & Problems—The hardy ice plant cannot tolerate wet soil in winter. In spring, a good trimming of the tattered, trailing leaves will improve its appearance.

Hardiness: Zones 5 to 10

Color(s): Hot pink/purple

Peak Season: Summer

Mature Size (H x W): 3 in. x 12 to 18 in.

Water Needs: Low

HARDY VERBENA

Verbena canadensis

Why It's Special—The gorgeous purple bloom clusters of the trailing verbena are 3 to 4 inches in diameter. As the verbena tumbles and rambles over garden walls and through rock gardens, it keeps blooming from May until frost. 'Homestead Purple' is sensational planted at the base of zinnias or Shasta daisies. A tough plant, trailing verbena likes full sun and can get by with minimal water. It is a colorful ground cover.

How to Plant & Grow—Hardy verbena likes to be planted in a good rich soil. Once it is established, it does not like a lot of water. Each plant will cover three to four square feet.

Care & Problems—When the blooming slows down in the heat of the summer, prune it hard to encourage fresh growth and to encourage continuing bloom. Not reliably winter hardy—it is good only to 20 degrees—verbena is still worth planting every year. Although this ground cover cannot withstand foot traffic, it looks great planted at the edge of a perennial bed.

Hardiness: Zones 7 to 9

Color(s): Purple

Peak Season: Summer through fall

Mature Size (H x W): 6 to 8 in. x 18 to 24 in.

Water Needs: Low to moderate

LADY'S MANTLE
Alchemilla mollis

Why It's Special—Mounding, velvety, light green leaves with scalloped edges, lady's mantle is a favorite cottage garden ground cover perennial. Raindrops are held as beads or teardrops in the center crux of the leaves. Huge heads of fluffy, lime green flowers tumble over the foliage mound.

How to Plant & Grow—Plant 18 inches apart in rich, moisture-retentive soil. Attractive as a blowsy edging plant for walkways and perennial border, *Alchemilla mollis* is a "must plant" in the cottage or English style garden, or as "knee socks" for roses to hide their spindly canes.

Care & Problems—Remove seed heads when the flowers start to fade. Shearing plants after blooming will neaten their appearance and may stimulate a second bloom period. Afternoon shade is important in hot, sunny sites.

Hardiness: Zones 3 to 8

Color(s): Green

Peak Season: June

Mature Size (H x W): 1 to 1½ ft. x 1 to 2½ ft.

Water Needs: Moderate

LILY OF THE VALLEY
Convallaria majalis

Why It's Special—The sweet fragrance of its bell-shaped flowers is one of the first signs of spring. An excellent, easy-to-grow ground cover for shady, moist, fertile areas, lily-of-the-valley spreads quickly through underground stems or rhizomes. This lovely woodland plant provides wonderful cut flowers.

How to Plant & Grow—Plant divisions of lily of the valley rhizomes or underground stems with two to three pips ("eyes" or shoots) in early spring, in well-drained but moist, humus-rich soil. Space plants 8 to 12 inches apart. Set divisions 6 inches apart, 1 to 1½ inches deep. Top-dress in the fall with well-aged manure or compost. Remove mature foliage and thin when flowers become sparse. Plant beneath shrubs and maintain a border with metal edging.

Care & Problems—Lily-of-the-valley does not tolerate foot traffic. It is susceptible to occasional leaf and stem rot, as well as anthracnose. Note: *All parts are toxic.*

Hardiness: Zones 3 to 8

Color(s): White and pink

Peak Season: May

Mature Size (H x W): 6 to 12 in. x 18 to 24 in.

Water Needs: Low to moderate

PLUMBAGO
Ceratostigma plumbaginoides

Why It's Special—In August, plumbago (also called leadwort) sends up clear blue flowers. As the foliage begins a colorful autumn transformation, rich green leaves turn red, then mahogany. It is deer resistant, fast growing, and looks great in a rock garden setting. Leadwort blooms over a very long time, but it is deciduous, disappearing in winter.

How to Plant & Grow—Leadwort is a warm-season ground cover, arriving on the scene as spring bulb foliage declines, making it a good planting companion to daffodils and tulips.

Care & Problems—Plumbago does well in most conditions but cannot tolerate wet, poorly drained soils. It's slow to emerge in spring; give it time to come up and remember where it is planted so you don't inadvertently rake it up. If desired, control its spread by removing unwanted plants in late spring or fall.

Hardiness: Zones 5 to 9

Color(s): Blue

Peak Season: August to September

Mature Size (H x W): 6 to 8 in. x 18 in.

Water Needs: Moderate

SERBIAN BELLFLOWER

Campanula poscharskyana

Why It's Special—Serbian bellflower is easy to grow with a long, prolific bloom period mid- to late spring. It will spread but not rampantly, and the upward-facing periwinkle blue flowers show up nicely against its dark green foliage. It pairs up well planted under white 'Iceberg' roses (or any other floribunda) or next to Japanese forest grass. It is very pretty cascading over rock walls. 'Blue Waterfall', 'Stella', and 'Blue Gown' are excellent performers.

How to Plant & Grow—Plant 6 to 12 inches apart in rich, well-drained soil. It will need some shade in the hotter parts of the Rockies. As with many ground covers, it is somewhat drought tolerant once it becomes well established.

Care & Problems—Serbian bellflower cannot tolerate wet soil in winter. In spring, a good trimming of the tattered, trailing leaves will improve its appearance.

Hardiness: Zones 3 to 8

Color(s): Hot pink and purple

Peak Season: Summer

Mature Size (H x W): 3 in. x 12 to 18 in.

Water Needs: Low

SNOW IN SUMMER

Cerastium tomentosum

Why It's Special—From late spring to early summer, this ground cover is awash in snowy-white flowers. A rock-garden favorite, snow-in-summer is easily grown in dry, infertile soil and heat. It is a beautiful, year-round choice for erosion control and difficult sites.

How to Plant & Grow—Plant new transplants from spring through early fall. Divide older clumps in early spring. Snow in summer freely reseeds. It requires full sun, good drainage, and aeration. Add a quality soil amendment such as compost or sphagnum peat moss in sandy and clay soils. Once established, it tolerates drought.

Care & Problems—Allow soil to dry slightly between waterings. Avoid using high-nitrogen fertilizer. Apply slow-release, 5-10-5 plant food in early spring. Shear faded flowers to encourage new growth of fuzzy, silvery white leaves. Overwatering results in leggy growth and possible crown rot. Slugs occasionally hide beneath thick foliage but they can be controlled.

Hardiness: Zones 3 to 7

Color(s): White and silver

Peak Season: Spring

Mature Size (H x W): 6 to 12 in. × 24 to 36 in.

Water Needs: Low

ST. JOHN'S WORT
Hypericum calycinum

Why It's Special—An exceptional ground cover, St. John's wort is undaunted by shallow tree roots. The flowers of St. John's wort are a bright, shiny, yellow with very showy sprays of bushy stamens rising from the center of the blossoms. The plants form a nice bushy mass, keeping weeds at bay. St. John's wort is also helpful for stabilizing slopes. 'Brigadoon' is highly recommended for its bright, chartreuse foliage, which turns orange-gold as the season progresses.

How to Plant & Grow—Plant 18 inches apart. St. John's wort can tolerate average, medium, rich, and sandy soils. Pinch the leaf tips the first couple of growing seasons; this encourages bushy growth. Grow it anywhere, as long as the roots aren't completely wet.

Care & Problems—*Hypericum calycinum* may be aggressive, but runners can be terminated by cutting a sharp edge around the plants.

Hardiness: Zones 5 to 9

Color(s): Bright yellow

Peak Season: July to August

Mature Size (H x W): 1 to 1½ ft. x 1½ to 2 ft.

Water Needs: Moderate

SWEET WOODRUFF
Galium odoratum

Why It's Special—Deceptively dainty in appearance, this is one tough ground cover. It has tiny, wispy, fragrant white blossoms in late spring. Good for dry, shady areas under pines and deciduous trees, its bright green leaves show up well in the woodland garden. The foliage smells like fresh-cut hay, and when dried, it is often used in herbal sachets.

How to Plant & Grow—Plant in soil enriched with some compost. It loves damp conditions but can handle some dryness. Plant 12 to 15 inches apart and water well. It will spread by creeping and sometimes self seed. Sweet woodruff provides nice textural contrast when planted with large-leaved hostas and ferns.

Care & Problems—The first year, water as soil becomes dry. If plants look tired in the spring, shear back to encourage new growth.

Hardiness: To Zone 3

Color(s): Green foliage with white blossoms

Peak Season: April to May

Mature Size (H x W): 6 to 8 in. x 18 to 24 in.

Water Needs: Low to moderate

HARDY VERBENA

JANUARY

- Think about problem areas in your garden and browse catalogues for interesting ground covers to alleviate these issues.

- Recently planted ground cover needs supplemental watering the first couple of years. On a day when temperatures are above freezing and the ground is not frozen, water for ten to fifteen minutes.

- If deer and elk are browsing on your ground covers, consider putting a screen of chicken wire over beds and plants.

FEBRUARY

- This is a good time to visit public gardens. See how they are dealing with issues you have in your garden. How do they use ground covers? Which varieties are working for them?

- It's still too early to plant outside, but if you know what ground covers you want for the garden in the spring, stop by your favorite nursery and ask them to order plants for you (if they don't already have them on their availability list). Ask them for recommendations for new varieties.

- If your ground covers hide spring bulbs, now is a good time to see what might be trying to come up. If it's really cold, leave the protective dry leaves in place as a protective mulch. But now you know, spring is headed your way.

- This is the perfect time to go to a tropical island. Get some sun and sand.

MARCH

- Bare-root ground covers that come via mail order can be planted as soon as you can work the soil. You may be able to start planting now, but ensure soil is not too wet. Grab a handful; it should crumble and not clump up.

- If you planted new ground covers last summer or fall, make sure they are nicely mulched to keep weeds at bay and to give them a running start on the new growing season ahead.

- If the ground is not frozen and the weather has been severely cold and dry, get some water on those newly planted ground covers to keep them from drying out.

- A slow-release, organic plant food can be sprinkled around the ground cover plants to give them a jump on the new season.

- Gently rake over ground covers to remove debris. Remember, some of them aren't up yet. You may trim tattered leaves and broken branches to make the area look tidy.

- and pull or dig weeds that might be showing up in the ground cover beds.

AJUGA

APRIL

- Now is the time to plant new ground covers. You will be giving them a great start on the new season. The best selections of all plants are now showing up in your local nurseries. Get there first!

- If it is still dry—and it often is in the interior West—pull out the hoses and give the ground covers a good drink.

- Be vigilant about pulling the weeds until the ground covers take over. You don't want weeds competing for moisture or nutrients.

MAY

- Now is an excellent time to divide your established, older ground covers and move them to parts of the garden where they can be of good use.

- If you discover dead patches in the ground cover areas, clean them out and wait for awhile. New growth will likely fill in and repair any holes.

- Quick! Get to the nurseries to see what new ground covers they might have that you did not know about. Check them out, do your homework, and decide it you are going to try the newbie.

JUNE

- At the first of the month, it is probably still cool enough for you to plant new ground covers and transplant divisions. Mulch them well and water them well.

- Give the existing ground cover plantings a good once-over, snipping back where needed to encourage fullness; train and pin bugleweed and creeping Jenny to send them into new territory.

JULY

- When the *Ajuga* (bugleweed) has finished blooming, shear off the tattered and faded blooms. The sooner, the better, as the bed will have a neat and tidy appearance.

- Avoid planting or transplanting ground covers in the heat of the summer.

- Check to make sure there is adequate moisture where the ground covers are planted. Sometimes we forget to check on them until it is too late.

- Continue removing any damaged or diseased parts of plants.

- At the end of the month, give the creeping thymes a serious haircut. Check under their mats and clean out the dead leaves and debris. This gives the plants a chance to gather their resources and put on a second, albeit slower, push of leaves later in the season.

AUGUST

- What worked and what didn't? Now is a good time to photograph and take notes of changes you want to make in all parts of the garden.

- Remove dead, damaged, or tattered ground covers. Clip them back, clean up the debris, and give them a good drink if necessary.

SEPTEMBER

- Hey, we live in the Rockies. This is a great time to go fly-fishing or camping when all the kids are back in school. Yellowstone National Park is awesome right now, before the snow flies!

- There will be great plant sales this time of year. If you have time and the inclination, now is a good time to purchase a few new ground covers for those nasty bare spots.

- Make sure your ground covers have adequate moisture now.

OCTOBER

- Rake and clean fallen leave from the areas planted with ground covers.

- Continue removing dead, dried foliage and stems, and cut back black, rotten, frozen plants, but leave grasses for winter decoration.

- Wait until ground is frozen to apply winter mulch.

NOVEMBER

- Enjoy this late season in the garden, especially the evergreen foliage of ground covers, conifers, dried grasses, and other plants with good winter "bones."

- If you have a prolonged dry spell, ensure plants have enough moisture. Water only when the ground is not frozen.

DECEMBER

- Go skiing.

- Plan modifications for next year's garden.

- Continue to monitor soil moisture content and water as necessary if the ground is not frozen. Work some compost into soil around plants.

LAWNS & ORNAMENTAL GRASSES
for the Rocky Mountain States

Rocky Mountain residents take great pride in their lawns. A healthy carpet of soft, green turf is both attractive and functional. Your lawn is a soft, cool area on which to throw out a blanket, enjoy a picnic, read a book, play croquet, toss a Frisbee®, or relax and appreciate the beauty of the world around you.

When selecting a turfgrass species for your lawn, consider how much time you want to dedicate to maintenance and what type of maintenance you're willing to provide. You may prefer pulling weeds, hoeing, deadheading, and maintaining perennials to watering, fertilizing, and mowing grass.

LIVE TO MOW ANOTHER DAY

With proper planning, you can have your lawn and enjoy it too! The Rocky Mountain Sod Growers Association recommends asking yourself these questions to choose the right turf for your lawn.

1. How will the turf be used? For recreation? Aesthetics? Ground cover? Near a house or a heavily used building? For outlying areas?
2. How much water do you want the lawn to consume? What is the cost of water in your area?
3. How much traffic will the lawn bear, and what wear tolerance do you need?
4. What are the mowing requirements?
5. How long do you want it to stay green?
6. What are the fertilizer requirements?
7. Will it be in shaded or sunny areas—or both?
8. How is the soil? Clay? Sandy? Salty?
9. How much time do you want to spend on lawn maintenance?

TURF CHOICES

Throughout most areas of our region cool-season grasses, such as Kentucky bluegrasses, improved cultivars of Kentucky bluegrasses, turf-type fescues, and perennial ryegrasses, are planted for home lawns, parks, and athletic fields. Seed germination is best at soil temperatures of 60 to 80 degrees Fahrenheit, and the optimum growth temperature is between 60 and 75 degrees Fahrenheit. The best growth quality for cool-season grasses occurs in the spring and fall; these grasses become dormant in summer when temperatures rise and drought periods occur. Full dormancy rarely occurs if you continue to water and fertilize lawns.

Kentucky bluegrass (*Poa pratensis*), which has a rhizomatous root system, goes dormant in summer without sufficient irrigation; but will start regrowth again when cooler temperatures and moisture return in late summer and autumn.

Some of the most drought resistant bluegrass cultivars include: 'America', 'Apollo', 'Baroness', 'Brilliant', 'Impact', 'Mallard', 'Midnight', 'Midnight II', 'Moonlight', 'Rugby II', 'Showcase', 'Total Eclipse', and 'Unique'. Bluegrass cultivars differ little in actual water use rate. It appears that enhanced drought resistance comes from the ability to form somewhat deeper roots than the other bluegrasses.

The Texas bluegrass × Kentucky bluegrass hybrids ('Reveille', 'Longhorn', 'Thermal Blue', 'Solar Green', 'Dura Blue', 'Bandera') have better than average drought resistance and excellent heat tolerance. These Texas hybrids form extensive root systems and produce large, aggressive rhizomes, making them well suited for heavy traffic areas.

The new, patented rhizomatous tall-fescue turfs were developed to withstand drought, heat, and foot traffic; maintain good color and a soft texture; and "self repair" bare spots. With minimal water, these blended grasses will require less water and will stay green until late in the season.

Perennial ryegrass (*Lolium perenne*) is used widely in grass mixtures because it germinates quickly from seed. Its leaf texture and color are compatible with bluegrass, it has good heat and wear tolerance, and if planted in deep, well-prepared soil, it goes dormant in extreme heat and short drought periods. It is important to have a sharp mower blade for a clean look. The presence of endophytic fungi in ryegrass improves its ability to resist some insect species, such as billbugs, cutworms, sod webworms, and possibly white grubs.

Fine fescue (*Festuca* spp.) grasses are best adapted to shady conditions. They are drought resistant, cold tolerant, and grow in soils of poor-to-average fertility. In extreme heat and drought periods, fine fescue goes dormant

FESTUCA GLAUCA

and rests until moisture becomes available. Fescues are well adapted for high-country lawns. Red, chewings, hard, or sheep fescues are typical fine fescues with fine, narrow grass blades.

Warm-season grasses include buffalograss and blue grama. Seed germination is best when temperatures are 70 to 90 degrees Fahrenheit, with optimum growth occuring between 80 and 95 degrees Fahrenheit.

Blue grama (*Bouteloua gracilis*) is a clump-forming grass that grows 10 to 16 inches tall. Buffalograss and blue grama are very drought tolerant. Blue grama needs little fertilizer and infrequent mowing. Left unmowed, it can grow to 15 inches and produce attractive seedheads. Blue grama cannot tolerate high-traffic or shady areas, nor does it perform well in elevations above 6,500 feet. In native stands, blue grama grows in association with buffalograss in short and mid-grass prairies. Combining the two in landscape use is recommended.

Buffalograss (*Buchloe dactyloides*) is a sod-forming grass that grows 6 inches tall, can be left unmowed, and can be maintained on 1 to 1¾ inches of water every two to three weeks during summer. This low-maintenance, water-thrifty grass is green to grayish green between May and October, and straw-colored at other times of year. Buffalograss doesn't tolerate shade or heavy traffic; if overwatered or overfertilized, it thins out and weeds invade. It is not recommended for elevations above 6,500 feet. A vigorous sod-former, buffalograss spreads by runners and stolons, requiring periodic edging to keep persistent runners in check. It can be planted from seed, sod, or plugs. "Vegetative" cultivars are available as sod or plugs and include '609', '315', 'Highlight', 'Buffalawn', and 'Prairie'. Other varieties can be planted from seed and include 'Plains', 'Topgun', 'Bison', and 'Sharp's Improved'.

Wheatgrasses (whose botanical names are synonymous with *Agropyron*), include crested (*Agropyron desertorum*), western (*Pascopyrum smithii*), thickspike, (*Elymus lanceolatus*), and streambank (*Agropyron riparium*). They are coarse-textured and bunch-type grasses adapted to tolerate precipitation as low as 10 inches per year. During dry spells, wheatgrass goes dormant, but makes a rapid recovery when moisture returns. It's a cool-season bunchgrass recommended for dryland lawns.

Smooth brome (*Bromus inermis*) is a cold- and drought-tolerant pasture grass with wide leaf blades. It greens in early spring and requires minimal water and fertilizer. When maintained as lawn, smooth brome loses some density. It can be used alone or with crested wheatgrass and western wheatgrass for soil-erosion control, a water-thrifty lawn, or a mountain lawn. Cultivars include 'Bromar', 'Lincoln', and 'Manchar'.

SITE PREPARATION

Proper soil preparation is crucial in establishing a drought-enduring lawn. Subsoil from basement excavation or "contractor dirt" that has been compacted by heavy equipment is not suitable for lawn establishment. A soil test will determine what nutrients your soil needs. Your state university or local soil-testing laboratory can help you prepare a soil sample for analysis.

Organic matter improves the soil's drainage ability and its capacity to retain moisture. If the organic content of the soil is less than 5 percent, incorporate 3 to 6 cubic yards of well-aged manure or compost per 1,000 square feet, depending on grass selection. Mix organic amendment into existing soil to a depth of 8 to 10 inches. Rake surface smooth before seeding, sodding, or hydroseeding.

PLANTING & CARING FOR YOUR LAWN

The best time to start cool-season grasses from seed is late summer to late September when nighttime temperatures are cooling down, days are still warm, and weeds are less competitive. These conditions are ideal for germination and establishment of grass seed. If you are unable to seed at these times, the second-best time is in early spring.

Warm-season grasses such as buffalograss and blue grama should be sown in May or June; they need warm soils to germinate successfully. Starting a lawn from seed is economical, but requires more

frequent watering and takes longer to achieve good results.

Sod, while initially more costly, provides an "instant" lawn. Install sod from spring through late fall, as long as the soil has been prepared properly and sod is available. Whether you seed or sod, the key to success is proper soil preparation.

Before planting seed or installing sod, eliminate weeds, especially difficult perennial weeds such as bindweed, quackgrass, bermudagrass, and Canada thistle, by spraying them with herbicide that has no soil residual, such as glyphosate, and allow it to fully translocate and kill weeds before you cultivate. Follow label directions.

After organic matter has been thoroughly incorporated into soil, install an in-ground automatic sprinkler system if your budget allows. It's the most efficient way to water larger lawn areas. Schedule sprinkling times so turf zones are separate from zones that water flowers, shrubs, and trees. Remember, shaded areas generally need less water than those with full sun exposure.

SEEDING A NEW LAWN

Prepare the area with quality organic matter, and rake the surface smooth. Apply 5 pounds of a starter fertilizer, such as diammonium phosphate (18-46-0), per 1,000 square feet of lawn, by raking it into the soil surface. Leave soil firm but not packed. If walking over prepared soil leaves footprints more than 1 inch deep, firm the soil with a roller. Spread grass seed in two directions at right angles, distributing half of the seed each direction. After planting, lightly rake or roll the area to make sure seed is in contact with soil. Water, then cover the surface with light mulch, such as clean wheat straw or pulverized compost, to conserve moisture. Water lightly and frequently to keep soil surface moist during the germination process. This may mean watering three to five times daily until the seeds have germinated; here's where an automatic sprinkler is most effective and efficient.

Once grass seed has germinated and seedlings begin to develop deeper roots, water the lawn less frequently, but increase the amount of water per application. Deeper, less-frequent watering encourages the development of a deeper root system, making lawn grasses more drought tolerant during summer heat. Young, tender seedlings can easily be damaged by weed killers. Although it can be frustrating to see weeds in a newly seeded lawn, it's common and shouldn't discourage you. If you accomplished preplanting weed control, most new-lawn weed sprouts are eliminated with several mowings and a thickened lawn.

Mow newly seeded lawn when it reaches 3 inches. Cut grass to remove no more than one-half inch off new grass plants. Mow cool-season grasses high—2, 2½, or even 3 inches tall. With more surface area, grass can manufacture more food energy to nourish roots and stems. Also, longer grass blades shade the soil surface, discouraging annual weed-seed germination.

Mow lawns frequently enough that no more than one-third of the grass blade is clipped. This may mean mowing every four to five days when the lawn is growing fast in spring. The lawn looks better and undergoes less stress, and the amount of clippings is smaller so they drop back into the lawn more easily. When clippings are returned to the lawn, nitrogen and other nutrients are recycled in an organic, slow-release form, promoting a healthier lawn. There is a myth that grass clippings cause thatch, which is actually the compacted, brown, spongy, organic layer of living and dead grass stems and roots that accumulates above the soil surface. It is usually a result of poor lawn management practices. As thatch layers thicken, the lawn is predisposed to drought stress, and insect, disease, and weed problems.

WATERING ESTABLISHED LAWNS

Soil type, weather conditions, turfgrass species, and the desired quality of lawn influence how much water you should apply and how often. Turf-type fescue lawns require as much or more water as the typical bluegrass lawn. Buffalograss and blue grama lawns look good for weeks without watering.

When you water, thoroughly wet the soil to the depth of the lawn's root system. Don't water again until it becomes dry at that depth. Deeper, infrequent watering promotes a deeper root system and drought endurance, and it conserves water. Rocky Mountain soils vary in how they accept water. Sandy soils require less water more often than loam and clay soils. Grasses growing in shade generally require less water, but more water is needed where tree roots compete with the lawn.

To avoid runoff and wasting water, practice "cycling" or "interval watering." Rather than trying to apply water all at once, water an area to the point of runoff (fifteen to twenty minutes), then allow it to soak in for thirty minutes or more before repeating the watering cycle in the same area to allow deeper percolation into clay soils. This technique is helpful for watering sloped areas where water naturally runs downhill.

THATCH

Thatch is a persistent problem in lawns throughout our area. Although some believe thatch is an accumulation of grass clippings in the lawn, it is actually a tightly intermingled layer of partially decomposed stems, roots, and leaves that slough off the crown between the actively growing grass blades and the soil surface.

Thatch should not be allowed to accumulate in lawns because it restricts the movement of water, oxygen, and nutrients into the soil. Since it also becomes resistant to water, drought stress occurs. Core aeration is a technique that aids water infiltration by reducing compaction and breaking through the thatch layer.

CORE AERATION

One of the most beneficial ways to reduce soil compaction while controlling thatch accumulation is by core aeration. Plugs or cores of soil and thatch, 2 to 3 inches long, are removed by a mechanical aerating machine and deposited on the lawn's surface. The resulting holes permit water, air, and nutrients to enter the soil and create a healthier root zone environment. Either rake the plugs off the lawn after aeration or leave them to disintegrate and filter back into the lawn. It may take several days to weeks before the plugs dissolve, depending on your soil type. Mowing over the plugs with a rotary lawn mower can break them down more rapidly, but this will dull the mower blade. The cores of thatch and soil can be collected and put into the compost pile.

HOW AND WHEN TO FERTILIZE THE HOME LAWN

What kind of lawn do you want? A low-maintenance or utility lawn won't look as uniform or deeply green as a higher maintenance lawn, but it won't need as much fertilizer, watering, or mowing.

Nitrogen is the most important nutrient for lawn grasses to maintain growth and good color; however, don't overstimulate your lawn with excess nitrogen, particularly during spring and summer. This can contribute to thatch accumulation and disease problems and will certainly increase mowing frequency.

Cool-season grasses such as Kentucky bluegrass, turf-type fescues, and perennial ryegrass need nitrogen fertilizer to produce an attractive, dense turf. Apply the equivalent of 1 pound of

actual nitrogen per 1,000 square feet of lawn per application every six weeks, depending on the quality of lawn you desire. Three to four applications are usually sufficient. The amount of product to use can be determined by dividing 100 by the nitrogen number (the first number on the fertilizer bag). For example, if you choose a regional formula of 20-10-5, you will need 5 pounds of fertilizer to equal 1 pound of actual nitrogen. Time your fertilizer applications around the following holidays: Memorial Day, Fourth of July, Labor Day, and Halloween.

Iron chlorosis—yellowing of the grass blades—is a common problem in our region. Our alkaline soils are the reason for this chlorosis because iron, while present in the soil, is not in a form available to turf grasses. To keep the lawn green, apply an appropriate lawn fertilizer containing iron or a separate iron supplement.

HOW LAWN FERTILIZERS STACK UP

The fertilizer you decide to apply is a matter of personal choice. Remember, nitrogen is the most

MISCANTHUS SINENSIS

PANICUM VIRGATUM 'HEAVY METAL'

important nutrient in lawn fertilizers. Organic fertilizers composed of natural products such as animal manures or plant components are not as concentrated, so more fertilizer is needed to achieve the recommended nitrogen rate. The nitrogen content is usually 5 to 15 percent on a weight basis. The lower concentration, however, means less danger of pollution from runoff. Also, organic fertilizers have less potential to "burn" the grass if over applied or applied under warm conditions. Organic and organic-based lawn fertilizers release nutrients slowly in conjunction with soil microorganisms. This reduces the growth surge that can occur when a straight chemical

fertilizer is used, providing long-term green without stimulating excessive top growth.

Nonorganic or so-called chemical fertilizers can be categorized into two types: synthetic organic fertilizers, which contain carbon, and inorganic types that are nutrients mined from the earth but which contain no carbon. Synthetic organic fertilizers include urea, sulfur-coated urea, ureaform, and IBDU®. These fertilizers are broken down by soil microbes to release nitrogen, carbon dioxide, and water. Most of the potassium, phosphorus, sulfur, and iron components are mined from the earth. Some fertilizers contain phosphorus derived from bone meal.

WEEDS IN THE HOME LAWN

Weed control in your lawn begins with the proper identification of the weed. Lawn weeds are classified as grassy types (crabgrass, tall fescue, quackgrass) or broadleaf (dandelion, plantain, spurge). Once you've determined the weed, find out whether it's an annual that grows from seed each year or a perennial that grows back from its roots year after year. Identifying weeds helps determine your control approach. You may use a chemical weed killer or just pull or dig the weeds by hand—"the cowboy way."

Before applying weed killers over the entire lawn, analyze the extent of the weed problem. It may be possible to deal with weeds on a spot basis rather than treating uninvolved sections of the lawn. If perennial weeds such as dandelions are a concern, uproot them with a dandelion digger, pull by hand, or spot treat them individually with an appropriate herbicide.

The easiest way to control annual weeds is with pre-emergent herbicides that prevent weed seed germination and rooting. Timing is important; apply these materials before seeds germinate. To control annual weeds that begin to grow in late spring or early summer (crabgrass, spurge, purslane), apply a pre-emergent in mid- to late April before warm weather causes seeds to germinate. Some annual weeds germinate in late summer (annual bluegrass, cheatgrass, chickweed); apply a pre-emergent to those in late August. Read product labels carefully to ensure the product will control weeds you are battling.

Perennial weeds such as Canada thistle, bindweed, plantain, and buckthorn grow from their roots each year and spread from seeds and underground roots. To control, use a post-emergent herbicide after the weed leaves have emerged. Know whether the weed is a grassy or broadleaf plant. Certain herbicides kill broadleaf weeds but are ineffective on grassy weeds, and vice versa. Read the product label to determine whether it will do the desired job.

WHEN IN DROUGHT

Some years, naturally occurring droughts can have a major impact on lawn care in the Rockies. These conditions often result in water restrictions. In most situations, to sustain your lawn in a dormant or semidormant state, you can reduce watering by two-thirds. Following are some lawn maintenance tips to help your lawn stay healthy when water is scarce:

- Reduce lawn fertilizer applications to decrease a lot of top growth. Avoid fast-release, high-nitrogen fertilizers. Use slow-release, organic-based lawn fertilizers that work in harmony with nature.
- Keep your lawnmower blade sharpened to provide a cleaner cut; this also reduces water loss from the leaf blades.
- Raise the mowing height of the grass to shade the roots and soil. This helps reduce soil moisture evaporation.
- Return grass clippings to the lawn by mowing often. Finely ground grass clippings help provide a natural mulch to the roots and help retain soil moisture.
- Reduce traffic on the lawn to prevent soil compaction and stress to grass plants. Compacted soils have decreased water absorption.
- To avoid runoff and wasting water, practice "cycling" or "interval watering."

THE BENEFITS OF LAWNS

Lawns do much more than consume water and grow. Properly chosen and maintained, a lawn contributes to our quality of life. Unlike gravel, concrete, asphalt, or bare dirt, the lawn cools the surrounding area. Temperatures are 10 to 15 degrees Fahrenheit cooler around a lawn; this ultimately reduces water consumption of nearby plants. A 2,000 square foot lawn provides enough oxygen for a family of four—every day! Turf areas reduce noise, air, and water pollution and provide excellent dust control. Well-established turf areas with extensive root systems control soil erosion and reduce glare. Finally, the properly selected lawn is one of the safest and softest natural playing surfaces for children, adults, and pets.

BLUE FESCUE
Festuca glauca

Why It's Special—Blue fescue is blue-gray, almost silver, and shaped like a porcupine or sea urchin. In midsummer, tufts of pale gold seed heads bloom, adding to the plant's airy texture. 'Sea Urchin' is very compact; 'Boulder Blue' is taller with much bluer blades.

How to Plant & Grow—Planted in average to sandy garden soil, the ornamental fescues will thrive in hot, dry conditions. Good drainage is a must.

Care & Problems—Cut them back in March for a "push" of clean fresh foliage. If the flower spikes are not to your liking, you may remove them as well. If the center of the crown appears to be dying back, dig, divide, and replant the healthy clumps.

Hardiness: Zones 4 to 8

Color(s): Steely blue-gray

Peak Season: July through October

Mature Size (H x W): 9 to 36 in. x 12 to 20 in.

Water Needs: Low

BLUE GRAMA
Bouteloua gracilis

Why It's Special—The seed heads of blue grama have the appearance of curly eyelashes. Blue grama is a native American prairie grass, that is very heat and drought tolerant and graceful in appearance.

How to Plant & Grow—Beautiful in beds, borders, or seeded through meadows, *Bouteloua gracilis* should be planted in full sun and watered only until it is established. Too much water will cause it to fail. Plant plugs 4 inches apart. Seed according to supplier's instructions.

Care & Problems—Blue grama benefits from one spring mowing a year. It may go dormant in dry conditions but it greens up quickly after watering.

Hardiness: Zones 3 to 10

Color(s): Green, fading to gold

Peak Season: June through August

Mature Size (H x W): 1 to 3 ft. x 6 to 12 in.

Water Needs: Low

BLUE OAT GRASS
Helictotrichon sempervirens

Why It's Special—A large, silver-blue, clump-forming grass, it is gorgeous as a specimen plant and dramatic when planted in large, hazy masses. In late June or early July, blue oat grass sends up slender wands with buff-colored seed heads. These are very airy in appearance, moving with the slightest breeze.

How to Plant & Grow—Plant 24 to 36 inches apart. Water until established. Best blue color develops under dry growing conditions. You may or may not choose to cut blue oat grass back in the spring.

Care & Problems—Good drainage is imperative. The crown may die out with severe cold or too much water. Lift and divide, discarding brown centers and replanting healthy divisions.

Hardiness: Zones 3 to 8

Color(s): Silver-blue foliage with straw-colored seed heads

Peak Season: June through autumn foliage; blooms July through autumn

Mature Size (H x W): 2 to 3 ft. (plus seed heads) x 3 ft.

Water Needs: Low

BUFFALO GRASS
Buchloe dactyloides

Why It's Special—Buffalo grass is a drought-tolerant, hardy ground cover and turf alternative. 'Legacy' is a premium turf variety that can tolerate f oot traffic, drought, and clay soils.

How to Plant & Grow—Best at elevations below 6,500 feet, the new, hybrid buffalo grasses need just 2 inches of water per month, an occasional mowing, and little or no fertilizer. These grasses can be started from seed, plugs, or sod. Follow supplier's instructions carefully for best results.

Care & Problems—Buffalo grass cannot tolerate too much shade or water. Take care not to overfertilize.

Hardiness: Zones 3 to 9

Color(s): Green

Peak Season: May through October

Mature Size (H x W): 4 to 6 in. x 6 to 12 in.

Water Needs: Low

CAREX
Carex spp.

Why It's Special—The mophead-shaped carex is not truly a grass, but its contribution to the garden in form and texture makes it a valuable addition to the border or shade garden. 'Evergold' and 'Beatlemania' are excellent cultivars.

How to Plant & Grow—Most carex prefer moist soils and do best in partial shade. Check the plant tag to determine proper spacing at planting time. When planting, enrich the soil with organic compost.

Care & Problems—Unlike ornamental grasses, carex resent springtime haircuts. If the blades are badly tattered from winter weather, trim neatly. It will take a while to grow back. We do not recommend the copper-colored *C. buchananii* because of its invasive tendencies.

Hardiness: Zones 6 to 9

Color(s): Green, gold, striped with cream, copper brown

Peak Season: April to July

Mature Size (H x W): 8 to 18 in. x 12 to 16 in.

Water Needs: Medium to high

FEATHER REED GRASS
Calamagrostis x acutiflora

Why It's Special—The upright form and narrow footprint of feather reed grass make it a valuable architectural plant for the landscape. Quick to green up and the first ornamental grass to set seed heads, this is a rugged yet tidy backdrop for the perennial garden.

How to Plant & Grow—Striking when used *en masse*, feather reed grass is handsome as a single exclamation point. Feather reed should be planted 24 inches apart. Prune to 12 inches in March.

Care & Problems—Excessive moisture will cause this grass to fall over. 'Karl Forester' is at the point of being overused. Look for new varieties 'Avalanche' and 'Overdam'.

Hardiness: Zones 5 to 9

Color(s): Green, with straw-colored seed heads

Peak Season: Late spring through fall

Mature Size (H x W): 3 to 5 ft. x 2 ft.

Water Needs: Low

FOUNTAIN GRASS
Pennisetum alopecuroides

Why It's Special—All the fountain grasses are known for their showy bottlebrush seed heads, movement, sound, and graceful shapes. They are deer resistant, drought tolerant, easy care, long blooming, and provide great winter interest. 'Karley Rose' has rose pink blooms over a five month period. 'Little Bunny', at 18 inches, is one of the smallest cultivars.

How to Plant & Grow—You will get extra beauty from these ornamental grasses if you can place them so that the sun rises or sets behind them. Space according to individual plant specifications.

Care & Problems—Fountain grass needs to be cut back to 12 inches in late March to early April. Divide and rejuvenate oversized clumps in the spring.

Hardiness: Zones 6 to 9

Color(s): Silver/gold, rose pink

Peak Season: July to February

Mature Size (H x W): ½ to 5 ft. x 2½ to 5 feet

Water Needs: Low to moderate

JAPANESE FOREST GRASS
Hakonechloa macra

Why It's Special—Japanese forest grass looks like an upside-down mophead in texture. It falls over itself, draping over the edge of perennial beds, walkways, and rock walls. The brightly variegated foliage makes it "pop" in the landscape. 'Aureola' makes a bold statement. Showiest in the summer, *Hakonechloa* also provides good fall and winter interest.

How to Plant & Grow—A very slow grower, Japanese forest grass may take forest grass up to three years to develop a showy sized clump, but the results are worth the wait. In the hottest, driest parts of the interior West, give forest grass afternoon shade so it does not scorch at the leaf edges.

Care & Problems—Forest grasses need a good raking/cleanup/haircut every spring. It seldom needs to be divided but if need be, do so in the spring. Give this plant plenty of moisture.

Hardiness: Zones 5 to 9

Color(s): Variegated bright green, yellow, and cream

Peak Season: Summer

Mature Size (H x W): 1 to 3 ft. x 1 to 3 ft.

Water Needs: Moderate

KENTUCKY BLUEGRASS
Poa pratensis

Why It's Special—The standard cool-season grass for American lawns, Kentucky bluegrass can be used successfully in small areas. It is lush, finely textured, a rich, deep green, and perfect for bare feet.

How to Plant & Grow—Easy to grow from seed or sod, the planting area must be well prepared. Incorporate weed free organic matter into the top 6 inches of the planting area soil. A starter fertilizer is often recommended, as is consistent moisture on the planted area.

Care & Problems— Improved bluegrass varieties are drought enduring and tolerant when planted in properly prepared soils and maintained with deep watering practices. The care and maintenance of Kentucky bluegrass lawns is a very big topic of discussion. Seek out a reputable turf company in your area for the latest local recommendations.

Hardiness: Zones 3 to 7

Color(s): Green

Peak Season: Spring through fall

Recommended Mowing Height: As permitted

Water Needs: High

LITTLE BLUESTEM
Schizachyrium scoparium

☀

Why It's Special—A native American prairie grass with outstanding cold and drought tolerance, little bluestem is well suited for the Rockies. This ornamental grass has fabulous winter characteristics as the fiery-orange to russet-red foliage accents the landscape. Its handsome growth habit, adaptability, fluffy white plumes, autumn color, and winter presence make this a grass worth growing.

How to Plant & Grow—Little bluestem grows in almost any soil, especially in dry and rocky sites, and it prefers full sun. Plant new plants so they can settle in before summer. Place plants 1½ to 2 feet apart. A good cover-up for spring bulb foliage, this grass can also help stabilize hillsides.

Care & Problems—Once-a-week waterings are adequate for *Schizachyrium scoparium*, and less may suffice. Cut back on watering in March or April.

Hardiness: Zones 5 to 9

Color(s): Silver-blue foliage turning rusty orange-red as it matures

Peak Season: Blooms late summer

Mature Size (H x W): 24 to 36 in. x 12 to 24 in.

Water Needs: Low

MAIDEN GRASS
Miscanthus sinensis

☀ ☽

Why It's Special—Maiden grass, with its long, arching, fine leaves, is a garden aristocrat. Its handsome growth habit, adaptability, fall coloring, silvery plumes, and winter presence make it a valuable plant. Of the many cultivars of maiden grass, 'Yaku Jima' is quite coarse and arching, 'Morning Light' has gorgeous seed heads, and 'Adagio' is a short version. Maiden grass is lovely with black-eyed Susans, tall sedums, and Japanese anemones.

How to Plant & Grow—Many cultivars are available; choose those well suited for your area. Maiden grass cannot tolerate excessive water or shade. When grass needs watering, leaf blades roll. Water as needed—sometimes that's as often as once a week.

Care & Problems—Maiden grass, like other ornamental grasses, needs a good, annual haircut in March or April, to within several inches of ground level. Avoid high-nitrogen fertilizers as they weaken the plant.

Hardiness: Zones 4 to 8

Color(s): Green, variegated with white/cream

Peak Season: Feathery plumes appear in August

Mature Size (H x W): 3 to 8 ft. x 2 to 5 ft.

Water Needs: Low

PINK MUHLY GRASS
Muhlenbergia capillaris

☀ ☽

Why It's Special—The pink, airy clouds created by the flowers of muhly grass are a sight to see. Pink muhly grass is tolerant of drought, heat, and poor soils, and stands out in the garden when planted alone. Pink muhly is breathtaking in mass plantings and is great for large containers as well.

How to Plant & Grow—A good choice for poor soils, pink muhly grass requires good drainage and a low water regimen. Space plants 3 feet apart. Prune to within 9 to 12 inches of the ground in late March. *Muhlenbergia capillaries* does best when planted in full sun but it can take some shade.

Care & Problems—There are rarely problems with pink muhly grass. Although it requires good drainage, water needs are low, once the plants are established.

Hardiness: Zones 6 to 10

Color(s): Pink and purple

Peak Season: Early fall through winter

Mature Size (H x W): 3 to 6 ft. x 1 to 3 ft.

Water Needs: Low

SWITCH GRASS
Panicum spp.

☀

Why It's Special—Native to the tall grass prairie, switch grass tolerates soil extremes. This warm-season grass starts slowly in the spring, growing 3 to 4 feet tall. By late summer, a hazy cloud of flowertops adds 1 to 2 feet to its height. Switch grass's early autumn colors—yellow, orange, and purplish red—add an incendiary glow to the landscape. It persists into winter, contributing a valuable silhouette to the landscape.

How to Plant & Grow—Best used in prairie-style gardens or naturescapes for wildlife cover, switch grass flourishes in full sun and moist, fertile soil but tolerates dryer soils. Plant 3 to 4 feet apart. Water new plants every five to seven days.

Care & Problems—Switch grass requires a spring haircut to 9 to 12 inches. Divide when center shows signs of decline. Remove entire clump, divide, and replant or reposition healthy divisions.

Hardiness: Zones 4 to 7

Color(s): Leaf color gray-blue to soft green

Peak Season: August through late fall

Mature Size (H x W): 4 to 6 ft. x 3 to 4 ft.

Water Needs: Low

TURF-TYPE TALL FESCUE
Festuca spp.

☀

Why It's Special—A relative newcomer to the lawn business, turf-type tall fescue is a patented grass which behaves like bluegrass but suffers none of bluegrass's shortcomings. It spreads by rhizomes, quickly filling in bare spots. It is drought and heat tolerant, withstands tough weather conditions, and maintains its green color very late in the season. Despite its drought tolerance, tall fescue can be easily killed or thins during extended dry periods, whereas bluegrasses go into a dormancy mode and survives quite well.

How to Plant & Grow—The optimal planting time for turf type fescues is fall—September and October. Because local conditions in the Rockies vary, consult a local turf/seed/sod expert for planting instructions and maintenance of a turf-type tall fescue lawn.

Care & Problems—A mowing schedule will depend on weather conditions but it is best to maintain grass height of 1 to 2 inches. Increase to 2 to 3 inches in hot weather. This grass needs approximately 1 inch per week.

Hardiness: Zones 2 to 11

Color(s): Green

Peak Season: Spring through fall

Recommended Mowing Height: 1 to 3 inches

Water Needs: Low

JANUARY

- Consider the possibility of removing just a small portion of your turf this year. Could you use some more perennial borders? Maybe you have a sunny space that would be perfect and productive if it were planted with small fruit trees.

- Did you remember to clean up the mower and sharpen the blade before you put it away for the season? If not, this is a good time to do so.

- If there is no snow on the ground, apply a pre-emergent weed-protection product now. Follow directions carefully.

FEBRUARY

- If you don't already have ornamental grasses, this is the year to add them. They get a haircut once a year. Start planning to incorporate them into your landscape.

- Keep your binoculars and birding lists close at hand. The seed heads of the grasses are a popular food source for the little birds that stayed behind. Make sure they have some fresh water too.

- Does your turf grass need renovation this coming growing season? Think about overseeding the bare and thinning spots.

MARCH

- Garden shows are everywhere and all the new lawn-and-garden toys and tools will be on display. Take in the shows. You will find new varieties of grass seed, plant foods, and great design ideas for your garden.

- On or about St. Patrick's Day is a good time to cut back the ornamental grasses. Cut them a few inches above the crown. A good clean cut is much nicer than a few whacks at the clump. Neatness counts.

- Post-emergent weed controls can be applied now to dandelions and weedy grasses. Carefully follow label instructions.

APRIL

- In some areas of the Rockies, it's time for the first pass over the lawn with the mower. If the blade is sharp and the mower was serviced, you are ready to go.

- Evaluate your irrigation system. There are dozens of new tools on the market for getting the water to the plants, such as Netafim™, microsprays, and noodleheads, to name a few. Investigate them.

- Watch as the grasses that are established in your lawn start to grow and cleverly hide the deteriorating foliage of your spring bulbs.

- If you use a granular fertilizer and follow the three-application method of fertilizing, now is the time for the first application.

MAY

- This is a good time to aerate your lawn. Leave the soil plugs where they fall, because they decompose, and add organic matter to the turf area.

- Top-dress the lawn with a thin layer—less than one inch—of organic compost.

- Ornamental grasses will be arriving in the nursery centers. They don't look like much, as most of them are still dormant, but they can be planted now.

- Keep those weeds under control.

- Reseed or install sod if you have bare spots; keep them moist.

JUNE

- Tune up and fine-tune your irrigation system. Do not set it and forget it. There are new moisture sensors on the market that will tell your sprinkler system when it needs to come on and when it is not needed.

JULY

- If you are going on vacation, make sure your lawn is kept up while you are gone and have someone check to make sure the sprinklers go off when they should, if they should.

- High temperatures and drought conditions are tough on turfgrasses in July. Do not aerate, do not apply fast-release fertilizers, and do not use weed killers now.

- Resist the temptation to lightly sprinkle the grass because it feels good to *you*. Water deeply and thoroughly to encourage the grass roots to grow deep.

AUGUST

- Keep the mower set high. Leave the grass clippings on the lawn as a light mulch to conserve moisture and add nutrients back to the soil.

- Mid- to late August is a good time to seed bluegrass or turf-type fescue.

- Drought stress is indicated when the normally green turf takes on a blue-gray tinge. Water deeply.

SEPTEMBER

- This month is a great time to repair bare spots in the lawn, using a premium lawn seed or turf from a reputable turf company.

- Apply your second application of organic fertilizer this month.

- As temperatures are cooler, check to see if you can get by with once-a-week irrigation. You can reset the timer on your sprinkler system accordingly.

- Keep the lawn mowed and the mower blade sharp.

OCTOBER

- If you didn't aerate in the spring, now is an excellent time to do so. You can topdress with a fine layer (less than 1 inch) of organic compost.

- Mow the last couple of times for the season. The turfgrasses are slowing down.

- As the leaves fall, mow them with a mulching mower. This wonderful leaf mulch can then be used to topdress the perennial borders, under trees, and for winter protection of roses.

- You may need to water one last time. Mid-October is the time to have your pressurized sprinkler system blown out. This will get the water out of the pipes and prevent freezing and breaking during the very cold weather.

NOVEMBER

- Gather up all the lawn and garden tools. Clean them up, sharpen those that need it, and put them away in good order.

- You may have a few piles of leaves to mulch with the mower. When that task is completed, clean the mower, sharpen the blade, and put it away until next year.

- It's a good time to find the snow shovel. Our work is never done, is it?

- Drain and store hoses. Insulate hose bibs/connections on the outside of the house to protect them from freezing in a cold snap.

DECEMBER

- Relax.

- Review your garden journal. The new seed catalogues will start showing up soon.

Grasses, flowers, and other plants combine to make an enticing landscape.

PERENNIALS
for the Rocky Mountain States

Perennials may be the most aesthetically rewarding of all landscape plants; in fact, perennials have become the standard of color in gardens. They are permanent and winter hardy, and it is not necessary to plant them each spring as you do annuals.

A perennial is defined as a plant having a life cycle lasting more than two years. They may be evergreen or deciduous, with the visible parts of the plant dying each winter and growing new plant parts each spring. Perennials can be shrubs and trees as well as tender plants such as geraniums and African violets.

NEWCOMERS AND NATIVES

The first settlers brought along their favorite plants, many of which we use now. Some imported plants felt so much at home here in America that they became weeds. The common daisy, dandelion, Devil's paintbrush, tansy, and others arrived as garden flowers or medicinal herbs, but spread rapidly.

However, not all perennials are immigrants. Some are native to North America's fields and woods—wildflowers such as lady's slipper, bee balm, and mountain bluebell were admired by early settlers and planted in their yards and gardens. But a great many of today's popular perennials bear little resemblance to those our ancestors grew, due to the efforts of amateur and professional horticulturists. Dedicated hybridizers have created literally thousands of varieties.

PLAN AHEAD

Because of their ability to last for long periods of time, it is wise to plan carefully before you install perennial plants. Although perennials are more expensive than most annuals, when you consider that they represent a long-term investment, the cost amortized over the years makes them very reasonable. With thousands of varieties available, you'll find a perennial suitable for every possible location and growing condition in your garden.

With some exceptions, most perennials are difficult to grow from seed. They often require special conditions to get them started. We recommend you purchase plants rather than s pend your time trying to start them from seed. In addition to the nurseries and garden centers that have large supplies available, vast numbers of mail-order garden supply centers offer an almost unlimited supply of perennial plants.

When planting perennials, carefully review the zone-hardiness designations for each plant. Some perennials are not appropriate for all areas. If you try to grow a perennial that is not suited for your area, it may produce nothing but long-term problems in a garden or landscape. Also, perennials that are designed for full sun need a location with no shade at all, or at least eight hours each day with no shade—reflective light bouncing off buildings doesn't do any good. There are those folks we refer to as being in "zonal denial" who regularly push their zone numbers to see how far they can go in either direction. There is nothing wrong with lusting after and trying to grow a night-blooming jasmine (Zone 9) in your Zone 4 garden. Just know your chances of success are slim.

PERENNIAL CRAZE

There has been a continuing and expanding interest in perennials. The craze isn't so surprising when you consider the great diversity these plants offer gardeners. They are fascinating in part because most bloom for only short periods and seldom look the same for two days in a row or for two years in succession. Perennial gardening has a facet to suit every interest or need, and perennials generally require less care than annuals.

Perennials play well with others too. They team up nicely with ornamental grasses, especially those with deep, rich colors. Consider planting tall sedums, Joe-Pye weed, daylilies, and rudbeckia with grasses.

Perennials can be useful as well as ornamental. Don't overlook the importance of perennials as "knee socks" for your roses. Catmint, daisies, and bellflowers are especially well suited for this little design trick.

REMEMBER TO HAVE SOME FUN

Have some fun when designing your perennial borders and gardens. Pick a color or colors you love and plant with abandon. There is no right or wrong in your garden.

ARTEMISIA
Artemisia spp.

Why It's Special—Artemisia surrounds us in the Rocky Mountain region. The iconic sagebrush, *Artemisia tridentata*, or tall western sage, is everywhere. Tamer varieties include 'Valerie Finnis', 'Powis Castle', and 'Silver Mound', which have pretty, fine, silver leaves, making them excellent plants for the mixed perennial border or water-wise landscape. Artemisia's soft gray foliage tempers bright colors and knits together all the hues in a colorful border, especially the greens. *A. tridentata* is the state flower of Nevada.

How to Plant & Grow—Plant artemisia anytime from spring to early fall, setting them in hot, dry spots in the garden. Prune to shape, but leave a few buds on each stem to encourage fullness. Most artemisias are deer resistant.

Care & Problems—There are few problems with artemisia. Avoid overwatering and provide excellent drainage.

Hardiness: Zones 4 to 9, some cultivars hardy only to Zone 5

Color(s): Silver-gray foliage, white or yellow blooms

Peak Season: Late spring through autumn

Mature Size (H x W): 2 to 6 ft. x 1 to 2 ft.

Water Needs: Low

ASTER
Aster spp.

Why It's Special—Asters appear late in the gardening season when annuals are winding down. They are tough, colorful, and carry the garden until the first hard frost. Asters come in a wide range of colors and sizes. Colorful cultivars include 'Anna Potschke' and 'Purple Dome'.

How to Plant & Grow—Asters should be planted 2 to 3 feet apart to allow for good air circulation, which helps prevent powdery mildew. Plant asters in combination with other showy, late-season perennials, such as Joe-Pye weed, ornamental grasses, sedum, and goldenrod.

Care & Problems—Avoid wetting foliage, as this may lead to problems with powdery mildew. Divide every three or four years. Pinch at least once by Memorial Day or the Fourth of July, or both, to slow their desire to bloom early. This will shorten plants slightly and create a fuller clump.

Hardiness: Zones 4 to 8

Color(s): Magenta, red, blue, lavender, and purple

Peak Season: Late August until frost

Mature Size (H x W): 18 in. to 4 ft. x 16 to 24 in.

Water Needs: Moderate

BAPTISIA OR FALSE INDIGO
Baptisia australis

Why It's Special—An American native, perennial baptisia has beautiful spikes of sweet-pea-shaped flowers that grow from neat, dense mounds of pretty clover-like foliage. Many new varieties have been introduced for the home gardener; 'Twilight Prairieblues', 'Carolina', 'Screaming Yellow', 'Solar Flare', and 'Purple Smoke' are colorful new cultivars. After the flowers finish their show, shiny, black, dried seedpods provide visual, ornamental interest into the fall. Baptisia pairs well with salvia 'May Night' and white peonies.

How to Plant & Grow—Baptisia is easily grown in full sun or with a little shade in well-drained, organically rich soils. It will tolerate drought once it is established. Baptisia develops a strong taproot, and it resents being disturbed once it settles in. Grow it with other hardy, drought-tolerant perennials.

Care & Problems—Taller plants may need support.

Hardiness: Zones 4 to 9

Color(s): Blues, purple, maroon, bicolor, and yellow

Peak Season: May and June

Mature Size (H x W): 3 to 4 ft. x 3 to 4 ft.

Water Needs: Low

BASKET OF GOLD
Aurinia saxatilis

☼

Why It's Special—Basket of gold is a sure sign of spring. The mounds of gray-green foliage are covered with clusters of bright yellow flowers for several weeks. Basket of gold is a perfect partner for spring-blooming bulbs. Imagine a planting of yellow and white tulips coming up through the masses of basket of gold. It also pairs up nicely with rockcress or aubretia, especially when they can tumble over a rock wall or hillside.

How to Plant & Grow—Grow in full sun with late-blooming white tulips for a sensational, late-spring show. Excellent drainage is a must. Once established, basket of gold is drought tolerant.

Care & Problems—After the plant has finished blooming, cut it back by half to keep plants neat and tidy.

Hardiness: Zones 3 to 8

Color(s): Yellow

Peak Season: April to May

Mature Size (H x W): 6 to 12 in. x 12 to 18 in.

Water Needs: Moderate to low

BEARDTONGUE
Penstemon spp.

☼ ☀

Why It's Special—The Rocky Mountain area is home to hundreds of native beardtongue species. Hummingbirds and humans alike adore their showy, tubular flowers. 'Palmer's Penstemon' grows to 5 feet tall with charming pink, puffy blossoms. The pineleaf penstemon, in red and yellow with wispy foliage, shines in rock gardens. Firecracker penstemon gets its name from its crimson red flowers.

How to Plant & Grow—Penstemons love sun and demand sharp, excellent drainage. A mulch of fine gravel will keep their crowns dry. When you plant beardtongue, you may want to add a handful of sand or scree to your backfill soil.

Care & Problems—Cutting back spent flower stalks to their base will prolong the life of the plant. Do not overwater.

Hardiness: Generally Zones 5 to 9 (some varieties are not as hardy, some more so)

Color(s): Red, pink, purple, blue, and white

Peak Season: Late spring to midsummer

Mature Size (H x W): Up to 5 ft. x 1 to 2 ft.

Water Needs: Low to moderate

BEE BALM
Monarda didyma

☼ ☀

Why It's Special—Bee balm's fantastic blossoms resemble a fireworks display—or Tina Turner's hairdo! Hummingbirds and butterflies flock to these floral explosions. The hybrid varieties are offspring of the North American native wildflower, sometimes called Oswego tea or bergamot. The essential oil from bee balm is the essence of bergamot in Earl Grey tea.

How to Plant & Grow—Bee balm should be planted 2 to 3 feet apart and divided every three years to prevent center die out. Deadheading (removing spent flowers) will encourage a longer bloom period.

Care & Problems—Some varieties of *Monarda* are prone to powdery mildew. Look for 'Jacob Cline', 'Petite', 'Raspberry Wine', and 'Coral Reef' as mildew-resistant varieties. Plant where individual plants will have good air circulation, and do not use overhead sprinklers.

Hardiness: Zones 3 to 9

Color(s): Red, pink, purple, and coral

Peak Season: Late June to August

Mature Size (H x W): 15 in. to 5 ft. x 18 in. to 5 ft.

Water Needs: Moderate

BELLFLOWER OR CANTERBURY BELLS

Campanula spp.

☼ ☀

Why It's Special—Canterbury bells are an old-fashioned perennial for the mixed border. Their cup-shaped flowers nod gracefully above the foliage. 'Hot Lips' is a pink variety and a short, aggressive spreader. *Campanula* 'Dickinson's Gold' has striking, yellow-green foliage set off with clear blue flowers. Glomerata has clusters of flowers; the Canterbury bell types have drooping blossoms resembling a teacup sitting in a saucer. Some peach-leaved *Campanula* have double blooms.

How to Plant & Grow—Bellflowers love fertile, moist, well-drained soil. If given some shade, they can do with less water. *C. glomerata* should be divided every few years to keep it vigorous. Follow label instructions for each variety.

Care & Problems—Deadheading spent flowers lengthens bellflowers' bloom period. Deter slugs and snails by sprinkling used coffee grounds around plants.

Hardiness: Zones 3 to 8 (depending on cultivar)

Color(s): White, pink, lavender blue, and clear blue

Peak Season: Late spring to early summer

Mature Size (H x W): 6 to 30 in. x 12 to 48 in.

Water Needs: Moderate

BLACK-EYED SUSAN

Rudbeckia spp.

☼ ☀

Why It's Special—Their distinctive, orange-yellow petals radiate from dark brown center disks. The dried seed heads are a winter food source for birds and add interest to the winter garden. Denver Daisy™ was created for Denver's 150th anniversary. 'Goldstrum' and 'Maxima' are two favorites, but don't overlook new double and triple blooms, those with green cones, and new bicolor varieties: 'Cherokee Sunset,' 'Green Wizard', and 'Indian Summer'.

How to Plant & Grow—*Rudbeckia* is especially pretty when planted with ornamental grasses and sedums, as their bold colors really stand out in a summer garden. New cultivars have bicolor flowers and 'Irish Eyes' sports a green center.

Care & Problems—Black-eyed Susan will wilt if not given regular water in the heat of the summer. They also tend to naturalize (spread). Regular deadheading will help prevent this.

Hardiness: Zones 3 to 9

Color(s): Yellow, red, orange, green, bronze, and bicolor

Peak Season: June through August

Mature Size (H x W): 2 to 3 ft. x 1 to 2 ft.

Water Needs: Low to moderate

BLANKET FLOWER

Gaillardia spp.

☼ ☀

Why It's Special—Native to the western U.S., the cheerful blanket flower shines in the home garden. It can take heat, drought and clay soils. 'Goblin' has red petals tipped in yellow, 'Burgundy' is a deep, rich red, and 'Oranges and Lemons' is taking the garden by storm with its luscious orange blossoms whose tips are lemon yellow. As flowers mature, they take on a peach and melon tone. A single plant of 'Oranges and Lemons' can have up to seventy-five blossoms at one time.

How to Plant & Grow—Plant in a sunny, well-drained location. Blanket flower pairs beautifully with ornamental grasses.

Care & Problems—*Gaillardia* prospers in well-drained soil and gently reseeds. Cutting spent flower stalks will encourage more blooms, but it is not required.

Hardiness: Zones 5 to 10

Color(s): Red, yellow, orange, burgundy, and bicolor

Peak Season: June through September

Mature Size (H x W): 8 in. to 3 ft. x 12 in. to 2 ft.

Water Needs: Low

BLAZING STAR
Liatrus spp.

☼

Why It's Special—Blazing stars draw butterflies and bumblebees to the sunny border. The different types of *Liatrus* have unusual purple flower heads: Meadow Blazing Star is covered with tight blossoms; scaly *Liatrus* has loose flowers, and punctata, native to the western short-grass prairie, resembles a purple bottlebrush. For a butterfly/hummingbird garden, plant some blazing star and a couple of hummingbird mint plants, sit back, and watch the action. 'Punctata' is comfortably xeric. 'Kobold' and 'Floristan White' are just two of the hybrids available.

How to Plant & Grow—*Liatrus* can be grown in normal, sandy, or even clay soils. A sun lover, it withstands high heat and low water. It performs well in "meadow" plantings and looks sensational popping up from ornamental grass plantings, especially through little bluestem or *Panicum* 'Shenandoah'.

Care & Problems—Too much water will result in floppy flower spikes.

Hardiness: Zones 4 to 9

Color(s): White and purple

Peak Season: Midsummer to late summer

Mature Size (H x W): 2 to 4 in. x 1 in.

Water Needs: Low to moderate

BLEEDING HEART
Dicentra spectabilis

◐ ☼

Why It's Special—Bleeding heart is an old garden favorite with graceful arching branches and many distinctive, heart-shaped, hanging flowers lined up along those branches. The drooping, white inner petals create the impression of bleeding hearts. 'Gold Heart' has dramatic, yellow-green foliage. The new 'King of Hearts' has lacy, parsley-like leaves and a smaller stature than the older varieties. 'Burning Hearts' has fine, silvery blue foliage with dainty, ruby hearts. Children enjoy making a "lady in the bathtub" from the flowers by turning the blossom upside down and separating it in half. The naked lady's "leg" will point up and over the edge of the "tub."

How to Plant & Grow—Easy to grow, bleeding heart prefers rich, well-drained, moist (not wet) soils.

Care & Problems—The foliage goes dormant in midsummer, often to the point of disappearing. The plant will reappear next year.

Hardiness: Zones 3 to 9

Color(s): Red, white, and bicolor

Peak Season: April to May

Mature Size (H x W): 1 to 3 ft. x 1½ to 2½ ft.

Water Needs: Moderate

BUTTERFLY WEED
Asclepias tuberosa

☼

Why It's Special—Butterfly weed brightens the perennial garden in the summer. Its upright clusters of orange flowers beckon butterflies in profusion. Later in the season, tapered seedpods appear. It grows well in poor, dry soils and is often grown from seed. Be patient; it often takes butterfly weed a couple of years to do really well.

How to Plant & Grow—Plant butterfly weed in spring through early fall. These temperamental plants have brittle, tuberous roots, so handle them carefully. Sandy loam is ideal, but some strains are suited for clay. Until established, water regularly when the soil dries out, then water deeply once every seven to ten days.

Care & Problems—The deep roots resent disturbance, so allow plants to develop into mature clumps. Since butterfly bush emerges late in spring, mark its position and work around it.

Hardiness: Zones 4 to 9

Color(s): Orange, red, pink, and yellow

Peak Season: June through July

Mature Size (H x W): 18 to 24 in. x 18 in.

Water Needs: Low

CATMINT
Nepeta spp. and hybrids

Why It's Special—Catmint has fragrant, minty foliage as well as pretty blue flowers. It is also somewhat deer resistant. Billowing mounds of rich blue flowers put on an impressive show in early summer. Paired with white or pale pink roses, or both, it makes a perfect cottage garden combination. 'Little Trudy' is a new, compact version just about 12 inches by 12 inches. 'Dawn to Dusk' is a pink variety.

How to Plant & Grow—Upright, tall, billowy, compact, matting, and trim describe different varieties of *Nepeta*. It can be planted in drifts or borders. Catmint appreciates good drainage, and once established, is very drought tolerant.

Care & Problems—A thorough pruning in early spring, before blooms set, will keep catmint plants tidy and full. Shearing again after the big May to June show will encourage a second, extended bloom.

Hardiness: Zones 4 to 9

Color(s): Blue, violet, and pink

Peak Season: May though June

Mature Size (H x W): 12 to 36 in. x 16 to 36 in.

Water Needs: Low

CHOCOLATE FLOWER
Berlandiera lyrata

Why It's Special—What's not to love about a flower with a chocolate fragrance? Charming mini-sunflowers are drought tolerant and highly adaptable to various soils. Yellow petals have a maroon center, red-striped undersides, and chocolate-colored stamens with velvety green leaves. The flowers start blooming in the evening, giving off their chocolate smell in the morning. Petals drop after a day, and the process repeats itself throughout the summer. It is sometimes called green eyes because of green calyxes left behind after petals fall. The dried seed heads are extremely attractive as well.

How to Plant & Grow—"Plant it and forget it" applies to chocolate flower. These tough and hardy little daisylike flowers pair well with winecups and globemallow for a hot-summer border. Planted *en masse*, this plant is gorgeous.

Care & Problems—Chocolate flower may reseed but it is easily removed. Plant it where its fragrance can be noticed.

Hardiness: Zones 4 to 8

Color(s): Yellow

Peak Season: June through August

Mature Size (H x W): 15 in. x 18 in.

Water Needs: Very low

COLUMBINE
Aquilegia spp.

Why It's Special—Colorado blue columbine (Rocky Mountain columbine) is Colorado's state flower. Columbine's exquisite flower shape and lacy foliage make it a must-have for any garden. New cultivars are available every year. Two of the many new cultivars coming to a nursery near you are 'Little Lanterns'— a diminutive variety with little red-and-yellow blossoms—and 'Black Barlow'— a tall one with double, drooping, dark purple blooms.

How to Plant & Grow—Columbine can be grown from seed or purchased as a plant in bloom. It self-sows, prefers part shade for best flower color, and is drought tolerant once established.

Care & Problems—In some areas, leaf miners can be a problem. Remove and discard damaged foliage. Clean plants by gently pruning in the fall or spring.

Hardiness: Zones 3 to 9

Color(s): Red, pink, yellow, white, pale blue, dark blue, and bicolor

Peak Season: May through July

Mature Size (H x W): 1 to 3 ft. x 1 ft.

Water Needs: Low to moderate

CORAL BELLS

Heuchera spp.

Why It's Special—There's been an explosion in *Heuchera* hybrids over the last decade and it's all about the variations in the foliage. They have luscious names, too, like 'Marmalade', 'Crème Brûlée', 'Georgia Peach' and 'Lime Rickey'. Coral bells put up a spike, similar to candelabra, of tiny little flowers. In many of the varieties, the flowers are the least important part of the plants.

How to Plant & Grow—Coral bells like rich, well-drained soils and morning sun. At higher, cooler elevations, they will tolerate full sun. Allow soil to dry out between deep, thorough waterings.

Care & Problems—Slugs and snails can be deterred with commercial baits or by spreading used coffee grounds around plants. Heuchera will not tolerate clay soils.

Hardiness: Zones 4 to 9 and Zone 3 with protection

Color(s): Bronze, purple, pink, orange, lime, apricot, and variegated foliage; cream to deep red flowers

Peak Season: June through August

Mature Size (H x W): 12 to 30 in. x 12 to 24 in.

Water Needs: Moderate

COREOPSIS

Coreopsis spp.

Why It's Special—Coreopsis, also called tickseed, is one of the easiest and brightest perennials to grow, and a must for wild gardens, meadows, and cottage-style gardens. Allow it to reseed for a naturalized, wildflower look. Watch for the new Fruit Punch varieties. 'Jethro Tull' has fluted, tubular petals, making it a real beauty in the flower border. The plant spreads low and flat, providing a solid mass of brilliant color in the early summer. It has a wonderful clove-like fragrance.

How to Plant & Grow—Plant coreopsis in full sun whenever possible (a little afternoon shade is fine) and water regularly until established. You may want to remove spent blooms to prevent reseeding. It endures drought and should be divided every three to five years.

Care & Problems—Coreopsis needs little care. Lean, light, sandy soils are necessary. After flowering, shear them back for a tidier appearance. Tickseeds are pest free.

Hardiness: Zones 5 to 9

Color(s): Cream, yellow, gold, and pink with burgundy accents

Peak Season: June through October

Mature Size (H x W): 10 in. to 3 ft. x 12 to 15 in.

Water Needs: Low

COTTAGE PINKS

Dianthus spp.

Why It's Special—Fringed flowers look as though they have been trimmed with pinking shears. There are thousands of cottage pinks cultivars; many new miniatures are wonderful rock garden, front-of-the-border plants. 'Tiny Rubies' has a hot magenta blossom and fine, grasslike, blue-green foliage. The plant spreads exceptionally low and flat, providing a solid mass of brilliant color in the early summer. It has a wonderful clove-like fragrance. Cottage pinks, also called Cheddar pinks, originated in Cheddar Gorge, England, a place known for Cheddar cheese.

How to Plant & Grow—While pinks like full sun, they can stand a little afternoon shade, and do well if divided every few years. Shear spent blossoms to keep a tidy, green appearance and neat shape.

Care & Problems—Cottage pinks should be divided when the center of the plant begins to die out.

Hardiness: Zones 4 to 9

Color(s): White, pink, red, rose, purple, and bicolor

Peak Season: June through July

Mature Size (H x W): 4 to 18 in. x 12 to 18 in.

Water Needs: Low to moderate

CREEPING HUMMINGBIRD TRUMPET

Zauschneria garrettii (syns. *Epilobium* spp.)

Why It's Special—Only 6 inches high but spreading quickly, Orange Carpet™ seeds were collected in Idaho. A colorful performer, creeping hummingbird trumpets are at home in high altitudes, cold climates, hot sun, and arid spots, making *Zauschneria* an excellent choice for a xeric landscape. It looks lovely planted in a rock garden or allowed to spill across a slope or rock wall. The hummers will find it wherever you plant it.

How to Plant & Grow—Plant creeping hummingbird trumpets with other drought-tolerant perennials for a summer show. They are awesome with orange agastache and bronze ninebark shrubs. *Zauschneria* likes well-drained soil and weekly watering. A little afternoon shade is all right

Care & Problems—Creeping hummingbird trumpet requires minimal care. A spring pruning will do; a second one will keep it shorter, but it seldom stops blooming and will go right up to the first hard frost.

Hardiness: Zones 3 to 9

Color(s): Orange-red

Peak Season: July to October

Mature Size (H x W): 10 in. x 18 in.

Water Needs: Low to moderate

DAYLILY

Hemerocallis hybrids

Why It's Special—Popular and incredibly easy to grow, daylilies come in many colors and sizes; there's a daylily for every garden. A daylily display is as close as you can get to a "plant it and forget it" garden. Thick foliage multiplies and crowds out weeds. Besides the snazzy cultivars, don't overlook the old-homestead, orange daylily. Passed along from gardener to gardener, it's nothing fancy, just bulletproof.

How to Plant & Grow—Plant "fans" in groups of three, 24 inches apart. Daylilies are beautiful in drifts and paired with Shasta daisies. 'Happy Returns' looks great planted in front of bronze ninebark shrubs or with shorter ornamental grasses. Several varieties of daylilies can tolerate some afternoon shade.

Care & Problems—*Hemerocallis* is virtually pest free. Water once a week when foliage appears. In the hottest, driest parts of the Rockies, they may need water twice a week.

Hardiness: Zones 3 to 10

Color(s): Orange, red, yellow, pink, salmon, maroon, and lavender

Peak Season: July through August

Mature Size (H x W): 1 to 4 ft. x 2 to 3 ft.

Water Needs: Low

EVENING PRIMROSE

Oenothera spp.

Why It's Special—Every evening and every morning, the evening primrose blooms, illuminating the garden with cheery flowers. *O. macrocarpa* has big, yellow, cupped flowers with glossy, green, narrow foliage on reddish, fuzzy stems. 'Siskiyou Pink' or Mexican evening primrose, *O. speciosa* has crepe-paper-like pink-and-white blossoms. It is quite drought tolerant and lovely when allowed to ramble over an embankment or rock wall. It does well in poor soils.

How to Plant & Grow—Grow evening primrose in full sun for the best blooms. Perfect drainage is a must. Do not mulch. Its long taproot allows it to withstand drought. *Oenothera* pairs well with short grasses.

Care & Problems—Regular deadheading will keep the plant tidy and blooming for a longer period. This plant prefers to be left alone and will spread fairly quickly if allowed to do so.

Hardiness: Zones 5 to 9

Color(s): Yellow, white, and pink

Peak Season: June through August

Mature Size (H x W): 6 to 12 in. x 1 to 4 ft.

Water Needs: Low

FERNS

Osmunda cinnamomea; Athyrium niponicum; Matteuccia struthiopteris

Why It's Special—Ferns have been around for millions of years. Several are native to our region, and many are well adapted to woodland settings. The Japanese painted fern is wildly popular and for good reason: its intricate, multicolor fronds with a silver-bronze flame make it a standout wherever planted. Ostrich ferns are biggies; some are as tall as 60 inches. The cinnamon fern, with its upright, "cinnamon stick" frond is graceful, slow growing, and prefers boggy sites.

How to Plant & Grow—Keep new ferns damp until they're in the ground; do not let their roots dry out. Plant ferns in rich, moist soils, keeping them moist until well rooted. As woodland treasures, ferns can take a little morning sun, but no more.

Care & Problems—If the proper site is chosen, ferns will live for many years with little more than an annual foliage clean up.

Hardiness: Zones 3 to 8 for all except Japanese painted fern—Zones 4 to 9

Colors: green, silver, brown, and bronze

Peak Season: Early summer until fall

Mature Size (H x W): 1 to 4 ft. x 1 to 5 ft.

Water Needs: High

FOXGLOVE

Digitalis spp.

Why It's Special—Foxglove's tall flower spikes are covered with tubular, funnel-shaped blossoms. The insides of the blossoms, particularly the white, pink, and rose-colored ones, are heavily speckled with dark purple and white spots. *Digitalis obscura* is a dwarf variety from Spain, and worth finding for its drought tolerance. *Digitalis lutea*, a shorty at just 3 feet tall, has slender, pale yellow flowers.

How to Plant & Grow—*Digitalis* is fine in the sun in cooler areas, but in the hotter, more arid parts of the Rockies, give it some afternoon shade. It performs well in moist, well-drained loam. Foxglove is one of those short-lived perennials, let it seed around and colonize so it comes back year after year.

Care & Problems—Foxglove may be subject to powdery mildew. Keep water off the foliage to discourage this.

Hardiness: Zones 3 to 8

Color(s): White, pink, rose, yellow, peach, and rusty copper

Peak Season: June through July

Mature Size (H x W): 3 to 4 ft. x 1 ft.

Water Needs: Moderate

GAZANIA

Gazania krebsiana linearis

Why It's Special—'Colorado Gold' is a brilliant yellow, hardy, daisylike flower well suited for borders and rock gardens. 'Tanager', recommended by Plant Select ® for the Rockies, is another tough, colorful variety. It is a brilliant orange, just 4 inches tall, and impressive when planted in large sweeps and masses. The leaves of this plant take on a purple tinge when the weather cools.

How to Plant & Grow—Excellent drainage is required. Removing spent flowers encourages more blooms and results in a tidy-looking plant. Consider planting 'Colorado Gold' with a deep blue *Allium* or catmint. The 'Tanager' would look right at home with hummingbird mint, *A. rupestris*. A little afternoon shade is acceptable.

Care & Problems—Gazania may need winter protection in colder parts of the Rockies.

Hardiness: Zones 5 to 9

Color(s): Orange, yellow, and maroon

Peak Season: May through June and again in September

Mature Size (H x W): 4 to 12 in. x 12 in.

Water Needs: Low to moderate

GENTIAN
Gentiana spp.

Why It's Special—The blue color of the gentian flowers is so intense and distinct that it competes for attention with our clear, blue Rocky Mountain sky. A favorite, everyman's gentian (*Gentiana septemfida*), can be grown in just about everyone's home garden. Plant in the front of a perennial border or tuck in next to a specimen rock for a great look.

How to Plant & Grow—Plant gentians in early spring to allow them plenty of time to root in. Spring is also the time to divide older plants. Locate gentian in full to partial sun to ensure the plants grow vigorously and show off their spectacular flowers. Most gentians perform at their best in sandy loam or gravelly loam soil, such as a rock garden or other well-drained area with humus-enriched soil.

Care & Problems—If given the humus-rich soil they prefer, gentians generally don't need fertilizer. Mulching is recommended. Water thoroughly after planting, and water weekly during extended dry periods.

Hardiness: Zones 3 to 7

Color(s): Blue

Peak Season: July through August

Mature Size (HxW): 8 to 12 in. x 10 to 15 in.

Water Needs: Moderate

GERMAN BEARDED IRIS
Iris germanica

Why It's Special—Bearded irises, sentimental favorites from grandmother's garden, are also called German irises or flags. Incredibly durable and long lived, their exotic blossoms are named for the Greek goddess of the rainbow. Some are heavily scented and reminiscent of grape soda or bubblegum. 'Dykes Medal' winners are cultivars with exceptional characteristics. 'Beverly Sills' is soft apricot, 'Batik' is splotchy—purple and white—and the list goes on; there are literally hundreds of hybrids.

How to Plant & Grow—Plant rhizomes (bulbs) with one-third above the soil. They will not tolerate wet feet. Space 12 to 18 inches apart. Iris will survive unattended for decades. A little shade is fine, but too much will result in poor blooms.

Care & Problems—Remove and discard rhizomes with soft, rotten spots. Do not overwater. Divide every three to five years to rejuvenate clumps if necessary.

Hardiness: Zones 3 to 9

Color(s): All colors but true red, green, or black and many bicolor combinations

Peak Season: May through June

Mature Size (H x W): 6 to 40 in. x 6 to 12 in.

Water Needs: Low

GOLDENROD
Solidago spp.

Why It's Special—Arching, bright yellow stems add pizzazz to the late summer garden. Stems are covered with hundreds of tiny, bright yellow flowers, giving the plant the appearance of exploding, yellow fireworks. Beautiful when paired with ornamental grasses, goldenrod is an easy perennial with architectural value in mixed borders. It is a good nectar source for migrating monarch butterflies, is loved by bees, and is good as a cut flower.

How to Plant & Grow—Plant with blue and purple asters for a dazzling, late summer show. *Solidago* does well in normal, sandy, even alkaline soils and full sun. 'Fireworks' is an exceptional variety.

Care & Problems—Often confused with ragweed because it blooms at the same time, *Solidago* does not send pollen into the air. You can cut *Solidago* back by half in early summer to keep size more manageable. This will delay blooming by about two weeks.

Hardiness: Zones 4 to 9

Color(s): Yellow

Peak Season: July through September

Mature Size (H x W): 3 to 4 ft. x 2 to 3 ft.

Water Needs: Moderate

HARDY GERANIUM

Geranium spp.

☼ ◑

Why It's Special—Hardy geraniums are not to be confused with the summer annual geranium, which is not a geranium, but a *Pelargonium*. Hardy geraniums are also called cranes-bill geraniums because their seed heads are shaped like, drumroll . . . cranes' bills! True hardy geraniums make great ground covers and tumble over stone walls and rock gardens. 'Jolly Bee', 'Rozanne', and 'Tiny Monster' are newer hybrids with superior, long bloom periods. Some varieties have bronze foliage and some take on a purple-bronze coloration when the weather cools.

How to Plant & Grow—Plant hardy geraniums in full sun or part shade in moderately fertile soil. They do well in alkaline clay loam of the Rockies and are excellent planted in waves or mixed containers.

Care & Problems—Shear geranium back to encourage more blooms (if they slow in late summer).

Hardiness: Zones 5 to 8

Color(s): White, pink, deep rose, and lavender blue

Peak Season: June through September

Mature Size (H x W): 6 to 18 in. x 6 to 18 in.

Water Needs: Regular

HARDY HIBISCUS

Hibiscus moscheutos

☼

Why It's Special—Sporting dinner plate-size flowers, the giant hardy hibiscus has the largest flowers of any cultivated perennial. Including them in the garden adds exotic, tropical punch. Hardy hibiscus are complemented by tall ornamental grasses. 'Kopper King' ups the wow factor with copper–colored leaves. 'Lord Baltimore' is readily available in a cha-cha shade of crimson red. 'Blue River II' has exquisite, clear white blossoms.

How to Plant & Grow—Hardy hibiscus is very easy to grow, requiring only full sun and average soil. Water regularly until it is established. Good mulch will keep the roots cool. Once established, they are somewhat drought tolerant.

Care & Problems—*Hibiscus moscheutos* is always slow to appear in the spring. Leave a small piece of the old flower stalk in place, and do not disturb. Feed it in late spring and midsummer with an all-purpose, water-soluble plant food.

Hardiness: Zones 5 to 9

Color(s): White, pink-red, pale yellow

Peak Season: August through September

Mature Size (H x W): 3 to 8 ft. x 4 ft.

Water Needs: Low to moderate

HARDY MUM

Chrysanthemum spp.

☼ ☀

Why It's Special—As the garden fades, mums come out to party. Plant in containers or borders with ornamental kales, and tuck inside hollowed-out pumpkins for a glorious autumn vignette. If planted in large swaths, stick to one color for maximum impact. Mums are available at your local nursery in September.

How to Plant & Grow—Plant hardy mums in draining, "humusy" soil. They require regular, even watering. Pinching back buds until mid-August will delay blooms and encourage foliage fullness. Plant them with tall sedums ('Matrona', 'Black Jack'), asters, and ornamental grasses for a pleasing display. They also look smart next to a red Japanese maple. Some late afternoon shade will prolong the bloom color.

Care & Problems—If aphids are a problem, hose off with a stiff spray of water. Deer love mums. For a homemade deer repellent, process 6 eggs with a little water in a food blender. Add 2 quarts warm water and 1 teaspoon dishwashing liquid; blend well. Apply to the ground around plants to keep deer away.

Hardiness: Zones 5 to 9

Color(s): White, pink, burgundy, purple, bronze, yellow, and orange

Peak Season: August to October

Mature Size (H x W): 1 to 2 ft. x 2 ft.

Water Needs: Moderate

HOLLYHOCK
Alcea rosea

☼

Why It's Special—The tall, cheerful hollyhock is required for the cottage garden. Varieties such as the 'Black Hollyhock', *A. nigra*, may do better grown from seed and treated as a biennial. 'Chater's Double' boasts double-ruffled blossoms. Hollyhocks look beautiful against a wall, old barn, or weathered fence where their towering silhouettes are shown to best advantage.

How to Plant & Grow—Plant hollyhock in hot, sunny spots in the garden. Seeds sown in August and September will bloom the following summer. Hollyhocks are short-lived perennials, but if allowed to seed around, they colonize bountifully.

Care & Problems—Rust and mites tatter hollyhock foliage. If you can bear it, cut plants back to the first basal leaves when they're approximately 2 feet tall. This forces the plant to bloom later, when the mites have moved on. Some newer varieties are rust resistant.

Hardiness: Zones 2 to 10

Color(s): White, pink, red, maroon, yellow, peach, and salmon

Peak Season: July through September

Mature Size (H x W): 2 to 8 ft. x 1 ft.

Water Needs: Low

HOSTA
Hosta spp.

☽ ☼

Why It's Special—There are few plants to rival hostas in the shade garden. Leaves vary widely and wildly from smooth to deeply crinkled, variegated, striped, and in shades from steel-blue to green. They come in all sizes, from the new 'Tiny Mice' to the fabulously large 'Empress Wu'. Hostas push a flower spike in July, but many folks remove them because they pale in comparison to the rich foliage display. Plant with foxgloves and ferns for a nice textural contrast.

How to Plant & Grow—Variegated hosta varieties need more shade than others but most hostas can handle sun until afternoon. Plant in rich, organic soil, and water thoroughly at least once a week.

Care & Problems—Slugs can devastate hostas, so be prepared to fight back with commercial baits. Follow the instructions carefully. Used coffee grounds sprinkled around the plant's base will help too.

Hardiness: Zones 3 to 10

Color(s): White, pink, and lavender blossoms top showy, green foliage

Peak Season: June through August

Mature Size (H x W): 6 to 60 in. x 10 to 72 in.

Water Needs: Moderate

HUMMINGBIRD MINT
Agastache spp.

☼

Why It's Special—The name says it all; hummingbirds cannot get enough of this perennial. Tall, airy stems and finely textured foliage make *Agastache* a water-wise garden staple. These plants have lovely mint- or licorice-scented foliage and come in a range of warm, sunset colors. 'Ava' is a gem with gorgeous, rich purple blossoms, each with a red calyx, which gives the appearance of the plant being in bloom long after the flowers have faded. 'Shades of Orange' and *A. rupestris* are wonderful varieties too. Folks are just catching on to the beauty and value of this plant.

How to Plant & Grow—*Agastache* requires excellent drainage and sandy soil. Prune to about 4 to 6 inches in the spring. Remove unwanted seedlings in the spring.

Care & Problems—Overwatering will kill hummingbird mint.

Hardiness: Zones 5 to 9, some are hardy only to Zone 6

Color(s): Orange, pink, blue, purple, yellow, salmon, and bicolor

Peak Season: July through October

Mature Size (H x W): 36 in. to 5 ft. x 36 in.

Water Needs: Low

JAPANESE ANEMONE
Anemone x hybrida

Why It's Special—A prized, late summer through autumn-blooming perennial, Japanese anemone spends most of the season as handsome foliage. Just as the garden is slowing down, the perfectly round buds open to reveal delicate flowers that sway in the breeze until frost. 'Queen Charlotte' and 'Prince Henry' have pink, double blossoms, while 'Honorine Jobert' is white.

How to Plant & Grow—Plant from spring to summer in moisture–retentive, rich soil. Locate plants 2 feet apart, and water regularly to establish, then once a week (deeply) during dry spells. Mulching helps protect plants in colder parts of the region. In mountainous, cooler climes, anemone can tolerate full sun. In the more arid, hot parts of the region, they must have some afternoon shade.

Care & Problems—Early frosts may nip anemone buds. Spring is a good time to remove plants that have spread into unwanted areas.

Hardiness: Zones 5 to 9

Color(s): White, pink, and rose

Peak Season: August through October

Mature Size (H x W): 3 to 4½ ft. x 2 ft.

Water Needs: Low

JOE-PYE WEED
Eupatorium purpureum

Why It's Special—For a bold, architectural statement in the garden, consider Joe-Pye. Its showy, rose-pink to purplish flower heads up to 18 inches across are pretty for several weeks. Joe-Pye creates a prominent focal point for the fall garden. 'Gateway' is an especially gratifying selection.

How to Plant & Grow—Use Joe-Pye weed for naturalizing the landscape where there is plenty of water or as a backdrop for the perennial border. *Eupatorium* is particularly stately when planted with ornamental grasses, but Joe-Pye has higher water needs; set the combo near a pool or pond or in a sprinkler zone set for more water. Space 2½ to 4 feet apart. Water as needed to prevent stress. Especially when planted in full sun, Joe-pie needs extra water to be happy.

Care & Problems—Cool nights, bright sun, and constant moisture allow Joe-Pye to thrive. Cut old stalks to the ground in late spring.

Hardiness: Zones 5 to 9

Color(s): Cream, rose-pink, and purplish

Peak Season: Late summer through fall

Mature Size (H x W): 4 to 6 ft. x 3 to 4 ft.

Water Needs: High

LAMB'S EAR
Stachys byzantina

Why It's Special—Lamb's ear is a textural, tactile treat with its velvety gray leaves that beg to be touched. It is luscious as an edging plant with blue or pink flowering plants. 'Helen Von Stein' does not flower, yet has the largest leaves of any of the lamb's ear cultivars. 'Silver Carpet' is just 4 to 6 inches tall and puts up a flower stalk. *Stachys* is Greek meaning "ear of grain," a reference to the look of the flower stalk.

How to Plant & Grow—Well-drained soils are mandatory for *Stachys byzantina*. Plant 12 to 18 inches apart, and divide when the center shows signs of decline. Remove flowering stems when flowers fade. Lamb's ear will tolerate some afternoon shade.

Care & Problems—Prune back tattered leaves anytime during the growing season. Lamb's ear responds well to a thorough pruning in the early spring.

Hardiness: Zones 4 to 9

Color(s): Silvery gray foliage, rose flowers

Peak Season: Late summer to early summer

Mature Size: (H x W) 12 to 18 in. x 12 to 18 in.

Water Needs: Low

LENTEN ROSE
Helleborus orientalis

Why It's Special—In February or early March, brush the snow off the evergreen leaves of *Helleborus* to reveal thick flower buds waiting to open. This plant blooms over an extended period, remaining attractive even after the petals have dropped.

How to Plant & Grow—Plant Lenten rose in early spring or fall knowing young plants can take two to three years to bloom. Space 1½ to 2 feet apart in rich soil. Water deeply once a week. *Helleborus* resent transplanting, but take heart— new seedlings will increase the colony over time.

Care & Problems—Remove old leaves in early spring to allow for new growth. All parts of *Helleborus* are poisonous to humans and animals. Hot, dry winds can cause scorching of the leaves. Cover the crowns with a layer of mulch for protection.

Hardiness: Zones 4 to 9

Color(s): White, lime-green, pink, rose, purple, maroon, pale yellow, and speckled

Peak Season: February through May

Mature Size (H x W): 18 to 24 in. x 12 to 24 in.

Water Needs: Low to moderate

LEWIS'S FLAX
Linum perenne (Linum lewisii)

Why It's Special—This wispy, airy, native wildflower softens a perennial border with its clear blue flowers. Beautiful when planted *en masse*, it is useful for erosion control on hillsides and pretty when allowed to naturalize amidst wildflowers or in cottage gardens. Noted in the journals of the Lewis and Clark expedition and named for Captain Meriwether Lewis, it is a favorite Western wildflower. It has multiple medicinal uses and is decent forage for range animals.

How to Plant & Grow—Best sown as seed four to six weeks before the average last frost. Lewis's flax is drought tolerant and reliable in most soils. Flax needs little attention and is a short-lived perennial, but it readily reseeds.

Care & Problems—*Linum* is virtually carefree. However, because it eagerly reseeds, you may wish to hoe out unwanted volunteers.

Hardiness: Zones 3 to 9

Color(s): Blue

Peak Season: May through July

Mature Size (H x W): 12 to 20 in. x 18 in.

Water Needs: Very low

LUNGWORT
Pulmonaria spp.

Why It's Special—Lungwort is a captivating woodland perennial deserving of more attention. The speckled foliage shines from the shade garden and combines delightfully with Lenten roses, ferns, and hostas. 'Pierre's Pure Pink', 'Bowles Red', and 'Mrs. Moon' are some of the earliest bloomers, generally appearing in April. Lungwort derives its name from the Doctrine of Signatures. In the sixteenth century, people believed that a plant's outward appearance indicated which physical ailments it cured. Apparently, lungwort's splotchy foliage indicated it would be helpful for bronchial issues.

How to Plant & Grow—Lungwort thrives in rich, moisture-retentive soil, appreciates some morning sun, and needs afternoon shade. It may be divided every three to five years.

Care & Problems—Slugs and snails can be problematic. Use commercial bait per instructions or sprinkle used coffee grounds around plants as a deterrent.

Hardiness: Zones 5 to 8

Color(s): White, pink, lavender-blue, and violet

Peak Season: Early spring, April and May

Mature Size (H x W): 6 to 10 in. x 18 in.

Water Needs: Low to moderate

LUPINE

Lupinus spp. and hybrids

Why It's Special—Since they prefer cooler conditions, lupines are among the most dependable plants at higher elevations. The showy, pea-like flowers are borne on columnar racemes in a wide variety of colors. The famous 'Russell' lupines were created from native plants in the Pacific Northwest. They are stately and rich in color, blooming in red, blue, yellow, and cream. Wild lupine seeds are available.

How to Plant & Grow—Plant container-grown lupines in the spring. They prefer full to partial sun, but require afternoon protection in the hot, dry parts of the Rockies. Rich, well-drained soil yields the best results. Plant 18 to 24 inches apart.

Care & Problems—Mulch *Lupinus* to conserve water and to keep the soil cool. Deadhead flower spikes to encourage rebloom. Hybrids often need staking and may be short-lived.

Hardiness: Zones 3 to 8

Color(s): White, pink, lavender, blue, purple, red, yellow, and bicolor

Peak Season: May through July

Mature Size (H x W): 18 in. to 3 ft. x 2 to 3 ft.

Water Needs: Moderate

MAXIMILIAN SUNFLOWER

Helianthus maximilianii

Why It's Special—An easy-to-grow, native wildflower, the striking, tall, bright Maximilian sunflower is a stunning back-of-the-border plant. A valuable wildlife plant for seed and cover, *Helianthus maximiliani* was used by Native Americans as a food source and for dyes. Pioneers planted the flowers near their homes to deter mosquitoes, and blossoms were added to bathwater to cure arthritis pain. The seeds can be eaten after drying. It was named to honor the German naturalist, Prince Maximilian, who led a scientific expedition through the American West in the 1830s.

How to Plant & Grow—Maximilian requires little maintenance and is drought tolerant. This sunflower prefers sunny, well-drained sites but tolerates a range of soils—moist, clay soils or on rocky ledges.

Care & Problems—Good even for clay soils, Maximilian sunflower has very few pests or problems. Give the plants room to flourish.

Hardiness: Zones 3 to 9

Color(s): Yellow

Peak Season: July through October

Mature Size (H x W): 6 to 8 ft. x 4 ft.

Water Needs: Low

ORANGE GLOBEMALLOW

Sphaeralcea spp.

Why It's Special—These clear orange blossoms resemble miniature hollyhocks. Mentioned in the journals of Lewis and Clark, globemallow is a native of the desert plains and lower mountain regions of the West. The bright orange flowers really stand out in their native habitat, which are primarily sagebrush steppes. When well-sited in the garden, globemallow will thrive in hot, arid climates.

How to Plant & Grow—*Sphaeralcea* is one plant that can stand heavy clay. Place in full sun, and cut back by half after the first heavy bloom in early summer. This will encourage the plant to fill out and put on another heavy bloom. Plant with winecups, little bluestem (its red tinge is a gratifying complement), and/or blue oat grass. It looks incredible planted near a bronze ninebark.

Care & Problems—Orange globemallow resents over-watering and is blissfully trouble free.

Hardiness: Zones 4 to 9

Color(s): Orange and watermelon-red

Peak Season: May through September

Mature Size (H x W): 36 to 42 in. x 24 in.

Water Needs: Low

ORIENTAL POPPY

Papaver orientale

Why It's Special—Oriental poppies are the quintessential perennial for the early summer garden, and they are drought resistant. Plump, hairy flower buds open to reveal thin, crepe-paper petals and a showy "boss" of purple-black stamens. With many colors and sizes to choose from, the big, old-fashioned, orange poppy now competes with other cultivars sporting huge, pale pink flowers, some of them 6 inches in diameter. 'Lauren's Grape', selected by Lauren Springer Odgen, author of *The Undaunted Garden*, is a purple showstopper. *Papaver nudicale*, the Iceland poppies (Zones 2 to 10), with a wide color range, are also worth a special mention.

How to Plant & Grow—Best grown from small, 4 to 6 inch plants or seeds sown in late fall or early spring, Oriental poppies need well-drained soil for winter survival. Poppies love sun, but a little shade is fine.

Care & Problems—Overhead watering will ruin attractive flower blossoms. When foliage has deteriorated after the spring bloom, carefully prune it away.

Hardiness: Zones 4 to 8

Color(s): White, pink, salmon, red, orange, and purple

Peak Season: June to early July

Mature Size (H x W): 2 to 4 ft. x 2 to 4 ft.

Water Needs: Low

PEONY

Paeonia lactiflora and hybrids

Why It's Special—Peonies, beloved by gardeners and non-gardeners alike, are an important addition to the cottage-type garden. Regal blossoms range from 3-inch singles to 10-inch singles, doubles, or semi-doubles. Spend some time selecting the varieties that really appeal to you.

How to Plant & Grow—Plant peony roots in late August through October; water well when buds are forming. They appreciate sunny, well-drained locations. Late afternoon shade prolongs blossoms. Plant the "eyes" no deeper than 1 to 2 inches below the soil surface, and space them 3 to 4 feet apart. A little afternoon shade will keep the blossoms looking good a little longer.

Care & Problems—In colder areas, mulching the first season will provide some protection to the crowns. Remove all old foliage and mulch in the spring. Don't worry about or spray ants, as they will take care of harmful insects.

Hardiness: Zones 3 to 8

Color(s): White, pink, salmon, red, rose, yellow, and bicolor

Peak Season: Late spring to early summer

Mature Size (H x W): 2 to 4 ft. x 3 ft.

Water Needs: Low to moderate

PERENNIAL SALVIA

Salvia x superba

Why It's Special—Perennial salvia, or violet sage, provides months of purple-blue blooms on sturdy upright spikes. 'East Friesland' has rich purplish blue flowers and grows to two feet; 'May Night' is a darker blue. There are pink and white hybrids as well: 'Pink Friesland' and 'Sensation Rose'. Pitcher sage, *Salvia pitcheri*, is a long-lived perennial loved by bees, butterflies, and moths.

How to Plant & Grow—These plants are well suited for a water-thrifty garden. Set out as early as possible. Salvia loves well-drained soil. During extended dry periods, water deeply every seven to ten days.

Care & Problems—Too much shade and/or water will cause stems to flop and the plant will languish. Shear spent flower stalks after first heavy bloom to encourage a flush of flowers.

Hardiness: Zones 4 to 8

Color(s): White, pink, lavender-blue, and purple

Peak Season: Late spring through September, heavy bloom in May and June

Mature Size (H x W): 18 to 24 in. x 18 to 36 in.

Water Needs: Low

PURPLE CONEFLOWER

Echinacea purpurea

☼ ☀

Why It's Special—Purple coneflowers are known to be butterfly magnets and a mainstay of the Rocky Mountain High Desert perennial garden. Now available in a riot of hybrid colors, they may well go by the simpler name coneflower. Cultivars on the market include 'Tomato Soup', 'Tiki Torch', 'Mac 'n Cheese', 'Gumdrop', 'Green Envy', 'Maui Sunset', 'Hot Papaya', and 'Fragrant Angel', and that's just for starters!

How to Plant & Grow—All coneflowers require a sunny planting site and excellent drainage. Plant as directed on label. Forfeit (cut off) the first flower stalk to develop a strong plant. While coneflowers thrive in full sun, a little late afternoon shade is fine.

Care & Problems—Deadheading encourages additional blooms. Newer hybrids should be given a thorough soaking once every seven to ten days in the hottest, driest climes. *E. pallida* likes extremely dry conditions.

Hardiness: Zones 4 to 9

Color(s): Deep pink, orange, red, melon, white, cream, lime-green, and bicolor

Peak Season: July through August

Mature Size (H x W): 2 to 4 ft. x 18 to 24 in.

Water Needs: Low to moderate

RED HOT POKER

Kniphofia caulescens

☼ ☀

Why It's Special—These striking, spiky plants add architectural drama to a perennial border. Their unique red and yellow flower spikes are reminiscent of torches, hence their other common name, "torch lilies." Recommended by the Plant Select™ program, 'Regal Torchlily' will look smashing in your garden. Plant as an exclamation or focal point in the perennial border. Consider pairing it up with some low, matted yellow ice plant, any of the drought tolerant yellow daisies, and the taller Maximilian's sunflower. Not the least bit subtle, it would be a dazzling display.

How to Plant & Grow—Plant in average, compost rich or sandy soils. Red hot poker can be a very successful waterwise plant with the occasional deep watering. Choose a spot where the sun shines most of the day.

Care & Problems—Very minimal. Remove spent flower stalks before winter.

Hardiness: Zones 4 to 9

Color(s): Bicolor red and yellow

Peak Season: Late July to September

Mature Size (H x W): 40 in. x 24 to 30 in.

Water Needs: Low

RUSSIAN SAGE

Perouskia atriplicifolia

☼

Why It's Special—Russian sage is a graceful, aromatic perennial with lavender-blue blossoms beloved by bees. The flowering effect lasts for months; combined with ornamental grasses and coneflowers, it makes an elegant statement in the landscape. The remaining branches make a pretty silhouette in the winter garden. An especially lovely combination includes black-eyed Susan, white coneflower, and Russian sage. The standard, old-fashioned Russian sage tops out at 5 feet tall; a new cultivar, 'Little Spire', is much shorter at 3 feet.

How to Plant & Grow—These fragrant plants preferlean soil that has not been amended with compost, dry conditions, and full sun. Set plants 2 feet apart, and water them regularly only to get them established. Despite its name, Russian sage is not edible.

Care & Problems—No serious pests are attracted to this plant. Russian sage should not be given supplemental water as it may reseed very aggressively. Do not plant near wildlands.

Hardiness: Zones 4 to 9

Color(s): Lavender-blue

Peak Season: June through September

Mature Size (H x W): 3 to 5 ft. x 4 ft.

Water Needs: Low

SEDUM MATRONA
Sedum telephium 'Matrona'

☼

Why It's Special—Incredibly dependable, tall sedum 'Matrona' offers a very long season of interest to the garden. In February, tiny little rosettes appear at the bases of the old stalks. The plants' fleshy pink-tinted leaves grow on dark burgundy stems and the dusty pink broccoli-type heads last into winter. Another tall sedum, 'Purple Emperor' has very dark foliage.

How to Plant & Grow—Space 18 inches apart in full sun and well drained soil. Older clumps may split in the center. Lift entire plant, divide into healthy clumps, discarding center. Replant. *Sedum* 'Matrona', and the tall cousins like 'Purple Emperor' and 'Black Jack', make great companions for the ornamental grasses and coneflowers.

Care & Problems—Avoid rich soils and overwatering, which will result in floppy, leggy plants. If aphids are a problem, wash with a strong spray of water from the hose.

Hardiness: Zones 3 to 9

Color(s): Pink, maturing to red, copper, or buff

Peak Season: August to frost

Mature Size (H x W): 18 to 36 in. x 12 to 24 in.

Water Needs: Low

SHASTA DAISY
Leucanthemum superbum

☼ ☼

Why It's Special—He loves me, he loves me not, he loves me, and daisy chains. You need not say the ditty or make the chains to enjoy this true, cottage-garden favorite. The white Shasta daisy stands out in the summer garden. Older varieties are notorious for flopping over after too much rain or when they need dividing. 'Becky' is a preferred cultivar with large blossoms and very strong stems; it seldom needs staking and it makes a wonderful cut flower. 'Crazy Daisy' has double, frilly petals; it is extremely eye catching in the perennial garden. 'Broadway Lights' opens yellow and fades to cream; it's a happy-faced, compact cultivar.

How to Plant & Grow—Plant Shasta daisies in average, dry-to–medium, well-drained soil. Light shade is welcome in hotter areas.

Care & Problems—Remove spent flower heads to encourage more blossoms. Divide every three years.

Hardiness: Zones 4 to 9

Color(s): White

Peak Season: June through July

Mature Size (H x W): 3 to 4 ft. x 2 to 3 ft.

Water Needs: Moderate

SIBERIAN IRIS
Iris sibirica

☼ ☼

Why It's Special—An elegant, graceful plant for the damp spot in your garden, the Siberian iris with its slender, upright foliage makes a design statement in the border. These flowers are perfect in the cottage garden. 'Caesar's Brother', a clear blue, and 'Gull's Wing', a white, are two superb cultivars. They multiply rapidly, dig easily, and make a perfect passalong plant.

How to Plant & Grow—Divide in spring or late summer, watering well until established. Iris may need to be divided every three or four years. Siberians will tolerate some shade, but they bloom more and have better color with at least six to eight hours of sun.

Care & Problems—In late autumn, cut back foliage to about 6 inches and remove debris. If rot or borers are discovered, remove and dispose of any infected parts.

Hardiness: Zones 3 to 9

Color(s): Blue, purple, maroon, white, pink, and yellow

Peak Season: May through June

Mature Size (H x W): 16 to 42 in. x 18 to 24 in.

Water Needs: High

SNEEZEWEED
Helenium autumnale

☼

Why It's Special—Sneezeweed, or Helen's flower, is heat tolerant with a long bloom season, augmenting the late summer garden palette. 'Moerheim Beauty', 'Mardi Gras', and 'Red Shades' are exceptional. The "cones" of sneezeweed are incredibly eye-catching, particularly those that have yellow tips. Sneezeweed was used by indigenous people to treat hay fever.

How to Plant & Grow—Sneezeweed prefers rich, moist soils and is intolerant of drought. To encourage thicker, more floriferous plants, cut the entire clump back by half in June. Yes, this will delay the bloom, but it makes a sturdier stand of sneezeweed, generally with more blossoms. Plant 18 to 24 inches apart.

Care & Problems—Too much shade or fertilizer will cause leggy, floppy plants. After a few years, the centers may die out. Dig entire plant, divide, and replant. Water in well.

Hardiness: Zones 3 to 10

Color(s): Orange, yellow, red, maroon, and bicolor

Peak Season: August and September

Mature Size (H x W): 24 to 36 in. x 12 to 24 in.

Water Needs: Moderate

SULPHUR FLOWER
Eriogonum umbellatum

☼ ☼

Why It's Special—Also called sulphur buckwheat, this little charmer is known for its bright yellow flowers. 'Kannah Creek' is a Plant Select® variety, well suited for the Rockies and high deserts of the West. Found throughout the entire region, it is named for the area of western Colorado near Grand Mesa. Buckwheat blooms are held like little umbrellas (hence the name *umbellatum*) above the foliage on single, skinny stalks. Buckwheat can be cut and dried for charming flower arrangements. It holds its color for a long time.

How to Plant & Grow—Plant sulphur flower in good loam, clay, or sandy soil. Buckwheat needs only occasional watering to look its best. Plant 12 inches apart. In large drifts, the mat-like foliage of buckwheat will make a showy ground cover. Full sun is recommended. A little shade late in the day is fine.

Care & Problems—Sulphur flower has very few problems, but will not survive overwatering.

Hardiness: Zones 3 to 8

Color(s): Yellow

Peak Season: May through July

Mature Size (H x W): 12 to 15 in. x 12 to 24 in.

Water Needs: Low to moderate

SUN DAISY
Osteospermum barberiae

☼

Why It's Special—Two cultivars of sun daisy have been awarded the Plant Select® designation: 'Lavender Mist' and 'Purple Mountain'. Both have beautiful flowers and rich green leaves, and they bloom all season long. 'Lavender Mist' flowers open white and turn lavender as they age. 'Purple Mountain' has bright purple flowers with a contrasting dark center. Sun daisy is attractive to bees and butterflies.

How to Plant & Grow—Sun daisies should be planted at least 12 inches apart in good garden loam. Both varieties have moderate water needs. They really show off in the garden when planted *en masse* and paired with the shorter ornamental grasses ('Little Bunny' or 'Hamelyn'), hot pink or yellow ice plants, and winecups. Thrives in total sun.

Care & Problems—Sun daisies are low-maintenance plants. New blossoms will cover old, so no deadheading is necessary.

Hardiness: Zones 5 to 9

Color(s): Soft lavender, bright purple, and white

Peak Season: April to August

Mature Size: (H x W) 10 in. x 12 in.

Water Needs: Moderate

SWEET WILLIAM
Dianthus barbatus

Why It's Special—Sweet William is a favorite in the perennial border or cutting garden. The fringed flowers have a soft clove fragrance. This short-lived perennial, if grown in optimal conditions, reseeds, colonizes, and does well for years. 'Sooty' has velvety, maroon flowers and red stems.

How to Plant & Grow—Best planted in deeply worked, organically rich, well-drained soil, sweet William does best with some afternoon shade, especially in the hotter parts of the West. Deadheading of spent flowers will prolong the plant's life. Plant in late spring or autumn for flowers next summer. Nurseries are now selling plants that will bloom the same year.

Care & Problems—*Dianthus barbatus* is susceptible to crown rust, rot, snails, earwigs and slugs. Excellent drainage is important.

Hardiness: Zones 3 to 9

Color(s): White, pink, red, maroon, bicolor, and picotee

Peak Season: May to frost

Mature Size (H x W): 1 to 2 ft. x 6 in. to 1 ft.

Water Needs: Low to moderate

VERONICA OR SPEEDWELL
Veronica spp.

Why It's Special—Veronica's blue flower spikes look great with Shasta daisies or 'Fragrant Angel' (white) coneflowers. 'Royal Candles' is a long-lived, long-blooming variety with clear blue spikes. *V. liwanensis*, or Turkish veronica, is a ground cover-type veronica without the blue spikes but covered with tiny, blue flowers. It is just a few inches tall and terrific rambling through the rock garden, planted on a slope or tucked near the edge of a perennial border.

How to Plant & Grow—Veronica performs best in full sun, but a little shade in the day is fine. They are intolerant of too much water. Spiky varieties do not like to be crowded.

Care & Problems—Speedwell is trouble free and somewhat drought tolerant. Divide every three to five years to maintain plant vigor. Remove spent flowers on spike forms.

Hardiness: Zones 2 to 9 (*V. spicata*), Zones 4 to 9 (Turkish)

Color(s): Blue and pink

Peak Season: Late May to mid-July

Mature Size (H x W): Turkish: 1 to 2 in. x 2 ft., spike varieties: 6 to 12 in. x 1 to 2 ft.

Water Needs: Low to moderate

WHIRLING BUTTERFLIES
Gaura lindheimeri

Why It's Special—Butterfly-shaped flowers nod and wave on the wispy, wand-like stems of *Gaura*. Whirling butterfly plants add a welcome airiness to the perennial border or a bit of whimsy to the cottage garden. Some of the new cultivars are quite compact: 'Blushing Butterflies' and 'Siskiyou Pink' are just 18 inches tall. 'Passionate Pink' has burgundy stems and foliage and deep rose-pink blossoms. All whirling butterfly plants can be used to great effect in containers. Try topping off a tall, narrow container with a cluster of one variety for a grand, "spouting" effect.

How to Plant & Grow—Plant *Gaura lindheimeri* in full sun in well-drained, loamy, or sandy soils. It likes the slightly alkaline soils of the Intermountain West and goes well with *Sedum matrona* or any echinacea.

Care & Problems—None serious. Remove seedlings to prevent unwanted plants.

Hardiness: Zones 5 to 9

Color(s): White, pink

Peak Season: June to October

Mature Size (H x W): 12 to 18 in. x 18 to 24 in.

Water Needs: Low to moderate

WINECUPS
Callirhoe involucrata

☀

Why It's Special—Sometimes called purple poppy mallow, winecups is a beautiful, sprawling, magenta-blossomed plant for the dry or xeric garden. It grows to 3 feet wide and looks great tumbling over rock walls.

How to Plant & Grow—*Callirhoe* likes it dry. Plant it in a well-drained site in full sun. It will tolerate clay soils and makes a colorful complement to chocolate flower and short, ornamental grasses. The magenta flowers are pretty pushing out of their mat near any of the artemesias, but especially with any of the fine-leaved varieties such as 'Powis Castle' or 'Valerie Finnis'.

Care & Problems—Winecups will die with too much water. Prune straggly ends when growth slows in high summer. It will generally push another set of blooms with cooler, September temperatures.

Hardiness: Zones 4 to 8

Color(s): Magenta

Peak Season: June to September

Mature Size (H x W): 6 to 9 in. x 36 in.

Water Needs: Low

YARROW
Achillea spp.

☀ ☽

Why It's Special—Yarrow shines in hot, dry climates, yet adapts well to gardens with moderate water. The flat-topped flower heads make perfect landing pads for migrating butterflies. With ferny foliage and unusual flower heads, yarrow adds a colorful, feathery dimension to the mixed border. It is well suited to elevations above 7,000 feet. The Western native yarrow is white but you will find plentiful, vivid cultivars in the nurseries.

How to Plant & Grow—Plant yarrow 18 inches apart in lean, dry, well-drained soils in full sun. It is striking when grouped with perennials of different textures, especially daylilies and ornamental grasses.

Care & Problems—Cut back *Achillea* after flowering to encourage branching and a second bloom period. It may self-seed if not deadheaded (cut back). Some people find the foliage irritating to their skin.

Hardiness: Zones 3 to 9

Color(s): White, pink, red, yellow, gold, lilac, salmon, and mixed

Peak Season: June to September

Mature Size (H x W): 2 to 3 ft. x 2 to 3 ft.

Water Needs: Low

YUCCA
Yucca filamentosa

☀

Why It's Special—Sometimes called Adam's needle, yuccas send up spectacular flower spikes each summer, sometimes 5 to 6 feet high. Covered with creamy, droopy bells mid-summer, some have a soft, pleasant fragrance. 'Color Guard' and 'Golden Sword' have striking gold-striped blades.

How to Plant & Grow—Yucca plants need free-draining soil and full sun. Consider using 'Color Guard' or 'Gold Sword' as a bold statement planted alone in a large container. Use a single yucca as a specimen plant or focal point; a grouping of three to five is stunning in a water-wise and/or contemporary planting. A mass of yellow ice plants sets off yellow-banded yucca leaves.

Care & Problems—Yucca requires little maintenance, and it is deer resistant. Remove flower stalks (with care) when blossoms fade. While they are extremely drought tolerant, they will appreciate a little extra water from time to time.

Hardiness: Zones 5 to 9

Color(s): Creamy white blossoms

Peak Season: July to August

Mature Size (H x W): 3 to 4 ft. x 3 ft.

Water Needs: Very low to low

JANUARY

- Evaluate last season's garden, and determine changes in plants and design.

- Plan a new perennial garden if you don't have one. Research plants and draw out bed size and shape.

- Start perennials from seed. The seedlings need 12 to 14 weeks indoors before outdoor transplanting.

- Avoid sidewalk and driveway deicing salts, especially where they can run off into beds. They will kill perennial roots.

- Perennials will need winter water during prolonged dry spells. Water during above-freezing temperatures.

- If some perennials are looking unattractive, they may be cut back.

FEBRUARY

- If you fell behind, you can still plant perennial seeds; it isn't too late! Ensure the seedlings have plenty of light, either natural or fluorescent. Lack of light will make plants weak.

- Check out your perennial plantings. Cover crowns and roots that may have been exposed by frost heaves, or mulch over them if the ground is frozen.

- Ensure perennials have enough moisture and water as needed when the ground is not frozen.

- Do not overwater seedlings.

- Be on the watch for weeds, and remove them before they go to seed.

MARCH

- You may be able to start planting now, but ensure soil is not too wet. A handful of soil should crumble and not clump up.

- Seedlings may need to be transplanted into soilless growing medium with mixed slow-release fertilizer.

- Seedlings can be moved outdoors during the day, and allow planting mix to dry slightly to harden off the plants. Bring seedlings inside at night to prevent freezing.

- March is a good time to apply a slow-acting fertilizer to the perennial bed.

- Begin garden cleanup. Cut off dried grasses, stems, and old blossoms.

- Stay on top of the weed control.

APRIL

- Plan and install support for taller perennials.

- Control height of perennials by pinching off 1 to 2 inches of top growth during this early part of the growing season.

- Ensure your transplanted seedlings are hardened-off for a week before planting.

- Plan your watering schedule. Perennials thrive on deep, infrequent watering.

MAY

- This is the month to plant after choosing your favorite and healthiest specimens.

- Plant perennials in containers in soilless growing mixture with slow-release fertilizer.

- Now is the time to divide perennials that are too large or are crowding other plants. It is best to divide them when new growth is only a few inches tall.

- Seedlings started indoors may be planted now, and all new plantings should be mulched with a 2 to 3 inch layer.

- Early blooming perennials may be deadheaded.

JUNE

- It is time to document progress of your perennial garden and make adjustments.

- Plant any remaining perennials, and divide those that need it. Do this before it gets too hot to prevent transplant shock.

- Water bed-planted perennials deeply, about 1 inch per week.

- Begin fertilizing perennials planted in containers with water-soluble fertilizer. These plants need more fertilizing because of leaching out of nutrients due to frequent watering.

JULY

- Add mulch as necessary to maintain a 2 to 3 inch layer.

- Avoid planting or transplanting perennials in the heat of the summer. However, if necessary, plant during the evening or on cloudy days. Cut plant back by one-third to one-half and mulch thoroughly.

- Continue deep, infrequent watering as needed.

- Continue removing any damaged or diseased parts of plants.

- Control pests by washing them off or using insecticidal soap.

- Remove weeds before they produce seeds. July is a big weed-control month!

AUGUST

- Perennial seed heads start to appear. If you don't want self-seeding proliferation, remove seed heads. However, consider that many perennial seeds are great food for birds.

- August is the right time to start perennials from soft wood cuttings. Use the healthiest branches available.

- Replenish mulch as needed. Thin plants and cut back dried flowers and foliage.

SEPTEMBER

- Consider leaving the variety of seed heads and pods for fall and winter interest.

- This is a good time to plant container perennials. Many may be rootbound after being in containers all summer so gently untangle their roots before planting.

- Prune dead and dying foliage and stems, and continue to eradicate weeds, especially before they go to seed.

OCTOBER

- You can still plant perennials, which is a better option than leaving them in the containers in which they were grown.

- Continue removing dead, dried foliage and stems, and cut back black, rotten, frozen plants but leave grasses for winter decoration.

- Wait until ground is frozen to apply winter mulch.

NOVEMBER

- Enjoy your evergreen foliage, dried grasses, and other dried, perennial structures.

- If you have a prolonged dry spell, ensure plants have enough moisture. Water only when the ground is not frozen.

- If you are not done yet, finish cleaning beds and cutting back all perennials that are not providing winter decoration.

DECEMBER

- Go skiing.

- Plan modifications for next year's garden.

- Continue to monitor soil-moisture content, water as necessary if the ground is not frozen, and work some compost into the soil around your plants.

DAYLILY

ROSES
for the Rocky Mountain States

Most of us instinctively love roses. But loving roses and knowing how to grow them are often two different matters. To be successful in the art of rose gardening in the Rockies, one must not forget about the practicalities. Roses pose a particular challenge for Rocky Mountain gardeners since many of the modern types cannot endure the cold, fluctuating winter conditions. How much coddling do you want to give to rose bushes in your landscape? Not only is it disappointing to buy roses each spring, only to have them die after the first winter, but it's hard on the pocketbook. Therefore, if you stumble upon an old variety that has stood the test of time, it deserves consideration. Though that old shrub rose from yesteryear was remarkably water thrifty and adaptable, it roots deeply and requires deep digging before planting, so don't expect a rose to do well if you just dig a hole, stick the bush in, and water it now and then. It takes some planning to find the logical location for specific rose varieties, and it takes time to properly prepare the soil.

THE WHO'S WHO AMONG ROSES

With so many roses from which to choose, it's a good idea to gain a basic understanding of how roses are classified. The American Rose Society (ARS) lists more than fifty categories. This can become quite confusing—even a bit intimidating. Rose aficionados are very serious about rose classification. That may be fine for them, but for average gardeners, growing roses should be fun and rewarding. In this chapter, you find brief descriptions of some of the more popular types of roses that can be grown successfully in our region. You can even grow many of these roses in pots if you have limited gardening space.

WHAT ROSES LIKE

Most roses perform best in full sun, but you can expect excellent results if they are planted in a spot where they receive six to eight hours of sun daily. The location should have good air circulation—avoid a "heat trap," where afternoon sun stresses the plants. Too much shade yields few flowers and early attacks from powdery mildew disease. Good soil drainage is essential to grow roses successfully. Poorly drained sites or locations where water accumulates result in short-lived rose bushes.

To test your soil's drainage, dig several 18-inch-deep holes in scattered locations where you intend to plant. Fill each hole with water. After twelve to twenty-four hours, fill the holes with water again. If the water drains away in eight hours or less, your soil is adequately permeable to air and water and will support plant life. Soils that drain as fast as the water enters are too permeable (sandy); soils that do not drain in eight hours are not permeable enough (clay) and will result in oxygen starvation to plant roots. The solution to both problems is similar—add a quality organic material such as compost, aged manure, sphagnum peat moss, or a combination of these materials. Organic matter helps hold moisture in sandy, fast-draining soils and helps open up clay soils to improve drainage and provide oxygen.

MAKING A GOOD INVESTMENT

Roses grow in a wide range of soil types, from heavy clay and crushed granite to sandy conditions. However, take the time to build a good soil; you'll grow more vigorous plants with more prolific

SHRUB ROSE

blossoms. Even the ugliest soil can be improved by adding quality organic matter, plus loosening and aerating it. If the planting location is new, infertile, compacted, and in need of improvement, then dig the planting hole 2 to 3 feet wide and 18 to 24 inches deep. The subsoil in the bottom of the hole should be thoroughly loosened. To your native soil, add one-third to one-half organic matter by volume and mix well. If your soil does not require such extensive treatment, it can be improved by spreading a 2- to 3-inch layer of compost over the soil surface and working it in to a depth of 10 to 12 inches. Then dig the appropriate-sized planting hole.

SELECTING ROSES

Rose bushes are available as bare-root plants, potted, and in packages. Mail-order nurseries usually send out bare-root, dormant plants. Local garden and nursery retailers sell container-grown roses. Department and grocery stores may offer both packaged and potted roses. Experience has shown that bare-root, dormant plants are excellent choices when planted in early spring. They successfully acclimate and adapt to local soil conditions. Potted roses are a good choice if the nursery has followed good cultural practices in potting and growing the plants. Packaged roses should be purchased before they send out long shoots or before they have had a chance to dry out in storage.

PLANTING TIPS

The preferred time to plant roses in the Rockies is spring, though container-grown plants can be planted successfully from spring through summer. The earlier you plant, the greater chance the plant has to develop a strong, vigorous root system before the heat of summer or before the soil freezes.

Prepare your planting location before buying the plants. If bare-root roses and packaged roses have dry roots when they arrive, put them in a 5-gallon bucket of tepid water to soak overnight. Avoid soaking the roots longer than twenty-four hours.

Bring the rose to the planting hole and prepare it for planting. Prune away any damaged or broken roots. Position the bush in the hole so that the graft or bud union (swollen knot or knob) is an inch below ground level. If needed, mound backfill soil in the center of the hole to position the bush properly. Gently add the prepared backfill soil around the roots and firm it with your hands. When you have filled the hole halfway, stop and water thoroughly. After the water has soaked in, finish adding the remaining soil and water again.

When planting is complete, the top of the bush can be pruned. To keep the center of the bush open for light and air circulation, prune the canes to an outward-facing bud. Pruning cuts should be made at a 30- to 45-degree slant above a bud, leaving 6 to 8 inches of the cane.

Next, cover the newly planted and pruned rose bush with a mound of the loose, prepared backfill soil. This prevents the canes from desiccation while the root system becomes established. In early spring, this technique protects the emerging shoots from frost damage. To prevent damaging the tender new growth, take care when removing the soil from around the stems.

Potted roses can be planted throughout the growing season. Dig the planting hole wide enough to accommodate the root system without crowding and deep enough to position the bud union 1 inch below ground level. If the roots have become rootbound, carefully loosen and spread them out into the planting hole or lightly score the rootball to encourage root development. Fill in with backfill soil, and water thoroughly.

WATERING TIPS

To grow vigorously and produce lots of blooms, roses need plenty of water. Dig into the top 2 to 4 inches of soil; if the soil is dry, it's time to water. Roses growing in clay soils require less watering than roses in sandy soils. Newly planted roses may need to be watered twice a week until they become well established. *When you water, do so thoroughly and deeply.* To reduce leaf diseases, water roses from the bottom rather than sprinkling overhead. To maintain

Climbing roses can be trained against a trellis or porch wall.

soil moisture and conserve water, mulch. Pine needles, coarse compost, and shredded cedar are good choices for mulching roses.

With fluctuating weather conditions in late fall and winter, dry air, and long periods without rain or snow, it is important to drag out the hose occasionally and water. Extended dry spells during fall and winter can result in the death of the root system. Water when air temperatures are above freezing and when the soil is not frozen solid. Water early in the day so the liquid has time to soak in before nightfall. Fall and winter watering may be needed every four to five weeks, depending on weather and soil conditions.

FERTILIZING TIPS

Some of today's modern roses need several applications of fertilizer to keep growing vigorously and blooming. Apply an appropriate rose fertilizer monthly beginning in mid-May and ending by mid-August. My favorite is an organic-based granular that can be applied monthly through mid-August. Follow label directions on the rose fertilizer package. Avoid the old adage, "If a little fertilizer is good, a bunch more will be even better." To reduce the chance of stressing the plant roots, water the soil the day before fertilizing.

PRUNING TIPS

Roses need to be pruned to maintain vigor and health and, in some cases, to keep the bush a desirable size. Depending on the effect you want, roses can be pruned in a variety of ways. In the Rockies, don't prune roses back severely in the fall. They need all the stored food energy possible to sustain them in our fluctuating climate. Here are some general guidelines for pruning established roses: prune hybrid teas, grandifloras, floribundas,

129

'LOUISE OELIER' BOURBON ROSE

and polyanthas in the spring; prune climbing roses after flowering; prune the nonproductive, old, heavy canes of climbing roses to ground level in early spring. Remember that roses are resilient and will benefit from proper pruning.

THE MOST WANTED LIST

Luckily, our semi-arid climate and higher altitude translate to relatively few pest problems on roses. But as we become more urbanized, pests soon follow. Early spring visitors may include aphids; these small and voracious pests cluster on the buds and young, tender growth to feed on the juices of the plant. They may be green, red, tan, or black and are easily banished by smashing them between your fingers and rinsing with clear water from the hose. If you prefer, Neem oil, home-made soap sprays, or insecticides can be used. Read and follow label directions.

Summer insects may include the curculio beetle, which drills holes in rose buds; if spotted, it drops from the bud to the ground and scurries away. If you're quick, hand picking keeps them at bay.

Spider mites are minuscule pests found on the undersides of the leaves; their feeding causes the foliage to develop a "salt and pepper" or stippled appearance. They can be kept under control by directing a forceful spray of water from the garden hose toward the underside of the leaves on a weekly basis. Watering from the bottom of the bush is also effective in thwarting other pests.

Thrips affect the buds and blossoms of roses and can be found at the base of the flower petals. They seem to prefer light-colored blossoms, and damage can be detected by discoloration of the flower petals. Some buds may not open normally because of their presence. Systemic insecticides can be used if thrips pose a threat in your rose garden.

The rose midge is perhaps the worst enemy; it causes the tips and buds to wither, blacken, and die. If rose midge becomes a problem, insecticide treatments may be necessary. Check with your County Extension Service.

Powdery mildew, blackspot, rust, anthracnose, and verticillium wilt are some common diseases that may attack stressed or weakened roses.

To help reduce the incidence of major disease and pest outbreaks, provide proper growing conditions, well-drained soil, and good air circulation. You must also provide the good cultural practices of watering, fertilizing, and pruning; removing yellow and diseased leaves; maintaining clean mulch around the plants; and inspecting the rose bushes weekly.

WINTER CARE

Some of the most popular roses, including hybrid teas, grandifloras, floribundas, and many climbing types, cannot endure cold, fluctuating weather conditions. After the first hard freeze, these types can be protected by applying a layer of loose soil at the base of each rose. Form a 6- to 12-inch, cone-shaped mound around the base of the canes. For additional protection, you can add evergreen boughs or straw on top of these mounds to protect the upper portions of the canes.

NOT SO NEEDY

Take a look at some of the new types of roses on the market. The Knock Out™ and Oso Easy™ brands have some incredible attributes that make them worth growing. Roses are a lot less demanding than many of the gardening books make them out to be. These floral favorites don't need an inordinate amount of care—just a little care on a regular basis. Well-drained soil, adequate moisture, occasional fertilizing, and regular maintenance make your roses thrive.

If you like roses, find a couple to try from the ones featured in this chapter. They were selected for their ability to survive our tough climate and to look good doing it.

AUSTIN ROSES
Rosa cultivars

Why It's Special—Rosarian David Austin created an entire series of beautiful roses by combining the best traits of heirloom (scent and rosette blossoms) with newer roses for hardiness and repeat blossoms. They are called "Austin" or "Austin English" roses. Cultivars 'Evelyn', 'Graham Thomas', and 'Abraham Darby' are among the strongest performers for the Rockies. 'Graham Thomas' has rich, deep, butter yellow blooms all summer. 'Evelyn' opens peach pink and fades to pale pink as it matures. 'Abraham Darby' is apricot.

Design Tips—Austin roses are perfect for interweaving clematis through their stems. Most roses require 6 to 8 hours of sun a day. In especially hot areas of the West, afternoon shade will prolong the color of the flowers.

Growing, Care & Problems—'Evelyn' benefits from deadheading as does 'Abraham Darby'. 'Graham Thomas' is well suited to a pillar. All like a couple of applications of organic fertilizer during the spring and early summer.

Hardiness: Zones 5 to 9

Peak Season: Summer; all will repeat bloom

Fragrance: 'Graham Thomas' has a very spicy fragrance; 'Evelyn', strong and sweet; 'Abraham Darby', rich and fruity

Mature Size (H x W): 'Graham Thomas', 5 to 8 ft. x 5 to 8 ft.; 'Evelyn', 4 ft. x 4 ft.; 'Abraham Darby', 5 ft. x 4 ft.

Water Needs: Moderate

CLIMBING ROSES
Rosa cultivars

Why It's Special—'Zephirine Drouhin' is a nonstop, fragrant bloomer that tolerates some shade. 'Blaze' is covered with masses of classic tea rose-shaped scarlet flowers. 'Dortmund' blooms are single petaled, clear red, with yellow stamens and a large white "eye." It's very showy and a prolific bloomer. 'New Dawn' was voted the most popular rose in the world in 1997. It sports soft pink, satiny blooms in lush profusion.

Design Tips—Train against a wall or up and over an arbor or pergola. Combine 'New Dawn' with blue and purple clematis and wisteria for a grand show. 'Red Blaze' and 'Dortmund' look great against neutral backdrops. 'Zephirine' should go where her fragrance can be enjoyed.

Growing, Care & Problems—Do not prune climbers the first two years. Trim diseased or broken canes in late spring. Climbing roses love full sun.

Hardiness: Zones 5 to 9, 'Blaze' and 'Zephirine Drouhin'; Zones 4 to 9, 'New Dawn' and 'Dortmund'

Peak Season: 'Blaze' and 'Dortmund', all season, heaviest in June; 'New Dawn' and 'Zephirine', May until frost

Fragrance: 'Blaze', soft and fruity; 'Dortmund', very light; 'New Dawn', fresh; 'Zephirine', strong "old rose" scent

Mature Size (H x W): 'Blaze' 10 to 15 ft. x 4 ft.; 'Dortmund' 8 to 10 ft. x 3 to 4 ft. (pruned); 'New Dawn':12 to 18 ft. x 6 to 10 ft.; 'Zephirine' 8 to 12 ft. by 3 to 6 ft.

Water Needs: Low to moderate (depending on weather)

FLORIBUNDA ROSES

Rosa cultivars

☀

Why It's Special—Floribundas are vigorous, prolific, and nonstop bloomers. They can handle the heat and tend to be somewhat drought tolerant—perfect for the Rockies. 'Iceberg' is available as a climber and as a pink floribunda. 'Livin' Easy' blooms are apricot-orange. 'Betty Boop' foliage emerges bright red, and its "picotee" edging (a different color on the tips) of the petals is very showy.

Design Tips—'Iceberg' is gorgeous planted *en masse* with a classic companion, lavender. 'Livin' Easy' pairs great with hot pink and white flowering perennials. While 'Iceberg' can take a bit of afternoon shade, most floribundas love full sun.

Growing, Care & Problems—Always leave some space around rose bushes to allow good air circulation. Like most roses, spring prune to shape and remove dead branches. Give floribundas a couple of applications of organic fertilizer (up until two months before first frost date).

Hardiness: Zones 5 to 9, 'Iceberg' and 'Betty Boop'; Zones 5 to 10, 'Livin' Easy'

Peak Season: May until early autumn

Fragrance: 'Betty Boop' has a mild rose fragrance; 'Iceberg', strong; 'Livin' Easy', moderate

Mature Size (H x W): All, 3 to 4 ft. x 3 to 4 ft.

Water Needs: Low to moderate (depending on weather)

GRANDIFLORA ROSES

Rosa cultivars

☀

Why It's Special—Grandiflora roses are similar to hybrid teas, but the shrubs are slightly shorter and the flowers are born in clusters on slightly shorter stems. They bloom throughout the summer, and can tolerate the high heat of the interior West. 'Gold Medal' has deep yellow flowers, and dark glossy green foliage. 'Love' is a fantastic bicolor with intriguing blossoms—rich scarlet red petals with silver-white reverses. 'Tournament of Roses' flowers begin as red buds, opening to reveal several shades of pink.

Design Tips—Grandifloras are meant for cutting and admiring, so position them near a patio or favorite seating area.

Growing, Care & Problems—In areas with late frosts, do not prune grandifloras until all danger of hard frost has passed. To support the shrub's blossoms and productivity, feed with an organic rose fertilizer according to the label instructions. Mulch in colder areas. Avoid overhead watering. Grandifloras enjoy full sun. Some darker reds will suffer in hot regions, so give them some shade in the late afternoon.

Hardiness: Zones 5 to 9

Peak Season: Late May until early autumn

Fragrance: 'Gold Medal' has a strong rich fragrance; 'Love', spicy and light; 'Tournament of Roses', little or no fragrance

Mature Size (H x W): 4 to 6 ft. x 3 to 4 ft.

Water Needs: Moderate

HYBRID TEA ROSES
Rosa cultivars

☀

Why It's Special—Large perfect blossoms with exquisite scents—that's why hybrid teas are widely grown roses. 'Peace' was named the day Berlin fell to the Allied forces in 1945. Robust, with dark green glossy foliage, the blooms are golden yellow tinged with pink. 'Double Delight' has creamy white blossoms that appear to have been dipped in strawberry red dye. 'Dainty Bess' has enormous pink blossoms with incredible maroon stamens.

Design Tips—Beautiful blooms on strong stems make hybrid teas perfect for cutting. Plant where you can see them every day. 'Dainty Bess' is a bit leggy and looks best with lavender hiding her knobby knees.

Growing, Care & Problems—Prune in late spring, after forsythia has bloomed. Feed with an organic rose fertilizer according to label instructions. Mulch to help them overwinter in colder areas. Deadhead for subsequent blooming. Hybrid teas enjoy full sun. Some darker reds will suffer in hot regions, so give them some shade in the late afternoon.

Hardiness: Zones 5 to 9, 'Dainty Bess' and 'Double Delight'; Zones 4 to 9, 'Peace'

Peak Season: May until early autumn

Fragrance: 'Double Delight' is strong and spicy; 'Dainty Bess' has a soft rose scent; and 'Peace' is sweetly scented

Mature Size (H x W): All, 3 to 5 ft. x 3 ft.

Water Needs: Moderate

MINIATURE ROSES
Rosa cultivars

☀

Why It's Special—These tiny shrubs are an excellent choice for rose lovers with small spaces. 'Gourmet Popcorn' is a popular rose with heavy cascades of bright white double blossoms. The flowers are set off by dark green foliage and lemon yellow stamens. 'Hot Tamale', as the name implies, is a snazzy mini with perfect little blossoms of rich pink and soft orange. The petals have a bright yellow reverse.

Design Tips—Minis are quite at home in large containers, and if mulched, will overwinter nicely in a pot. 'Gourmet Popcorn' is an excellent choice for a White Night Garden, planted as a short hedge near a patio. Their diminutive size makes these roses nice additions to window boxes.

Growing, Care & Problems—Miniature roses are known for their prolific blooming habits. Deadhead to encourage repeat blooming. Prune in late spring to shape. Both of these are disease resistant and strong performers. While they are full sun lovers, these small beauties would take some shade in the hottest part of the day.

Hardiness: Zones 5 to 9, 'Hot Tamale'; Zones 4 to 9, 'Gourmet Popcorn'

Peak Season: May until early autumn

Fragrance: 'Gourmet Popcorn' has a soft honey fragrance; 'Hot Tamale' has a mild scent, if any

Mature Size (H x W): 18 to 30 in. x 18 to 24 in.

Water Needs: Moderate

MODERN SHRUB ROSES

Rosa cultivars

☀

Why It's Special—The Knock Out ™ series is incredibly disease resistant, drought tolerant, self-cleaning, and bloom from late spring until the first frost. Wow! They also come in nice clean colors—red, yellow, clear pink—and do not fade in the heat. The entire series of Explorer are hardy to minus 35 degrees, making them an excellent selection for the interior West and high elevation gardens.

Design Tips—The Explorers are available as shrubs or climbers. 'Morden Centennial', 'John Cabot', 'William Baffin', and 'Alexander MacKenzie' are standouts.

Growing, Care & Problems—Plant in a well prepared garden spot. In Zones 5 and colder, the bud union should be one inch below the soil line. An annual meal of organic fertilizer is enough. Knock Out roses are self-cleaning. A spring shaping and removal of any dead branches will suffice.

Hardiness: Zones 5 to 11, Knock Out; to Zone 4 (even 3), Explorer Series

Peak Season: May until first hard frost

Fragrance: Explorer Series roses have a slight rose scent; only the yellow Knock Out has a mild fragrance

Mature Size (H x W): Explorers: 2½ to 10 feet x 3 to 5 feet; Knock Outs: 3 to 4 feet x 3 to 4 feet.

Water Needs: Low

OLD GARDEN ROSES

Rosa cultivars

☀

Why It's Special—Old roses, those grown before 1867 (the date the first hybrid tea was developed), have a rich and varied history. Also known as antique roses, the types include several forms. 'Mme. Hardy ' is double, fragrant and white with a noticeable green "pip" or center eye. It flowers in clusters and single damask style blossoms.

Design Tips—They are highly fragrant so plant them where you can enjoy them. 'Louise Odier' is an ideal "Old Rose" with cupped blossoms and double petals that flatten as they age. 'Louise Odier' has excellent form, is very sturdy, and sometimes blooms again in fall.

Growing, Care & Problems—With 'Mme. Hardy', slight "balling" may occur during extended rains. This means the roses don't open completely. Avoid watering using overhead sprinklers. After the heavy blush of bloom in early summer, cut back canes by one-third (at least) to one-half. These roses need fertile, well-drained soil and full sun.

Hardiness: Zones 5 to 9, all

Peak Season: 'Louise Odier', summer and fall; 'Mme. Hardy', June

Fragrance: Both are intensely fragrant

Mature Size (H x W): 'Louise Odier', 4 to 6 ft. x 3 to 4 ft.; 'Mme. Hardy', 6 ft. x 3 to 4 ft.

Water Needs: Moderate

RUGOSA ROSES
Rosa rugosa

☀

Why It's Special—Rugosas are brilliant garden roses with incredible fragrance. Their "hips" can be used for jelly or eaten right from the shrub. Heat is a rugosa's friend and it will continue its show when lesser roses have slowed down. 'Hansa' is a deep rich pink. The whitest of white roses, 'Blanc Double de Coubert' is hardy to Zone 3. 'Purple Pavement', despite its name, is a dark raspberry. 'Therese Bugnet' is delicate looking with pink double blossoms.

Design Tips—The downside to rugosas: their wild side makes them wickedly thorny so plant them where they will not attack you. These are tough, stout plants, seldom bothered by deer, so they make a good, not-so-friendly fence when you need one.

Growing, Care & Problems—Rugosas are disease resistant and need only a good sunny place to grow and a spring pruning to keep them healthy and nicely shaped.

Hardiness: Zones 3 to 7

Peak Season: May until the first hard frost

Fragrance: All rugosas are very richly scented

Mature Size (H x W): 5 to 7 ft. x 4 to 7 ft.; a few cultivars are more compact

Water Needs: Low

SPECIES ROSES
Rosa spp.

☀

Why It's Special—Tall, gangly, and wild looking, species roses are the parents of all modern roses. Austrian copper (*Rosa foetida bicolor*) has bright orange flowers with bright yellow reverses. Suckers may produce all yellow blooms, giving the impression of two plants in one. The red-leaved rose, *Rosa glauca rubrifolia*, has reddish purple foliage and star-shaped pink flowers in late spring or early summer.

Design Tips—Austrian copper will grow almost anywhere and prefers to be left alone. It fits best in a naturalized, wild setting.

Growing, Care & Problems—Drought-tolerant Austrian copper will sulk for years if it's pruned. The red-leaved rose responds very well to pruning and shaping after flowering; it is somewhat drought tolerant. There are virtually no problems with either, and they grow in sandy to clay soils.

Hardiness: Zones 3 to 8

Peak Season: June

Fragrance: Sorry; they have a slight and, to some, unpleasant odor (*foetida* = fetid)

Mature Size (H x W): Austrian copper, 6 to 9 ft. x 6 to 9 ft.; red-leaved, 6 to 10 ft. x 5 ft.,

Water Needs: Low

JANUARY

- If you are considering roses for your garden, keep in mind placement, types, number, and the size of the space you can devote to growing them.

- If you have mulched your roses, inspect their winter mulch and make sure it is still in place. Replenish if needed.

- Water roses occasionally but deeply when the ground is not frozen.

FEBRUARY

- Order bare-root roses and designate the shipping time to coincide with the proper planting time for your area.

- Grafted roses are quite susceptible to frost heaving, so make sure yours are still properly mulched.

- Apply a layer of compost over the root zone if you didn't have time to apply mulch. It will begin to break down.

- Apply horticultural oil to canes that have a history of insect or disease problems.

MARCH

- Transplant roses that need relocating. Do not plant a rose where one has been before unless you remove nearly all of the soil the previous rose inhabited.

- Remove protective, winter mulches as plants begin to grow.

- Prune roses according to type. Use clean, sharp, and disinfected tools.

- Remove all dead canes and old leaves.

- Apply a granular, slow-release fertilizer to your established roses.

APRIL

- Now is the time to purchase container-grown roses at your local nursery. The selection is wide, and this is a good time to get the new plants in the ground.

- Begin the training of climbing roses. Peg them to rock walls and fences. Pegs are available at nurseries.

- Inspect roses for pests—aphids especially. Knock them off with a strong spray from the hose.

MAY

- It's too late to plant bare-root plants, but timing is still all right for planting container-grown roses.

- Consider the gift of a rose for Mother's Day.

- Do not overwater your roses. Allow the soil to dry out between watering. While roses do need ample water, they prefer a deep, regular soaking. Avoid overhead watering.

- Remove new shoots originating below the graft or at the crown.

- If you have powdery mildew or blackspot, remove the affected leaves, buds, and flowers, and dispose of them in the trash.

JUNE

- June is the peak season for roses. They will be in full bloom. Enjoy them, pick them, and share them.

- Sit back with your notebook and your camera; record what you like and dislike about your roses. Is that one just way too orange? Does it clash with its garden neighbor?

- Keep roses trimmed of faded flowers. Some new varieties are self-cleaning, meaning the new blossoms will push the old petals off the plant.

- Water deeply at least once a week.

JULY

- Continue to evaluate the rose plantings. Dig up and dispose of any that are sickly or diseased; eliminate those that are not making a strong comeback.

- As always, keep an eye on the soil moisture. Remove dead leaves and faded blossoms.

- Stay on top of the insect issues. Use an insecticidal soap if necessary.

AUGUST

- This is the last month for planting container roses. Remove blossoms so the plant's energy is directed to root development. Roses need to be in the ground and developing their root systems before winter sets in. It may be August now, but yes, winter will set in.

- If you want pretty and edible rosehips, stop deadheading the flowers and removing faded blossoms. Allow those hips to grow.

- Be vigilant about weeds and keep grass pulled from around the base of your rose bushes. It is hard to do when there are thorns everywhere, but it is crucial for best performance and highest visual impact.

SEPTEMBER

- Which roses worked well this year and why? Do you need more of a particular type? Make a note in your garden journal.

- Do *not* prune roses any more this season. Pruning at this time will stimulate new growth, which won't have time to harden off before the frosts come.

- Light frost will not adversely affect your roses. Some will continue to bloom until a very hard frost.

OCTOBER

- Get ready to spread the winter mulch on the rose beds.

- Keep the soil moisture adequate.

- Sign up for specialty rose catalogs.

NOVEMBER

- Get the mulch in place to protect the rose bushes from harsh winter weather. Make sure the mulch covers the crown and graft knob as well as lower parts of the canes. This encourages plant dormancy and protects from continuous freezing and thawing.

- Water all the roses once more before the ground freezes.

DECEMBER

- Get some sticky notes and make some lists of new roses for the new year.

SHRUB ROSE

SHRUBS
for the Rocky Mountain States

At one time shrubs were simply those plants that homeowners automatically planted around the foundation because every other house in the neighborhood used them that way. But you don't have to continue to install shrubs in this antiquated fashion. Shrubs are as diverse as the gardeners who grow them, and they can serve several different functions. They provide a solid background for perennial and annual flowerbeds. Many shrubs have unique flowers, handsome bark, or fruit that add color and texture to the landscape.

SMALLER TREES

Generally speaking, the classification shrub refers to that group of plants that are woody like trees, but smaller in stature. Some are deciduous, losing their leaves in winter, while others are evergreen. Some shrubs are grown for their flowers and some for their berries; others, such as burning bush, are noted for their brilliant autumn color. Among the many pleasures of growing shrubs is discovering ways to combine different kinds so that they complement the other plants in the landscape. Many shrubs live to a ripe old age, so allow them space in which to grow and spread their branches. Keep in mind the shrub's mature, landscape size when choosing its location.

ADAPTABLE SHRUBS

Shrubs are among the most adaptable and easy-to-care-for landscape plants. Like trees, most shrubs develop root systems that help them endure during periods of drought, yet their small size allows them to be movable if needed. Growing shrubs successfully begins with making the right choices—be sure to select a shrub whose needs match the special growing conditions in your area. Most shrubs are relatively resistant to insects and diseases. If a problem develops, it's generally the fault of the gardener, not of the shrub. The presence of spider mites on a *Euonymus* probably indicates that the shrub's natural defense system is stressed from being planted too close to a house, fence, or other "heat trap."

LESS IS MORE

As with most plants, shrubs thrive in well-drained soils that have been enriched with compost or other quality, organic matter. Most soils throughout the Rocky Mountain region are both alkaline (high pH) and low in organic matter, but don't overamend the soil with too much organic matter. When it comes to supplementing the backfill soil, less is better. If your soil is of poor quality, you can mix 25 to 30 percent by volume of compost to the native soil and blend it in uniformly. Adding excessive amounts of organic amendments or fertilizer to the planting hole creates a "bathtub" effect—the roots of a newly planted shrub may decide to remain within the planting hole and never explore the surrounding native soil. Roots grow and move into soil that contains a balance of oxygen and moisture, so the best advice is to dig the planting hole wide rather than deep and loosen the soil.

A TIP ON PLANTING

Container-grown shrubs that have a tight mass of roots encircling the rootball with no soil visible are considered extremely rootbound. In these situations, use the "split ball" or "butterfly" root-pruning technique. Lay the plant on its side, and slice through the rootball vertically from the bottom about halfway to the top. Spread the two halves, like butterfly wings, over a mound of soil in the planting hole. Add the backfill soil, and water slowly. With this technique, you bring the roots, which had grown to the bottom of the container, nearer the surface where soil conditions are more favorable for vigorous root development. Caution: Don't use this technique on larger balled-and-burlapped shrubs, newly potted specimens, or containerized plants where the roots are not rootbound.

FERTILIZING SHRUBS

After their first growing season, shrubs can be fertilized in spring as growth resumes. Use an organic-based, granular 5-10-5 or 10-10-10 fertilizer at the rate of one-quarter cup per each foot of the shrub's height. Use a crowbar or metal rod to make a series of holes 8 to 10 inches deep and 12 inches apart around the shrub's drip line. Broadcast the fertilizer in the area where the holes were made, and water thoroughly.

PRUNING WITH A PURPOSE

While many trees never need pruning once they reach a mature shape, shrubs benefit from regular pruning. Prune to achieve specific results—to keep the shrub the proper size and shape, to help it produce more flowers, or to rejuvenate a tired, old shrub into youthful vigor. Pruning can simply mean removing three to five of the oldest stems each year, almost to ground level (leaving stubs of only 3 to 4 inches). New buds on the stubs then become activated to grow into new, vigorous stems. Such "renewal" pruning keeps the shrub youthful with healthy stems that produce more flowers. Pruning to limit a shrub's size is generally reserved for

OREGON GRAPE

those plants that have outgrown their space. It may be a result of having selected the wrong shrub to fit the planting site. Make the pruning cuts just beyond a healthy bud or small branch that you want to preserve on the shrub. Use a sharp pair of bypass hand pruners. If larger stems need to be cut off, a long-handle lopper makes this task a breeze. Forget about those electric hedge trimmers—the problems they cause usually outweigh their benefits. Shearing the tops of shrubs with trimmers and clippers turns your favorite shrubs into "green meatballs." The resulting dense shell of green foliage on the top and outside of the shrub causes the inside to be dark, dead, and lifeless. You always get the best results and maintain the shrub's natural shape by using hand tools.

Prune flowering shrubs to promote more blooms. Those shrubs that bloom on last season's growth, such as lilacs and forsythia, should be pruned right after flowering. Pruning in the fall or winter removes next spring's flower buds!

Those that bloom on the current season's growth, such as butterfly bush, blue mist spirea, summer spirea, and potentilla, should be pruned in early spring. Many of these perform at their best if cut back to the ground in March.

TREASURED MEMORIES

Shrubs can provide privacy, screen out unsightly views, or even serve as a windbreak to protect our more tender and vulnerable plants. They can provide shelter and food to attract birds, an important asset for those of us who believe that the landscape should be heard as well as seen. The sweet fragrance of Grandma's lilacs at the back door is a treasured memory. With the right planning, shrubs offer beauty and versatility in our landscapes in every season for many years. The shrubs chosen in this chapter are among the best for our region, but many more can be used here. Experiment to discover the ones that may soon become your favorites.

MOCK ORANGE

AMERICAN PLUM
Prunus americana

Why It's Special—A common native plant, American plum is frequently seen growing and thriving along the roadsides from the High Plains to the Foothills. It is a harbinger of spring. It blooms profusely before leaves emerge, abuzz with bees busily gathering nectar and pollen from the fragrant blossoms. You can harvest the fruit to make jam and jelly. *Prunus americana* is a tough, widely adaptable shrub that endures drought conditions quite well.

How to Plant & Grow—Plant container-grown shrubs in the spring through early fall. Transplant bare-root plants in early spring. This shrub does best in full sun and well-drained soils. Keep it pruned to maintain a more formal look, or let it grow in its natural form for a naturescape or wildlife-friendly garden.

Care & Problems—Unlike many other of the *Prunus* species, native American plum is resistant to pests known as crown borers.

Hardiness: Zones 3 to 8

Peak Season/Color: Spring; white

Mature Size (H x W): 10 to 20 ft. x 8 to 12 ft.

Water Needs: Low

APACHE PLUME
Fallugia paradoxa

Why It's Special—Apache plume grows as an arching, lacy shrub with finely dissected leaves. It is drought enduring and can be planted in dry, sunny locations. Attractive single, white, rose-like flowers appear during early summer and continue through late summer. As the flowers mature, feathery, silver-pink, rounded seedheads develop. These seed plumes are quite decorative on the shrub, particularly when backlit by sunlight. Exfoliating, whitish bark adds winter interest. This shrub is an excellent choice for a xeric garden.

How to Plant & Grow—Plant in the spring. This plant is an excellent choice for open, dry, sunny locations. Loosen compacted soils, and amend with scoria (crushed volcanic rock) to improve drainage.

Care & Problems—Water deeply, but infrequently. This shrub does not tolerate "wet feet," so be careful not to overwater.

Hardiness: Zones 6 to 10

Peak Season/Color: Summer; white, silver-pink seedheads

Mature Size (H x W): 3 to 6 ft. × 3 to 6 ft.

Water Needs: Low

ARBORVITAE
Thuja occidentalis

Why It's Special—Arborvitae has many uses in the garden: windbreaks, screens, or as a single exclamation or focal point. Look for those with interesting shapes or foliage. Style choices are globe, pyramidal, and columnar, all with soft scales instead of prickly needles. 'DeGroot's Spire' is gold-green, 6 feet x 24 inches, with thick ruffled foliage, 'Pyramidalis' tops out at 25 feet tall x 6 feet wide.

How to Plant & Grow—Tough as they are, arborvitaes need plenty of moisture to become well rooted. Once they settle in, they are somewhat drought tolerant. They enjoy full sun and take some shade. Alkaline soils are a plus.

Care & Problems—Spider mites may show up in the heat of the summer, particularly when plants are stressed. Give the plant a strong blast from the hose to knock them down.

Hardiness: Zones 3 to 7

Peak Season/Color: Cold season; several varieties turn coppery orange

Mature Size (H x W): 2 to 25 ft. x 18 in. to 6 ft.

Water Needs: Moderate

BARBERRY
Berberis spp.

☼

Why It's Special—Barberry is an excellent choice for color contrast in the garden. 'Rose Glow' is a pink and red variety that forms a nice, rounded mound. 'Helmund's Pillar' is columnar, which makes it a good vertical accent plant. Leaves grow in small clusters and turn a brilliant orange, red, or yellow in autumn. Red berries appear in late summer. Use for screening, an impenetrable barrier, or an informal hedge.

How to Plant & Grow—To get the most intense leaf color, plant barberry in full sun. Most are adapted to Rocky Mountain soils, though Japanese barberry is notorious for chlorosis (yellowing leaves) in highly alkaline soils.

Care & Problems—Water deeply, but infrequently. Once established, barberry is quite drought tolerant. Pruning out the oldest canes to ground level rejuvenates the shrub to grow fresh, colorful stems and brightly colored leaves.

Hardiness: Zones 4 to 9

Peak Season/Color: June to October; wine-red, yellow, or variegated (pink or green) foliage

Mature Size (H x W): 3 to 6 ft. × 3 to 6 ft.

Water Needs: Low

BEAUTY BUSH
Kolkwitzia amabilis

☼

Why It's Special—An old-fashioned shrub that has withstood the test of time, beauty bush can survive years of utter neglect. Its bloom is spectacular, with bright-pink, yellow-throated, tubular flowers in early June. Clusters of feathery, brown seeds follow the flowers and persist into winter. The gray-brown bark exfoliates, providing an interesting winter texture.

How to Plant & Grow—Plant in borders, informal hedging, or windbreaks. Beauty bush provides a nice contrast to evergreen plantings. In really hot regions, a little shade is appreciated.

Care & Problems—Beauty bush endures with little care once it becomes established. Renew older, overgrown shrubs by pruning them completely to the ground in the spring. To keep this shrub a desirable size and shape, thin out the oldest stems to ground level; that also helps it maintain vigor after flowering. New growth emerges from the base.

Hardiness: Zones 5 to 9

Peak Season/Color: Early summer; pink, tubular flowers with variegated (pink or green) foliage

Mature Size (H x W): 6 to 12 ft. × 8 to 12 ft.

Water Needs: Low

BLUEBEARD or BLUE MIST SPIREA
Caryopteris incana spp.

☼ ☼

Why It's Special—When few other shrubs are in bloom, blue mist is covered in abundant blue blossoms and nectar-seeking bees and butterflies. Gorgeous, especially when planted with ornamental grasses and fall-blooming magenta and purple asters.

How to Plant & Grow—Plant in full to partial sun for the best foliage and prolific flowering. Avoid areas that are too wet or poorly drained or crown rot will result. Do not overamend the soil with organic matter; doing so causes rank growth with few flowers. This shrub is adapted to dry conditions, but can suffer severe wilt in the heat of summer. Water thoroughly, but infrequently.

Care & Problems—Each year, the branches die back to the woody center or crown of the plant. Cut the shrub back to near ground level in early spring before growth begins. Seedlings are common and can be removed or transplanted to other areas.

Hardiness: Zones 5 to 9

Peak Season/Color: July through August; light to dark blue

Mature Size (H x W): 2 to 4 ft. × 2 to 3 ft.

Water Needs: Low

BUCKTHORN
Rhamnus frangula

Why It's Special—A very attractive, fast-growing screen or hedge for Rocky Mountain landscapes, buckthorn features lustrous foliage that grows densely from near ground level to the top of the plant. This shrub is strongly columnar, which makes it an excellent choice for landscapes with limited space. 'Fineline' has a dense growth habit and works well as a screen for privacy or as the center of a large container. It is deer resistant, drought tolerant, and low maintenance.

How to Plant & Grow—Locate in full sun to partial shade. Buckthorn prefers a moderately rich, organic soil that is well drained. It needs plenty of water to become established.

Care & Problems—Buckthorn requires minimal care. Prune this shrub in the spring to thin out crisscrossing branches or broken limbs. Pests do not generally bother buckthorn—birds frequent the plant for berries.

Hardiness: Zones 2 to 7

Peak Season/Color: Fall; brilliant-yellow foliage

Mature Size (H x W): 5 to 7 ft. x 3 to 5 ft.

Water Needs: Low to moderate

BURNING BUSH
Euonymus alatus

Why It's Special—Fire-red autumn leaves give this shrub its common name, burning bush. During spring and summer, the foliage is dark green. Burning bush's unique stems feature corky ridges called wings. In winter, these winged stems collect snow to create an interesting plant sculpture for the winter garden. 'Compactus' is a dwarf form that grows to 5 feet with crimson fall foliage.

How to Plant & Grow—The best color is achieved in full sun, but a little shade in the late afternoon never hurts. Amend the soil with compost to improve soil porosity and drainage.

Care & Problems—Burning bush grows in somewhat horizontal tiers, which gives it a flat-topped look. Pruning is generally not recommended; when done improperly, frequent pruning or shearing destroys this plant's natural shape. Spider mites can become a nuisance; control by washing them off with a strong stream of water.

Hardiness: Zones 4 to 8

Peak Season/Color: Fall; fire-red foliage

Mature Size (H x W): 5 to 15 ft. x 10 to 12 ft.

Water Needs: Low

BUTTERFLY BUSH
Buddleia davidii

Why It's Special—A profusion of white, pink, red, purple, or lavender flowers borne in racemes graces the plant in the summer. The woodsy and sweet fragrance of its blossoms draws butterflies like a magnet. Look for 'Black Knight' with dark purple blooms, 'Charming' with pink flowers, and 'Harlequin' with variegated foliage and magenta flowers.

How to Plant & Grow—Plant butterfly bush in full to partial sun for colorful and abundant blossoms. A butterfly bush growing in the shade or rich soil soon becomes leggy and has few, if any, flowers.

Care & Problems—During most winters, the plants die back to the ground but the roots survive. If it does not die back, it is advisable to cut the stems back to within 12 inches of the ground each spring for the best shape and good bloom.

Hardiness: Zones 5 to 10

Peak Season/Color: June through September; purple, lavender, pink, rose, or white

Mature Size (H x W): 4 to 6 ft. x 4 to 6 ft.

Water Needs: Low

COTONEASTER
Cotoneaster spp.

Why It's Special—Cotoneaster is a coarse, tough shrub for the mountainous West. It grows low and horizontal to the ground, creates shelter for birds, provides erosion control for slopes, and boasts good-looking foliage and bright red berries. 'Coral Beauty' is so named for its abundant coral berries, which stand out in the winter landscape. 'Willow Leaf' cotoneaster has finer leaves and the same, fine traits as the standard cotoneaster. In the fall, bright green leaves take on a bronze cast. 'Tom Thumb' is but 8 to 10 inches tall and just two feet wide, making it a sweet mini version for the smaller garden.

How to Plant & Grow—This shrub works best when planted on a hillside or where it can drape pleasingly over a wall. It loves full sun, can take a little shade, and needs only occasional watering once established.

Care & Problems—Cotoneaster is a nice, easy-to-care-for plant.

Hardiness: Zones 5 to 8

Peak Season/Color: Autumn through winter; green with red berries

Mature Size (H x W): 1 to 2 ft. x 4 to 6 ft.

Water Needs: Low

CURRANT
Ribes spp.

Why It's Special—Our native buffalo currant (*Ribes odoratum*) has fragrant, yellow blooms, followed by red–black, teardrop-shaped, edible fruit. Currants are excellent shrubs for naturescape, providing fruit for birds. *Ribes sanguineum* 'King Edward VII' has rose-colored flowers and blue-gray fruit. If you live in the High Country, this shrub is a must.

How to Plant & Grow—Plant currants in full sun or partial shade. They tolerate most garden soils.

Care & Problems—Trim out the oldest canes after flowering to keep the shrub growing vigorously. Prune currant in the spring to shape and to keep the plant in bounds for hedge purposes.

Hardiness: Zones 3 to 8 ('King Edward VII' hardy to Zone 6)

Peak Season/Color: Golden currant: May through June; yellow blossoms; 'King Edward VII'; May through June; pink blossoms

Mature Size (H x W): 3 to 6 ft. x 3 to 6 ft.

Water Needs: Low to moderate

DAPHNE
Daphne spp.

Why It's Special—Daphne is a beautiful, small to medium shrub with dense clusters of white, pink, or lilac blossoms, primarily grown for its incredible, sweet fragrance. 'Carol Mackie' has rich green leaves with creamy white or yellow margins and sports clusters of light pink flowers. Daphne is beautiful planted amid evergreens and conifers, as well as in the perennial border.

How to Plant & Grow—Locate in full sun to partial shade. When removing from the pot, do not disturb roots. This shrub does best in well-drained soils; it does not tolerate wet feet. Avoid planting near rooflines where snow and ice loads might fall on fragile stems and branches.

Care & Problems—Established daphnes need little maintenance. An occasional pruning in spring to thin out crowded stems keeps shrubs tidy. Pests and diseases are seldom problems.

Hardiness: Zones 5 to 8

Peak Season/Color: April through early June; white, pink, or lilac

Mature Size (H x W): 3 to 4 ft. x 2 to 5 ft.

Water Needs: Low to moderate

DWARF ARCTIC WILLOW

Salix purpurea nana

Why It's Special—Dwarf arctic willow features slender, gray-green leaves on purplish branches. Another harbinger of spring, its yellow-green catkins appear before the leaves. This shrub thrives near the downspout of the house in foundation plantings. 'Hakuro Nashiki' is even more beautiful, with rich red stems in early spring followed by new leaves, which emerge cream and green with a pink overtone. It's stunning when trained on a standard.

How to Plant & Grow—Locate in full sun to partial shade. Dwarf Arctic willow prefers moist soil, so amend heavy clay, sandy, or gravelly soils with moisture-retentive compost.

Care & Problems—Willows need proper moisture to grow and look good. Extreme periods of drought cause them to perish. Mulching around the plants can conserve and maintain moisture. A good haircut in the spring will force fresh new growth and good color.

Hardiness: Zones 4 to 6

Peak Season/Color: Early spring; yellowish green catkins

Mature Size (H x W): 6 to 8 ft. × 6 to 10 ft.

Water Needs: Low to moderate

ELDERBERRY

Sambucus spp.

Why It's Special—Native elderberries brighten a drive through the Rocky Mountains. Our native *Sambucus cerulea* has creamy white, summer-flower plumes followed by drooping umbels, or clusters, of blue or purple berries. Several new varieties of elderberry are 'Black Lace', 'Black Beauty', and 'Sutherland Gold'. The black (or *nigra*) cultivars have dark-bronze foliage and rich-pink blossoms in early spring. The gold variety has cream-colored flowers and bright red fruits.

How to Plant & Grow—Elderberries thrive when given supplemental water, and in a season or two, they can top 6 feet. After blooming is done, prune to shape and keep it a manageable size. If it's berries you are after, do not prune. It looks great in a large patio pot. The gold varieties need afternoon shade, especially after 3 p.m.

Care & Problems—All parts of elderberry are reported toxic to pets. Keep that in mind when planting it in your garden.

Hardiness: Zones 3 to 8

Peak Season/Color: Late spring; cream-pink flowers; autumn-winter, blue, purple, and red berries

Mature Size (H x W): 6 to 10 ft. × 6 to 10 ft.

Water Needs: Low

FERNBUSH

Chamaebatiaria millefolium

Why It's Special—Native to the Great Basin and Colorado Plateau, fernbush, or desert sweet, has upright panicles of white flowers and finely cut ferny, aromatic foliage. It is a soft gray-green and has the appearance of an evergreen in the landscape. Pairing well with ornamental grasses and penstemons, it's perfect for the water-wise garden and makes a nice, informal hedge. Lovely in small groupings of 3 to 5 plants, fernbush blooms from July until August, and the stems are a handsome, cinnamon color. Native Americans prepared tea from the leaves to settle upset stomachs.

How to Plant & Grow—Plant fernbush from spring through early fall. Locate in full sun or partial shade. Though it tolerates a wide range of soils, fernbush requires excellent drainage.

Care & Problems—*C. millefolium* has no known pests or diseases. It responds well to pruning and shaping in early winter.

Hardiness: Zones 4 to 8

Peak Season/Color: July to August; white

Mature Size (H x W): 3 to 5 ft. x 3 to 5 ft.

Water Needs: Low

FIRETHORN
Pyracantha coccinea

Why It's Special—Firethorn's showy white spring blooms become bright red to orange fruit in autumn. Lustrous, dark green leaves make it a desirable hedge, barrier, or screen. Birds use it for nesting and eat the fruit. Train firethorn on a trellis or espalier.

How to Plant & Grow—Be sure the planting site is large enough to allow this shrub to grow and spread, and permanent; firethorn is difficult to move once it's established. Firethorn tolerates dry conditions well, but it will succumb to root rot if watered too heavily in clay. It likes partly shady areas.

Care & Problems—Thorns make pruning difficult; if necessary, prune soon after flowering. Firethorn may be prone to bacterial fire blight. Prune out infected stems in late winter. Pests include aphids and spider mites; scale can be a problem. Early detection and control prevent severe problems.

Hardiness: Zones 6 to 9

Peak Season/Color: Early summer, white flowers; fall, bright red to orange berries

Mature Size (H x W): 4 to 12 ft. × 4 to 12 ft.

Water Needs: Moderate

FLOWERING QUINCE
Chaenomeles speciosa

Why It's Special—The most common flowering quince has brilliant, scarlet-red flowers, which bloom on two-year-old or older wood. Its fruit looks somewhat like a pear. The stems and twigs have large spines, so be careful not to plant it where you might brush against it. 'Cameo' has no thorns, but features attractive apricot-pink flowers. 'Red Charlot' grows to 8 feet high with double, rose-red flowers. 'Jet Trail' has white flowers and forms a low, compact plant. Force a branch into bloom indoors in early spring.

How to Plant & Grow—Quince does well in the high desert and in all but the coldest parts of the mountainous regions. You can plant anytime. It flowers best in full sun but grows in any soil.

Care & Problems—Prune heavily right after it blooms. Flowering quince is easy to maintain and is not bothered by pests.

Hardiness: Zones 5 to 9

Peak Season/Color: May to June; apricot, red, and pink

Mature Size (H x W): 3 to 12 ft. x 3 to 10 ft.

Water Needs: Low to moderate

FORSYTHIA
Forsythia x intermedia

Why It's Special—Standing tall above flowering spring bulbs, the bright yellow blossoms of this shrub announce the arrival of spring. You can easily coax forsythia branches into bloom indoors in late January and February. This shrub features a multitude of spreading, arching branches in an upright growth habit.

How to Plant & Grow—Locate in full sun to partial shade. Be sure the site is both large enough to allow this shrub to spread and permanent. This shrub tolerates dry conditions well.

Care & Problems—Forsythia can become unruly, so it is a good idea to thin out the older stems and renew this shrub every three years to maintain a handsome, healthy plant.

Hardiness: Zones 4 to 8

Peak Season/Color: Early spring; bright yellow blossoms

Mature Size (H x W): 6 to 9 ft. x 6 to 12 ft.

Water Needs: Low

HYDRANGEA
Hydrangea spp.

Why It's Special—New hydrangeas are coming to market every year. Some newbies are 'Limelight', 'Pinkie Winkie', 'Pee Gee' and 'Endless Summer'. They need part shade, where they really make a splash. The show begins mid-summer with dinner plate-sized blossoms. A favorite is the oakleaf hydrangea; its lobed leaves emerge a grayish green with felt undersides in the spring becoming a striking wine-purple by fall. Flowers are creamy beige tinged with pink.

How to Plant & Grow—Hydrangeas enjoy the sun until midafternoon. Amend and enrich their soil, and mulch well. Give them plenty of water to become established, then water as necessary, generally once a week.

Care & Problems—The new cultivars will shine if you forgo the first season of blossoms. Gently prune the plant to a pleasing shape, pinching out flower buds. This encourages fullness and more blossoms the second year.

Hardiness: Zone 4 to 9

Peak Season/Color: July to September; cream, white, pale green, blue, and pink

Mature Size (H x W): 3 to 10 ft. x 3 to 8 ft.

Water Needs: Moderate

GLOSSY ABELIA
Abelia x *grandiflora*

Why It's Special—This fountainlike, mounding shrub is at home in any garden, and deserves a home in yours. Its leaves change from a bronzy color when they are new to a rich green in summer and bronze-purple in fall. Three seasons of foliage color! Tiny, pale pink bell-shaped flowers grow all along the branches. The blooms occur in the late summer and are there until frost. Glossy abelia just lights up a shady corner in a garden, though it will grow in full sun too. 'Edward Goucher' is a good variety. 'Kaleidoscope' and 'Confetti' have variegated foliage with pink tones, but they are hardy only to Zone 6. Another type, 'Prostrata', is low growing, only to 18 to 24 inches high and 4 feet wide.

How to Plant & Grow—Locate in full sun to partial shade. Glossy abelia likes a moderately rich, organic soil that is well drained. These shrubs need plenty of water to become established; so water as necessary, which is generally weekly.

Care & Problems—Abelia has few needs. It may need a branch pruned here or there.

Hardiness: Zones 5 to 9

Peak Season/Color: July to October; soft pink flowers

Mature Size (H x W): 2 to 6 ft. x 3 to 6 ft.

Water Needs: Moderate

KERRIA
Kerria japonica

Why It's Special—*Kerria japonica* is a handsome, no fuss, landscape plant. In April and May, the variety 'Floraplena' is covered with rich yellow double or triple blossoms, which resemble button mums or Lady Banks roses. 'Picta' has variegated foliage. 'Honshu' and 'Golden Guinea' are sought-after single-petal varieties. The foliage is a rich green. The stems have the added bonus of being bright yellow-green in winter; they're pretty on a dull, cloudy day or against a snowy backdrop. It's an excellent woodland plant.

How to Plant & Grow—Plant from spring through early fall in a partially shaded area or one with dappled light. Kerria likes well-drained, moist soil. Kerria needs very little tending.

Care & Problems—Kerria has few known problems. Selective pruning can be done to shape the plant. Removed dead or crossed twigs.

Hardiness: Zones 4 (with snow cover) to 8

Peak Season/Color: April to May; yellow

Mature Size (H x W): 5 to 6 ft. x 4 to 8 ft.

Water Needs: Moderate

LILAC
Syringa vulgaris

☼ ☀

Why It's Special—Endearing, memory-filled shrubs, lilacs are often found in long-abandoned homesteads. Common lilacs have purple flowers borne in 4- to 8-inch terminal panicles. Today, many species, sizes, hybrids, and cultivars are available, including the compact shrub 'Miss Kim'. Perfumed flowers can be enjoyed for weeks if you plant different species with varied blooming times.

How to Plant & Grow—Plant from spring through early fall. Lilacs love full sun, but some shade in the afternoon is fine.

Care & Problems—Powdery mildew, leaf blights, and wilt may attack stressed plants. Maintain shrubs well to reduce the onset of such problems. If you deadhead old flowers, be careful not to remove next year's flower buds; they develop on the same branch just below the spent flower heads. Rejuvenate crowded older plants by removing the old stems to ground level. New growth then comes from the base.

Hardiness: Zones 2 to 9

Peak Season/Color: May to June; white, blue, violet, lilac, magenta, pink, reddish purple, and deep purple

Mature Size (H x W): 4 to 15 ft. x 4 to 12 ft.

Water Needs: Low

MOCK ORANGE
Philadelphus spp.

☼ ☀

Why It's Special—Native to our region, and Idaho's state flower, the incredibly fragrant Lewis's mock orange thrives in the tough conditions at the Cheyenne Research Station in Wyoming. It's hardy at higher elevations and develops into a rounded, upright form. It produces an abundance of 1- to 1¼-inch, pure-white flowers in early summer. 'Miniature Snowflake', 'Cheyenne', and 'Belle Etoile' are recommended.

How to Plant & Grow—Plant from spring through early fall. Though it tolerates a wide range of soils, mock orange performs best in well-drained locations. It needs at least six hours of sun each day.

Care & Problems—Mock orange is a dependable shrub that provides years of aromatic blossoms. If overcrowded, prune out the oldest stems to rejuvenate the shrub and induce new growth from the base. Remove as much as 30 percent of the older wood every two to three years. These shrubs are seldom bothered by insects or diseases.

Hardiness: Zones 4 to 9

Peak Season/Color: White flowers in early summer

Mature Size (H x W): 4 to 15 ft. x 4 to 12 ft.

Water Needs: Low

MOUNTAIN MAHOGANY
Cercocarpus montanus

☼

Why It's Special—One tough native shrub for a water-thrifty landscape is mountain mahogany. The foliage, though sparse, is a thick and leathery gray-green. The wedge-shaped leaves curl under slightly around the edges. The tiny, yellow flowers in mid-spring are followed by fuzzy, twisted seed tails that add an interesting texture. One of the best features of mountain mahogany is its evergreen nature in the winter. In the summer, its white, feathery plumes are quite attractive. Curlleaf mahogany, *C. ledifolius*, is also recommended.

How to Plant & Grow—Plant mountain mahogany in the spring in a sunny site with well-drained soil. Break up any areas of compacted soil to help improve drainage.

Care & Problems—Once mountain mahogany is established, it requires little care or water. Occasional pruning in late winter or early spring keeps the plant in bounds. Pests and diseases do not bother this shrub.

Hardiness: Zones 2 to 7

Peak Season/Color: July; olive green

Mature Size (H x W): 3 to 10 ft. x 4 to 8 ft.

Water Needs: Low

MUGO PINE
Pinus mugo

☀ ◐

Why It's Special—Compact, pretty needles, evergreen, nice shape, no maintenance—all are attributes of the mugo pine. Ranging in size from tiny, dwarf collector specimens to imposing 12-foot-tall shrubs, there is a mugo for every garden. A couple of narrow columnar varieties can be found in local nurseries. Conifers such as mugo look good when positioned with plants of strikingly different foliage texture and color, such as ornamental grasses, blue spruce, silver buffaloberry, or tall bearded iris. And don't relegate the mugo to a stand-alone plant. If space permits, try planting a drift of the dwarf cultivars for an intriguing ground cover.

How to Plant & Grow—Exceptionally drought tolerant, mugo needs full sun, but can tolerate light shade. Once it is settled in, it gets by on very little water. Like most garden plants, it appreciates decent soil and drainage.

Care & Problems—It will not tolerate overwatering or inadequate drainage.

Hardiness: Zones 3 to 7

Peak Season/Color: All seasons; green

Mature Size (H x W): 3 to 12 ft. x 18 in. to 6 ft.

Water Needs: Low

NINEBARK
Physocarpus opulifolius

☀ ◐

Why It's Special—A hardy, deciduous shrub with pretty bronze foliage and upright, arching branches, the common ninebark is native to parts of the Rockies. As it matures, it becomes open and leggy. Ninebark's flowers are quite showy and are followed by purple fruit that birds savor. As the bark matures, it exfoliates in thin, coarse sheets adding winter interest. 'Dart's Gold' features attractive, lime green leaves. 'Coppertina', 'Little Devil', and 'Summerwine' are smaller varieties.

How to Plant & Grow—Plant ninebark in full sun or partial shade. The gold cultivars need afternoon shade. Although it prefers moderately fertile, well-drained soil, this shrub tolerates dry situations.

Care & Problems—Prune established plants to thin out branches that die back. Renew an older shrub by cutting it to the ground in late winter or early spring. This extremely hardy plant resists pests and diseases.

Hardiness: Zones 2 to 7

Peak Season/Color: June; creamy pink

Mature Size (H x W): 4 to 10 ft. x 3 to 6 ft.

Water Needs: Low

OREGON GRAPE
Mahonia aquifolium

◐

Why It's Special—Oregon grape is an upright-growing, broadleaf, evergreen shrub. The glossy, leathery foliage is highlighted by bright yellow flowers in May, followed in late summer by clusters of deep blue berries. The green, holly-like leaves are spiny, turning a purplish bronze with cold weather. This somewhat aggressive grower spreads by underground stems, and over time, it forms irregular colonies. Our Rocky Mountain native, creeping mahonia (*Mahonia repens*), makes a useful, woody ground cover with handsome foliage, flowers, and fruit.

How to Plant & Grow—Oregon grape is useful as a foundation plant in a north or east exposure. Provide ample moisture for good root establishment. Add compost to native soils when planting.

Care & Problems—If exposed to persistent wind and sun, the leaves tend to develop scorch and turn tannish brown. Plant where protected from the wind. Pests and diseases do not generally bother this shrub.

Hardiness: Zones 3 to 7

Peak Season/Color: Spring; yellow

Mature Size (H x W): 3 to 6 ft. x 3 to 5 ft.

Water Needs: Low

POTENTILLA OR CINQUEFOIL

Potentilla fruticosa

☀ ☀

Why It's Special—Bright yellow blooms are complemented by fine-textured, grayish green leaves. Cinquefoil grows into a dense shrub with soft, slender, upright branches. Some varieties have arching branches that make them effective for use in informal hedge or barrier plantings. A flush of bloom occurs in May, with flowers continuing until frost. Use on rocky slopes to help stabilize the soil and to provide colorful accents. Potentillas have become a mainstay in many Rocky Mountain landscapes, and sadly, they aren't shown off to their advantage. They are strong performers and good bloomers. Treat yourself by clustering three or more.

How to Plant & Grow—Plant in the spring to allow them to settle in before fall. This native shrub performs best when located in areas that receive full to partial sun. Potentilla shrubs are very hardy and drought-enduring once established.

Care & Problems—Very little maintenance is required; prune to shape in spring.

Hardiness: Zones 2 to 8

Peak Season/Color: Summer; white, yellow, orange, and pale pink

Mature Size (H x W): 3 to 4 ft. x 3 to 4 ft.

Water Needs: Low

RED TWIG DOGWOOD

Cornus sericea

☀ ☀

Why It's Special—Red twig dogwood is widely adaptable to the diverse climate and soil conditions of the Rocky Mountains. It prefers moist conditions, but grows successfully in moderately dry soils too. Both red twig and yellow twig bear clusters of small, sweet smelling, creamy-white flowers in the spring. The colorful stems are a striking feature, with some red, some yellow, some mixed. They stand out beautifully against the winter snow. 'Ivory Halo' has interesting green- and cream-variegated foliage.

How to Plant & Grow—Water new plants thoroughly every five to seven days for the first month after planting. Plants may need a deep soaking during the heat of summer to prevent leaf scorch.

Care & Problems—To maintain the plant's height and to promote brightly colored stems, prune out one-fourth to one-third of the oldest canes each year. Remove these canes to ground level, and new growth will emerge from the base.

Hardiness: Zones 2 to 8

Peak Season/Color: Winter; bright stems

Mature Size (H x W): 6 to 8 ft. x 8 to 10 ft.

Water Needs: Moderate to low

ROCK SPIREA OR OCEANSPRAY

Holodiscus dumosus

☀ ☀

Why It's Special—A Rocky Mountain native, rock spirea features handsome sprays of white to pink flowers in late June. As the flowers mature, they transform and deepen to russet in the fall, then persist through the winter. The attractive, fine-textured foliage is even more magnificent when it turns reddish. The leaves, when crushed, have a spicy scent. Rock spirea tolerates both heat and drought. It is an excellent, upright-spreading shrub for a water-thrifty or xeric garden.

How to Plant & Grow—Plant in the spring to allow it to become settled before fall. This native shrub performs best when located in areas that receive full to partial sun. Rock spirea is not fussy about soil as long as it is well drained.

Care & Problems—Rock spirea is a relatively carefree shrub needing only periodic pruning. Pests and diseases do not generally bother rock spirea.

Hardiness: Zones 4 to 8

Peak Season/Color: June; white or pink

Mature Size (H x W): 3 to 4 ft. x 3 to 4 ft.

Water Needs: Low

ROSE OF SHARON
Hibiscus syriacus

Why It's Special—An old-fashioned favorite, Rose of Sharon's blossoms appear midsummer. Flowers range from 2½ to 4 inches and can be single, semi-double, or double. It's a focal specimen in the perennial border. It may die back to ground level in winter, but it endures erratic climatic conditions well and grows new, vigorous stems the following spring. 'Diana' and 'Aphrodite' are favorites.

How to Plant & Grow—Plant in early spring as soon as the soil can be worked. Rose of Sharon tolerates light shade, but prefers a site with full sun.

Care & Problems—Rigorous pruning in late spring to thin out crowded branches encourages vigorous and floriferous stems. Prune the previous season's growth to two or three buds for fewer but larger flowers. It's slow to start in the spring; be patient for the leaves to emerge.

Hardiness: Zones 4 (with protection) to 8

Peak Season/Color: August to October; white, pink, red, purple, or lavender

Mature Size (H x W): 8 to 12 ft. x 6 to 10 ft.

Water Needs: Low to moderate

SAND CHERRY 'PAWNEE BUTTES'
Prunus pumila var. *besseyi* 'Pawnee Buttes'

Why It's Special—A graceful form of the native sand cherry, this is an excellent choice for the water-wise landscape in the Rocky Mountain region. In April, loads of fragrant, white flowers attract bees, and when pollinated, the shrub will produce heavy crops of black cherries in summer. Wildlife adores this plant. Sand cherry makes a nice, woody ground cover and works in foundation plantings or mixed borders. A Plant Select™ Selection, it is hardy up to 9,000 feet.

How to Plant & Grow—Sand cherry is not fussy; it will grow in sandy soil or clay loam. This shrub needs some water, a thorough deep soaking from time to time is recommended.

Care & Problems—Prune lightly, and only to remove dead wood or to softly shape the plant.

Hardiness: Zones 2 to 8

Peak Season/Color: May to June; white flowers, black cherries

Mature Size (H x W): 18 in. x 4 to 6 ft.

Water Needs: Low to moderate

SILVER BUFFALOBERRY
Shepherdia argentea

Why It's Special—Leathery, silvery green leaves make native buffaloberry a handsome addition to the Rocky Mountain garden. Drought and cold resistant, this shrub tolerates conditions other shrubs will not survive. The dense, upright, rounded growth habit of this shrub provides a good screen, informal hedge, or mass planting for a windbreak. The ends of the branches have 1- to 2-inch thorns. This excellent, naturescape plant has orange-red berries favored by wildlife. Both male and female plants are required to produce fruit.

How to Plant & Grow—Place in a sunny spot with open exposure. It is a good plant for dry, alkaline soil conditions. No soil amendment is necessary as long as the soil has been broken up to relieve soil compaction.

Care & Problems—Silvery buffaloberry is able to use atmospheric nitrogen; do not add fertilizer. Prune out dead wood in early spring and remove any branches that may be crisscrossing.

Hardiness: Zones 2 to 7

Peak Season/Color: Fall; bright-orange berries (if pollinated)

Mature Size (H x W): 8 to 15 ft. x 6 to 12 ft.

Water Needs: Low

155

SMOKE BUSH
Cotinus coggyria

☼ ☀

Why It's Special—The beautiful, smooth, oval leaves of the smoke bush are pretty by themselves; add the "smoke" (tiny flower puffs), and you have one intriguing garden shrub. There is also a lime-green cultivar, 'Golden Spirit', with white smoke puffs. The purple shrub will have scarlet leaves in autumn, and the green one changes to orange, yellow, and red. It's excellent as a focal point in the garden.

How to Plant & Grow—Smoke bush likes an afternoon respite from the hot desert sun, but six hours a day gives the plant the best coloring. Good, moist, well-drained soil is a necessity. This plant is terrific in a container.

Care & Problems—In the spring, cut all the stems back, leaving two or three buds from the base. Always remove dead or crossed stems.

Hardiness: Zones 5 to 9

Peak Season/Color: Late spring, early summer; white, pink

Mature Size (H x W): 15 ft. x 15 ft.

Water Needs: Moderate

SPIREA, BRIDAL BREATH
Spirea x vanhouttei

☼ ☀

Why It's Special—A sentimental favorite, bridal wreath spirea can still be found, unattended, near old homesteads and cemeteries. Its longevity in Rocky Mountain gardens is a testament to its hardiness and drought tolerance. With graceful, arching branches that curve back to the ground, each one covered with clusters of tiny white blossoms, this spirea is still used to make garden "headdresses" for little girls. 'Renaissance' is a recent cultivar.

How to Plant & Grow—Bridal wreath spirea loves full sun, but it can tolerate some shade. It needs regular watering the first and second year, but after it is well established, it is drought tolerant. Give it room to be a show-off in the garden. It blooms in tandem with peonies and German bearded irises. A bouquet of all three plants makes a lovely gift.

Care & Problems—Spirea needs good drainage. It should be pruned after blooming to remove old dead canes and to shape if necessary. Pests and diseases do not generally bother this great old-fashioned shrub.

Hardiness: Zones 3 to 7

Peak Season/Color: Late May to early June; white

Mature Size (HxW): 5 ft. x 6 to 10 ft.

Water Needs: Low

SUMMERSWEET
Clethra alnifolia spp.

☼ ☀

Why It's Special—Summersweet is unique in that it blooms well in part shade and has the ability to attract lots of butterflies and bees. The pretty white or pink bottlebrush flowers bloom in July and August and are followed by peppercorn-like, brown seed heads giving it nice winter interest. It's a modest-size shrub and looks great when planted in groupings of three, five, or seven, if space allows. The added bonus is that the glossy bay-leaf type foliage will become brilliant, yellow-orange foliage in the autumn. Many folks know this plant as sweet pepperbush. 'Ruby Spice' and 'Hummingbird' are well-liked cultivars.

How to Plant & Grow—Summersweet likes moist sites, but won't survive with poor drainage. It will be happiest in part shade, particularly during the hottest part of the day.

Care & Problems—Those who seek a popular, easy-to-care-for plant can stop here!

Hardiness: Zones 3 to 8

Peak Season/Color: Summer; pink, white

Mature Size (H x W): 4 to 8 ft. x 4 ft.

Water Needs: Moderate

VIBURNUM
Viburnum spp.

Why It's Special—Viburnums comprise a large group of adaptable, valuable shrubs that feature handsome foliage and attractive flowers. These easy-to-grow plants tolerate most soils throughout our region. The berrylike fruits of viburnum are among wild birds' favorites. *Viburnum* × *rhytidophylloides* 'Alleghany' thrives in arid conditions, as well as in fertile, cool soils near evergreens. Snowball bush, or *V. opulus*, is a tried-and-true favorite. Its grapefruit-sized blossoms start lime green and fade to white.

How to Plant & Grow—Viburnums prefer moist soils. Amend the soil with compost at the rate of 30 percent by volume to the native soil. Mulch well and water throughout the summer to prevent scorch or severe wilting. In the hottest areas of the region, afternoon shade is a plus.

Care & Problems—Once established, viburnums need only minor pruning to keep them in shape; prune after flowering. If aphids appear, a strong spray of water will knock them down.

Hardiness: Zones 2 to 7

Peak Season/Color: Spring, pink/cream bloom; autumn, red berries

Mature Size (H x W): 4 to 12 ft. x 3 to 10 ft.

Water Needs: Low to moderate

WEIGELA
Weigela florida

Why It's Special—When weigela blooms, it's covered with rosy pink, one-inch blossoms from the ground to each twig tip. Weigela is a vase-shaped plant with branches that eventually arch to the ground. The leaves are burgundy or green (depending on the cultivar) in summer and turn slightly yellow in fall. *Weigela florida* 'Polka' will withstand temperatures to -40 degrees Fahrenheit. Wine & Roses™ has burgundy leaves and rose pink flowers.

How to Plant & Grow—You can plant this shrub anytime of the year in a container. Weigela makes a colorful filler shrub under tree canopies, but it also grows in full sun. This shrub thrives in moist, well-drained soils.

Care & Problems—Prune after flowering to keep weigela compact. It should bloom all summer if well pruned. No pests attack it.

Hardiness: Zones 3 to 8

Peak Season/Color: Summer, pink and white blooms, burgundy or green foliage; fall, yellowish foliage

Mature Size (H x W): 4 to 10 ft. x 4 to 12 ft.

Water Needs: Low to moderate

JANUARY

- Study your garden to evaluate shrub placement and varieties that did or did not do well last season, or those you just didn't like.

- Some shrubs may need protection from winterburn by shading them if they have a southern exposure.

- Remove heavy, wet snow from shrubs by lifting branches gently, from underneath.

- Monitor soil moisture and water if necessary and if the ground is *not* frozen.

- When shoveling snow, shovel it up under the shrubs under the eaves of the house where no snow accummulates.

FEBRUARY

- Don't be in a hurry to plant new shrubs. It is still too early.

- Dig out diseased, dead, or too-old shrubs (old foundation plantings come to mind) and plan for replacements.

- If leaves and branches are iced over, do not disturb them—let the ice melt. Take your camera out and capture the way light plays with dripping ice.

- Maintain soil moisture as necessary, only if the ground is not frozen.

- You can start pruning shrubs now, but wait to prune spring bloomers until after they bloom.

- Patience is a virtue all year long, but for the gardener in February, it is a job requirement.

MARCH

- Purchase those new shrubs now, and if the soil is ready, plant them.

- Clean out planting beds and remove the winter mulch.

- Renovate shrubs now by removing overgrown, tangled, and dead wood. As new growth emerges, selectively eliminate the weaker branches.

- Control pests now by spraying shrubs with dormant oil spray before buds emerge.

APRIL

- Evaluate spring-blooming shrubs and make notes of what you might want to add for *next* year.

- Replenish mulch so it is 2 to 3 inches deep, but do not let it touch the stems or trunks of shrubs.

- Water needs for established shrubs is about 1 inch per week. Do not overwater newly planted shrubs but make sure they have enough water by thoroughly soaking them as needed.

- Be alert for insect problems and wash them off with a strong spray of water or use an insecticidal soap. Pull those weeds!

MAY

- Plant container-grown shrubs this month. Garden centers have the latest cultivars and new plants are arriving daily.

- Finish pruning spring-flowering shrubs after they bloom and before they set next year's buds.

- Replenish mulch and water as needed.

- Deadhead spent flowers from shrubs.

JUNE

- You can still plant container-grown shrubs but it's too late to transplant existing shrubs.

- It's time to move indoor shrubs outdoors but protect them for a week or so to let them acclimate.

- Once again, do not water excessively but do water adequately. Mulch assists greatly in retaining moisture.

- The only pruning you should be doing now is to remove dead or broken branches.

JULY

- If you are going on vacation, line up someone to take care of your garden while you are away.

- Do not plant new shrubs now. Hot, dry weather causes new plantings a great deal of stress.

- Weed garden beds.

- Replenish organic mulch as needed.

- Stay on top of the watering chores.

- Keep weeding garden beds.

AUGUST

- Toward the end of the month or during several days of cool weather, new shrubs can be planted.

- Shop for healthy shrubs at your local garden center. Most will be on sale.

- Provide adequate water and continue weed and pest control.

- No fertilizer should be applied after the middle of August. Shrubs need to harden off for the upcoming winter season.

SEPTEMBER

- Plant any new shrubs you've purchased.

- Root-prune shrubs you are planning to move next spring. With a sharp shovel, cut down around the outer edges of the shrub (that is, along the drip line).

- Bring indoor shrubs back inside before the first frost.

- Clean pots of all insects and inspect the plants before you bring them in.

OCTOBER

- Deeply water all shrubs before the ground freezes.

- Tie up loose-branched evergreens to prevent them from spreading apart under heavy snow.

NOVEMBER

- Apply winter mulch, 3 to 4 inches deep, but not touching the stems or trunks of the shrubs.

- Monitor moisture content of the soil and water deeply as needed when the ground is not frozen.

DECEMBER

- Go skiing.

- Selectively cut evergreen boughs and stems of other attractive shrubs for indoor decorations and outdoor containers.

- Put holiday lights on shrubs.

DWARF ARCTIC WILLOW

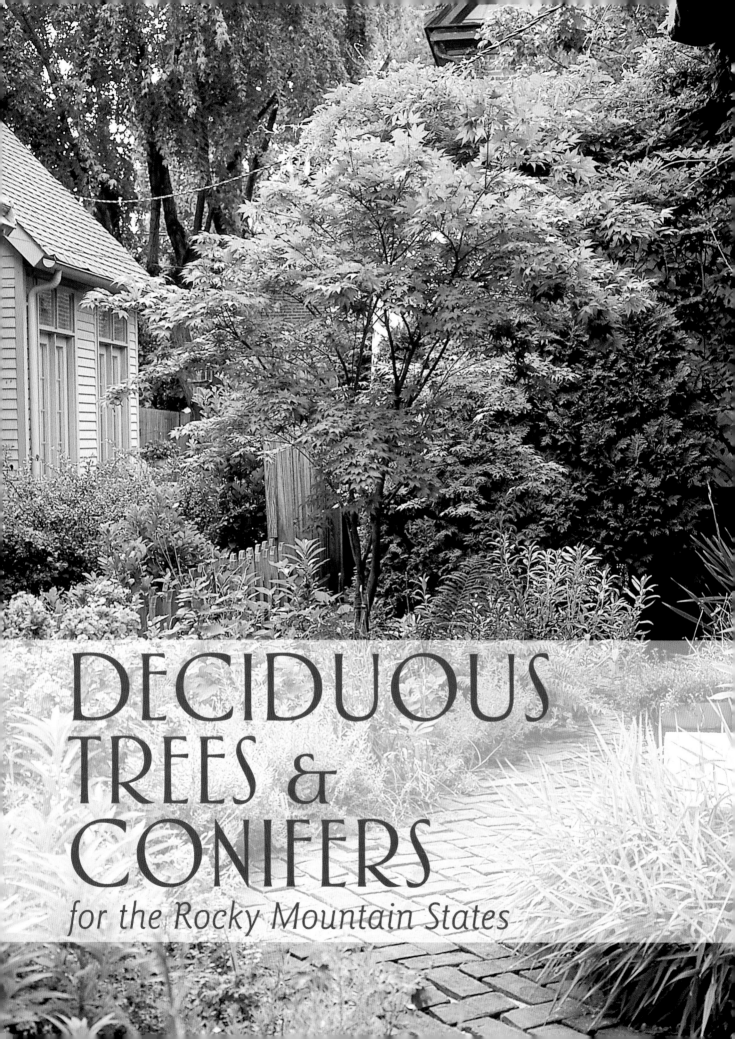

DECIDUOUS TREES & CONIFERS

for the Rocky Mountain States

DECIDUOUS TREES

Planted in the proper location, a tree will live for generations, silently cleaning the air while providing shade, beauty, and shelter for wildlife. Trees are a living link between the past and the future.

Deciduous trees give us shade in summer, cooling our living environment by blocking out the hot sun. Bare of their leaves in winter, the same trees allow sunlight and warmth to reach us when we need it most. They remove carbon dioxide and pollutants from the air, and return oxygen to the air we breathe. They are one of nature's gifts.

MAKING GOOD CHOICES

The most important consideration for growing trees successfully in the Rockies is choosing the right type of tree for your specific site and needs.

What is it that you are looking for? Maybe a tree that has an ever-changing, seasonal display?

A tree just for shade? Or is it a tree that will grow fast for privacy and shade? After a long, chilly winter, who doesn't look forward to the beauty of a flowering plum or crabapple?

PLANTING TIPS

Trees are transported and sold in one of three ways. Bare-root trees are grown in a nursery field, harvested when dormant (early spring or late fall), and made available to gardeners. Once dug, these trees should be planted as soon as possible, so the roots don't dry out and preferably, before the leaves emerge in the spring.

Specimen trees are often sold balled and burlapped (their rootballs wrapped and secured with a wire basket and twine). It is important to remove at least the top one-third to one-half of the wire basket after the tree is situated in the planting hole. Use a bolt cutter to cut through the stiff wire, and then carefully pull it away. This allows the upper portion of the rootball to develop healthy roots. The top of the rootball should be planted level with the surrounding grade. Also, remove any nylon twine around the trunk; this material does not decompose and can girdle roots and the trunk of the tree even years later.

Container-grown trees are also available. Look for signs of healthy new growth when selecting these trees. When planting containerized trees, check the root system. If the roots have grown into a mass encircling the rootball, they should be teased or even cut at planting to encourage lateral growth. The nice thing about container-grown trees is they can be planted just about any time of the year, but spring is the ideal time, as soon as the ground can be worked. A note about those so-called "plantable" containers—they aren't! When you take the tree out of its container for planting, carefully remove the plastic or fiber pot.

THE SECRET TO SUCCESS

As with all types of plants, the secret to growing trees successfully is to start with good soil. Few trees thrive in clay, heavy, compacted, or poorly drained soils. The lack of available oxygen to the roots results in stunted growth or eventual death. Nor do trees survive drought in sandy or rocky soils that have no ability to retain moisture. Trees produce vigorous, healthy growth if they are planted in soil that is well drained, loosened as deeply as possible, and amended with some organic matter. But there is one caveat: Don't over-amend the soil with too much "stuff"! If a mixture of too many amendments or too much of one amendment is added to the planting hole, the tree's roots may decide to remain within the hole, growing in circles and never exploring the surrounding soil. This causes a "bathtub" effect. Remember, roots will grow and move into soil that contains oxygen. After years of research, gardeners have learned the best rule is to dig the planting hole much wider than deep. And be sure to take time to loosen the soil around the planting hole thoroughly.

So how much organic matter should be added to your native soil? A guideline is to use up to 4 yards

Trees are spectacular when left alone, but with some careful pruning and training you can achieve very dramatic effects.

of organic matter for every 1,000 square feet of area to be planted. This varies, of course, depending on what kinds of trees you select; some species prefer less pampering with special soil amendments.

If you are moving to a new homesite that is not yet landscaped, the ideal way to prepare the soil is to incorporate organic amendments into the soil as deeply as possible and adjust the planting height. A tractor with plow or disk attachments works best for large areas; a heavy-duty Rototiller is good for smaller areas. When planting trees in an existing landscape or when replacing trees, amend the soil taken from the planting hole; be careful not to make the soil too rich in organic material.

URBAN LEGENDS

You don't have to cut the branches back by one-third to balance the top of the tree with the roots. The branch tips on a small tree produce plant hormones that direct the growth of roots. If you prune to compensate for lost roots, the tree's energy goes into replacing the lost foliage. While this happens, root growth stops temporarily.

This is exactly the opposite of what the new tree really needs. Except to remove broken, damaged branches or to correct shape, don't prune a new tree for a year after planting.

You don't need to feed the tree with vitamins and hormones at the time of planting. This is a myth that, at worst, impedes root growth by increasing the soluble salt levels in the planting hole. A tree manufactures its own vitamins and hormones, so why waste your money?

Don't fertilize trees during transplanting; allow the roots to become established the first growing season so they are able to use supplemental nutrients in future years.

MUCH ABOUT MULCH

After planting, spread a 2- to 3-inch layer of organic mulch over the root zone, but not up against the trunk. Piling mulch on or over the base of the tree trunk can keep the bark soft and wet (conditions that favor diseases); it may also encourage rodents to gnaw on the bark. Appropriately applied mulch helps to reduce weed growth, keeps the soil cooler, and maintains and conserves moisture. Water deeply and thoroughly to moisten the rootball and the surrounding soil. This encourages new roots to grow into your native soil.

IMPORTANT WATERING TIPS

WATERING NEWLY PLANTED TREES

Watering the first year is critical—transplanted trees need ample moisture to become established. With backfill soil, build a dike about 3 inches high around the root zone. This forms a reservoir to hold water and allows it to soak down to the roots. Apply 1 to 2 inches of water to the root zone each week, but do not overwater. A good way to determine whether the tree needs water is to dig down around the root zone (to a depth of 4 to 6 inches) and feel the soil. If the soil is dry, it's time to water. If the soil is still moist, wait a few days.

WATERING ESTABLISHED TREES

As trees grow and mature, watering practices vary, depending on the species and their tolerance for drought. It is important to saturate the soil deeply around the drip line (the area on the ground beneath a tree's outermost branches). For larger, maturing trees, the area beyond the drip line should be watered too. The most effective way to provide water is to place a "frog-eye" sprinkler at the outer edge of the drip line. Move the sprinkler around this zone every ten to fifteen minutes to allow for overlap and to cover the root zone completely.

How much water does a tree need? An easy way to determine this is to measure the tree's trunk diameter at knee height, then multiply by ten. For example, a tree with a 7-inch diameter tree trunk needs 70 gallons of water.

How long should you water? When using the frog-eye sprinkler, set a medium pressure and multiply the trunk diameter by five to calculate total watering time. For example, that 7-inch tree should be watered for thirty-five minutes, moving the sprinkler as needed for overlap. Slow watering allows water to percolate deeply where roots can use it more efficiently.

FALL AND WINTER WATERING

Lack of available subsoil moisture can take its toll on trees during the fall and winter seasons. When there is little or no rain or snow, it is critical to winter-water trees when temperatures are above freezing and as long as the ground remains unfrozen. This may need to be done every four to five weeks, depending on weather conditions. After winter watering, don't forget to drain your hoses and return them to storage for use later as needed.

THE ABCs OF FERTILIZING TREES

If you're uncertain about applying fertilizer to trees, a soil test can help you determine when it becomes necessary to do so. You can also look for symptoms of nutrient deficiency, including small leaves, light green or yellow leaves, stunted or short shoot growth, dead twigs at the ends of branches, and general lack of vigor. If these symptoms are present and are not a result of other variables such as drought stress, root injuries, herbicide damage, or diseases, then tree fertilization may be necessary.

Apply tree fertilizer when environmental conditions are most favorable for root growth. This is best done in late spring or early summer when the soil is moist and temperatures are between 68 and 84 degrees Fahrenheit.

Tree fertilizer is most effective and best used by the root system when applied to the soil surface over the root system of the trees (the tree's drip line and several feet beyond). Research has shown that surface placement of a complete fertilizer (N-P-K such as 10-10-10) is as good as, or better than, subsurface applications to shade trees growing outside of lawn areas. Trees growing within lawn areas benefit from lawn fertilizer (but do not use weed-and-feed formulations) and generally do not need additional tree fertilizer applications. Trees can absorb nutrients applied to the soil surface because the nutrients move downward with water that percolates through the soil; tree roots near the soil surface can absorb the migrating nutrients. A rate of 1 to 2 pounds of actual nitrogen per 1,000 square feet per growing season supplies the nutrient needs of most trees.

Just remember, fertilizer applications are not to be used as a rescue effort for stressed, injured, or declining trees.

Since the root zone of most trees lies just below the soil surface (6 to 12 inches), applying fertilizer to the surface of the soil is the easiest and most effective method of getting nitrogen to the root zone. Scatter the fertilizer at the drip line of the tree and several feet beyond this area, using the required amount to cover the area. Water thoroughly after fertilizing to allow the nutrients to reach the root system. Caution: Do not use too much fertilizer. If you apply more than the manufacturer's recommendations, tree roots can be burned or killed.

THE KINDEST CUT

PRUNING—MORE HARM THAN GOOD . . . SOMETIMES

You'll be surprised how much outdated information about pruning trees can still be found in gardening books. Two common, outdated pruning procedures are these: "Prune flush with the trunk," and "Paint the cut to prevent the wood from rotting." Both of these old recommendations have been shown by research to cause more harm than benefit to the tree.

Here's why: by pruning flush with the trunk, the larger cut that results takes longer to heal or close over. You are also eliminating the growing "point." Another name for the branch growing point is the branch collar. When pruning branches, try to cut the branch to maintain the branch collar.

PRUNING WOUNDS AND WOUND CLOSURE

Trees do not heal wounds the way people do. Trees grow callus tissue in response to pruning. This tissue grows over the wound or injured area, but the damaged tissues are not repaired. Trees chemically wall off the wounded tissue, a process called compartmentalization. Make pruning wounds as small as possible so the tree can close the wounds more quickly. The longer a wound remains open, the greater the chances decay will occur. Research has shown flush cuts may open large wounds that are unable to close rapidly.

Wound dressings or paints inhibit the tree from healing itself and should not be applied. If a tree is pruned at the proper time and pruned correctly, the plant heals itself quickly. So do not paint cuts. Also, do not leave stubs sticking out from the trunk. They will die back into the trunk and cause the heartwood to decay.

WHEN TO PRUNE

Trees can be pruned anytime of year, but pruning during different seasons results in different plant responses. Late winter and early spring—after a general warming trend—is a good time to prune because callus tissue then forms rapidly. This is the period of fastest redevelopment and readjustment to pruned limbs. Even though outwardly the cut may look the same, under-neath the tree has sealed off that cut to prevent decay, insects, and diseases from invading.

Prune trees that "bleed" from wounds (dripping sap), such as maples, birches, and walnuts, in late summer or early fall. Bleeding, however, does not generally harm the tree.

Removing large quantities of foliage after (not during) a flush of growth, such as late spring or early summer, tends to dwarf a tree. If that's the effect you desire, this is a good time to prune. For more rapid development, pruning before leaf emergence in the spring is better.

Pruning in late summer or early fall can cause vigorous regrowth, which in some species does not have time to harden off by winter. Late-fall or early-winter pruning subjects the tree to a greater incidence of dieback around the cut, and the wound closes more slowly.

WHAT TO PRUNE

Prune to remove dead, diseased, or damaged wood; to eliminate rubbing, interfering, or poorly placed branches; and to shape the tree. Dead wood should be cut back to—but not into—live wood. Sometimes you may prune out diseased wood to stop the disease's spread. When pruning diseased wood, make a thinning cut well below the infected site into the healthy wood. Disinfect your pruning equipment between each cut with 70 percent alcohol or rubbing alcohol. Do not use chlorine bleach because it rusts tools.

Cut back damaged branches to another branch. This damage includes previous poor pruning cuts or stubs. Eliminate poorly placed branches. Cut off branches that are or will eventually rub or grow in the wrong direction.

Narrow "V" crotches (bark incursions) occur when a layer of bark is squeezed between two branches growing very close together. Cut off one of the trunks or branches. Bark incursions may cause one of the limbs to split under strong winds or under a heavy snow or ice load.

Prune the tree to the shape you want. Such pruning is done to accentuate the tree's normal shape.

When planting young or new trees, do not prune off one-fourth to one-third of the top as is sometimes recommended. Severe pruning at the time of planting reduces shoot and root growth the following year. When planting a tree, prune out the dead, diseased, and damaged branches and cut the rubbing, interfering, and badly placed branches. Select the main scaffold branches as early as possible.

Water sprouts or suckers sometimes emerge when a tree has been severely pruned, and they usually grow from a stub cut. Some species of trees are notorious for producing many vigorous shoots. These shoots are generally poorly placed and interfere with growth. Prune them off when young or physically rub them off when they are quite small.

PROTECTING YOUNG TREE BARK

Protect the tree trunk bark of young trees by wrapping 1½-inch diameter or wider, white, plastic swimming pool hose around the trunk. Cut the hose to a length equal to the distance between the ground and the first branch. Make a vertical cut the length of the hose, pry it open, and snap the hose around the trunk.

Rocky Mountain Gardening Tip: Apply reflective tree wraps around Thanksgiving, and remove the wrapping around Easter.

THE BEAUTY OF TREES

Trees are functional all year. They sharpen our awareness of the changing seasons, from the first, green buds in spring through the cool, lush summer foliage. The brilliant autumn yellow and gold colors of native aspen trees stir visitors and residents alike to enjoy a drive to the High Country. As winter arrives, deciduous trees can be dramatic and sculptural as they bring interest to the otherwise stark landscape.

CONIFERS

The diversity of those hardy evergreens that endure cold and drought is apparent from the high peaks of the Rocky Mountains at tree line—that ragged line where trees stop and tundra begins—where the twisted bristlecone pines reside, to the subalpine forests, where spires of firs rise to the sky, to the montane forests, where ponderosa pines grow on the south-facing slopes and Douglas firs reside on wetter, north-facing exposures. Some of the wind-sculptured bristlecone pines on Mount Evans in Colorado have survived for more than two thousand years.

THINKING LIKE A NATIVE

When you plan to plant evergreens in your landscape, keep their native habitat in mind. A pinyon pine planted in the middle of the lawn soon develops weak branches, falls under attack by borers, and is on its way to plant heaven. Similarly, Colorado blue spruce becomes stunted and struggles to survive if planted in the corner of the yard where snow seldom remains and water never reaches. Finding an evergreen that looks good is a waste of time if the tree does not survive.

WEEPING
NORWAY SPRUCE

One important consideration is the tree's winter hardiness. The U.S. Department of Agriculture (USDA) has divided the country into areas called Hardiness Zones based on the average minimum winter temperatures of that region. These regional zones are identified numerically. These hardiness zone numbers are not always an exact guide because within a particular zone, significant variations in soil, rainfall, exposure, and humidity can affect a plant's ability to acclimate to a certain locale. If you can simulate the growing conditions for native evergreens in your landscape, experiment by growing various species.

Know the ultimate height and spread of an evergreen before you plant it. If you value your view of the mountains, don't plant a spruce in front of the living room window. It eventually blocks the view. Look up, as well; growing evergreens can interfere with overhead power lines and utility areas. The spread of an evergreen is often referred to as the "skirt," and without proper planning, it can have consequences in your landscape. The skirt of our native spruces can grow to 25 feet or more. What a shame it is to have to prune a beautiful spruce by removing the lower branches to open up a view or clear a driveway. Cutting away a large portion of the lower branches

destroys the spruce's fulcrum of balance. It becomes more prone to blowing over when high winds hit your neighborhood.

PLANNING FOR SUCCESS

Evergreens have the best chance of success when planted in the spring, though fall planting can be successful if you get it done by mid-October. Root growth slows down as soil temperatures approach 45 degrees Fahrenheit. Trees planted in the fall need to be mulched heavily (4 to 6 inches) in an effort to delay the freezing of the soil and allow more time for root development.

Autumn and winter watering is essential before the soil freezes; even after a freeze, continue to monitor moisture in the soil, watering monthly when there is no snow cover throughout the winter.

Planting evergreens is relatively simple: Dig a wide, shallow hole; add backfill soil; water slowly to eliminate air pockets under the roots; cover the soil with an organic mulch; and water only as needed after planting. In heavy-clay soils, score the side walls of the planting hole to break up the soil compaction created from the digging process. You don't need to loosen the soil below where the rootball is to rest; doing so can cause the evergreen to settle too deeply after planting.

Transplanted evergreens acclimate to their new environment if planted in concert with native soil conditions.

MAKING THE MOST OF YOUR SOIL

Few plants thrive in "contractor dirt," compacted clay, or poorly drained soils. Such soils lack the oxygen needed for root growth. The old method of planting was to amend the entire planting area prior to digging the planting holes. However, horticulture experts now advise against amending planting sites prior to planting.

Instead, loosen the native soil thoroughly to alleviate soil compaction. This preparation creates a more suitable environment for root growth. Adding some organic matter helps improve drainage and aeration, but don't add large amounts of organic matter into the backfill soil. If the soil is too rich, the tree's roots may decide to remain within the planting hole and never attempt to explore the surrounding native soil. Roots grow into soil that has a balance of oxygen and water, so the best recommendation is to dig the hole wider rather than deeper and loosen the soil thoroughly.

ABCs OF PLANTING

If you're planting in heavy-clay soil, dig the planting hole 1 to 2 inches shallower than the height of the tree's rootball. Shallow planting in clay soils prevents the tree from sinking too deeply. If your soil is sandy, the hole should be no deeper than the rootball. Here, the idea is to place the rootball on a solid foundation so the roots can grow in the top 15 to 18 inches of soil.

Now you're finally ready to plant. Handle the rootball with care; breaking the rootball is often fatal to young trees and shrubs, especially evergreens. Remove the tree from its container and place it in the hole. If the roots have become potbound, growing in circles and compacted, tease out the roots by hand or score (nick) the sides of the rootball with a sharp knife. This stops the roots from growing in a spiral pattern (girdling each other) and encourages them to spread out into the soil.

On larger, balled-and-burlapped evergreens, remove at least the top half of the wire basket after the tree is situated in the planting hole. Cut off remaining nylon twine and rope as well. Cut off as much of the burlap wrap around the top of the ball as possible or tuck it back into the soil. Cut several slits through the remaining material to permit the roots to venture into the new soil. Shovel backfill soil into the hole about halfway up, and gently firm it to keep the tree from tipping over. Then water slowly and allow the soil to settle in, eliminating air pockets. Once the water has soaked in, add more backfill soil to complete the planting. Water again. Use the extra soil to construct a dike at the edge of the planting hole. In four to five days, fill this reservoir with water. Don't overwater—more evergreens die from over-watering than under-watering. Give the soil a good soaking when it begins to dry out at 4 to 6 inches deep.

Mulch the planting area 3 to 4 inches deep with old pine needles, compost, or shredded wood chips. In later years, an appropriate ground cover can be planted as living mulch.

You don't have to add fertilizer during the planting operation or afterwards. Research has shown that no fertilizer is needed for the first growing season. Evergreens planted in turf areas generally receive adequate nutrients from regular fertilizing of the turf grasses during the growing season. After the second or third spring, you may apply a slow-release, organic fertilizer around the drip line. Apply 1 cup of fertilizer per inch of trunk thickness; measure the thickness of the trunk 4 feet from the ground. Use a crowbar or an old ski pole to punch holes 8 to 10 inches deep at 12-inch intervals, and scatter the fertilizer granules where the holes were punched. Water until the fertilizer granules dissolve or wash into the holes.

ALL-SEASON INTEREST

Choose a variety of evergreen trees for your home landscape for privacy screening, wind abatement, and year-round accent. Evergreens make highly effective windbreaks to buffer the force of the wind, absorbing it rather than redirecting it over a fence or wall. Combined with deciduous trees and shrubs, evergreens provide ornamental interest and wildlife habitat throughout the seasons.

AMUR MAPLE
Acer ginnala

Why It's Special—Many gardeners are not familiar with the amur, but it is an excellent choice for the home garden and landscape. Small, fragrant, yellow flowers appear in the spring. The foliage is very attractive, deeply lobed, and dark green. It creates a dazzling red display in the fall. The amur maple is multi-trunked, making it an excellent choice for screening or as a specimen plant in the larger landscape. This maple is both heat and drought tolerant. 'Ember' has outstanding fall color.

How to Plant & Grow—Spring and fall are excellent planting seasons. See the beginning of this chapter for detailed tree planting instructions. Keep trees watered adequately until well established, which is generally two to three years. Amur maple will tolerate afternoon shade, but truly dislikes soils with a high alkalinity.

Care & Problems—Pest and disease free, *Acer ginnala* may need a light pruning in the summer months.

Hardiness: Zones 2 to 8

Peak Season/Color: Autumn; red

Mature Size (H x W): 15 to 20 ft. x 15 to 20 ft.

Water Needs: Low to moderate

ASH
Fraxinus spp.

Why It's Special—White and green ash trees have become popular and dominant trees in Rocky Mountain landscapes. They are adaptable to alkaline soils, drought tolerant, and grow relatively quickly. The pyramidal young tree becomes broadly oval as it matures. Dark green, compound foliage turns purple in autumn. White ash will be one of the first trees to color up in the fall, and will drop its leaves by mid-October. 'Autumn Purple' has excellent color and is disease resistant. If you choose a green ash for your garden, choose either 'Marshall' or 'Patmore'.

How to Plant & Grow—Spring and fall are excellent planting seasons. See the beginning of this chapter for detailed tree planting instructions. Keep trees watered adequately. Ash trees should be situated in full sun.

Care & Problems—Ash trees are prone to borers. Check with a reputable nursery or your county extension office for recommended tree treatments.

Hardiness: Zones 3 to 9

Peak Season/Color: Autumn; bronze/purple

Mature Size (H x W): 50 to 60 ft. x 35 to 45 ft.

Water Needs: Moderate

EASTERN REDBUD
Cercis canadensis

Why It's Special—In April the branches of the Eastern redbud will be covered with tiny, pea-like, rose-colored blossoms, which give way to new, reddish purple leaves. As the season progresses, the foliage will turn green. Finally, in the fall, those heart-shaped leaves will fade to gold. The cultivar 'Forest Pansy," will retain the reddish purple leaf color throughout the season.

How to Plant & Grow—Redbud, especially 'Forest Pansy', does better when given some afternoon protection, especially in the high desert regions of the Intermountain West. In fact, 'Forest Pansy' would do well with an eastern or morning exposure and benefits from afternoon shade. Once well established—in about three years—redbuds are somewhat drought tolerant. When planting, amend soils with moisture-retentive compost.

Care & Problems—If scale is a problem, apply insecticidal soap according to the label directions.

Hardiness: Zones 4 to 9 ('Forest Pansy', 5 to 9)

Peak Season/Color: Early spring, pink blossoms and reddish-purple leaves; summer, green leaves; fall, gold foliage

Mature Size (H x W): 20 to 30 ft. x 25 to 30 ft.

Water Needs: Moderate

EUROPEAN HORNBEAM (PYRAMIDAL)

Carpinus betulus 'Fastigiata'

☀

Why It's Special—European hornbeam has been in cultivation for centuries. The columnar, or 'Fastigiata' cultivar, is perfectly suited to narrow city lots and makes a dashing screen between neighboring, two-story houses or a prominent, stately specimen. It is a recommended tree for fire-wise and windbreak plantings. Hornbeam turns a handsome yellow in the autumn and sports smooth, gray bark.

How to Plant & Grow—European hornbeam should have a regular watering schedule during the first two growing seasons to establish a deep and extensive root system. After that, it should be watered regularly and deeply. Always plant in full sun.

Care & Problems—'Fastigiata' hornbeam withstands regular and tight pruning. In Europe it is regularly planted in grand allees and often pleached, or trained, in the flat, espalier style. It has few pests or diseases.

Hardiness: Zones 4 to 8

Peak Season/Color: Fall; yellow foliage

Mature Size (H x W): 35 to 45 ft. x 25 ft.

Water Needs: Low, once it is established

FLOWERING CRABAPPLE

Malus spp.

☀

Why It's Special—The frothy flowers of crabapples are a welcome spring vision. There are dozens of varieties—rounded, tall or small, and weeping; white or pink blossoms both single and double; red, yellow, or purple fruit; and green or bronze leaves. In other words, there's one for your garden. The best way to choose is to visit a nursery in the spring, admire them all, and select the one best suited to your climate, space, and taste.

How to Plant & Grow—Spring and fall are excellent planting seasons. See the beginning of this chapter for detailed tree planting instructions. Keep trees watered adequately. Prune lightly when the trees are young to define their shape.

Care & Problems—Give crabapples a deep watering about once every ten to fourteen days, using 2 inches of water each time. To enhance flower and fruit production, apply a nitrogen fertilizer in early spring.

Hardiness: Zones 3 to 10

Peak Season/Color: Spring; pink and white

Mature Size (H x W): 8 to 30 ft. x 10 to 20 ft.

Water Needs: Low to moderate

GOLDENRAIN TREE

Koelreuteria paniculata

☀

Why It's Special—Goldenrain tree is spectacular, with bright yellow flowers hanging in foot-long panicles above the leaves. The bell-shaped, one-half-inch flowers completely cover a tree when it's in bloom. In late summer and early fall, the fruit develops into three-sided, bladder-like, yellow husks that look like miniature Chinese lanterns. Goldenrain's fall foliage coloration is yellow. It will grow anywhere and is very tolerant of drought and wind.

How to Plant & Grow—Goldenrain grows best in full sun but is well adapted to partial shade. Spring and fall are excellent planting seasons, but you will find the best selection in the spring. See the beginning of this chapter for detailed tree planting instructions. Keep trees watered adequately until well established, which is generally two to three years.

Care & Problems—Pest and disease free, goldenrain tree prefers light pruning in the summer months, if needed.

Hardiness: Zones 5 to 7

Peak Season/Color: Autumn; red

Mature Size (H x W): 20 to 30 ft. x 40 ft.

Water Needs: Low to moderate

HAWTHORN
Crataegus phaenopyrum

☀

Why It's Special—Hawthorns are tough, hardy, and easy to grow where few other trees survive. They are splendid specimen trees, and they work in small spaces. Showy white flowers are followed by apple-like fruit in late summer and fall. Many wild birds favor the fruit. 'Lustre' is a popular cultivar. Russian hawthorn, *C. ambigua*, sports garnet red autumn fruit.

How to Plant & Grow—Plant hawthorns in spring through early fall, but avoid late-fall planting. Water 2 inches deep about every ten to fourteen days. Hawthorns thrive in the sun.

Care & Problems—Once established, hawthorns are low maintenance and need only periodic pruning in late winter or early spring. Some suckering around the base of the tree occurs occasionally, but these can be pruned away as soon as they appear.

Hardiness: Zones 4 to 8

Peak Season/Color: Spring, white blossoms; fall, red fruit and red, maroon, yellow, and gold foliage

Mature Size (H x W): 20 to 30 ft. x 20 to 25 ft.

Water Needs: Low to moderate

HONEY LOCUST
Gleditsia triacanthos var. inermis

☀

Why It's Special—Honey locust is perfect for the spot that needs dappled, not heavy shade. The small leaves develop late in the spring, unfolding in a distinctive, lemon-lime cloud. These leaves drop early in the fall, as do the long, curving pods. 'Moraine', 'Shademaster', and 'Skyline' are recommended. Though taller than others, 'Sunburst' will grow to 70 feet, but it is fruitless and podless.

How to Plant & Grow—Plant container plants anytime, although they do best planted in fall to allow more root growth before summer. These trees will grow in any soil, provided it has good drainage. They like full sun.

Care & Problems—Water new trees twice a week until established, then weekly until the foliage drops. After that, water monthly until the new leaves unfold. Give trees near sidewalks extra water to keep surface roots from heaving walkways up in search of moisture.

Hardiness: Zones 4 to 8

Peak Season/Color: Spring, lime green foliage; fall, bright yellow foliage

Mature Size (H x W): 25 to 35 ft. x 35 ft. (70)

Water Needs: Moderate

JAPANESE MAPLE
Acer palmatum

☀

Why It's Special—Japanese maples have been called the aristocrats of deciduous trees. These are always "attention getters" and should be selected and placed accordingly. Dome- or vase-shaped, their branches are layered, often weeping or pendulous. The leaves are exquisite and may be pale green or deep burgundy—often some variation or combination of both. There are too many cultivars to list but 'Bloodgood', a dark red, is well suited to our hot dry summers and easy to find. 'Sango Kaku', the coral bark maple, is not hardy in all parts of the Rockies, but where it can be grown, it is sought after for its incredible hot pink bark.

How to Plant & Grow—Spring and fall are excellent planting seasons. Smaller varieties will do well planted in an large container (giving them adequate room for root development and winter insulation). Japanese maples make good patio plants.

Care & Problems—Japanese maples are generally free of pests and diseases. Prune lightly in the summer if needed. Afternoon shade is important—site accordingly.

Hardiness: Zones 5 to 8

Peak Season/Color: Vibrant new growth in spring followed by colorful autumn displays

Mature Size (H x W): 5 to 30 ft. x 4 to 15 ft.

Water Needs: Moderate

KENTUCKY COFFEETREE

Gymnocladus dioica

☀

Why It's Special—Kentucky coffeetree is one of the stateliest trees in the winter landscape. Its distinctive rough bark is deeply furrowed. The mature bark has great winter interest. Female trees bear greenish white panicles of flowers followed by long, beanlike pods that last through the winter. Male flowers are smaller and less fragrant. Late to leaf out in the spring, it is seldom damaged by late-spring frosts. It makes an excellent shade tree with superior drought endurance.

How to Plant & Grow—Plant this tree in the early spring or early fall. Even though the Kentucky coffeetree grows slowly, it eventually becomes quite large and needs plenty of room to develop. Place this beauty where it will receive full sun.

Care & Problems—Bear in mind that the fruits on female trees and large leaf stalks that support the many leaflets drop in mass and require periodic cleanup.

Hardiness: Zones 3 to 8

Peak Season/Color: Fall; yellow-gold

Mature Size (H x W): 50 to 60 ft. x 40 to 50 ft.

Water Needs: Low to moderate

LINDEN

Tilia spp.

☀

Why It's Special—With their heart-shaped leaves and delicious sweet summer fragrance, linden trees make attractive, dense, shade trees for the home landscape. The fragrant flowers, drooping from the branches in midsummer, are nectar magnets for honeybees. The little-leaf linden, *Tilia cordata*, and the American linden, *Tilia americana*, are recommended and tolerant of our region's alkaline soil conditions. In autumn, the linden's handsome foliage turns yellow and gold. 'Redmond', 'Legend', and 'Greenspire' are exceptional cultivars.

How to Plant & Grow—Plant lindens in the spring or early autumn so they will become well established before the onset of winter. Provide ample moisture to prevent stress and subsequent leaf scorch. Locate in full sun.

Care & Problems—Lindens do attract large numbers of bees when they are in blossom, so heads up!

Hardiness: Zones 3 to 7

Peak Season/Color: Fall; yellow

Mature Size (H x W): 50 ft. x 30 to 40 ft.

Water Needs: Moderate

MAPLE

Acer spp.

☀

Why It's Special—Maples are a favorite shade tree known for their bright, autumn foliage. 'Autumn Blaze', with its vibrant, orange-red, fall color, and 'October Glory' are showstoppers. Japanese maples, *Acer palmatum* spp., come in myriad sizes (generally less than 12 feet in height) and have a graceful structure, often in the weeping style. There are many leaf colors and shapes from which to choose.

How to Plant & Grow—Maples are limited to the high desert and mountainous regions of the Rockies and should be planted in full sun for best coloration. They succumb to leaf scorch in the hot region around Las Vegas, and the temperatures there are too hot in fall to develop vivid, fall color.

Care & Problems—All maples need a deep watering to a soil depth of 12 inches about every ten to fourteen days; use about 2 inches of water. All maples have shallow roots, and silver maple is the worst; don't plant them next to sidewalks, patios, or driveways because the roots will crack the concrete.

Hardiness: Zones 3 to 7

Peak Season/Color: Fall; brilliant red foliage

Mature Size (H x W): 40 to 50 ft. x 20 to 30 ft.

Water Needs: Moderate

MAYDAY
Prunus padus commutata

☀

Why It's Special—*Prunus padus commutata*, or Mayday tree, is prized for its modest height and spring-fresh, fragrant, drooping flower clusters in late April to early May. Small, black fruit ripens in July to early August and is a favorite of visiting birds. Mayday tree has nice fall color with foliage turning yellow-gold to bronze-red. The "bird cherry" is a good choice for a shelterbelt and wildlife plantings.

How to Plant & Grow—Plant Mayday tree in early spring. For the best flowering and growth form, locate in full sun with good air circulation. It does best in well-drained soils, so be sure to condition clay soils with a good soil amendment.

Care & Problems—Overwatering can cause stress and poor root growth. Most ornamental cherries are shallow rooted, so be sure to provide ample moisture and keep the root zone cool.

Hardiness: Zones 3 to 7

Peak Season/Color: Autumn; yellow foliage

Mature Size (H x W): 18 to 25 ft. x 20 to 30 ft.

Water Needs: Low to moderate

OAK
Quercus spp.

☀

Why It's Special—Our native Rocky Mountain oak, *Q. gambelii*, is noted for its durability and adaptability to dry conditions and alkaline soils. It can be grown as a small tree or large shrub and is hardy to 8,000 feet. Bur oak (*Q. macrocarpa*), the majestic one at 80 x 80 feet, is one of the best suited for alkaline soils and drier conditions. It offers fringed acorns as a wildlife delicacy. English (*Q. robur fastigiata*) columnar oaks are perfect in narrow spaces, with handsome foliage and reaching to only 15 feet wide.

How to Plant & Grow—Plant oak trees in the early spring. Allow plenty of room for them to grow. Oaks need deep watering, occasional fertilizer and full sun.

Care & Problems—Aphids may be an occasional pest; hose off with a strong stream of water.

Hardiness: Zones 3 to 8

Peak Season/Color: Autumn; yellow, orange and red

Mature Size (H x W): 20 to 80 ft. x 15 to 80 ft.

Water Needs: Moderate

ORNAMENTAL PEAR
Prunus calleryana

☀

Why It's Special—Ornamental pears are widely used in residential and commercial landscapes because of their rapid growth, uniform shape, and beautiful, white, spring blossoms. They can be used for screening, street plantings, and garden focal points. Fall coloration is outstanding, when leaves turn a shiny crimson red. Ornamental pears are relatively drought tolerant, with good disease resistance. 'Chanticleer' is an excellent choice in limited lateral space. 'Jack' is a new smaller cultivar, topping out at 20 feet.

How to Plant & Grow—Ornamental pears perform best in full sun with good air circulation to reduce the onset of powdery mildew disease. Though adapted to a wide range of soils, ornamental pears prefer well-drained soils.

Care & Problems—Most varieties do not need pruning because of their uniform growth habit. Remove only broken, damaged, or rubbing branches. Protect trunks of young trees the first few growing seasons to prevent sunscald injury.

Hardiness: Zones 5 to 8

Peak Season/Color: Spring; white flowers; fall, red

Mature Size (H x W): 20 to 35 ft. x 15 to 30 ft.

Water Needs: Low to moderate

QUAKING ASPEN
Populus tremuloides

☼

Why It's Special—Pale white, smooth bark and leaves that quake in the breeze, followed by golden yellow fall foliage, make aspens a Rocky Mountain icon. Yes, they are native to our region, but there are limitations for their use. Aspen trees do best at elevations of 7,000 feet and above. When planted at lower elevations, aspen trees are exceptionally vulnerable to borers and seldom survive more than a decade.

How to Plant & Grow—The best time to plant aspens is in the spring to allow for good root establishment. In their native habitat, aspens grow in soils naturally enriched with lots of leaf mold. When planting these trees in your landscape, amend the soil with a moisture-retentive compost to simulate mountainous conditions. Locate in a sunny spot.

Care & Problems—As these trees grow, roots expand into the surrounding area and "suckers" appear everywhere. Prune as needed or allow trees to colonize. At lower elevations, they are infested with poplar twig gallfly—a pest for which there are no effective controls.

Hardiness: Zones 2 to 5

Peak Season/Color: Autumn; yellow foliage

Mature Size (H x W): 20 to 30 ft. x 25 to 30 ft.

Water Needs: Moderate

RIVER BIRCH
Betula nigra

☼

Why It's Special—The river birch is cherished for its amazing bark. As the tree matures, it begins to peel and exposes its rich inner bark with colors of buckskin to cinnamon brown. River birches are very showy during the fall and winter. The fall leaves are a rich yellow. The male tree produces slender, dark brown catkins that add to its ornamental value. The river birch is not bothered by bronze birch borers. 'Heritage' is an excellent selection.

How to Plant & Grow—Single-stem trees can be spaced 15 feet apart and the canopies allowed to intertwine. Lower branches can be removed to permit foot traffic. Plant river birch trees in early spring through early summer in full sun.

Care & Problems—Provide ample water during the summer heat for good root establishment. In late fall and winter, watering is a must to ensure this tree's survival. Prune in the summer.

Hardiness: Zones 4 to 7

Peak Season/Color: Autumn; yellow foliage

Mature Size (H x W): 25 to 35 ft. x 20 to 30 ft.

Water Needs: Moderate

SERVICEBERRY
Amelanchier alnifolia

☼ ☼

Why It's Special—One of our native plants, serviceberry is an attractive tree with fragrant white flowers and serrated foliage. The blooms appear before leaves fully emerge. Its sweet blue fruit is treasured by birds and humans alike. In autumn, leaves range from yellow to orange-red. The small size of *Amelanchier* makes it perfect for smaller landscapes and for use in patio plantings and as a foundation plant. 'Saskatoon' and 'Autumn Brilliance' are fine tree selections; 'Regent' is a shrub, only 3 feet tall.

How to Plant & Grow—Serviceberry grows as a multistemmed shrub or small tree in dry conditions and grows taller in moist, semi-shaded locations. Trees planted in full sun have more blossoms and more intense fall colors.

Care & Problems—Provide regular deep watering during long, dry spells. Relatively low maintenance, serviceberry requires periodic pruning of suckers at the base if you intend to keep it as a single-stemmed specimen.

Hardiness: Zones 2 to 7

Peak Season/Color: Autumn; yellow foliage

Mature Size (H x W): 25 to 35 ft. x 20 to 30 ft.

Water Needs: Low to moderate

SWEET GUM
Liquidambar styraciflua 'Cherokee'

☀

Why It's Special—Sweet gum 'Cherokee' is a sterile cultivar of *Liquidambar*, which produces few or no seed balls, a huge plus for this tree. Most folks would rather not have to deal with sweet gum's notorious, sputnik-like pods in the fall. 'Cherokee's' fall foliage is a varnished red or burgundy, stunning in the home landscape. The bark is unique; it is corky and springy to the touch, and toothed, or winged around the branches.

How to Plant & Grow—Sweet gum is a resilient colorful tree. Once it takes hold, it can withstand the heat and drought of the Rockies. Water it well to help it settle in. Once it is established, sweet gum is quite drought tolerant. 'Cherokee' is somewhat intolerant of alkaline soils, so amend the planting space accordingly when planting on your property. Locate this tree in a sunny spot.

Care & Problems—Sweet gum is easy to care for, with few pests or diseases.

Hardiness: Zones 5 to 9

Peak Season/Color: Autumn; red and burgundy foliage

Mature Size (H x W): 50 ft. x 25 ft.

Water Needs: Low to moderate

TULIP POPLAR
Liriodendron tulipifera

☀ ☀

Why It's Special—This American native shade tree is an excellent slow growing, long-lived tree with intriguing yellow, tulip-shaped blossoms and blue-green leaves. A member of the magnolia family, it deserves to be used more often in our gardens and landscapes. Birds love it for nesting and it sports lovely fall foliage.

How to Plant & Grow—Plant tulip poplar in the spring as it needs the entire season to develop a decent root system. Give the tulip tree room to grow and adequate water. It is not drought tolerant and needs weekly, regular, deep and thorough watering. It can be planted in full sun, but a position with late afternoon shade is fine.

Care & Problems—Tulip tree is easy to care for with few pests or diseases. It's not salt tolerant, so plant it where it will not be damaged by winter road salts.

Hardiness: Zones 5 to 9

Peak Season/Color: In summer, large yellow-green tulip-like blossoms with orange blaze markings

Mature Size (H x W): 50 ft. x 30 ft.

Water Needs: Moderate to High

WESTERN CATALPA OR INDIAN BEAN TREE
Catalpa speciosa

☀

Why It's Special—Catalpas have gorgeous orchid-like blossoms in the spring followed by huge heart-shaped bright green leaves. When they are in full bloom, you can see them across as city's tree canopy rising up like developing thunderheads. Later, they develop bean-like long, dark, dry seedpods. Catalpas are great shade trees.

How to Plant & Grow—Allow catalpa plenty of space in your landscape and locate it in full sun. Western catalpa tree tolerates both wet and dry alkaline soil conditions.

Care & Problems—The small branches are quite brittle and break off easily in ice and snowstorms or during high winds. Avoid planting near sidewalks and driveways since the seedpods can accumulate, and, if crushed, they stain concrete surfaces.

Hardiness: Zones 4 to 8

Peak Season/Color: Late spring; white flower clusters

Mature Size (H x W): 40 to 60 ft. x 25 to 30 ft.

Water Needs: Low

YELLOWWOOD
Cladrastis kentukea

☼ ☼

Why It's Special—Yellowwood is a handsome, drought tolerant shade tree that should be used more often. It puts on an incredible display of blossoms in June when four to sixteen inch, white, wisteria-like blooms drip from the tree. The blossoms are heavy in alternate years and very fragrant. The heartwood is a deep yellow and was used as a source of yellow dye. The bark is beautiful—with the texture and appearance of smooth gray steel. The leaves, in early spring, are a soft green, developing into a rich green color over the course of the season.

How to Plant & Grow—Plant this tree with a protected eastern exposure to avoid scorching by the afternoon sun. Prune only in midsummer, as the tree tends to bleed other times of the year.

Care & Problems—Yellowwood is free of major pests.

Hardiness: Zones 3 to 9

Peak Season/Color: Spring, white; autumn, golden yellow

Mature Size (H x W): 30 to 50 ft. x 30 to 50 ft.

Water Needs: Low to moderate

AUSTRIAN PINE
Pinus nigra

☼

Why It's Special—One of the most adapted and hardiest pines for the Intermountain West landscape is the Austrian pine. This pine withstands dry windy climates, heavy clay soils, and alkaline conditions throughout the region. It is well adapted to sandy soils of the High Plains. Austrian pine's stout, pyramidal growth makes it an excellent choice for windbreaks, shelterbelts, screening, or as a splendid specimen tree.

How to Plant & Grow—Container-grown and balled-and-burlapped specimen pines should be transplanted in the spring to early summer. Avoid late-fall planting. Austrian pine prefers well-drained soils, but adapts to clay soils that are made to drain by proper soil preparation and modifications. Planting on raised berms in heavy-soil sites helps ensure survival and prevents overwatering. Plant in a sunny location.

Care & Problems—This pine is easily stressed from too much watering and fertilizing, particularly when planted in a lawn. These issues are easily prevented.

Hardiness: Zones 3 to 7

Color(s): Evergreen

Mature Size (H x W): 30 to 60 ft. x 20 to 40 ft.

Water Needs: Low

BRISTLECONE PINE
Pinus aristata

☼

Why It's Special—The bristlecone pine is a beloved native that grows in the subalpine forests and at tree lines. Its dark brown cones have small prickles on the scales, giving this pine its common name. Some specimens are among the oldest trees in the world at over 2,000 years old! The dark-green needles densely cluster along the stems and branches and are covered with tiny pitch nodules often mistaken for insect pests.

How to Plant & Grow—Plant bristlecone pine in spring and provide excellent drainage. Use it as a focal point, a backdrop for a perennial garden, or an unlikely addition to a rock garden. This plant is right at home in full sun.

Care & Problems—Bristlecone pines have unique growing characteristics—they would look right at home in Dr. Seuss's yard—and should not be pruned. Allow them to develop naturally. This pest-resistant species endures in alkaline, rocky, poor, and well-drained soils and wind.

Hardiness: Zones 2 to 7

Color(s): Dark blue-green

Mature Size (H x W): 10 to 30 ft. x 8 to 20 ft.

Water Needs: Low

COLORADO SPRUCE
Picea pungens

☀

Why It's Special—The majestic Colorado spruce is noted for its silvery blue needles that form a pyramid, its stiff, horizontal branches sweeping the ground. Some of the magnificent blue spruce cultivars have outstanding color variations and growth characteristics. My favorites include 'Hoopsii', 'Fat Albert', 'Iseli Fastigiate', 'Montgomery', and 'Thompsenii'.

How to Plant & Grow—Plant your spruce trees where they will receive adequate moisture. Do not apply weed-and-feed fertilizers near spruce trees; herbicides can accumulate near the root zone and result in distorted growth and possible dieback. This conifer loves sunny sites.

Care & Problems—In the summer heat, spider mites can become a problem, causing the needles to develop a salt-and-pepper appearance. Control them by spraying the tree with water or an appropriate miticide. Be very cautious when using dormant sprays on spruce; oil sprays remove the bluish green coloration. Pruning alters the spruce's natural growth habit, which is generally not recommended.

Hardiness: Zones 2 to 7

Color(s): Gray-blue

Mature Size (H x W): 60 to 100 ft. x 20 to 30 ft.

Water Needs: Low, once it is established

CONCOLOR FIR
Abies concolor

☀

Why It's Special—The concolor fir is one of the most beautiful conifers. This native's dense growth is displayed in beautiful, tiered branches to create a bold look in the landscape. Among the firs, *Abies concolor* is noted for its outstanding tolerance of hot, dry conditions. There are several cultivars of dwarf concolors for smaller spaces and conifer collections.

How to Plant & Grow—Concolor fir requires a spot with full sun or afternoon shade, with plenty of room to grow. It prefers moist, well-drained soils, but endures drought if watered properly.

Care & Problems—In windy and exposed sites, construct a burlap screen on the windward side of the tree to reduce windburn and needle desiccation. Giant conifer aphids may visit the needles and twigs in late summer, attracting ants and yellow jackets. Control them with insecticidal soap.

Hardiness: Zones 3 to 7

Color(s): Bluish green

Mature Size (H x W): 30 to 60 ft. x 15 to 20 ft.

Water Needs: Low to moderate

DOUGLAS FIR
Pseudotsuga menziesii

☀

Why It's Special—Douglas fir can be used as a garden backdrop or as an ornamental conifer in the landscape. The short, thin needles are shiny green above with a whitish band beneath. One of this evergreen's best features is its downward hanging cones with decorative three-pronged bracts. Douglas fir grows into an open pyramidal form, with upper branches that grow upright and lower branches that descend. With age, this fir prunes itself, creating a more open appearance. Look for the blue-needled *P. menziesii* var. *glauca*, a slow-growing type whose form is somewhat more pyramidal. *P. menziesii* 'Glauca Pendula' is the weeping cultivar.

How to Plant & Grow—It does best in moist, well-drained soils, and it does not tolerate dry sites.

Care & Problems—Douglas fir can be long lived, provided it receives adequate moisture. Soak the soil deeply on a regular basis with a soaker hose.

Hardiness: Zones 4 to 7

Color(s): Green

Mature Size (H x W): 30 to 60 ft. x 15 to 20 ft.

Water Needs: Moderate

EUROPEAN LARCH
Larix decidua

☼

Why It's Special—Larch is a deciduous conifer. In the autumn, the needles turn a vivid school bus yellow, then drop to the ground. In spring, it pushes forth tender, lime green needles. For a satisfying effect, underplant with spring-flowering bulbs and ground covers like *Galium odoratum* or *Ajuga reptans*. Use this unusual deciduous evergreen as a specimen tree or as an elegant background for a group planting.

How to Plant & Grow—Choose an open area with full sun and plenty of space; larch has considerable spread. Provide consistent moisture during the growing season. It does not tolerate extreme drought, but it does tolerate alkaline soils.

Care & Problems—Water periodically throughout winter, particularly when there is little or no snow cover but only when temperatures are above freezing and soil is not frozen. Watering may be necessary every five to six weeks during extended late-fall and winter dry spells.

Hardiness: Zones 3 to 7

Color(s): Unusual, bright yellow needles in autumn

Mature Size (H x W): 70 to 80 ft. x 25 to 30 ft.

Water Needs: Moderate, more in extreme heat

LIMBER PINE
Pinus flexilis

☼

Why It's Special—A Rocky Mountain native, limber pine fits well in a smaller landscape setting as a specimen tree, accent, or background planting. It develops real character as it matures and creates a stunning silhouette with silvery gray bark. Some cultivars are especially grand. 'Extra Blue' has intense blue needles. 'Nana' is a dwarf form that works well in rock gardens. A distinctive, densely branched specimen, *Pinus flexilis* 'Vanderwolf's Pyramid' features bluish green needles accented underneath with a pale blue line.

How to Plant & Grow—Limber pine prefers well-drained soils but can adapt to clay soils that are made to drain with good soil preparation and modifications. Plant in a sunny spot.

Care & Problems—Keep newly planted pines healthy by providing adequate moisture during establishment. After planting, add 2 to 3 inches of organic mulch. It's especially important to supply water in the fall and winter months when rain or snow is lacking.

Hardiness: Zones 2 to 7

Color(s): Green

Mature Size (H x W): 30 to 45 ft. x 25 to 30 ft.

Water Needs: Low to moderate

NORWAY SPRUCE
Picea abies 'Cupressina'

☼ ☼

Why It's Special—'Cupressina' was discovered in Germany almost a century ago. Because it is tall and slender, this tall, slim evergreen is sought after for small gardens and contemporary urban landscapes. The branches are dense and slightly upturned, like a perfect Christmas tree. This strong branch structure makes them less susceptible to breakage from heavy snow loads.

How to Plant & Grow—A matched pair of 'Cupressina' looks stately when planted on either side of an entryway, or you may choose to plant a single tree as an elegant focal point. Norway spruce can tolerate full sun but a bit of afternoon shade is acceptable.

Care & Problems—In windy and exposed sites, construct a burlap screen on the windward side of the tree to reduce windburn and needle desiccation. Giant conifer aphids may visit the needles and twigs in late summer, attracting ants and yellow jackets. Control them with insecticidal soap.

Hardiness: Zones 3 to 7

Color(s): Green

Mature Size (H x W): 6 ft. x 25 ft.

Water Needs: Low to moderate, once it is well established

PINYON PINE

Pinus cembroides var. *edulis*

☀

Why It's Special—This southern Rocky Mountain native prefers south-facing slopes and thrives on neglect. When cutting firewood, it's great fun to collect the pine cones for a bountiful harvest of delicious pinyon nuts. Pinyon pine (the two-needle pinyon) is very drought tolerant. It grows into picturesque forms with twisted trunk and limbs. The resin deposits and needles release an enjoyable pine fragrance during hot summer evenings.

How to Plant & Grow—In home landscapes, pinyons do best planted on berms or raised island beds where drainage is good. Pinyons planted in heavily watered turf areas often fail. Combine it with our native sumac, *Rhus trilobata*, for a spectacular Rocky Mountain autumn display. These pines need full sun.

Care & Problems—Pinyons are often treated with too much love and care and quickly become stressed from over-watering, overfertilizing, and improper pruning. Resist pruning and allow it to grow into its natural form.

Hardiness: Zones 5 to 8

Color(s): Green

Mature Size (H x W): 12 to 20 ft. x 12 to 15 ft.

Water Needs: Low

ROCKY MOUNTAIN JUNIPER

Juniperus scopulorum

☀

Why It's Special—Tough as nails, drought tolerant, loved by birds and butterflies—what more could you ask for? The Rocky Mountain juniper and its ornamental cultivars perform extremely well in the home garden. Cedar waxwings and other migrating feathered friends feast on the abundant, white-coated blue berries. 'Witchita Blue' and 'Skyrocket' are two easy-to-find columnar varieties for narrow, tight spaces and excellent choices for hedging. They work well in Mediterranean-style landscapes.

How to Plant & Grow—After the first growing season, junipers are quite drought tolerant. They do especially well on sandy, rocky hillsides and in mountainous areas.

Care & Problems—Spider mites can be a nuisance during hot dry weather. Knock them off with a sharp blast from the garden hose. If desired, you can lightly shear the trees to give a "refreshed" look to the steel blue color of the blue varieties, and to shape any of the cultivars.

Hardiness: Zones 3 to 8

Color(s): Evergreen or bluish cast

Mature Size (H x W): Native 30 to 40 ft. x 3 to 15 ft. Cultivar dimensions will vary.

Water Needs: Low

179

SERBIAN SPRUCE

Picea omorika

☼

Why It's Special—Serbian spruce comes in several shapes and sizes. A fine specimen for a focal point, it is upright, narrow, and tall. It may be difficult to find, but it is worth the effort. The blue-green needles are exceptionally pretty with silver undersides. 'Bruns Pendula' is a shorter but wider cultivar with a graceful weeping form and the same, unique needle coloration. There are several handsome dwarf cultivars available. In late summer, the cones appear with a deep purple-bronze coloration.

How to Plant & Grow—The Serbian spruce is drought tolerant once it settles in. Plant in well-drained soil in full sun.

Care & Problems—Spider mites may be problematic during hot, dry spells. Spray the tree down with a blast of water from the hose to knock them down or treat with a miticide. Follow all directions carefully.

Hardiness: Zones 4 to 8

Color(s): Silver

Mature Size (H x W): 30 to 35 ft. x 8 to 10 ft.

Water Needs: Low

WESTERN WHITE PINE

Pinus monticola

☼ ☽

Why It's Special—The weeping form of our native western white pine, *Pinus monticola* 'Pendula', is an elegant, graceful specimen tree for any landscape. Its long green needles, in clusters of five, drape over the twisting branches of this majestic evergreen. Handsome long cones develop each season and add an interesting dimension to this beautiful conifer. The western white pine is the state tree of Idaho.

How to Plant & Grow—White pine should be planted in full to partial sun, afternoon shade is a plus. This tree works especially well when sited near a rock wall where its graceful profile will be showcased. It performs best when planted below an altitude of 8,500 feet.

Care & Problems—Spider mites can be a nuisance during hot dry weather. Knock them off a tree with a sharp blast from the garden hose. Do not plant where reflected heat from a building or wall will cause undue stress on this northern beauty.

Hardiness: Zones 4 to 7

Peak Season: Evergreen

Mature Size (HxW): 8 to 20 ft. x 8 to 10 ft.

Water Needs: Moderate

DOUGLAS FIR

JANUARY

- This is a good time of year to develop a plan to replace any trees that aren't working in your landscape and to add new trees for shade and color.

- Check recently planted trees for proper staking. Adjust the supports accordingly.

- Water trees when the temperature is above freezing and the ground is not frozen.

- Study your leafless trees and make your pruning plans. What is dead? Broken? Crossed? Those will have to go.

FEBRUARY

- Remove any storm-damaged limbs or branches.

- Remove heavy, wet snow from loosely formed evergreens by gently brushing branches upward. Do not bat at them to knock the snow down.

- Do not pile snow around the trunks of your trees. Instead, spread it around, working from the drip line in.

MARCH

- If you have insect damage, apply dormant or horticultural oil to your trees when the daytime temperatures are above freezing, but below 70 degrees.

- Plant bare-root trees now, before they leaf out. This helps prevent transplant shock.

- Water trees as needed and build a basin around the base of the tree, a couple of feet in radius from the trunk outward. When you water, fill this basin and let the water soak in. The basin should be just high enough (3 to 6 inches) to hold the water. Do not build volcanoes of mulch up to the tree trunk.

APRIL

- Early in the month, before the buds break on the trees, you can still apply dormant oil spray to your trees.

- Prune unwanted "suckers" or "water sprouts" from the tree before they get any bigger.

- Celebrate Arbor Day by planting a tree.

- The selection of container-grown and balled-and-burlapped trees is good right now. Shop for the perfect new tree, and get it planted.

- Deeply water all the trees in your garden. Do this every two or three weeks. When you are doing this deep watering, it is a good time to apply an organic fertilizer as directed on the label.

MAY

- This month you can transplant evergreens in your garden.

- Continue planting container-grown trees.

- Fertilize trees that are showing signs of nutrient deficiency. The alkaline soils of the Rockies may cause trees to look chlorotic (yellowish). Talk to your local extension office for recommendations on treating this condition.

JUNE

- Refrain from planting new trees or transplanting existing trees from now until the end of the year. If you do plant, extra care is required.

- Remove stakes and supports from trees planted last year.

- Trees planted last year and this year will need up to 2 inches of water per week.

- Organic mulch will reduce watering needs, so replenish as needed.

- Prune any errant or broken branches.

JULY

- At this time of the year, many trees drop twigs, leaves, and bark—this is normal.

- Keep an eye out for insect pests. Hose them off with a sharp blast of water, or apply an insecticidal soap as per the manufacturer's instructions. If pests are truly problematic, consult a certified arborist in your area for assistance.

- Avoid planting and transplanting now due to hot, dry weather.

- Give those trees a nice big drink, allowing the water to soak in around the drip line.

AUGUST

- If certain trees aren't performing well, consider removing and replacing them with new trees well suited for your landscape. Do some serious research, as trees are important investments paying off in added property value and reduced cooling bills.

- You can still plant container-grown trees toward the end of the month.

SEPTEMBER

- Plan a compost pile for all the fallen leaves you will be gathering soon.

- Wrap young trees' trunks with hardware cloth for protection from small, chewing critters. Leave in place through the winter and possibly the next year.

- Install fencing to deter deer and elk from munching on your trees.

- Water requirements may lessen as the temperatures cool and natural precipitation increases, but monitor the moisture content of the soil around your trees.

- Do not prune unless you must remove dead or diseased branches.

OCTOBER

- Make a note of the fall colors in your landscape, and notice which colors your trees contribute to the palette. Do you need to add some more red for next year?

- You can still plant deciduous trees during the first part of October.

- Evergreens may shed needles this time of year. This is normal.

- Start raking and shredding the leaves from your garden. This is free, organic mulch.

NOVEMBER

- If you are planning to have a live Christmas tree this year and will be planting it later, dig the hole now and cover the soil pile with a tarp to keep it from freezing solid.

- Wrap loose-growing evergreens with twine to keep the branches together. This helps prevent breakage from heavy snow loads.

- Give all the trees in your landscape another good soaking.

DECEMBER

- Wax those skis and check your bindings. Ski season is just around the corner.

- Living Christmas trees should not be indoors for more than five days. Any longer and they will break dormancy, making them ill suited for planting out in the freezing temperatures. Move the tree back outside to a protected location, and be ready to plant as soon as the soil is workable.

- Inspect newly planted trees for proper support, staking and moisture.

COLORADO SPRUCE

VINES
for the Rocky Mountain States

Vines are opportunistic plants that extend their growth vertically using neighboring trees, shrubs, walls, or manmade supports to reach up towards the light. They provide vertical cover, shade, privacy, and landscape accent in a variety of colorful forms. Many vines have handsome foliage, beautiful flowers, and edible fruits, and their clinging, twining, or upright growth habits make a nice visual contrast with the other plants around them.

CONSIDERING VINES

Vines offer many choices. Some are annual (living for just one growing season), while others are perennial and will last a lifetime. Some are herbaceous with soft stems, and some are woody. Some are tender and may die back each winter, while some are rather aggressive and long-lived. Some vines are fast growing, and some are more restrained. Annual vines are a good way to start—you can experiment by adding certain colors and textures to the landscape without making a long-term commitment. Many are easy to grow from seed in the spring, such as morning glories, sweet peas, and moonflowers. At the end of the season, many of these annuals produce seed that will self-sow and germinate the nexg spring, if conditions are right. Annual vines produce the largest leaves and bear more flowers when planted in full sun.

Perennial vines reward you with flowers, interesting foliage, and often, ornamental stems and bark for winter interest. Once established, vines do not like to be disturbed, so select your perennial vines thoughtfully and consider the best location for them to grow and prosper.

LET'S DO THE TWIST

Vines vary in the way they climb. Clematis vines use tendrils, or leaf-like appendages, that grow out from the stems and wrap themselves around some kind of support. Several vines, including Boston ivy, Virginia creeper, and trumpet vine, have non-coiling, clinging tendrils with a different mechanism—an adherent pad. Like a super-strength adhesive, their stems bond to a rough surface or support structure.

PORCELAIN VINE

Other vines, such as English ivy and climbing hydrangea, have aerial rootlets called holdfasts that cement themselves to walls, trees, or other objects in their path as the vines grow. Most vines climb by twining themselves around a structure. In the wild, they use a tree for climbing; in your landscape, it could be a post, a pillar, a downspout, or a dead tree. The vine will start to twine when it touches an object, producing growth faster on one side of the vine than the other. This causes the vine to twist as it grows, so it continues to bend round and round the object. Just as people are right- or left-handed, so are twining vines. They twist around the support either clockwise (to the right) or counterclockwise (to the left). This growth habit is easy to see when you observe a honeysuckle, which grows clockwise, and bittersweet, which grows counterclockwise. It helps to know this so that when a vine starts to grow, you won't inadvertently twist it in the wrong direction. Instead, let nature take its course.

HOW TO GROW A HAPPY VINE

If you want vines to establish more rapidly, heavy clay or sandy soils should be amended with organic matter. You may add one-third volume of compost or well-rotted manure to the soil removed from the planting hole. These organic amendments will improve soil structure and drainage. Dig the

HYACINTH BEAN

WISTERIA

planting hole as deep as the rootball and two to three times as wide. Drive a stake into the planting hole before setting the vine in the hole. This will prevent damage to the developing roots later. Loosen the rootball, and gently untangle the longest roots so they can be spread into the hole. Position the vine in the hole so that the crown will be planted at the same level it was in the container. Fill in the planting hole with the prepared backfill soil; gently firm the soil around the plant, and water in thoroughly to eliminate any air pockets. Tie the stems loosely to the stake using soft twine or plastic-coated wire.

Most vines need an object to climb or twine on, and matching the vine to the support is one of the secrets for success. A twining vine will not grow up a brick wall, and you can't expect ivy to climb a wire. Vines can be trained on arbors, trellises, pergolas, gazebos, fence posts, lattices, and trees. Clematis are often at their best when climbing through trees and shrubs. Some vines can be left to grow as a ground cover to hold the soil,

and they are attractive when cascading over stones and embankments. Vines can dress up chain-link fences, and annual vines can be easily trained and grown on twine or string.

AN IMPORTANT RULE

The vines covered in this chapter represent some of our favorites and include some of the best, tried-and-true vines for the Rockies, but they are by no means an exhaustive list. Most are hardy throughout our area; it is helpful, however, to provide some protection to newly planted vines by applying a winter mulch in late November or early December. Evergreen boughs, shredded cedar mulch, or coarse compost at the base of the vines will help protect the roots and crown from heaving. *Gardening with an Altitude Tip:* Be sure to water vines periodically in the absence of rain or snow. During a dry fall and winter, water monthly as long as the soil remains unfrozen and will accept moisture, and when temperatures are above freezing.

CHOCOLATE VINE
Akebia quinata

☀ ☀

Why It's Special—Chocolate vine's blossoms do indeed smell like chocolate! The interesting "split" blossoms droop in clusters of three to five. They are often difficult to see under the abundant blue-green foliage. It is deciduous, but one of the first plants to awaken in the spring. Occasionally, it produces 4-inch long, sausage-like fruit. 'Alba' is the white variety, while 'Purple Bouquet'™ is more compact. 'Purple Rose' has pink flowers. *Akebia* is also called five-leaf akebia or monkey vine.

How to Plant & Grow—Plant in the spring. The sunniest locations suit chocolate vine, but this vine also does just fine in some shade. It may grow 25 feet in a season, and can be used as a ground cover. It's not fussy about soil or water.

Care & Problems—Prune hard and as needed to keep the vine manageable and to your liking.

Hardiness: Zones 4 to 10

Peak Season/Color(s): Early summer; purple or rose-brown blossoms and blue-green leaves

Mature Size (H x W): 15 to 30 ft. x as permitted

Water Needs: Low

CLEMATIS
Clematis spp.

☀ ☀

Why It's Special—Clematis produces exquisite blooms on vigorous, fast-growing vines. *Clematis* × *jackmanii* is extremely popular, with its rich purple blossoms. Sweet autumn clematis (*C. terniflora*) produces clusters of small, sweet-smelling, white flowers. It really loves to ramble.

How to Plant & Grow—Clematis vines usually require two seasons before blooming. Mulching the base of the plant is essential to maintain cool moist roots. An east- or northeast-facing site is ideal. When planting vines, bury the roots and the first 6 inches of the vine. This will force the clematis to send out additional roots as anchors. If you don't know which type you planted, ask for help identifying the variety before pruning.

Care & Problems—Pruning methods are tricky and vary by type: A, B, and C. Check the information tag that came with your plant to determine which type you have and the proper pruning technique. Plant clematis where they can have their feet in the shade and their faces in the sun.

Hardiness: Zones 4 to 8

Peak Season/Color(s): June to frost, varies by type; red, white, blue, pink, plum, purple, and bicolor blossoms

Mature Size (H x W): 15 to 20 ft. x as permitted

Water Needs: Moderate

CLIMBING HONEYSUCKLE
Lonicera spp.

☀ ☀

Why It's Special—Hardy and vigorous, honeysuckle vines thrive with a minimum of care. Tubular flowers of red, orange, coral, yellow, and white release a sweet fragrance. 'Halliana' (Japanese honeysuckle), known as Hall's, is a favorite, dependable variety. Goldflame honeysuckle (*Lonicera* × *heckrottii*) has blue-green foliage and red buds opening to blossoms with yellow corollas and pink outer petals. 'Kintzley's Ghost'™ is a Plant Select™ pick.

How to Plant & Grow—Plant from spring through fall. Bare-root plants transplant easily in early spring. Choose a site with full sun to partial shade.

Care & Problems—Prune when the blooms fade. Prune back growth in the spring to maintain desired shape; thin out the oldest stems to ground level to encourage new growth from the crown. Aphids may invade some varieties; control them with homemade soap sprays or by hosing them off the plant.

Hardiness: Zones 3 to 8

Peak Season/Color(s): Late spring to frost; red, pink, scarlet, orange, white, and yellow blossoms

Mature Size (H x W): 15 to 20 ft. x as permitted

Water Needs: Low

CLIMBING HYDRANGEA

Hydrangea anomala var. petiolaris

☀

Why It's Special—Climbing hydrangea is an excellent vine for north and northeast walls. A true clinging vine, it cements itself to just about any structure by aerial rootlets called holdfasts. As it matures, the vine requires a strong support for its weight and to keep it somewhat tamed. Faintly scented, lacy, flat, white flower clusters appear among the dark green, serrated leaves in June and July. Peeling, reddish brown bark adds winter interest. Though this vine is somewhat slow to get started, it is worth the effort.

How to Plant & Grow—Climbing hydrangea prefers partial shade with a rich, moist, well-drained, slightly acidic soil.

Care & Problems—Prune regularly in the spring to keep the vine shapely and within bounds. Older, neglected hydrangea vines tend to lose their vigor and produce few flowers. This vine is generally not bothered by pests or diseases.

Hardiness: Zones 4 to 8

Peak Season/Color(s): Summer; white blossoms, dark-green leaves, and reddish brown bark

Mature Size (H x W): 15 to 20 ft. x as permitted

Water Needs: Moderate

HYACINTH BEAN

Dolichos lablab

☀

Why It's Special—Hyacinth bean, an annual vine, has pretty purple stems, a purple cast to the leaves, and velvety purple bean pods. A fast grower, it is lovely on arbors, along wooden fences, and when grown for shade on trellises near a patio. It looks great when allowed to grow and twine through other upright plants in the garden. It's also known as Egyptian bean, Indian bean, or lablab. Do not eat the beans.

How to Plant & Grow—Sow hyacinth bean seeds outside in the soil after your last frost date. Before sowing, soak seeds in water for 24 hours. Plant water-soaked seeds 1 inch deep and 6 inches apart. Plant as close as possible to the support structure you will be using. They may take two to three weeks to germinate. Hyacinth bean prefers full sun.

Care & Problems—Somewhat drought tolerant, hyacinth beans appreciate well-drained soil.

Hardiness: Annual

Peak Season/Color(s): Early summer; purple or rose-brown

Mature Size (H x W): 15 to 30 ft. x as permitted

Water Needs: Low

MOONFLOWER

Impomea alba

☀

Why It's Special—Moonflower unfurls its exotic, ghostly white blooms early in the evening. It has a delightful, intoxicating fragrance. The leaves are heart shaped. This romantic glory of the night dates back to the 1700s and is considered a must-have for cottage and white night gardens. It is perfect when planted with 'Heavenly Blue' morning glory or one of the other heirloom favorites. Since they bloom at different times of day, they put on quite a show. Moonflower is an annual; it will begin blooming about sixteen weeks from seeding and will continue until the first hard frost.

How to Plant & Grow—Sow outside in the soil after your last frost date. Soak seeds in water for 24 hours before planting. Plant one-quarter to one-half inch deep and 1 foot apart in amended, well-drained garden soil, near the support it will climb. Locate in a sunny spot.

Care & Problems—Moonflower is poisonous.

Hardiness: Annual

Peak Season/Color(s): Mid- to late summer; white blossoms

Mature Size (H x W): 20 ft. x as permitted

Water Needs: Low

MORNING GLORY
Impomea purpurea

☀

Why It's Special—Morning glories are right at home in the cottage or heirloom garden. A mainstay of pioneer gardens, they scramble up trellises and through other vining plants. Position them to wander through climbing or pillar roses, espaliered fruit trees, and clematis. 'Heavenly Blue' is indeed heavenly with its ethereal ice-blue blossoms and their clear-white throats. Other recommended varieties: 'Grandpa Ott's', 'President Tyler', 'Scarlett O'Hara', 'Carnevale di Venezia', and 'Flying Saucers'.

How to Plant & Grow—Sow after your last frost date. Soak seeds in water for 24 hours before planting. Plant one-quarter to one-half inch deep and one foot apart in amended, well-drained soil near its intended support. Create a rustic trellis for a collection of heirloom morning glories by lashing together old twigs and branches. It needs full sun for the best display of flowers.

Care & Problems—Morning glories are easy to grow, which makes them a colorful choice for weekend gardeners.

Hardiness: Annual

Peak Season/Color(s): Mid- to late summer; white, blue, pink, red, and bicolor blossoms

Mature Size (H x W): 20 ft. x as permitted

Water Needs: Low

PORCELAIN VINE
Ampelopsis brevipedunculata

☀ ☀

Why It's Special—Porcelain vine will extend 12 to 18 feet a year. 'Elegans' has visually striking, turquoise berries. Its leaves are splashed creamy white and tinged pink. Porcelain vine is deciduous, so whatever it covers in summer will be bare in winter.

How to Plant & Grow—Porcelain vine is easy to transplant from spring through early fall. For the most abundant and colorful fruit, plant this vine where it gets full sun or filtered shade. Be sure the soil is well drained, and provide a support for the vine to climb. If you plant near a tree or post, fasten chicken wire loosely around the support to help the vine's tendrils cling.

Care & Problems—Somewhat slow to establish, porcelain vine is long-lived and prolific. Prune as needed in spring to direct vine growth. Pests and diseases don't bother this vine.

Hardiness: Zones 4 to 8

Peak Season/Color(s): Late summer; green, splotchy white-and-pink leaves, and turquoise berries

Mature Size (H x W): 15 to 20 ft. x as permitted

Water Needs: Moderate

PURPLE ORNAMENTAL GRAPE
Vitis vinifera 'Purpurea'

☀ ☀

Why It's Special—Grown for its plum, burgundy, and purple foliage, ornamental grape is a garden showstopper. The foliage pairs well with pink, blue, or lime green perennial flowers or foliage. New growth emerges green, becomes bronze red during the summer and will have variations on a purple theme in the autumn. It may set small purple fruits, but the skins are tough and bitter, so plant it for its looks, not for eating.

How to Plant & Grow—Plant ornamental grape in the garden where it can be a focal point or a dramatic backdrop for other perennials. Provide strong supports for this rambler. Trim the wispy new growth to keep it in check during the season. It likes our western soils. Make sure the soil is well drained, but it should be watered regularly and deeply. These vines would do well to have some afternoon shade in the hottest parts of the Rockies.

Care & Problems—Do any pruning in late winter or early spring to avoid "weeping" sap later in the growing season.

Hardiness: Zones 5 to 9

Peak Season/Color(s): From late spring to the first hard frost; leaves of red to purple

Mature Size (H x W): 20 to 30 ft. x as permitted

Water Needs: Moderate

SWEET AUTUMN CLEMATIS

Clematis terniflora

Why It's Special—When most of the garden has started to wind down, this stunning clematis puts on the show of shows. Commonly called "virgin's bower," sweet autumn clematis is covered with masses of tiny, fragrant white blossoms. It will clamber 30 feet or more through apple trees or pergolas. It looks *spectacular* growing through evergreen shrubs. Another Latin name for it is *Clematis paniculata*.

How to Plant & Grow—Fast-growing sweet autumn clematis may cover an arbor or unsightly stump in its very first season. This vine will thrive in full sun if it gets consistent, moderate moisture. It also does well with afternoon sun.

Care & Problems—Sweet autumn clematis flowers on new growth, so cut this one back to just 12 inches in early spring. Feel free to clip it back throughout the season to maintain its size and shape. It is rarely bothered by pests or diseases.

Hardiness: Zones 4 to 9

Peak Season/Color(s): August until the first really hard frost; white

Mature Size (H x W): 15 to 20 ft. x as permitted to spread

Water Needs: Moderate

TRUMPET VINE

Campsis radicans

Why It's Special—Driving through the West, you may have seen these bright orange flowers and their lush, leafy vines scrambling up telephone poles. Trumpet vine's orange-scarlet, trumpet-shaped blossoms highlight the summer landscape at a time when other vines have finished flowering. The abundant flowers attract hummingbirds and sphinx moths. Its compound leaves are glossy green. 'Madame Galen' has salmon-red flowers.

How to Plant & Grow—Plant bare-root vines, root suckers, or container-grown vines in the spring in well-drained soil. The sunniest locations suit trumpet vine, which continues flowering into fall. Some afternoon shade is acceptable. Be sure to put vine supports in place before planting.

Care & Problems—Once established, trumpet vine is trouble free and hardy. Don't be afraid to prune—pruning is necessary to keep this vine a desirable size. It may die back over the winter, but will return the next season.

Hardiness: Zones 4 to 8

Peak Season/Color(s): Midsummer; orange, scarlet, or salmon-red flowers

Mature Size (H x W): 15 to 20 ft. x as permitted

Water Needs: Low

WISTERIA

Wisteria spp.

Why It's Special—In full bloom, wisteria is glorious with its foot long racemes (flower clusters) dripping lilac, fragrant, pea-like blossoms. Chinese and Japanese cultivars are common, but native wisteria cultivars are now available. 'Blue Moon' is a repeat bloomer, and 'Amethyst Falls' is a shorter variety for small gardens and container gardens.

How to Plant & Grow—When purchasing a new plant, it's best to purchase a plant *in bloom* from a reputable nursery. Plant in the spring in well amended soil with good drainage. Provide a substantial support in the beginning. Wisteria loves a bit of late afternoon shade but it is not mandatory.

Care & Problems—Wisteria is easy to grow, but needs careful, regular pruning to direct its energy toward the blossoms and to keep it from overtaking the house. Prune in late winter and again in the middle of summer to remove excess tendrils and foliage. If your wisteria has failed to bloom, apply a triple-phosphate fertilizer according to the label directions.

Hardiness: Zones 4 to 9

Peak Season/Color(s): April through June; white, lavender, and pink blossoms

Mature Size (H x W): 20 ft. x as permitted

Water Needs: Low

CHOCOLATE VINE

JANUARY

- Take your time and go through the gardening catalogs; read up on vines and determine how you could add one or two—or a few—more. Is there room on that arbor for a new clematis?

- Most vines are just fine in the winter. Cut back branches or tendrils that whip in the winter wind.

- Order your seeds for annual vines. It's still too early to plant them, but you want to be ready.

FEBRUARY

- Do a little homework. Get out your calendar and mark the last average frost date for your area, then count backwards through the weeks to determine when you should be starting the annual vines indoors. You don't want to start them too early.

- When you are inspecting the garden for adequate moisture, check the vines too. Water if needed.

- Order bare-root vines and specify delivery in March.

- Grapevines can be pruned now. Save the prunings for wreath-making projects.

MARCH

- Those bare-root vines you just ordered? They will show up any day and can be planted anytime you can work the soil.

- In late March, prune back your 'Jackmanii' clematis and any others that bloom on new wood. If you don't know what variety of clematis you have, ask for help in identifying it.

- Do not prune the spring-blooming clematis varieties that bloom on last year's wood. Those can be pruned in July.

- Stake out some new planting spots for new vines. In your garden journal, work out some great new combinations. How about a sweet autumn clematis in an apple tree? Or a purple clematis climbing through a blue atlas cedar? Do you have climbing or rambling roses? Clematis are perfect companions for them.

- Vertical gardening is very popular. Did you start those annual vine seeds?

APRIL

- Use vines to break the monotony of a wooden fence or to screen and improve the view of a chain-link fence.

- Repair, paint, and add arbors, pergolas, and trellises. They need to be sturdy, well grounded, and have no loose bits flopping in the breeze.

- Now is an excellent time to shop for vines at the garden store. Pick some nice ones, take them home, and get them in the ground!

- Buds will begin to expand and leaves to emerge on clematis, honeysuckle, Virginia creeper, and trumpet vine. To stimulate more growth, cut them back by 30 to 50 percent. For wisteria, cut back excess growth, being careful to leave the new flower buds to bloom next month.

MAY

- Check trellises and other supports to make sure they are securely fastened to a wall or post. Vigorous vines are heavy. Ensure adequate air circulation behind trellises and screens so vines won't bake in the sun. They should be positioned 12 to 18 inches from a solid wall.

- Vincas, ivies, Virginia creepers, and trumpet vines are taking off right now. Prune unruly shoots and branches and redirect the growth where you want it. These vines can be pruned aggressively to keep them in check.

JUNE

- Go into the garden armed with twist ties, old panty hose, and other tie back devices. Old panty hose (who wears those anyway?) make terrific tiebacks for vines. They can be cut in strips, and when used to tie up heavy branches, they still have enough give and will not girdle the bark on the plant.

- There is still time to plant new vines!

- Look for exquisite tropical vines at the nursery: bougainvillea, mandevilla, angel's trumpet, black-eyed Susan vine, jasmines. They can go outside now. Put them in a sheltered location at first and slowly move them into their summer positions on the patio.

JULY

- When the wisteria has finished blooming, prune the excess growth back right away before the buds for next year start to develop. Do this by mid-July.

- The hummingbirds will have found the vines full of nectar. Take some time to sit and watch them zip from one flower to the next. Did you know hummingbirds have the ability to remember how long it takes for a flower to refill with nectar?

- Large, flowering clematis can be pruned now. Check your garden journal notes so you know which clematis belongs to which pruning group. You can prune it 30 to 50 percent.

- Climbing hydrangeas should be pruned so new growth is no more than 12 inches from the main stem. This prevents it from becoming top-heavy and breaking.

AUGUST

- Spider mites target stressed plants including vines. Hold a piece of white paper under a leaf, and shake the leaf. If there are tiny, red dots scurrying across the paper, your vines have spider mites. Hose them off.

- Check on your Boston ivy, English ivy, and Virginia creeper. Snip them back to where you want them. Prune out dead leaves, and keep the plants clean. Good air circulation is important.

SEPTEMBER

- Mid-month, bring in the tender, annual vines that "summered" out of doors. Hose them down well before you bring them in and check them over for signs of spider mites and other insects. If those bad bugs come inside, you may have to resort to using an insecticidal soap.

- After the first hard frost, remove the tattered and blackened annual vines from the garden. Don't prune perennial vines unless you are removing dead or damaged branches.

OCTOBER

- Virginia creeper is a sensational vine for autumn. The leaves turn hot pink and scarlet, and the vines should be allowed to ramble through flowerbeds and over walls. It often shows up uninvited from a seed dropped casually by a bird or rodent. You can purchase plants or ask for a start from a friend who has more than one.

- Cut pieces of ivy for your fall decorations. Run several long vines down the dining room table. Add an ornamental gourd here and there. Voila! Instant fall.

NOVEMBER

- Secure the stems of established vines before winter sets in. This will prevent them from suffering winter storm damage.

- Make sure the vines get one more deep watering before the ground freezes.

DECEMBER

- Wax the skis.

- Ask for or give a gift certificate to the garden center of your choice. You can buy vines in the spring.

- Using some of your grapevine prunings from last February, deck those halls!

PURPLE ORNAMENTAL GRAPE

MORE GREAT PLANT OPTIONS
for the Rocky Mountain States

INTRODUCTION

There are hundreds of wonderful plants for your garden and no way to share them all with you in a single volume. We profiled almost 300 plants that do really well in our area, but left many more on the cutting room floor.

In this section, we've added a few more terrific plants we just can't live without. You'll find lists of annuals for specific uses, a few more grasses, an homage to the pretty penstemon, perennial lists, lesser known trees, vines, and information on plants that attract pollinators.

Some of you will want to try them all. And you should. Inquiring minds want to know! Ask your neighbor what they love to grow and why. Take a free class on perennials at your local garden center and nursery. Take a master gardener class to boost your skills. Gardening can be a lifelong love affair with the world of chlorophyll and photosynthesis. Don't hesitate to mix it up, try it out, and watch the garden grow.

LAVENDER WITH EUPHORBIA

ANNUALS

WITH COLORFUL FOLIAGE
- Alternantha (*Alternantha* cultivars)
- Beefsteak plant (*Acalypha wilkesiana*)
- Burning bush (*Bassia scoparia forma trichophylla*)
- Coleus (*Solenostemon* x *hybridus*)
- Coppertone mallow (*Hibiscus acetosella*)
- Dusty miller (*Senecio cineraria*)
- Jacob's coat (*Acalypha wilksiana*)
- Joseph's coat (*Amaranthus tricolor*)
- New Guinea impatiens (*Impatiens hawkeri* hybrids)
- Polka dot plant (*Hypoestes phyllostacha*)
- Snow on the mountain (*Euphorbia marginata*)
- Variegated impatiens (*Impatiens walleriana* varieties)
- Variegated zonal geranium (*Pelargonium* 'Ben Franklin', 'Vancouver Centennial')

WITH OUTSTANDING FRAGRANCE
- Four o'clocks (*Mirabilis jalapa*)
- Evening stock (*Matthiola triscupidata*, *M. bicornis* 'Starlight Sensation')
- Flowering tobacco (*Nicotiana sylvestris*)
- Heliotrope (*Heliotropium arborscens*)
- Large white petunia (*Petunia axillaris*, P.F2 hybrids)
- Mignonette (*Reseda odorata*)
- Moonflower (*Ipomea alba*)

- Nicotiana hybrids (*Nicotiana* x *sanderae*)
- Sweet alyssum (*Lobularia maritima* 'Sweet White')
- Sweet pea (*Lathyrus odoratus* 'Cupani', 'Old Spice', 'Old Fashioned Scented Mixed')

EASY TO GROW FROM SEED
- Bachelor buttons (*Centaurea cyanus*)
- Calendula or pot marigold (*Calendula officinalis*)
- California poppy (*Eschscholzia californica*)
- Cosmos (*Cosmos pinnatus*)
- Flowering tobacco (*Nicotiana sylvestris* and spp.)
- Four o'clocks (*Mirabilis jalapa*)
- Larkspur (*Consolida ambigua*)
- Love lies bleeding (*Amaranth*)
- Marigold (*Tagetes*)
- Morning glory (*Ipomoea tricolor* and spp.)
- Nasturtium (*Tropaeoleum majus*)
- Love in a mist (*Nigella damascena*)
- Snapdragon (*Antirrhinum majus*)
- Spider flower (*Cleome*)
- Sunflower (*Helianthus annuus*)
- Zinnia (*Zinnia* spp.)

GOOD FOR HANGING BASKETS AND CONTAINERS
- Bacopa (*Sutera cordata*)
- Bidens (*Bidens feulifolia*)
- Black-eyed Susan vine (*Thunbergia alata*)
- Cuphea (*Cuphea llavea*)
- Fan flower (*Scaveola*)
- Ivy geranium (*Pelargonium*)
- Lantana (*Lantana camara*)
- Licorice plant (*Helichrysum petiolare*)
- Lobelia (*Lobelia erinus*)
- Million bells (*Callibrachoa* spp.)
- Moss rose (*Portulaca*)
- Nasturtium (*Tropaeoleum majus*)
- Parrot beak vine or lotus vine (*Lotus berthelotti*)
- Silver falls (*Dicondra argentea*)
- Sweet potato vine (*Ipomoea batatas*)
- Verbena (*Verbena* hybrids)
- Wave petunia (*Petunia* spp.)
- Zinnia (trailing) (*Zinnia angustifolia*)

CLEOME

MORE GRASSES FOR THE INTERMOUNTAIN WEST

ORNAMENTAL GRASS WITH RHUS 'TIGER EYE'

Ornamental grasses have so much going for them, it is no wonder they have taken the gardening world by storm. Their single best attribute—in many a gardener's mind—is their minimal maintenance. Give them a haircut in the early spring, and every 5 years divide and share the clump. Maiden grasses, *Panicum* species, *Pennisetum* species—all shine in Western gardens.

So many of the grasses are winners, it's easier to point out the ones that aren't as well behaved as some. Lyme grass, northern sea oats, ribbon grass, and bloodgrass are all very invasive if planted in the right place. Use them with great care and consider yourself warned. Note, too, annual purple fountain grass is just that, an annual, and it won't survive our winters here although you sometimes find it sold as a perennial.

Western gardeners are getting really savvy to the usefulness and beauty of native grasses as ornamentals. You may have to look a little harder to find these beauties, but they are worth it.

Indian rice grass, *Achnatherum hymenoides* 'Nezpar', was used as a food source by Native Americans. While it does not like clay soils, it is otherwise well suited for cold hardiness in the Intermountain West. It has beautiful lacy seed heads. Zones 3 to 8.

Prairie dropseed, *Sporobulus heterolepsis*, is native to the American prairies. It needs a little more water than some of the drought tolerant varieties, but the warm golden orange fall color and airy seed heads make it a keeper. Zones 3 to 8.

Angel hair dwarf clumping fescue, *Festuca tenuifolia* 'Angel Hair', is a smallish ornamental grass, just 10 inches tall and 6 inches wide. It is evergreen with airy little seed heads that float above the grass blades and stems. It's nice in smaller suburban settings, and it can be used in groupings to add texture and movement. Zones 4 to 8.

PENSTEMON

PENSTEMON: A PERFECT PERENNIAL

There are so many perennials that work well in our gardens in the Rocky Mountain region it is foolhardy to single out one particular family. But, the penstemons truly stand out. They work well in firewise plantings, waterwise and xeric gardens, rock gardens, and any perennial border. More than 250 different penstemons have been identified. They even have their own society, The American Penstemon Society. Find them on the Web at www.apsdev.org and at their Facebook page! Some great ones, with their colors, are noted.

- *Penstemon angustifolius* broad-beard beardtongue, narrowleaf penstemon: sky-lavender blue
- *Penstemon arenarius*, sand dune penstemon: pale pink
- *Penstemon attenuatus*, sulphur penstemon: blue, purple, yellow, white
- *Penstemon barbatus*, golden-beard penstemon, beardlip penstemon: soft pink or red
- *Penstemon caespitosus*, mat penstemon: pale blue
- *Penstemon concinnus*, Keck Tunnel Springs beardtongue, Tunnel Springs penstemon: scarlet
- *Penstemon davidsonii*, Greene Davidson's penstemon, timberline penstemon: soft pink-violet
- *Penstemon davidsonii* var. *praeteritus*, Steens Mountain penstemon: soft pink-violet
- *Penstemon eatonii*, Eaton's penstemon: hot red
- *Penstemon fruticosus*, Greene bush penstemon: blue-purple

- *Penstemon parryi*, Parry penstemon, Parry's beardtongue: red and pink
- *Penstemon pinifolius*, pineneedle beardtongue: red or yellow
- *Penstemon pseudospectabilis*, desert penstemon: coral
- *Penstemon richardsonii*, cutleaf beardtongue: pink
- *Penstemon rydbergii*, meadow beardtongue, Rydberg's penstemon: blues
- *Penstemon spectabilis*, showy penstemon: lavender
- *Penstemon strictus*, Rocky Mountain beardtongue, Rocky Mountain penstemon: blues to purples
- *Penstemon superbus*, Superb beardtongue: vivid coral
- *Penstemon triflorus*, Heller's beardtongue: rich rose
- *Penstemon triphyllus*, Riggin's penstemon: pale pink
- *Penstemon tubiflorus*, White wand beardtongue: white
- *Penstemon uintahensis*, Uinta Mountain beardtongue: blue-violet
- *Penstemon unilateralis*, oneside penstemon: pink
- *Penstemon utahensis*, Utah penstemon: hot red or pink
- *Penstemon venustus*, Venus penstemon: purple
- *Penstemon virens*, Front Range beardtongue: soft blue
- *Penstemon wrightii*, Wright's beardtongue: coral

PERENNIALS

FOR SMOKIN' HOT, DRY SITES

- Artemisia (*Artemisia* cultivars)
- Basket of gold (*Aurinia saxatalis*)
- Beard tongue (*Penstemon* cultivars)
- Blanket flower (*Gaillardia x grandiflora* and cultivars)
- Blazing star (*Liatris* spp.)
- Butterfly weed (*Asclepias tuberosa*)
- Catmint (*Nepeta* spp. and hybrids)
- Chocolate flower (*Berlanderia lyrata*)
- Coreopsis (*Coreopsis* spp. and hybrids)
- Creeping hummingbird plant (*Zauschneria garrettii*)
- Evening primrose (*Oenothera macrocarpa* and spp.)
- German bearded iris (*Iris germanica*)
- Hollyhock (*Alcea rosea*)
- Hummingbird mint (*Agastache* spp.)
- Lambs ears (*Stachys byzantine*)
- Lewis's flax (*Linum perenne* or *Linum lewisii*)
- Maximilian sunflower (*Helianthus maximilianii*)
- Orange globemallow (*Sphaeralcea* spp.)
- Perennial salvia (*Salvia x superba* spp.)
- Purple coneflower (*Echinacea purpurea* and cultivars)
- Russian sage (*Perovskia atripicifolia*)

BLACK-EYED SUSAN

- Sulfur flower (*Eriogonum umbellatum* and spp.)
- Winecups (*Callirhoe involucrata*)
- Yarrow (*Achillea* spp. and cultivars)
- Yucca (*Yucca* spp.)

FOR A SHADY AND NOT SO DRY SPOT

- Bellflower (*Campanula* cultivars)
- Bleeding heart (*Dicentra spectabilis* and spp.)
- Columbine (*Aquilegia* and hybrids)
- Coral bells (*Heuchera* and hybrids)
- Ferns (*Athyrium, Osmunda*)
- Foxglove (*Digitalis* spp. and hybrids)
- Gentian (*Gentian fremontii*)
- Hosta (*Hosta* spp.)
- Lenten rose (*Helleborus orientalis* and cultivars)
- Lungwort (*Pulmonaria* and cultivars)
- Lupine (*Lupinus* spp. and hybrids)

TO ATTRACT POLLINATORS
(HUMMINGBIRDS, BUTTERFLIES, BIRDS, AND BEES)

- Aster
- Baptisia
- Bee balm
- Blanket flower
- Butterfly bush
- Butterfly weed
- Chives
- Coral bells
- Coreopsis (tickseed)
- Four o'clocks
- Glossy abelia
- Guara (whirling butterflies)
- Hardy hibiscus
- Hollyhock
- Hummingbird mint (*Agastache*)
- Hummingbird trumpet (*Zauschneria garretti*)
- Lavender
- Lupine
- Phlox
- Rose of Sharon
- Sage
- Sedum
- Shasta daisy

ROSES FOR THE ROCKY MOUNTAIN REGION

HYBRID TEA ROSES (CULTIVAR NAME, COLOR)

- Brigadoon, pink blend
- Dainty Bess, light pink
- Duet, medium pink
- Garden Party, white, near white, and white blend
- Legend, medium red
- Midas Touch, deep yellow
- Miss All American Beauty, deep pink
- Olympiad, medium red
- Peace, yellow blend
- Pristine, white, near white, and white blend
- Sheer Bliss, white, near white, and white blend
- Touch of Class, orange-pink and orange-pink blend
- Tribute, deep pink
- White Masterpiece, white, near white, and white blend
- Dolly Parton (HT), orange-red and orange-red blend
- Double Delight (HT), red blend
- Fragrant Cloud (HT), orange-red and orange-red blend
- Hansa (Hrg), medium red
- Mister Lincoln (HT), dark red
- Perfume Delight (HT), medium pink
- Pink Parfait (GR), pink blend
- The Prince (Shrub), dark red

POLYANTHAS (CULTIVAR NAME, COLOR)

- China Doll, medium pink
- Dick Koster, deep pink
- Margo Koster, orange and orange blend
- Mothersday, dark red
- The Fairy, light pink

GRANDIFLORAS (CULTIVAR NAME, COLOR)

- Gold Medal, medium yellow
- Love, red blend
- Olé, orange-red and orange-red blend
- Queen Elizabeth, medium pink
- Sonia, pink blend
- Tournament of Roses, medium pink

FLORIBUNDAS (CULTIVAR NAME, COLOR)

- Europeana, dark red
- Eyepaint, red blend
- French Lace, white, near white, and white blend
- Gene Boerner, medium pink
- Iceberg, white, near white, and white blend
- Nearly Wild, medium pink
- Purple Tiger, mauve and mauve blend
- Showbiz, medium red
- Simplicity, medium pink
- Singin' in the Rain, apricot and apricot blend
- Sunsprite, deep yellow

SHRUB ROSES (CULTIVAR NAME, COLOR)

- All That Jazz, orange-pink and orange-pink blend
- Ballerina, medium pink
- Bonica, medium pink
- Carefree Delight, pink blend
- Golden Wings, light yellow
- John Cabot, medium red
- Linda Campbell, medium red
- Morden Centennial, medium pink
- Oranges "n" Lemons, orange and orange blend
- William Baffin, deep pink

CLIMBING ROSES (CULTIVAR NAME, COLOR)

- America, orange-pink and orange-pink blend
- Blaze, medium red
- Golden Showers, medium yellow
- Jeanne Lajoie (Cl Min), medium pink
- Joseph's Coat, red blend
- New Dawn, light pink

MINIATURE ROSES (CULTIVAR NAME, COLOR)

- Acey Deucy, medium red
- Crazy Dottie, orange and orange blend
- Cupcake, medium pink
- Dee Bennett, orange and orange blend
- Light of Broadway, red blend
- Millie Walters, orange-pink and orange-pink blend
- Minnie Pearl, pink blend
- Party Girl, yellow blend
- Rainbow's End, yellow blend
- Simplex, white, near white, and white blend
- Snow Bride, white, near white, and white blend
- Starina, orange-red and orange-red blend
- Valerie Jeanne, deep pink

MORE CHOICE SHRUBS AND TREES FOR THE ROCKIES

Several very special native shrubs deserve a shout out for their usefulness in our gardens. Try to incorporate them into native, wildlife, drought-tolerant, and fire-wise plantings. They also add a nice dimension to any standard perennial border.

Serviceberry, *Alemanchier alnifolia*, is found in every state but Hawaii. George Washington grew these shrubs at Mt. Vernon. You may know it as shadblow, shadbush, or Juneberry. One of the finest for our region is the 'Saskatoon', which lent its name (via Cree Indians) to the city in Saskatchewan, Canada. The beautiful berries resemble blueberries and make delicious pies and jams. Their fall color is a brilliant yellow. They grow 10 to 20 feet tall and about 6 to 8 feet in diameter, and it's drought tolerant.

Netleaf hackberry, *Celtis reticulata*, is one tough plant. Tolerant of dry, windy conditions, it's capable of surviving range fires because of its long deep taproot. A slow, steady grower, the shrub is generally 20 to 30 feet tall (often much shorter) and 6 to 15 feet in diameter. Drought and tough living keep them on the short side. The bark of hackberry is curious, corky, and flanged. Native peoples used the drupes (fruits) as we would use pepper to flavor meat. Wildlife love these berries.

Snowbush or Buckbrush, *Ceanothus velutinus*, with its shiny deep green leaves, is a wonderful addition to the Intermountain West garden. It is one of the very few durable broadleaf

FRINGE TREE

evergreens that can take the heat, drought, and cold of our region. It grows about 3 to 10 feet in height and as wide. It is covered with sprays of very sweet flowers late spring to early summer. Snow cover is needed in the colder parts of the West to help it survive the winter. Zones 3 and 4 (with snow cover) to 7.

Golden Currant, *Ribes aureum*, makes a great native alternative to the spring forsythia. Its sulfur yellow, bright flowers sing to the bees; it sports rich green foliage throughout the growing season; and it has a very nice shape, easily trimmed to a hedge. The berries go from pale green to gold to orange and then to red (if there are any remaining after the birds work it over). These berries are delicious. One more great thing—the currant bush has striking fall foliage of hot pink to orange leaves.

Chinese Fringe Tree, *Chionanthus virginica*, is an American native shrub or small tree and is an absolute favorite of nurserymen, botanical garden staff, and people who love great plants. A Great Plant Pick™, in late spring it explodes with a frothy display of white panicles, six to eight inches long. The flowers give way to medium or dark green semi-glossy leaves and small dark blue drupes in the fall. If that isn't enough, it has handsome gray-brown bark patterns, a lovely open vase shape, and muted yellow autumn foliage. It's best for zones 4 to 9, and grows to 20 feet tall by 10 feet wide. It loves moist soil but it's fairly drought tolerant once it is well established.

Chinese Pistache, *Pistacia chinensis*, is not as widely known as it should be in our region. It can handle alkaline, acid, loamy, moist, droughty, and clay soils. It starts out kind of scrawny, but it develops over time into a beautiful shade tree, 25 to 35 feet tall and as wide. Heat is not an issue. The green blooms are not particularly showy, but occur in April and may develop into small orange-red nuts. Its seeds and flowers make it a valuable wildlife habitat tree.

HUMULUS

MORE GOOD VINES FOR THE INTERMOUNTAIN WEST

Cypress vine or cardinal creeper, *Ipomea quamoclit*, is a fast-growing annual vine covered with red, star-shaped blossoms over lacy, ferny foliage. It will grow 15 to 25 feet in one season.

Ornamental kiwi, *Actinidia kolomitka*, has unbelievable foliage colors. The medium green, heart-shaped leaves look as if they have been dipped in pink and white paint. It needs full sun (or some shade for best color in the hottest parts). Do not fertilize. It needs well-drained soil. If you are hoping for fruit, you will need both male and female plants. The fruits are pale green, and about 1 inch long. This is a good plant for a trellis and arbors, growing to 15 to 20 feet tall. It is a perennial.

Spanish flag, *Mini lobata*, also goes by the fantastic name "exotic love." It is exotic with beautiful sprays of crimson to yellow tubular flowers appearing at the same time. It is an annual,

growing 15 feet tall, blooming from summer until autumn. It requires full sun (or some shade in the hottest parts of the West), and give it rich, moist soil.

Black-eyed Susan vine, *Thunbergia alata*, has either bright yellow or deep orange blossoms with a very distinctive dark eye. It loves full sun, and does beautifully when trained up a mini-trellis in patio pots or left to cascade over window boxes or hanging baskets. It grows to 6 feet long.

Cup and saucer vine, *Cobea scandens*, is an heirloom showstopper. The blossoms begin creamy white or pale green and mature to purple, becoming somewhat striped white and purple. The blossoms are fragrant and will cover the plant from summer to fall. Give it full sun and adequate support, it is especially well suited be trellised behind purple eggplants. It lends itself equally well to white picket fences in cottage-type gardens.

MORE GARDENING TIPS & DESIGNS

for the Rocky Mountain States

ELEMENTS OF GOOD GARDEN DESIGN

Some folks garden to put food on the table, others are enamored with the beauty of the blossoms of perennials. Some folks are *totally* captivated by garden design. But a lot of us fall somewhere in-between. For those of you obsessed with design (you know who you are!), here are some tips on creating a well-designed garden.

THE ESSENTIAL ELEMENTS

There are six components to good garden design. If you follow these principles, I (Mary Ann) assure you that you will be pleased with the results. (And even if you're not, you can still change it later—most of the time. There are very few plants that cannot be moved, at least once in their life.)

FOCAL POINT

There should be a central design feature to define a garden's personality. It can be a sculpture, a specimen tree, a tastefully designed water feature, or an architectural element such as an arbor or pergola. Focal points are generally "on-axis" with major sight lines. In other words, it's the first thing you see or that you want other people to see as they enter the garden. You can create a focal point to view from inside your home too.

THEME

Does your garden have a particular style? Is it cottage, modern, prairie, woodland, mountain, tropical, country, or contemporary? Maybe it is plant driven with a focus on foliage, evergreens, perennial collections, or roses? Is the overall look and feel of the garden cohesive? Decide on a theme.

REPETITION

One of the best design tips is all about simplicity. Keep this mantra in mind, "Simplify and repeat;

HYDRANGEA

simplify and repeat." Less truly *is* more, especially when you use fewer *types* of plants, but *more* of each type. Swaths and masses are easy on the eye. Swaths of "one" are not acceptable. Singletons are best used in terms of specimen plants: one spectacular weeping white pine, an exceptional flowering shrub, or a single grand shade tree.

GOOD PLANTSMANSHIP

Are plants well situated and well spaced? Have plants been installed with healthy practices? Have you chosen the right plant for the right place? You can have the best design in the world but it will fall apart if you don't practice good plantsmanship.

COLOR

What is your color theme (scheme)? Consider these elements of color—are you using primary, secondary, or tertiary colors? Primary colors are red, yellow, and blue—they cannot be created from secondary colors. Secondary colors are orange, green, and violet, made by mixing the primary colors in different combinations. The tertiary colors are made by mixing primary and secondary colors to create

colors such as red-orange, red-violet, blue-green, and so forth. Are you drawn to monochromatic, similar, or high-contrast color combinations? Does color continue in the non-floral elements of your landscape such as artwork, architecture, bark, berries, or foliage? Pick a color palette you like.

SCALE AND PROPORTION

Does your garden reflect the architectural scale of your home? Are the landscape materials (wood, stone, concrete, and so forth) "respectful" of the home's original architecture? Do built elements hold their own in relationship to front porch, deck, or patio architecture? Proportion and scale are important.

A smattering of botanical curiosities do not make a well designed garden, nor are unusual plants required in order to have a well designed garden. Gardens should have limited ornamentation, because it's about the green stuff, not the ornaments.

Remember, first and foremost, gardening is a very personal undertaking and you should garden in a way that brings joy and happiness to you. So, go out there and create your own style!

A bronze urn planted with purple wave petunia, trailing verbena and bacopa

ALLIUM

BULBS LOOK BETTER WITH BUDDIES

You may not be thinking of partners for your bulbs, particularly when it's late autumn, and gardening has lost its luster for the season. But consider planting spring bulbs and tubers with a supporting cast for added color dimension and a smooth seasonal transition. Here are some tips:

- Camas bulbs and dog tooth violets bloom at precisely the same time. Their blue, yellow, and pink colors look great with lilacs.
- The earliest of early bulbs, the little dwarf iris can be a real show-off when planted next to hellebores and snowdrops.
- Sicilian honey lilies dip their pretty bells next to dark red peonies. The dark purple in the bells picks up the darker tones of the peony blossoms.
- Ladies mantle frothing under 'Purple Sensation' alliums is a gorgeous combination. Both look good for an extended period of time.
- White and yellow tulips (mid and late varieties) and daffodils, planted right next to basket of gold, gives a nice contrast in textures and heights. Add some wispy white windflowers if possible.
- Daffodils with blue glory-of-the-snow and grape hyacinths are a plant-it-and-forget-it combination that will return year after year.

- For a late, hot summer hurrah, elephant ears and cannas put on a tropical show.
- Consider planting the darker foliaged dahlias ('Bishop of Landaff') near a purple smoke bush or dark ninebark.
- The slender hardy gladiolas make a surprising textural statement popping out of creeping thyme or purple iceplant.
- Plant spring bulbs as close to perennial ornamental grasses as possible. Nice groupings of bulbs, not singletons or soldier lines, need very little water after they are done blooming. Grasses, once they are established, need very little water as well. The added bonus is that grasses fill out after spring bulbs have bloomed and do a terrific job of hiding the unsightly, but important, decaying foliage of the bulbs.
- Lilies—all kinds of lilies—do well in our region. They are at home tucked into borders (remember, some get as tall as 6 feet!) or equally happy in large patio pots. They must have good drainage and prefer a dry spell in late summer and autumn. Stake them for stability. Investigate the Martagon, Aurelian, Orientpet, Oriental, and trumpet types to expand your horizons.

"DELICIOUS" COMBOS OF EDIBLES AND ORNAMENTALS

Several years ago, I (Mary Ann) came across some brilliant container gardens. They were planted in the plainest of plain, jumbo black plastic pots, and yet they exuded magic for the entire gardening season. When I tracked down the designer and asked her how she did them, she told me, "I can't stop at one plant so I crammed them all into one big pot!"

She put in one tomato plant, a dill and maybe a basil, a couple of petunia plants, a black-eyed Susan vine, a couple of onion sets, and some snapdragons. And every other combination she could manage.

In that same vein, folks have taken to tucking their edibles in with their beloved ornamentals. I call this planting idea a bountiful, beautiful border. Here are some ideas:

- A dwarf apricot tree underplanted with strawberries and pansies.
- Sugar snap peas on a trellis with eggplants and leeks. As the snap peas fade in the heat, the eggplants will come on strong and will take up the space. Stick a couple of purple hyacinth beans in next to the peas for height. The purple bean blossoms and subsequent beans will look terrific with the eggplants "shrubs."
- Tomatoes *love* basil. They both need regular, deep watering. Basil does much better planted in this manner than with the other, drought-tolerant herbs.
- In a long narrow planter, or along a hot, sunny sidewalk or driveway, plant your tarragon, thyme, oregano, and pot marigolds (*Calendula*). These Mediterranean herbs will soak up the heat, plus, the herbs all like to be on the dry side as does the pot marigold. If they're grown without pesticides or herbicides, you can toss the petals of the flowers and some of the herbs' leaves into a salad for some real sparkle.
- Dill and fennel are hosts for insect pollinators. They also add an airy, ferny texture to the garden. Tuck them in among your shrubs and vegetables for added dimension, good eating, and potentially increased yield.
- To create an all silver-and-white evening garden, and one with fragrance, combine the following: 'Only the Lonely' nicotiana (an annual), silver-leaved artichokes, cooking sage, lavender, and annual moonflower vines.

But don't stop here—try different combinations on your own. It's quite fun! And you get to eat your "mistakes."

Geranium in a terra cotta planter

GROUND COVERS: LOOKING GOOD WHILE HARD AT WORK

PACHYSANDRA

Ground covers keep the soil cool, help retain moisture, and fend off weeds. Here are some ways to use them in good-looking combinations:

- Use 'Black Scallop' bugleweed under a red- or green-leaved Japanese maple. The clear blue flowers of the bugleweed will open the same time as the maple's new leaves emerge.
- Hardy 'Homestead Purple' verbena looks amazing with the hot pink or yellow iceplants. Adding Shasta daisies will cool it down a bit.
- Ladies mantle and hostas pair up nicely with completely different textures. The frothy blossoms of ladies mantle liven up the coolness of the hostas. Add some short yellow foxglove (*Digitalis lutea*) for a real treat.
- In a high mountain setting where aspens flourish, plant bearberry underneath them for a nice "carpet." Seed some columbine in as well.

- Lily of the valley is not only fragrant, but it looks fetching with the new dark purple and pink hellebores.
- Creeping thyme, in pink, makes a great welcome mat for blazing star (purple or white), and hummingbird mint in blue or pink.
- The short, creeping veronica with its tiny blue flowers will make small species tulips, especially *Tulipa clusiana*, shine.
- Pair dead nettle with yellow and blue varieties of columbine. Pair the pink-flowering nettle variety with pink columbine.
- Pachysandra, sweet woodruff, and bleeding heart make beautiful companions. For an all white look, use the white bleeding heart or 'Alba' variety with the white flowering sweet woodruff.
- The gorgeous leaves of Siberian bugloss 'Jack Frost' (*Brunnera*) will be pretty with a blue flowering bugle flower or foamflower.

MAKE THE MOST OF ORNAMENTAL GRASSES

Much attention is paid to the turf-type grasses, but the ornamental grasses have taken a starring role in the gardens of Rocky Mountain gardeners. There are several reasons for this. Here are a few reasons we love ornamental grasses.

- The single biggest advantage of ornamental grasses: You give them a haircut once a year. How easy is that?
- Most of them are fairly drought tolerant once they become established in the garden.
- They add the elements of texture, movement, and sound to a garden. Plus, when sited just right, a setting sun behind a mature grass seed head is a gorgeous thing to behold.
- In the winter, they add structure and texture to the garden, plus their seed heads are fancied by birds.
- They mimic the soft grasslands of our region.

FOUNTAIN GRASS

Some handsome planting combinations and ideas for using ornamental grasses are:

- Pair coneflowers, hardy hibiscus, rose of Sharon, and Russian sage with fountain grasses.
- Little bluestem turns a soft pinkish brown later in the growing season. This is nice with the bronze foliage of ninebarks or the dark elderberries.
- Japanese forest grass or the bright green carex varieties are good looking when juxtaposed with the bold leaves of oakleaf hydrangeas.
- Pink muhly grass was destined to be paired with the coneflowers.
- Create a bold, small-space garden with just these three plants: 'Karl Forester' feather reed grass, *Clematis tanguitica*, and a (yellow) Sunny Knock Out™ rose. Wow!
- Tuck bulbs next to ornamental grasses. As the grasses fill out in late spring, they conveniently hide the unsightly foliage of the spring bulbs.
- To soften the abrupt edge of a hardscape, say a patio or a driveway, large, varied plantings of grasses will do the trick. Try using them in clumps: one large silver maiden grass, three 'Karl Forester' feather reed grass, and seven 'Little Bunny' fountain grass. Repeat if needed.

PENNISETUM

GLOBEMALLOW

PERFECT PARTNERS FOR PERENNIALS

- *Artemesia* 'Powis Castle' or 'Valerie Finnis' with Rocky Mountain beardtongue
- German bearded iris (any cultivar) with snow in summer
- Creeping hummingbird trumpet with ganzania and Maximilian sunflower
- Bleeding heart with peonies, and dark purple or blue German bearded iris
- White or pink or red peonies with catmint
- Japanese anemones with autumn asters and 'Karl Foerster' grass
- Red hot poker with orange globe mallow and Mersea Yellow beardtongue
- 'Moonshine' or 'Coronation Gold' yarrow with *Yucca baccata*, especially 'Gold Sword'
- 'Paprika' yarrow with 'Chicago Apache' red daylily and firecracker penstemon

- *Sedum* 'Matrona' and 'White Swan' coneflowers, plus Russian sage
- Sulfur flower with 'Oranges and Lemons' Indian blanket flower and yellow ice plant
- Jupiter's beard planted side by side with 'Siskyou Pink' evening primrose and mockorange
- Yellow evening primrose with 'Burgundy' blanket flower and silver maiden grasses

FRAGRANT PERENNIALS

- Lavender
- German bearded iris (generally the dark blue-purple and yellow)
- Catmint
- Peonies (check the cultivars to make sure)
- Bee balm
- Cottage pinks (heirloom varieties have a strong clove scent)

SHRUB COMBINATIONS THAT SHINE

For many of us, our gardens have gotten smaller and for several reasons: we have smaller suburban lots, we are downsizing, and we want to spend less time on maintenance and more time enjoying the scenery. We want our landscapes to work smarter so we don't have to work harder. Creating long-blooming, colorful combinations with shrubs, especially flowering shrubs, is a smart way to deal with smaller spaces. Here are some design options.

Mockorange, with its heady jasmine-like fragrance, blooms at the same time as the beautiful sky blue Lewis's flax. Catmint and rich yellow tickseed (*Coreopsis*) would add another dimension.

AMERICAN PLUM

American plum, with its rich burgundy foliage, is wonderful paired up with the briefly blooming but amazing old man's whiskers, or *Geum trifolum*.

Kerria, or the yellow Japanese rose shrub, likes a little afternoon shade, and really shines next to bluish toned or bright lime green hostas. A variegated Japanese forest grass adds another layer to the look.

Glossy abelia, especially the new 'Kaleidoscope', echoes the colors of the hot new coneflowers. Look for cultivars 'Harvest Moon', 'Hot Papaya', and others.

Ninebarks, particularly the bronze-foliaged varieties 'Summerwine' and 'Diabolo', make a great backdrop for the single red or double red Knock Out™ roses or the rich pink rugosas.

Use silver buffaloberry as a backdrop for Rocky Mountain penstemon for a silver and blue look. Snow in summer would be a nice addition to this grouping. To change it up a bit, grow buffaloberry with the charming sulfur buckwheat and a midsized perennial like 'Oranges and Lemons' blanket flower.

Fineline buckthorn works really well in a container. Its finely cut foliage and upright stature adds some height to a patio planting. Tuck bright red annual geraniums around the base of the shrub. You will have the added benefit of the buckthorns pretty yellow autumn color well into October.

If blue is your favorite color, you can do an all blue combination. Start with blue mist spirea and pair it up with a large blue or blue and white rose of Sharon. Underplant with hardy geranium 'Rozanne'.

The beautiful round leaves of a purple smokebush are accentuated when it is partnered with the dark purple seathrift or creeping pink thyme.

A design trick: to create successful shrub combinations, look at the color of the foliage as well as the color of the stems and the blossoms. *Sedum* 'Matrona' has a dark red stem that is picked up and echoed in the dark reddish purple of smokebush or the dark ninebarks. You get the idea.

FIREWISE LANDSCAPING

Wildfires are a part of life in the great American West. You can greatly reduce the risk of wildfires burning your home by practicing "firewise landscaping." This is the practice of creating a "defensible space" around your home and across your property, as much as 60 to 100 feet from the house. The Bureau of Land Management and municipal fire agencies have put together some guidelines and safety tips for homeowners.

CREATE ZONES OF DEFENSE

Zone 1, from the house outward, 30 or more feet

Use fire-resistant plants only (a list follows). These are primarily low-growing, fire-resistant plants, particularly ground covers and vines. Keep plants *and* the area near the house well maintained, removing "duff," or dead plant material. Keep grasses mowed and well irrigated. A gravel mulch is recommended and has several other benefits: it will reduce water loss, keep plant roots cool, and discourage weed growth. Break up the plantings near the house by incorporating hardscapes—stone patios and walkways—to minimize the ability of fire to run along continuous fuel sources. Be certain to clean out gutters and rake up leaves.

Zone 2, 30 to 60 feet from the house or farther

Reduce plant density. Use only low-growing and fire-resistant plants and shrubs. Keep tall grasses and shrubs well groomed. It is recommended they be spaced apart at a ratio of two times their height. For instance, a shrub that will reach 10 feet of height at maturity should be spaced 20 feet from its neighboring shrub.

Zone 3, 60 to 100 feet from the house

Thin and prune existing plants. Prune tree limbs 6 to 10 feet up the trunk of the tree and minimize overlapping branches between trees and shrubs.

FIRE RESISTANT PLANTS

All plants are flammable, but some plants are more fire resistant than others. They have high moisture content, are low growing, have high salt or soap content, and are non-resinous. They will generally have large leaves and green stems too.

In the following list, the plant groups are from the top to bottom, the most flammable to more fire resistant. Note that conifers and grasses are at the *top* of the list.

HARDY ICE PLANT

- Conifers (the least fire resistant)
- Grasses
- Shrubs
- Deciduous trees
- Perennials
- Annuals
- Vines
- Ground covers
- Succulents (the most fire resistant)

Note that fire resistant vines and ground covers are generally inexpensive and relatively easy to maintain. Vines can be trained on metal fences to create a "green fence" that may stop or at least slow down a wildfire.

FIRE-RESISTANT GROUND COVERS

- Ajuga — *Ajuga reptans*
- Basket of gold — *Aurinia saxatalis*
- Bearberry or kinnikinnick — *Arctostaphylos uva-ursi*
- Caucasica sage — *Artemisia caucasica*
- Creeping phlox — *Phlox subulata*
- Creeping thyme — *Thymus praecox*
- Giant flowered soapwort — *Saponaria x lempergii*
- Green mat penstemon — *Penstemon davidsonii*
- Groundcover rose — *Rosa* hybrids
- Hardy iceplant — *Delosperma* spp.
- Hardy plumbago — *Ceratostigma plumbaginoides*
- Hens and chicks — *Escheveria* spp.
- Hummelo lamb's ear — *Stachys monieri* 'Hummelo'
- Japanese pachysandra — *Pachysandra terminalis*
- Lamb's ear — *Stachys byzantina*
- Lily of the valley — *Convallaria majalis*
- Mat penstemon — *Penstemon caespitosus*
- Mother of thyme — *Thymus serphyllum*
- Poppy mallow — *Callirhoe involucrata*
- Pussytoes — *Antennaria* spp.
- Rock soapwort — *Saponaria ocymoides*
- Rockcress — *Arabis* spp.
- Silver-edged horehound — *Marrubium rotundifolium*
- Snow in summer — *Cerastium tomentosum*
- Turkish speedwell — *Veronica liwanensis*

FIRE-RESISTANT VINES

- Chocolate vine — *Akebia quinata*
- Clematis — *Clematis* spp.
- Climbing hydrangea — *Hydrangea anomala petiolaris*
- Dragon Lady crossvine — *Bignonia capreolata* 'Dragon Lady'
- Grapes — *Vitis* spp.
- Honeysuckle — *Lonicera* spp. and hybrids
- Hops vine — *Humulus lupulus*
- Kiwi vine — *Actinidia kolmikta*
- Matrimony vine* — *Lycium barbarum*
- Purple leaf grape — *Vitis vinifera*
- Silver lace vine* — *Polygonum aubertii*
- Sweet autumn clematis — *Clematis terniflora*
- Sweet pea — *Lathyrus latifolius*
- Trumpet honeysuckle — *Lonicera sempervirens*
- Trumpet vine — *Campsis radicans*
- Virginia creeper* — *Parthenocissus quinquefolia*
- Wisteria — *Wisteria* spp.

*Can be invasive

FIRE-RESISTANT SHRUBS AND TREES

- Aspen — *Populus tremuloides*
- Birch — *Betula* spp.
- Buckthorn — *Rhamnus* spp.
- Buffalo berry — *Sheperdia* spp.
- Currant — *Ribes* spp.
- Lilac — *Syringa vulgaris*
- Maple — *Acer* spp.
- Mountain mahogany — *Cercis ledifolius*
- Serviceberry — *Amelanchier* spp.
- Skunkbush sumac — *Rhus tribolata*
- Snowberry — *Symphoricarpos* spp.
- Western sandcherry — *Prunus basseyi*
- Willow — *Salix* spp.

Avoid sage, pine, and juniper, which are high in resins and volatile oils making them *extremely* flammable. Plants that are deciduous are preferable to conifers. Drought-tolerant plants have thick succulent leaves.

HIGH AND OH, SO DRY

DROUGHT-TOLERANT GARDENING FOR THE ROCKIES

One of the single biggest challenges facing gardeners in the Rocky Mountains is the looming prospect of persistent drought. Water is like gold in this parched area, with many years drier than others. Snowfall—should we be so lucky to have it—makes up 75 percent of our water supply. Changes in our climate and variances in our weather patterns, coupled with significant population increases, have put incredible strain on our water supply. While some areas of this geographic region experience no shortage of water, in most of America west of the 100th meridian, water is scarce and sacred.

WATER RESTRICTIONS: SIGN OF THE TIMES

Some cities and areas of the region have been under water restrictions and in extended drought conditions for *years*. Colorado has been dealing

NINEBARK

with the issue for decades. In the 1970s, Colorado developed and trademarked a program called Xeriscape™. It means dry, not *zero* water use. There are seven principals of xeriscaping that can help you better use the water you have available to you.

PRINCIPLES OF XERISCAPING

1. **Start with a good plan.** Take a long, hard look at how you will use your land. Plan accordingly. In areas where you are paying for treated, municipal water, you will, in fact, pay quite a lot for it. You can end up with a water bill of a couple hundred dollars a month.

2. **Install an efficient irrigation system.** One that is properly designed (for different zones) and well maintained is critical. Deliver the water to the *plants*, not to the sidewalks and the streets. The newest systems have moisture sensors that can adjust for rain and variances in temperatures.

3. **Use mulch and use it wisely.** A two- to three-inch layer of mulch will help retain the moisture in the soil and will cool a plant's roots, both reducing water needs. Keep mulch *away* from tree trunks and plant stems. This mulch will decompose, adding to the tilth and fertility of your soil. And that's a great thing.

4. **Improve your soil.** It is good to have a professional soil test. For about $40, you can have your soil tested at a reputable lab, through the County Agricultural Extension office or another qualified entity. They will recommend how much—if any—amendments your soil will need to support a vegetable and/or perennial garden. You want to create a soil comprised of at least 5 to 10 percent organic matter.

5. **Plant appropriate turf grasses.** Lawns, while beautiful, use in excess of 65 percent of the drinking water in most cities and towns. In the last few years, incredible improvements have been made in the turf grass industry.

(However, Kentucky blue grass is *not* suitable to our region. It is not the least bit drought or heat tolerant.) Check out the new rhizomatous fescue blends, and the newest development: Xerilawn™. If you don't feel the need to mow, figure out how to replace your turf area altogether. (Check zoning regulations first, though.) In the last few years, incredible improvements have been made in turf grass selections for home landscapes. Improved varieties of drought and heat tolerant bluegrass varieties allow us to grow and maintain a healthy and water conserving lawn.

6. **Use appropriate plant materials.** Select plants that are adapted to our region and those with a favorable history in your area. Don't get sentimental about rhododendrons, Hinoki cypress, or jasmine here. What worked in Seattle or San Francisco is not adapted for this climate. Study new introductions of adapted plants and cultivars of natives from Plant Select™, Utah's Choice™, and other horticultural groups. These organizations have greatly increased the number of pretty plants available to homeowners.

7. **Take good care of your landscape and garden.** Please, do not "set it and forget it" with the automated sprinkler systems. Seasonal clean-up, fresh mulch, and good pruning techniques will all contribute to a successful and beautiful garden.

BUT XERIC GARDENS ARE GRAY AND SPINEY AND ALL GRAVEL!

Not anymore, they're not. A lush, abundant garden is totally doable with waterwise plantings. Just because you live in an area with little rainfall does not mean that, as a gardener, the desert plant palette is all you have to work with.

The first and easiest way to move away from the gravelly, boney look is to go for color. Gardeners must exercise wild abandon with color when planting their gardens. Think tropical: hot pinks, purples, oranges, reds, and golds. Use bold colors for garden walls, garden art, and outdoor furniture. Look at firecracker penstemon, geranium 'Rozanne', roses, ninebarks, and elderberries in the plant palette. If

you use only a few of the gray-leaved, furry plants, you'll really show off the hot colors of other perennials and shrubs.

Next, plant in groupings of three or five, or plants of each variety, and plant as a "drift" for a cottage garden look. Waterwise/adapted/xeric plants can be used the same way traditional perennials can be used.

Add water. Don't provide more water to the plants, but installing a self-contained, recirculating water feature uses very little water, yet provides the cool, refreshing sound of water.

Waterwise gardens should be designed like well-executed Impressionist paintings. Think of a Monet: you know it's a water lily even if you can't clearly see the water lily form. You can give the impression of abundance and lushness without using the water typically required to create "abundant and lush."

And don't fertilize very often. Fertilizing encourages tender new growth, which is subject to drying and attractive to nuisance insects.

It is possible to have a colorful and beautiful garden and still be waterwise.

BUTTERFLY GARDENING

The Rocky Mountain region is an excellent place for viewing and attracting butterflies. The West's differing habitats and climates allow for a good variety of butterfly species. Besides being beautiful to watch, butterflies play a part in the food chain, and to a small extent, they pollinate flowers.

SOME GOOD CHOICES

To attract butterflies, you need plants on which their caterpillars can feed and flowers from which the adult butterflies can sip nectar. Find a sunny location sheltered from strong winds; butterflies cannot feed well in windy conditions. Some of the best nectar-producing flowers planted in my garden—and ones sure to attract these winged beauties—include:

- Butterfly bush (*Buddleia* spp.)
- Aster (*Aster novae-angliae*, *Aster 'September Ruby'*)
- Butterfly weed (*Asclepias tuberosa*)
- Coreopsis (*Coreopsis* spp.)
- Joe-pye weed (*Eupatorium* spp.)
- Liatris (*Liatris* spp.)
- Black-eyed Susan (*Rudbeckia* spp.)
- Purple coneflower (*Echinacea purpurea*)
- Globe thistle (*Echinops exaltatus*)
- Phlox (*Phlox* spp.)

Many of these flowers also attract hummingbirds and provide a food source for those acrobatic flying jewels as they migrate to warmer climates.

For an excellent butterfly garden, plant these flowers in large clusters sheltered by shrubs or a hedge, with the taller flowers in the back. Adding rocks and evergreens help to hold heat; the butterflies can perch on them to warm themselves.

In a separate area, plants that can feed the larva or caterpillar stage of butterflies will encourage egg laying and a larger number of butterflies. Many butterfly species are very specific about which species of plant the caterpillar will eat.

Larval food plants include: quaking aspen, cottonwoods, hackberry, white ash, clover, alfalfa, vetch, winter cress, willow, cabbage, and milkweed.

Some of the families of butterflies that you can attract to your landscape include: swallowtails, whites, sulphurs, coppers, hairstreaks, blues, snout butterfly, hackberry butterfly, longwings, angelwings, tortoiseshells (mourning cloak), painted ladies, red admiral, buckeye, fritillaries, crescents, admirals, satyrs, milkweed butterflies (Monarch), and skippers.

Avoid the use of pesticides. Since butterflies are insects, pesticides kill them in the larval and adult stages. To control such pests as aphids in other areas of your landscape, use a homemade spray of soapsuds, garlic, chives, and hot sauce.

PLANTS FOR BUTTERFLIES

A complete butterfly garden should contain plants that butterflies use during each stage of their life cycle—egg, larva (caterpillar), pupa (chrysalis), and adult (butterfly).

Unlike adult butterflies, young caterpillars are particular about their diet. Caterpillars prefer wild plants such as chokecherry, milkweed, hackberry, nettle, or Queen Anne's lace. When possible, let some of the native or wild plants flourish in a corner of your landscape. Some domestic plants, such as parsley, carrot, fennel, dill, and nasturtium, are also favorites for caterpillars. The idea is to have a balanced menu—host plants for caterpillars and nectar-producing plants for adult butterflies.

A mixture of annuals, perennials, and biennials provides a variety of combinations to attract a wide range of butterfly species to your garden. Choose old-fashioned or heirloom varieties since many of the newer hybrids have been bred for larger, showy flowers, but are not noted for better nectar production.

PERENNIALS

- *Asclepias*—Milkweed B
- *Alcea*—Hollyhock B
- *Aster*—single-flowered asters N
- *Achillea*—Yarrow N
- *Coreopsis*—Tickseed N
- *Dianthus*—Sweet William, Dianthus N

- *Echinacea*—Coneflower N
- *Eupatorium*—Joe-pye weed N
- *Helenium*—Sneezeweed N
- *Hemerocallis*—Daylilies N
- *Linum*—Flax H
- *Lupinus*—Lupine H
- *Lychnis*—Maltese cross, Campion N
- *Mentha*—Mints N
- *Penstemon*—Beardtongue N
- *Perovskia*—Russian Sage N
- *Phlox*—Perennial phlox N
- *Rudbeckia*—Black-eyed Susan N
- *Scabiosa*—Pincushion flower N
- *Sedum*—Stonecrop N
- *Verbena*—'Homestead Purple' verbena N

ANNUALS
- *Alyssum*—Sweet alyssum B
- *Tropaeolum*—Nasturtium B
- *Cosmos*—N
- *Dianthus*—Annual pinks N
- *Lantana*—N
- *Pentas*—Starflower N
- *Phlox*—Annual phlox N
- *Salvia*—N

- *Tagetes*—French marigold (single-flowered types) N
- *Tithonia*—Mexican sunflower N
- *Verbena*—N
- *Zinnia*—N

HERBS
- *Allium*—Chives N
- *Anethum*—Dill H
- *Borago*—Borage N
- *Foeniculum*—Fennel H
- *Lavendula*—Lavender N
- *Mentha*—Mint N
- *Monarda*—Bee balm N
- *Nepeta*—Catmint N
- *Petroselinum*—Parsley H
- *Salvia*—Sage N
- *Thymus*—Thyme N

TREES AND SHRUBS
- *Buddleia*—Butterfly bush N
- *Caryopteris*—Blue mist spirea N
- *Chrysothamnus*—Rabbitbrush N
- *Cornus*—Dogwood H
- *Crataegus*—Hawthorn H

- *Fraxinus*—Ash H
- *Prunus virginiana*—Chokecherry H
- *Salix*—Willow H
- *Syringa*—Lilac N
- *Viburnum*—B

KEY: N = Nectar Producing, H = Host plant for caterpillars, B = Both nectar and host plant

NATURE'S LITTLE HELPERS

Beneficial bugs keep your garden's insect population under control. Not everything that creeps, crawls, and flutters into your landscape and garden is an unwelcome pest or enemy. Many creatures that visit help to keep insect populations in check. Summer is a great time to observe, learn more about the life in your garden, and make friends with the many insects and other of Nature's little helpers. Get to know the friendly creatures before reaching for the bug killer. You soon learn to appreciate their contributions to a healthy yard and garden. Here are just a few to help you get started.

PARASITIC WASPS There are thousands of parasitic wasp species from more than a dozen insect families. These tiny wasps are highly specific in their habits, attacking only one kind of insect. Some prey on aphids, others develop only on scale insects, while other wasps parasitize caterpillars.

Like the creature from the movie *Alien*, female parasitic wasps insert eggs into the body of these insect hosts. The eggs hatch within the host, and the developing wasp grubs usually kill the host insect within seven to ten days. Several generations of wasps are produced during one growing season.

LADY BEETLES Better known as ladybugs, lady beetles are among the most widely recognized beneficial insects. Visit some of your local garden outlets; you'll find convergent lady beetles for sale in packets of five hundred or more. These are the classic reddish orange beetles with bright black spots. Voracious eaters, lady beetles consume large quantities of soft-bodied insects, including aphids, small caterpillars, and scales.

At the immature or larval stage, the lady beetle looks nothing like the adult. Only ¼ to ½ inch long, the black and orange larvae resemble miniature orange and black Gila monsters. But you want these tiny larvae around because they eat hundreds of aphids a day.

Some gardeners bring insect samples to nurseries and clinics to identify them and discover they have mistakenly killed the "ugly creatures" after finding them resting on the foliage and stems of evergreens. Upon closer examination, they learn that the creatures they've killed are the larval stages of the lady beetles.

So don't reach for the bug killer until you've identified the creature in your garden. Pesticides kill lots more than you think and upset the natural balance in your garden.

Tip: If you purchase lady beetles, open the container and sprinkle a little water over them. Then close the container back up and keep them in the refrigerator until you're ready to release them. The best time to turn them loose is late evening, preferably after a rainstorm. Release them where there is a food source, preferably aphids, but pollen and nectar from flowers work temporarily.

SPIDERS Misrepresented by nursery rhymes and folklore, spiders have become feared and often hated in the home and garden. But most spiders should be welcomed to the yard and garden. Their webs trap hundreds of unsuspecting insect pests that would otherwise destroy plants.

Summer is a great time to watch for spiders finding new home sites. If you look at the right time of day—early morning when the sun is bright or early evening—you may spot the fine webs floating in the air.

After hatching, the tiny spiderlings climb onto a high perch (fence posts, tree branches, and so forth). and spin fine threads of silk. When the summer breeze catches the threads, the tiny spiders are carried great distances to a new home. If they don't like where they land, they can take up residence elsewhere by simply repeating the process.

DRAGONFLIES You don't need a pond in your backyard to attract dragonflies. These fascinating

MOCK ORANGE

creatures of the insect world can be found in most gardens zigzagging over flowers and shrubs.

Dragonflies are fun to observe as they hover over garden plants like miniature helicopters, often moving rapidly in all directions—even backwards. They have the ability to capture insects on the wing, using their strong front legs as a scoop; then stuffing helpless victims into their mouths without even stopping. Once the task is completed, dragonflies land on the tip of a plant and rest, motionless, for long periods.

Dragonflies don't sting or bite, as many of us have been led to believe. But from an insect's perspective, the dragonfly is a monster with the skill to capture and devour an unsuspecting visitor.

LACEWINGS One of the most delicate-looking insect predators found in the garden is the lacewing. Their iridescent green wings shimmering in the sunlight, lacewings feed on aphids, thrips, small caterpillars, and spider mites. Both larvae and adults feed on insect pests.

Lacewings occur naturally throughout the Rocky Mountain region, but you can also buy them in the egg stage. Scatter about a thousand lacewing eggs around each 500 square feet of garden area.

HOW TO ENTICE FRIENDLY CRITTERS TO YOUR GARDEN

- Lay off the use of pesticides at the sign of a bug in your garden. Many pesticides kill beneficial insects, as well as the pests.
- Provide a source of water in the garden—a small birdbath, a shallow pond, or a small dish filled with gravel and water.
- Have a spot for shelter from wind and rain. A row of tall perennials, such as sunflowers, shrubbery, or ornamental grasses, provides a buffer zone for insect predators to hide and later come out to hunt down the "bad guys."
- Grow plants that are a source of nectar and pollen for beneficial insects. These plants attract the insects to the garden and give them something to eat while they wait for the insect prey to arrive or hatch from eggs. Some of the common herbs, such as dill, fennel, lemon balm, and spearmint, are favorite plants of beneficial insects. They also favor many wildflowers, daisies, cosmos, clovers, and other legumes.

GREEN GARDENING

A day rarely goes by that we don't hear some reference to going green, climate change, greenhouse gases, carbon neutral, eco-friendly, environmental footprint, or global warming.

WHY SHOULD WE CARE?

Our unique perspective as gardeners has allowed us personally to witness the environmental impact of our actions. As we create natural environments in our own little spot on the planet, we glean insights into a bigger picture. The changing conditions present themselves in many ways: Higher than average temperatures are causing plants to leaf out and bloom earlier than ever. Birds and butterflies are breeding and migrating earlier as well. Many wildlife species are being found at higher elevations and farther north than in previous years.

COMPOST YOUR GARDEN WASTE

Picture any landfill. Have you ever seen one that didn't look like a small mountain? Now imagine that landfill at only one-third its original size. The two-thirds that you just vaporized in your mind is the portion of that mountain that could have been composted or recycled. Paper accounts for over 40 percent of landfill mass on average, while an additional 25 percent is made up of yard trimmings and food scraps. All of that could have been compost!

If you think there's no difference in depositing paper, yard trimmings, and food scraps into the landfill versus recycling or composting them, think again. For organic material to break down, it must have carbon, nitrogen, moisture, and oxygen. The better the ratio among those

ingredients, the faster the process of decomposition occurs. At home, we can control those variables rather easily. With the right combination, we can have finished compost as quickly as several weeks to several months.

In a landfill environment, the ideal combination for decomposition rarely if ever exists. The compaction that occurs from the addition of more and more material and the weight of heavy equipment at the surface deprives potentially decomposing matter of sufficient oxygen and prevents moisture from reaching the material as well. In fact, the breakdown process happens so slowly that one researcher was able to excavate newspapers from the 1960s that were still intact and readable.

This massive amount of organic material creates an even greater problem in a landfill. As organic matter attempts to decompose, in the absence of sufficient oxygen, *methane* is created. A powerful greenhouse gas, methane is twenty-three times more effective at trapping heat in the atmosphere than carbon dioxide. It's no surprise that solid waste landfills are the single largest man-made source of methane gas in the United States.

In addition to organic matter taking up unnecessary space, many items that may never break down, like heavy plastics from garden containers, metal, stone, and concrete, find their way into landfills. Many of these products can be repurposed in some form or another. In fact, the garden has many uses for these very materials.

THERE IS PROGRESS

For every item that you can throw in the compost pile, that's one less for the landfill.

Fortunately, there is measurable progress in reducing the amount of yard waste we are keeping out of our landfills, and there are a number of reasons why. First, many municipalities no longer allow yard debris to be included with other household waste. Instead, trimmings are set aside in biodegradable paper bags and collected separately. They're then taken to a municipal composting site where they are deposited for the slow decomposition process.

Elsewhere, many cities and counties across the country offer curbside pickup of items too bulky for paper sacks. Tree limbs, shrubs, and other such items are the usual components of this part of the recycling campaign. Even fall leaves are bagged and taken to composting facilities by some municipalities.

When you're outside working in the yard, it's always surprising how much yard debris accumulates so quickly. Can it all go into the compost pile? Yes, it probably could, but should it? Well, that's another story.

WHAT GOES IN THE COMPOST PILE?

Outside, anything that was growing is fair game . . . almost. A few exceptions are mentioned here. First, however, great additions to a compost pile from outside the house include grass clippings, hay, straw, pine needles, leaves, wood chips, bark, and other yard trimmings.

You may have heard that for compost to break down quickly, there needs to be the right ratio between carbon (the brown stuff) and nitrogen (the green stuff). Although that is true, compost happens in nature with no help from us, although it may take longer.

Rather than get bogged down in trying to provide the perfect ratio, just be sure always to have some of both working all the time. The rate of composting can be accelerated by simply keeping the pile moist (like a damp sponge) and turning it often to provide oxygen to the center of the pile.

Now, the outdoors has a few limitations on what not to put in a compost pile. First, **avoid adding weeds that have gone to seed**. Weed seeds often survive the decomposition process, only to be spread next season under the cloak of perfect compost.

Diseased plant material also poses risks to your compost. The pathogens may survive the composting process and infect other plants later as they are distributed about your garden. Play it safe and remove this material from your property completely. Although burning would destroy the pathogens and infected plant material, it's not an option in the eco-friendly garden.

Fireplace ashes present yet another problem. Ashes are highly alkaline. More harm could be done by raising the soil pH of acid-loving plants than the small benefit from potassium inherent with ash. Leave them out of the compost.

Don't add twigs or branches to the pile that are thicker than a pencil. It's not that they won't become compost; it's just that we're usually too impatient. Instead, toss all thicker branches into a pile of their own. As they slowly break down, the added benefit is that they provide cover and protection for birds and many of the smaller wildlife that live in the area. Keep thorny branches and twigs such as roses and briars out of the compost pile. They go into that separate pile and provide additional protection for the smaller animals.

So although there are some *don'ts* when it comes to what to put into your compost, the exceptions are very few. Just remember this: for every item that you can throw in the compost pile, that's one less for the landfill. If that's not motivating enough, know that what you are putting in your compost pile will provide the very best soil amendment you can give to your garden, and no store-bought product can match it!

COMPOST GRASS CLIPPINGS AS A VALUABLE RESOURCE

Can you imagine how many bags of grass clippings are collected on any spring or summer day? The EPA tells us yard clippings make up over 20 percent of the entire waste stream entering public landfills. Keep them. Grass clippings are loaded with nitrogen, a key nutrient to lush growth and deep green color. They're also a necessary part of helping other organic material break down quickly.

Nitrogen provides the food source for microorganisms to decompose carbon, that brown waste in our compost such as twigs and leaves. You only need about 20 percent as much nitrogen as carbon, but it is essential that you have both for efficient decomposition. In fact, a compost pile without green waste will seem to just sit there. It will eventually break down, but it takes *much* longer.

Add some grass clippings to the mix and watch that pile start to cook. That heat is from the microbes hard at work again, nourished and fortified from the addition of their essential food source.

In an eco-friendly garden you do not want to add clippings that have been doused with herbicides and pesticides. Some of those chemicals don't break down in the heat of composting, and you do not want tainted compost in an otherwise chemical-free garden.

The same goes for grass containing a lot of weeds. It's not the weeds as much as the seeds they make. Weed seeds have the ability to survive some pretty harsh conditions, including a hot compost pile. The seeds could remain viable, only to germinate later in other parts of the garden where you apply the finished compost. If the grass is cut often enough, weeds are rarely a problem since frequent mowing cuts off emerging seed heads.

Finally, too much of a good thing can be, well . . . too much. If you've ever placed a large amount of grass clippings in a pile, added water, and come back later, you may have noticed a strong and not so pleasant aroma much like the smell of ammonia. It's simply a matter of chemistry—too much moisture and not enough oxygen to process the decomposition of the nitrogen-rich grass clippings. But it's an easy fix. Just spread the pile out to allow more oxygen in, add some carbon-based brown ingredients, and then mix it all together. The problem should resolve itself within a day or two.

COMPOST KITCHEN WASTE, PAPER, AND OTHER ITEMS TO REDUCE LANDFILL COSTS

One of the easiest ways to add to your compost is to toss in those food scraps from salads, vegetables, and fruits. So just what can and can't go into the compost bin?

From inside the house, just about anything that once came from a living source can be composted. From the *kitchen*, add all fruit and vegetable scraps, coffee grounds and filters, paper towels and the roll, paper napkins, oatmeal, banana peels, eggshells, and tea bags.

From *around the house*, add vacuum cleaner bags and contents, dryer lint, cardboard rolls, clean

Shredded paper is a compostable resource most of us overlook.

paper (shredded is best), newspaper, cotton and wool rags, hair and fur, and houseplants.

As with everything in life, there are exceptions to the rule, including household compost. First, don't add meat products, bones, fats, grease, oils, or dairy products to compost. They create odors that can attract pests such as rodents and flies. And don't compost pet or human wastes. These can contain parasites, bacteria, germs, pathogens, and viruses that are harmful to humans.

THE THRILL OF SHREDDING

Inside the house, the shredder is the equivalent to the compost bin outdoors, based on how much it is working. Shred everything: bills, junk mail, school papers, printed emails and articles—oh the list goes on, and so does the pleasure.

Shredders are readily available today from many sources—drug stores, office supply stores, and the big warehouse clubs all sell them. You can purchase a high quality, home/office version for about $80. It can take about fifteen sheets at a time, cuts paper into confetti, and handles a large volume.

As long as there is junk mail, school work, and bills, there will be an endless source of compostable material from inside the house.

MULCH OR COMPOST LEAVES— DON'T SEND THEM TO THE LANDFILL

Leaves contain more than half the nutrients they took in during the season.

Fallen autumn leaves contain 50 to 80 percent of the nutrients that their trees extracted from the earth this past season. Use them to replenish the soil and nourish all that grows within it.

Earthworms will feast on this debris, burrow deeper into the soil, and then deposit the matter as castings, adding even more valuable nutrients, oxygen, and drainage in the process. Beneficial fungi and bacteria will assist in the decomposition process, consuming this raw leaf material and returning it in a nutrient-rich form that can be utilized by plant and tree roots more efficiently and effectively than anything man has ever created.

Mere months after these shredded leaves are applied to the garden, they'll transform into matter that promotes the life of soil-dwelling organisms, which in turn will fortify the plants and trees to be more pest- and disease-resistant.

Have you ever stopped to consider that no matter what condition soil is in, leaf compost will help make loose soil retain moisture and compacted soil drain better?

Rather than being viewed as unnecessary trash, these leaves, grass clippings, and other garden trimmings should be going into our own gardens to enrich the soil while reducing the need for supplemental fertilizers and other harmful chemicals.

USE A MULCHING MOWER AND GRASSCYCLE

Grasscycling does not cause thatch, and it reduces nitrogen fertilizer needs.

With the arrival of spring, cutting the grass becomes another weekly ritual to promote the health and beauty of a great-looking lawn and landscape. But many homeowners don't realize it's not necessary to bag those grass clippings. In fact, leaving them on your lawn offers several advantages.

Grasscycling is the natural recycling of grass clippings by leaving them on your lawn when mowing, rather than bagging and removing them.

Grasscycling does not promote thatch. It is a common misconception that grass clippings are a major cause of thatch buildup in lawns. Thatch buildup is caused by grass stems, shoots, and roots—not grass clippings. Clippings, which consist of about 75 percent water, decompose quickly while adding nutrients to the soil.

Grasscycling contributes valuable nutrients. Studies indicate that as grass clippings decompose on your lawn, they contribute enough organic matter and nitrogen to reduce lawn fertilization needs by about 25 percent per year.

Grasscycling does not promote weed growth. One of the keys to proper grasscycling is to remove only one-third of the grass blade each time you mow, always keeping in mind the recommended height for your type of grass. This may necessitate that you cut your grass a bit more frequently, especially during peak growing times. Consistent, regular mowing reduces the chances of weeds going to seed and dispersing throughout your yard.

It's also important to use a sharp blade. Sharp blades make clean cuts, thus reducing the chance for lawn diseases and pests. A healthy lawn is a lush lawn and one that does not create a favorable environment for weeds to grow and flourish.

Grasscyclng leaves no visible residue. The key to having a freshly cut lawn free of unsightly clippings is to make note of the comments above. Again, always use a sharp mower blade to ensure a clean cut. Avoid cutting off more than a third of the grass blade any time you mow. This not only reduces the size of the clippings, it is also less stressful on the grass. Finally, don't mow when the grass is wet. Clumps will ultimately develop, no matter how hard you try to avoid it.

USE A CHIPPER TO BREAK DOWN TREE BRANCHES

To get great compost faster, you want your yard debris to be as small as possible from the start.

It's simply the "law of the compost pile"— smaller particles decompose faster than larger ones. So, to achieve great compost faster, you want your yard debris to be as small as possible. The solution for large stems, vines, and branches is a chipper/shredder.

When choosing your chipper/shredder, electric models are the more eco-friendly choice. Besides not spewing pollutants into the air, they are quieter than most gas-powered models. And, if you are not chipping debris that is larger than about two and a half inches in diameter, electric models work fine.

RECYCLE THOSE PLASTIC POTS

Of most of the plastic recycled today, very little is garden garbage.

When we think about the act of gardening, we often assume we are doing wonderful things for the environment. But many of us don't realize the amount of trash we generate at the same time we are creating that beautiful garden.

Recycling bins offer an eco-friendly disposal option for plastic pots in most areas.

Take plastic pots, for instance. They come in all sizes from little cell packs to very large containers. Once we've planted the beauties that came in them, where does the pot go? Into the trash, or at best it's into the curbside recycle bin or municipal recycling center.

According to the EPA, of the nearly 27 million tons of plastic generated in the United States in 2003, only 3.9 million tons of it was recycled. But as Beth Botts, a writer for the *Chicago Tribune* points out in her article "Beauty and the Plastic Beast," most of that was soda, water, and milk bottles; very little was garden garbage.

Looking deeper into the issue, we find that one main problem is the variety of plastics that are used in making garden containers in the first place. Even if everybody sent their containers to the recycling center, most are not accepted and end up in the landfill instead.

SOLVING THE PLASTIC PROBLEM

So what's an eco-friendly society to do? Solutions range from asking manufacturers to standardize the type of plastic they use for garden containers and for growers to use, to creating biodegradable pots and asking municipalities to segregate plastic pots for recycling. While these and more ideas are being researched, progress isn't going to happen overnight.

Still, there are some things we as individuals can do to help. Ask your local garden center if you can return empty containers. We can also request programs that offer garden container recycling for all types of plastic pots, including recycling numbers 2, 4, 5, and 6. Or we can seek out garden centers or botanic gardens that make this service available. Maybe you can begin a program in your community.

In 2007, the Missouri Botanical Garden successfully recycled over one hundred thousand pounds of horticultural plastic originally destined for the landfills. The Garden's successful Plastic Pot Recycling program in St. Louis is the most extensive public garden recycling program in the U.S., collecting over three hundred tons of waste in the past ten years. Think what would happen if every city in the United States followed suit.

BUY PLANTS IN POTS MADE FROM BIODEGRADABLE MATERIAL

Eco-friendly garden containers are nothing new. But what is new is what they're made from.

It is mind-boggling to consider that every product we consume, from the foods we eat to the items we use every day, took energy to make, package, ship, store, and sell to us. A big part of that energy is the fossil fuels consumed in the process.

As gardeners, we have a number of opportunities to conserve energy from products. One of the more interesting choices is the use of biodegradable plant containers. It may be only a small factor in the big picture, but it is one way to reduce the pressure on landfill space and fossil fuel consumption.

Eco-friendly garden containers are not new. Terra cotta pots have been around forever, but in our lifetime, plastic pots are the ubiquitous choice by the nursery industry. In terms of water retention, weight, durability, and cost, they have no equal, which is unfortunate.

OPTIONS BESIDES PLASTIC

For seedlings and smaller plants such as annuals and perennials, pots made from pressed paper pulp, peat moss, and even composted cow manure are an eco-friendly option to plastic. They can be planted directly in the ground, making it easier on us and easing the risk of transplant shock to the seedlings.

Composted cow manure pots have the added advantage of fertilizing plants as they break down. Coir, a product made from coconut hulls, has been used extensively as liners for open-weaved hanging baskets and window boxes. Now this natural material is being translated into compostable garden pots.

Similarly, a material made from a combination of grain husks (rice shells) and coconut shells offers other decorative options. Its products last from three to five years, as long as the pot is not broken. Once broken, they will compost in nine to nineteen months.

Even old wine barrels that have outlived their original purpose can be pressed into service as planters. The wood will eventually break down over time, making them an eco-friendly alternative to plastic.

Finally, one of our favorite recyclable pots is a good old-fashioned toilet paper or paper towel tube. They make a great way to start seeds indoors. Just fill it with your favorite potting soil, place a seed or two inside, and plant it directly into the ground once the seedlings are ready for the great outdoors. If seedlings are susceptible to cut worms, leaving the top of the tube out of the ground a bit acts as a protective collar. How's that for recycling?

GARDENING TO PROTECT THE ECOSYSTEM

Protecting ecosystems and maintaining biodiversity are so critical to keeping the earth in balance; it's hard to even comprehend the complexities of the concept in words. Just try to imagine a balanced ecosystem as a web of connections from one living organism to other living and non-living things. The web connects them, providing the necessary resources for survival, like food and shelter.

Due to the highly complex nature of ecosystem relationships, the removal or disruption of a single one of its members could throw the entire system out of balance. Unfortunately, we have yet to fully understand these complex relationships, so the exact cause and effect of disturbances is many times still unpredictable.

Maintaining natural habitats also provides protection for breeding and migrating populations of birds, as well as offering shelter from predators. Insect pests are kept in check, reducing the need for chemical control measures. The gene pool of plants vital for food and medicine is preserved, while pollinating insects continue to sustain these ecosystems as they work and breed in their diverse habitat.

Today, virtually all of the earth's ecosystems have been altered through human actions, and yet the interruptions seem to continue at a faster rate than ever before. As our interference persists, many plant and animal species have declined in populations and scope, and the rate of extinction has increased by at least a factor of one hundred over natural rates. Biodiversity loss has occurred more rapidly in the last fifty years than at any other time in history, and these changes are expected to continue at the same pace or even accelerate. But slowing down the loss of biodiversity is not sufficient.

PROMOTE COMPLEXITY AND AVOID MONOCULTURES

Any time we plant too much of one thing, we're setting ourselves up against Mother Nature, and for problems that can have far-reaching implications. The potato famine happened when a devastating potato blight raced through the plantings of Irish peasants. It was the reliance upon one crop, and especially one variety of one crop, that led to massive crop failure. Had they planted several types of potatoes or rotated them with other crops, thousands of deaths could have likely been avoided.

The Dust Bowl was in large part the result of repeated large-scale plantings of the same crop year after year. When we don't plant a variety of crops in alternate growing seasons, land is dormant and exposed, and populations of pests and diseases can build up to decimate the same host crop when it is replanted in subsequent seasons. In the case of the Dust Bowl, tons of soil were blown into the air after a drought killed off crops that had already been weakened.

Here's a more recent example: The thornless honey locust—an excellent shade tree in many ways—was overplanted along streets and highways all over the eastern U.S., in part because it had virtually no known pests. Today these massive plantings are being attacked by several highly damaging and opportunistic pests. The abundance of trees provided ample opportunities for pests and diseases by supplying food and shelter and a resulting population explosion in the absence of natural predators.

Mini-monocultures of turfgrass are a ubiquitous feature in just about every landscape in America.

MISCANTHUS IN MIXED BORDER WITH PINE AND SEDUM

Few are the homes that don't have some amount of turf occupying a portion of their landscape. As lovely as a well-manicured lawn can be to look at, it replaces the habitats of native plants and wildlife and food sources for birds or beneficial insects.

The balance of nature is indeed a concert of all of its inhabitants. The natural environment around us is never a monoculture on its own. When biodiversity is protected and promoted in our own yards and neighborhoods, so is the stability of the ecosystems that give us fresh water, clean air, productive soil, and healthy forests.

PROTECT THE GENE POOL

Saving heirloom or sentimental favorite seeds is a significant way to prevent their extinction.

America has been the great melting pot in more ways than one. With each wave of immigrants came a wave of new plants, many in the form of a packet of generations-old seed tucked carefully into a pocket. Each settler planted a favorite tomato, a favorite apple, a particular type of morning glory or an especially striking sunflower, and as a result, they added to the amazing horticultural variety in our country.

In the middle part of the last century, however, people stopped saving seeds from year to year. With the advent of hybridization, large seed companies began selling seeds that didn't come from seeds saved year after year. Hybrid varieties have many advantages to farmers and home gardeners in terms of consistency, yields, or pest and disease resistance, but there was also a disadvantage. They had to be purchased new each year or whenever current supplies were exhausted. This method of seed acquisition replaced much of the traditional swapping and passing on to the next generation of our treasured seeds.

Typically the results from planting a hybridized plant from seed will be iffy. That snapdragon that was such a gorgeous peach-yellow blend this year might reseed next year, but the flower color can be dramatically different. This is not necessarily a bad thing, just something to be aware of. And don't expect that hybrid tomato seed to produce offspring identical to its parent.

Check out the Seed Saver's Exchange online. It's a nonprofit organization in the U.S. dedicated to the preservation of heirloom seeds, where members swap and receive open-pollinated seeds. http://www.seedsavers.org/

Open-pollinated varieties are different. These seeds have not been manipulated by man. Their pollination takes place naturally through insects, birds, wind, and other means. The seeds of open-pollinated plants *can* produce new generations of the same plant, which is how we can save and plant seeds from one generation to another. So if your grandmother had some wonderful russet signet marigolds that she grew in her garden decades ago and she saved the seed each year, your parents could save and grow them, and today, so could you.

233

Many vegetables and flowers we enjoy today are the product of open-pollination and seed saving.

If you aren't lucky enough to have a grandparent who saved seeds, check out the Seed Savers Exchange online. It's a non-profit organization in Iowa dedicated to the preservation of heirloom seeds, where members swap and receive open-pollinated seeds to grow in order to prevent some wonderful plants from being lost.

There's another reason for saving seeds that reaches far beyond our flower or vegetable gardens. The entire diversity of plant life on our planet is shrinking rapidly. Climate change is expected to exacerbate the loss of plant diversity and increase the risk of extinction for many more species, especially those already at risk from other threats. Regions of the planet that provide much of the genetic material for our cultivated crop plants are quickly being damaged or destroyed. Many times the effects are irreversible.

Unfortunately, pressures on the environment no longer allow plants to remain protected in their natural habitats. Saving their seeds is a significant way to preserve these plants from one generation to the next.

In response to this pressing issue, seed banks have been established all over the world to effectively guarantee the survival of individual plant species. Their primary mission is to collect, store, and convert the stored seeds back into plants for reintroduction or habitat rehabilitation whenever necessary. This worldwide collaboration aims to save twenty-four thousand plant species around the globe from extinction. With the proper storage methods provided by seed banks, seeds can survive for hundreds and possibly thousands of years.

DISCOURAGE POACHING OF PLANTS FROM THE WILD

Gardeners should be aware that this happens all too often. A big concern is the gathering of orchids, cacti, and tropical plants. Some species within these groups are very rare, and collecting them from their native habitats is seriously threatening their existence. If you are seeking these rare plants and find them in a nursery, check to see if it carries the Convention on International Trade in Endangered Species (CITES) certification, part of a United Nations watchdog program to protect rare species of plants and animals.

DO YOUR HOMEWORK BEFORE USING TRAPS FOR INSECT PESTS

But just because it's not in a bottle doesn't make it an eco-friendly option.

In an eco-friendly garden, the more chemicals you can keep out of your landscape, the better, even organic and natural ones. So what do you do to control those destructive Japanese beetles, pesky flies, and annoying mosquitoes? Do we trap, zap, or gas these creatures with a botanical-based insecticide?

BUG ZAPPERS

Remember the sound of success on a summer evening? You know the sound, and you loved it. It made for some very entertaining evenings. But what were those zappers cooking, anyway? In 1996, Timothy Frick and Douglas Tallamy collected and identified the kills from six bug zappers at various sites throughout suburban Newark, Delaware, during the summer of 1994. Of the nearly 14,000 insects that were electrocuted and counted, only 31 (0.22 percent) were mosquitoes and biting gnats. The largest group made up 48 percent (6,670). They consisted of midges and harmless aquatic insects from nearby bodies of water. Too bad, because those insects are vital to the aquatic foodchain.

Another important group caught in the traps were predators and parasites. These biological control organisms (consisting of ground beetles and parasitic wasps) are the very insects that help keep pests populations down naturally. This group accounted for 13.5 percent (1,868).

So how good are bug zappers in the eco-friendly garden, or any garden for that matter? They're terrible! By design, they are nonselective and kill many harmless and beneficial insects. The authors even extrapolated their findings and determined that four million bug zappers (four years of approximate sales in the U.S) operated for forty nights each summer, would destroy seventy-one billion non-target insects each year.

MOSQUITO MISTERS

One of the newer products to hit the market are misters designed to eliminate mosquito populations around a certain perimeter from the unit. They work by periodically disbursing an organic or synthetic pesticide, usually pyrethrin or permethrin. Marketers of these systems defend the use of the organic spray version because pyrethrum is organic and natural. Yes, but it's also *nonselective*, making it a very bad option. The indiscriminant application can destroy beneficial insects, pets, and especially fish.

Another concern expressed in a letter to the U.S. Environmental Protection Agency by the American Mosquito Control Association warned that the indiscriminant use of pyrethroids (the synthetic and very potent version of pyrethrin) by misting systems could result in widespread resistance, seriously compromising the capability to control adult mosquito populations.

A better approach is to eliminate all standing water and use safe larvicides with *Bt* dunks and repellents.

MOSQUITO TRAPPING WITH CO₂

On a more positive note, another technology waging war on mosquitoes includes the use of carbon dioxide (CO_2), a gas found to attract mosquitoes. Although studies do show success in controlled and mostly enclosed environments, the question of their effectiveness in a half- or full-acre outdoor setting remains a question.

BUILD PROJECTS WITH SUSTAINABLE WOOD

Some of the most beautiful woods are harvested from threatened sources.

The giant redwood—it's the tallest tree in the world. The tree is valued for its beauty, light weight, and resistance to decay. It's redwood's ability to withstand the elements that makes it particularly attractive for use in outdoor landscapes. This popularity as a building material has reduced

redwood's total population by 40 percent in just three generations. That's more than enough to place it on The World Conservation Union's Red List of Threatened Species.

Since the early 1800s when redwood logging began, some 90 to 95 percent of old growth forests have been felled. The remaining stands are almost entirely in parks and reserves.

There are also endangered exotic wood species, the ones that lure us with irresistible grain patterns and interesting colors. Teak is the best known of these. Ironically, it became a popular and exclusive wood in Britain, when they recycled teak ship masts that had been crafted in foreign ports into beautiful garden furniture back home. The American and European appetite for this strong and beautiful wood has nearly eradicated it from its natural range in Southeast Asia and Central America.

Today, teak is a wood to choose with caution because of its impact on the tropical rainforests where much of it is harvested. Be aware of other rainforest woods most often used for patio and garden furniture (which includes tropical woods) such as mahogany, nyatoh, balau, jatoba (also called Brazilian cherry), parapera, kempas, iroko, and ipê.

LOOKING FOR THE FSC LABEL

Environmental groups such as the Sierra Club, Greenpeace, and The World Wildlife Fund endorse just one label in the marketplace—that of the Forest Stewardship Council (FSC). Its label certifies that the wood in a product has been sustainably produced. The timber industry has answered with its own certification program called the Sustainable Forestry Initiative (SFI). Consumers Union (CU) doesn't give it as high marks as the FSC, but it still indicates some progress in protecting forest environments at home and abroad.

LOOKING FOR RECYCLED OR SALVAGED WOOD

In stores, look for recycled wood products that are certified by the SmartWood's Rediscovered Wood Program. The program utilizes wood that, until its rediscovery, would otherwise have been destroyed through natural decay, burning, or disposal. Inventory is derived from old buildings, fallen or removed trees, or other tree culling events. You can identify "SmartWood Rediscovered" by its label on finished products.

LOOKING FOR ENVIRONMENTALLY SOUND WOOD SUBSTITUTES

There's a new wave of products made from alternative materials that lets more trees stand. The new so-called synthetic lumber made from recycled wood and plastics (sold by brand-names such as Trex® and Timbertec®) is a more forest-friendly alternative.

AVOID INVASIVE NON-NATIVE PLANTS

The introduction or use of invasive exotic plants is listed as one of the biggest threats to biodiversity in the United States and worldwide.

What novice gardener or uninformed weekend warrior hasn't uttered these words, "I want something that grows *fast!*" It's a natural desire to crave instant gratification in all areas of our life, even gardening. But be careful what you wish for because, in some cases, that fast grower could become your worst nightmare.

If you've ever taken a drive through the countryside of the northern United States and seen vast open pastures carpeted with brightly colored purple loosestrife, you've seen what an invasive plant can do. If you've ever taken a drive through the South and seen entire buildings and patches of woodlands smothered by kudzu, you've seen an invasive plant in action. And in the Pacific Northwest, neon yellow Spanish broom lights up slopes, often growing so thick that nothing else can.

Invasive plants are introduced species that can thrive in areas beyond their natural range of dispersal. These plants are characteristically adaptable, aggressive, and have a high capacity to propagate. These exotics often have few natural enemies and contribute little to the support of native wildlife. Their vigor combined with a lack of natural enemies often leads to outbreaks in populations. Invasive plants can totally overwhelm

BINDWEED

and devastate established native plants and their habitats by out-competing them for nutrients, water, and light—and because they offer so little food value to native wildlife, they are destructive of biodiversity on every level.

Despite huge government efforts to control them, invasive plants continue to spread. Aggressive weeds spread to an estimated four thousand acres (over six square miles) each day on public lands managed by the Bureau of Land Management (BLM) and the Forest Service. They are also spreading on private lands and parklands, but no one has calculated the extent of those infestations.

The best way to stop invasives dead in their deep-rooted tracks is to first find out what's invasive in your area; check with your Cooperative Extension Service or do some online research (www.invasive.org and www.invasivespeciesinfo. gov are excellent sources).

You can also ask a trusted source at your local garden center. However, too many garden centers still sell highly invasive plants simply because we still buy them. As always, it's simply a matter of supply and demand. If you see invasive plants for sale at your nursery or garden center, please inform the manager and make them aware of the risks of promoting the sale of these environmentally destructive plants to unwitting consumers.

PROTECT STANDING DEAD TREES WHENEVER POSSIBLE

It may look like a dead tree to you, but to eighty-five species of birds and other wildlife, it's home.

Dead trees are a vital part of an ecosystem that makes the perfect home for some woodpeckers and are a magnet for the wood-devouring insects that woodpeckers love to peck.

Certainly, it is sometimes critical to remove a large dead tree if there is any possibility that people may be in harm's way, especially children who frequent the area. Dead trees may also be at risk for falling on a house, driveway, or sidewalk. Nor would you want a limb in a windstorm to take out a window or your minivan. But if it's in the back of the yard or especially if it's in a wooded spot, leave the tree alone once all safety risks have

been assessed. Dying trees and branches are all part of the cycle of a natural woodland habitat.

PROVIDE A VARIETY OF WATER SOURCES FOR WILDLIFE

The presence of water can mean the difference between life and death for animals in the wild.

Natural water supplies are of course the obvious first choice. Wetlands are common, but in the face of increasing drought and shrinking sources, that option is not as easy to come by anymore.

Adult animals are better equipped to handle extended periods without water, yet almost all wildlife can be found within a couple miles of a water source. As these sources become less available, animals can become weakened, and female mammals may be unable to produce milk for their young, exacerbating the problem. As limited water sources dry up, animals can be reluctant to leave their only known supply

Birds are the obvious consideration. When you create a watering spot that birds enjoy, you might be surprised at just how many of them take advantage of it. You may also be surprised to see what else shows up there! Even a simple birdbath can attract a number of birds just in the first few hours after you fill it.

USING WATER TO ATTRACT BIRDS

If attracting birds to your backyard habitat is important to you, here are a few things to know that will make the experience more enjoyable for you and the birds.

Provide shallow water. Have you ever seen robins splashing in puddles after a rain? Birds love shallow water that they can easily splash in. Birdbaths serve this need, as does a shallow ledge just a few inches deep in a water garden or a shallow stream. The height of the water source also plays a role. Some birds that normally might not come to your yard will stop and visit if they can find water at ground level (this includes a stream).

The basic birdbath is still a classic. Don't think you need a fancy water feature to attract birds. The most basic, concrete birdbath on a pedestal works great to attract those birds that prefer their water higher up.

Include rocks and small boulders. A flat rock, placed just in the center of a birdbath, can create a welcomed island of safety for birds to survey their surroundings from a slightly more secure position. A flat stone placed just so its top is at the water level is an ideal height.

Boulders and rocks, depending on how they are set up, also create a natural point of entry to a water garden, especially if the boulder is rough or craggy and has a good foothold.

And don't forget that, once frozen, these water sources might as well be dried up. In areas of the country where the water freezes, look for birdbath heaters and deicers. No matter what time of year, a fresh water supply is necessary and appreciated.

PARTICIPATE IN THE NATIONAL WILDLIFE FEDERATION'S WILDLIFE HABITAT PROGRAM

This is an easy way for you to help raise awareness about the importance of gardening with the environment in mind.

Perhaps you've seen them. Those small but attractive signs posted near a school yard, a backyard, or by the street. The people that display them are proud to show that they are one of the National Wildlife Federation's "Certified Wildlife Habitats." And chances are if you're an environmentally aware gardener, you're already doing many of the things in your landscape that could get it certified as a Backyard Wildlife Habitat too.

The guidelines for certification require you to provide elements from each of the following areas:

Food sources. This means planting native plants or other plants that feed wildlife, such as those that produce seeds, fruits, nuts, berries, or nectar.

Water sources. Have in place a water feature such as a birdbath, pond, water garden, or stream.

Cover. Provide cover in the form of a thicket, a rock pile, or a birdhouse.

Places to raise young. These could be dense shrubs, vegetation, nesting boxes, or a pond.

Sustainable gardening. Garden in a way that assists nature, by mulching, composting, creating a rain garden, or fertilizing without chemicals.

All it takes to become certified is to fill out an application and send it along with a small fee to cover costs. You'll even receive a yard sign from the National Wildlife Federation that announces your certification.

Contact the National Wildlife Federation at 1-800-822-9919, visit its Website at www.nwf.org, or email info@nwf.org for more information.

(Adapted from *The Green Gardener's Guide*, Joe Lamp'l, Cool Springs Press 2007)

ROCKY MOUNTAIN STATE TERRAINS

COLORADO

Colorado is the highest state in the United States, with an average elevation of 6,800 feet. About 40 percent of the state is the High Plains, which slope gently higher as you move westward from the eastern border at elevations of 3,350 to 4,000 feet, through the Front Range. The High Plains are usually hot on summer mornings and cool during an afternoon thunderstorm. Those thunderstorms can sometimes be severe and the hail they contain can destroy gardens in minutes. The daily maximum summer temperature is about 95°F at elevations below 5,000 feet but cools at higher elevations to the west. There are wide variations in temperatures within short distances. For example, the difference in average annual temperature between two gardens only 90 miles apart can be equivalent to differences in temperature between Florida and Iceland. About 85 percent of the state's annual precipitation falls in summer. Gardeners in the northeastern areas enjoy a respectable growing season of about 140 days; those in the southeastern areas, an even longer season of about 160 days; and the fortunate few in the extreme southeastern corner of Colorado relish their 180-day seasons.

About 200 miles west of the eastern border lie the Foothills, with elevations of about 7,000 to 9,000 feet. Gardening here becomes challenging, with an average July temperature of 60°F and daily highs in the 70s and 80s°F. Nights are particularly cool all summer long, which will limit your vegetable selection. Cool-season crops will do well but warm-season crops will be more of a challenge. Beyond the Foothills lie the mountains, rising from 9,000 to 14,000 feet, and beyond them is the high plateau that extends to the western border at elevations above 10,000 feet. While there may be some gardens in the low western valleys, much of the mountainous area simply does not have a growing season long enough to make it worthwhile. Nights are so cool above about 8,000 feet that many folks simply do not garden. Gardeners in the valleys of the Gunnison, Dolores, and Colorado

Rivers enjoy especially long growing seasons, with the area around Grand Junction having up to 221 frost-free days in some years. Summers are wet in the eastern areas of the state but they are pretty dry in the western areas.

Productive Colorado soils, like those throughout the lower elevations of our region, have low acidity, which can cause some nutrient deficiencies. Front Range soils tend to be heavy clays that need amendments. Adding coarse sand equal to about 50 to 80 percent of the top eight inches or so of garden soil will go far to amend what you have.

The soils along river valleys are most productive, as are soils in the moister northeastern parts of the state. Drier soils on the plains of southern Colorado and on the mountain slopes and plateaus are thin and can be relatively unproductive.

IDAHO

Idaho's elevation rises from north to south, with the lowest location at the confluence of the Clearwater and Snake Rivers (738 feet) and the highest at Mt. Borah in Custer County (12,655 feet). Large parts of the state, especially northern areas, are strongly influenced by Pacific Ocean air, though eastern Idaho is not. Temperatures are highest at the lower elevations of the Clearwater and Little Salmon River basins and along parts of the Snake River Valley from Bliss to Lewiston. Gardeners in Swan Falls enjoy the highest annual average temperature for the state (55°F) while those in Obsidian, at 6,780 feet, experience the lowest (35.4°F). Daily temperature fluctuations are most extreme in the high valleys and the semi-arid plains of the Snake River. In fact, the daily temperature from July to September can vary by more than 30°F at Boise.

Idaho precipitation patterns are complex. Average valley precipitation is greater in the southern sections, with large areas of the Clearwater, Payette, and Boise River basins getting 40 to 50 inches or more per year. On the other hand, large areas in the northeastern valleys, much of the

Upper Snake River plains, the Central plains, and the lower elevations of the southwestern valleys receive fewer than ten inches per year. In the northeastern valleys and the eastern highlands less than half the rain falls between April and September, while in the Boise, Payette, and Weiser River drainage basins less than a third falls in those same months. Low relative humidities throughout the state mean dry air and rapid drying of soils and plants.

Wind throughout the state can be highly destructive, and savvy Idaho gardeners plant in protected areas. As in other states, the growing season varies greatly depending on elevation, soil type, topography, and vegetation cover. Lewiston and its immediately surrounding areas have the longest seasons in the state. The central Snake, and lower Payette, Boise, and Weiser River basins enjoy about 150-day seasons, while upstream areas of the Snake near Pocatello and Idaho Falls have about 125-day growing seasons. Some high valleys have no growing season at all.

The most productive Idaho soils are the desert soils along the Snake River and the prairie soils in the western part of the state around Lewiston and Moscow. In general, the rest of the state has relatively poor soil.

MONTANA

Montana has great climatic variations. The western part of the state is mountainous while the eastern two-thirds is part of the Great Plains. Elevations vary from a low of 1,800 feet in the northwestern part of the state where the Kootenai River enters Idaho to 12,850 feet at Granite Peak near Yellowstone Park. About half the state lies above 4,000 feet. Land west of the Continental Divide enjoys a modified northern Pacific Coast climate, with milder winters, more even distribution of annual precipitation, cooler summers, stronger winds, more cloudiness, higher relative humidity, and shorter growing seasons than those of eastern Montana. In western Montana hot spells are rare in summer and of relatively short duration, though temperatures can sometimes top 100°F in the low valleys. Above 4,000 feet it is almost never "very hot." Eastern Montana has a more extreme climate with average

July temperatures of 74°F in southern areas. Midsummer days are warm but nights cool into the 50s and 60s°F. Miles City is one of the warmest parts of the state, having a July minimum of 60°F and an average maximum temperature of 90°F.

Precipitation is highly variable. The western mountains are the wettest area and nearly half of the annual precipitation falls from May to July. Heron is the wettest location, receiving 34.7 inches of rain on average each year. North-central Montana is the driest part of the state, although the absolute driest spot is near Belfry along the Clark Fork of the Yellowstone River in Carbon County. Belfry receives an average annual precipitation of only 6.59 inches.

Summer storms are frequent, with hailstorms in July and August causing about five million dollars of crop damage annually.

The average growing season for Montana is about 130 days. Most of the agricultural areas enjoy a growing season of more than 120 days, while the middle Yellowstone River Valley in the area around Miles City can expect a 150-day season. The higher valleys of western Montana have no growing season at all.

Soils in the eastern parts of the state are rich and can be quite productive, as can be the soils along major rivers like the Yellowstone, the Milk, and the Missouri.

NEVADA

Nevada is 313 miles wide (east to west), 483 miles long (north to south), and the seventh largest state. It lies within the geographic area known as the Great Basin, with a small part of the southern end of the state in the Mojave Desert. There are mountain ranges alternating between flat basins from one side of the state to the other.

The climate of the state is variable, but generally arid. Summer temperatures range from 105°F in Las Vegas, the hot region (elevation 2,162 feet), to a brief high of 87°F in Ely, the mountainous region (elevation 6,253 feet), and 95°F in Reno, the high desert region (elevation 4,404 feet) in between. There is a wide fluctuation from daytime to nighttime temperatures in many communities, as well. As in the other Rocky Mountain and Great Basin states, temperatures can and do vary 50 degrees from morning to night. In towns above 6,000 feet, frost can occur anytime during the summer.

Precipitation also differs greatly throughout the state. In the low-elevation areas or the hot region of southern Nevada around Las Vegas, the annual precipitation is 4 inches. In most of the valleys or high desert regions of the rest of the state, the annual precipitation is 8 to 9 inches, and in the mountainous regions (those areas above 5,000 feet), up to 20 inches. In parts of the Sierra Nevada Range, over 200 inches of precipitation fall annually.

Wind is something to be aware of and common in all the valleys across the state. In Las Vegas, the wind starts around ten in the morning. The wind is hot and dry and can stress plants in a matter of hours. If a plant is listed as a high water user, it needs to have protection from the wind.

Nevada soils are considered mineral soils: they are low in organic matter and nutrients. They are somewhat alkaline, and many are saline, as well; both of these factors affect plant growth. The soil is also generally clayey and poorly drained. Soil tests will tell the home gardener how to adequately amend the soil for productive garden beds and borders.

UTAH

Most of Utah is mountainous, varying from an elevation of about 2,500 feet in the Virgin River Valley in southwestern Utah to 13,498 feet at Kings Peak in the Uinta Mountains. Most of the state receives only light precipitation throughout the year.

The lower elevations generally are warmer than elevated valleys and mountains. In general, the southern counties are 6 to 8°F warmer than the northern counties. There are wide daily fluctuations in temperatures, and in winter on clear nights the cold air settles in the valley bottoms while the benches and foothills remain warmer. Experienced gardeners know that thebest growing areas are the higher lands at the valley edges. Although there

is no orderly or extensive zone of equal length growing season, most agricultural areas of the state enjoy 130- to 150-day seasons.

Precipitation is highly variable, ranging from fewer than five inches per year over the Great Salt Lake Desert to more than forty inches in some areas of the Wasatch Mountains. The annual average for agricultural areas is about ten to fifteen inches. Areas of the state below 4,000 feet receive less than ten inches. Northwestern and eastern Utah are also quite dry.

The loam soils in the narrow belt at the base of the Wasatch Range are highly productive, as are the dry soils and the gray desert soils in much of western and some parts of eastern Utah.

WYOMING

Wyoming's elevation rises from north to south, with an average elevation of 6,700 feet. The lowest elevation is 3,125 feet near the northeastern corner of the state; the highest is the 13,785-foot Gannet Peak in the west central part of the state. Eastern Wyoming has an average elevation of 4,500 feet while the foothills to the west rise to 6,000 feet and more.

The entire state is relatively cool and areas above 6,000 feet rarely experience temperatures of 100°F. The average maximum temperature in July is 85 to 95°F, though areas above 9,000 feet have an average July maximum of only about 70°F. The lower part of the Big Horn basin, the lower elevations of central Wyoming, and the northeastern and eastern sections along the border are the warmest. Summer nights are cool.

Late spring and early fall frosts are common. The average growing season in the main agricultural areas is about 125 days. Areas along the eastern border west to the foothills can experience growing seasons from 100 to 130 days, while Farson, near Sandy Creek off the Green River, has only a 42-day season. There is practically no growing season for tender plants in the upper Green River Valley, Star Valley, and the Jackson Hole area.

Elevations greater than 7,000 feet receive annual precipitation of up to thirty inches, with about a third of that falling during the growing season. Southwestern Wyoming at elevations of 6,500 to 8,500 feet receives 7 to 10 inches. Lower elevations at 4,000 to 5,500 feet in the northeastern parts of the state and along the eastern border can expect about 12 to 16 inches per year. The southwestern sections are very dry. The lower part of the Big Horn Basin, with 5 to 8 inches, is the driest. Seaver, at 4,105 feet, receives 5.5 inches. Worland, near the southern part of the basin, receives 7 to 8 inches; Thermopolis, 11 to 12 inches; and Laramie, in the southeast corner of the state at 7,236 feet, about 10 inches. As an example of how quickly conditions change in the West, Centennial, only thirty miles west of Laramie but at an elevation of 8,074 feet, receives about 16 inches per year. The High Plains area receives about 10 to 15 inches per year, with 9 to 12 inches of that falling during the growing season.

Gardeners along the eastern border below 4,500 feet can expect a growing season of 130 to 150 days. The area from the eastern border to the foothills at elevations of 4,500 to 6,000 feet usually has growing seasons of 100 to 130 days, while elevations of 6,000 to 7,000 feet can experience seasons ranging from 80 to 100 days. Shorter seasons of about 80 days or fewer prevail above 7,000 feet. In some areas frost can occur *every night*. Both hail and wind can cause problems.

The lowlands of eastern Wyoming have some very fertile moist and dry soils but low precipitation and low temperatures limit their usefulness. You can modify these with careful irrigation and season extenders and you will have a great garden.

PUTTING IT ALL TOGETHER

Gardening becomes increasingly more challenging the higher the elevation, and the cool summer nights, short growing seasons, and poor soils make gardening at elevations above 7,000 to 8,000 feet very difficult. Site characteristics vary so widely that you must understand your specific garden conditions, based upon the soils, precipitation, and climatic conditions within a few hundred yards of your garden. Pay close attention to your location and choose your varieties wisely. And remember, following some good neighborly advice will go a long way toward making you a successful gardener.

RESOURCES

Listed below are some resources you might find helpful as you venture along the garden path. Remember, too, that your neighbors and friends can be excellent sources of information, particularly about local conditions. And don't forget about the services that are free, such as university and Extension Service programs.

AGRICULTURAL EXTENSION OFFICES

United States Department of Agriculture
1400 Independence Avenue SW., Stop 2201
Washington, DC 20250-2201
www.csrees.usda.gov/Extension

(Look in your local phone directory under Government listings, County offices for your nearest extension office.)

AMERICAN HORTICULTURE SOCIETY

7931 East Boulevard Drive
Alexandria, VA 22308
Tel: 703-768-5700, (toll free): 800-777-7931
Fax: 703-768-8700
www.ahs.org

AMERICAN PUBLIC GARDENS ASSOCIATION

351 Longwood Road
Kennett Square, PA 19348
Tel 610-708-3010
www.publicgardens.org

THE DROUGHT MONITOR

P.O. Box 830749
Lincoln, NE 68583-0749
Tel: 402-472-6707

Drought monitor map: www.drought.unl.edu/dm/monitor.html

GARDEN CLUBS OF AMERICA

www.gcamerica.org

PLANT SELECT

Colorado State University
1173 Campus Delivery
Fort Collins, CO 80523-1173
Tel: 970-481-3429
Fax: 970-491-7745
www.plantselect.org

UNITED STATES NATIONAL ARBORETUM

3501 New York Avenue, NE
Washington, D. C. 20002-1958
Tel: 202-245-2726

USDA HARDINESS ZONE MAP

www.usna.usda.gov/Hardzone/ushzmap.html

FLAX

BLANKET FLOWER

PLANT NURSERY LOCATOR

MAIL-ORDER PLANT SOURCE

High Country Gardens
2902 Rufina Street
Santa Fe, NM 87507-2929
Tel: 800-925-9387
www.highcountrygardens.com

IDAHO

Idaho Nursery and Landscape Association (INLA)
P.O. Box, 2065
Idaho Falls, ID 83403
Tel: 800-462-4769
www.inlagrow.org

NEVADA

Nurseries and Landscape Association (NLA)
P.O. Box 7431
Reno, NV 89510-7431
Tel: 775-673-0404
www.nevadanla.com

COLORADO

Colorado Nursery and Greenhouse Association
959 S Kipling Pkwy, # 200
Lakewood, CO 80226-3904
Tel: 303-758-6672
www.coloradonga.org/gardener

UTAH

Utah Nursery and Landscape Association
1174 E. 2700 S., #16
Salt Lake City, UT 84106-2678
Tel: 801-484-4426
www.utahgreen.org

MONTANA

Montana Nursery and Landscaping Association
P.O. Box 1366
Bigfork, MT 59911-1366
Tel: 888-220-1569 (toll free)
Local Tel: 406.755.3079
www.plantingmontana.com

WYOMING

Wyoming Nurseries and Garden Centers
www.gardenguides.com/local-nurseries/wy

BIBLIOGRAPHY

Abbott, Marylyn. *Gardens of Plenty: The Art of the Potager Garden*. New Line Books (2004)

Anisko, Thomasz. *When Perennials Bloom: An Almanac for Planning and Planting.* Longwood Gardens (2008)

Austin, Clair and James Waddick. *Irises, A Gardener's Encyclopedia*. Timber Press (2005)

Bartley, Jennifer. *Designing the New Kitchen Garden: An American Potager Handbook*. Timber Press (2006)

Bennett, Jennifer. *Dryland Gardening: Plants that Thrive and Survive in Tough Conditions*. Firefly Books (2005)

Brickell, Christopher. *American Horticulture Society Encyclopedia of Plants and Flowers*. DK ADULT (2002)

Brickell, Christopher. *RHS New Encyclopedia of Plants and Flowers* (RHS). Dorling Kindersley Publishers Ltd. (2008)

Chalker-Scott, Linda. *The Informed Gardener*. University of Washington Press (2008)

Chalker-Scott, Linda. *The Informed Garden Blooms Again*. University of Washington Press (2010)

Creasy, Rosalind. *The Edible Rainbow Garden* (Edible Garden). Periplus Editions (2000)

Cretti, John. *Month-by-Month Gardening in Idaho*. Cool Springs Press (2008)

Cretti, John. *Month-by-Month Gardening in Montana*. Cool Springs Press (2008)

Cretti, John. *Month-by-Month Gardening in the Rocky Mountains*. Cool Springs Press (2005)

Cretti, John. *Month-by-Month Gardening in Utah*. Cool Springs Press (2008)

Cretti, John. *Rocky Mountain Gardener's Guide*. Cool Springs Press (2003)

Darke, Rick. *The Encyclopedia of Grasses for Livable Landscapes*. Timber Press (2007)

DeSabato-Aust, Tracy. *Well Tended Perennial Garden: Planting and Pruning Techniques*. Timber Press (2006)

Druse, Ken. *The Collector's Garden: Designing with Extraordinary Plants*. Clarkson Potter (1996)

Fillipi, Oliver. *The Dry Gardening Handbook: Plants and Practices for Changing a Climate*. Thames & Hudson (2008)

Gough, Robert and Cheryl Moore-Gough. *Rocky Mountain Vegetable Gardening*. Cool Springs Press (2010)

Kuhns, Michael. *A Guide to the Trees of Utah and the Intermountain West*. Utah State University Press (1998)

Lancaster, Brad. *Rainwater Harvesting for Drylands (Vol. 1): Guiding Principles to Welcome Rain into Your Life And Landscape*. Rainsource Press (2006)

Meyer, Susan E., Roger K. Kjelgren, Darrel G. Morrison, William A. Varga, Bettina Schultz. *Landscaping on the New Frontier: Waterwise Design for the Intermountain West*. Utah State University Press (2009)

Miller, Diana. *400 Trees and Shrubs for Small Spaces*. Timber Press (2008)

Morash, Marian. *Victory Garden Cookbook*. Knopf (2010)

Nold, Robert. *High and Dry: Gardening with Cold-Hardy Dryland Plants*. Timber Press (2008)

Ogden, Scott. *Plant-Driven Design: Creating Gardens that Honor Plants, Place and Spirit*. Timber Press (2008)

Oudorf, Piet. *Designing with Plants*. Timber Press (2008)

Pavord, Anna. *Bulb*. Mitchell Beazley (2009)

Phillips, Judith. *Natural by Design: Beauty and Balance in Southwest Gardens* (Paperback). Museum of New Mexico Press (1995)

Plant Select®. *Durable Plants for the Garden*. Fulcrum Publishing (2008)

Quest-Ritson, Charles and Brigid Quest-Ritson. *American Rose Society Encyclopedia of Roses*. American Rose Society

Rice, Graham. *RHS Encyclopedia of Perennials* (Hardcover). Dorling Kindersley Publishers Ltd (2006)

Robb, James J., William E. Riebsame, and Boulder Center of American West University of Colorado. *Atlas of the New West: Portrait of a Changing Region*. W. W. Norton & Company (1997)

Roberts, Johnathan. *The Origins of Fruits and Vegetables*. Universe Publishing (2001)

Solomon, Steve. *Gardening When It Counts Growing Food in Hard Times* (Mother Earth News Wiser Living Series). New Society Publishers (2006)

Springer Ogden, Lauren. *The Undaunted Garden: Planting for Weather Resilient Beauty*. Fulcrum Publishing (2011)

Tatroe, Marcia and Charles Mann. *Cutting Edge Gardening in the Intermountain West*. Johnson Books (2007)

Tannehill, Celia and James E. Klett. *Best Perennials for the Rocky Mountains and High Plains*. Colorado State University Publications (2002)

Thomas, Graham S. *The Graham Stuart Thomas Rose Book: Enlarged and Thoroughly Revised*. Frances Lincoln (2004)

Woodward, Joan. *Waterstained Landscapes: Seeing and Shaping Regionally Distinctive Places* (Center Books on Contemporary Landscape Design). The Johns Hopkins University Press (1999)

GLOSSARY

AERATION: A term to describe methods of introducing air movement into compacted or tight soils.

ALKALINE SOIL: Soil having the properties of a high pH above the neutral rating of 7.0.

AMENDMENT: Material added to soil that helps improve drainage, moisture-holding capacity, or nutrient-holding capabilities.

ANNUAL: A plant that starts from seed, flowers, and produces seed to complete its life cycle in one growing season.

BACKFILL SOIL: Soil removed from the planting hole that is returned to the hole during the process of planting.

BALLED AND BURLAPPED: A method of wrapping the rootball of a large tree or shrub with burlap, rope, twine, and wire basket so that the plant can be brought to the nursery or transported to the planting site.

BARE-ROOT PLANT: A plant harvested without soil around the roots. This is done in the early spring or fall.

BIENNIAL: A plant that has a two-year life cycle. The first year it grows from seed and produces foliage. During the second year, it resumes foliage growth, blooms, develops seeds, and dies.

BLEEDERS: A term used to describe trees that drip sap from a pruning cut or wound; especially trees such as maple, birch, cottonwood, aspen, and walnut.

BLOOM: 1. The flower of a plant. 2. The bluish gray coating on evergreen needles, fruit, or foliage that can be wiped off or removed by certain pesticide sprays.

BRACT: A modified leaf at the base of a flower or flower clusters.

BROADLEAF WEED: A weed having flattened, broad leaves, as distinguished from thin, grasslike foliage.

BULB: A horticultural term for an underground leaf bud with fleshy scales; the tulip and onion are true bulbs. The term is often used to include corms, tubers, and thickened rhizomes.

CALCAREOUS SOIL: A soil that is alkaline because of the high amounts of calcium carbonate.

CANOPY: The height and width of a tree's branch area.

CHLOROSIS: A condition when plants develop a yellowing of otherwise normal green foliage.

COMPACTION: The compression of soil particles, collapsing air spaces in between.

COMPOST: A mixture of decomposing and decomposed organic waste materials that have been layered in a pile, turned periodically to hasten decomposition, and used to condition garden soil. It provides a source of humus and slow-release nutrients.

CORM: A solid, bulblike underground stem, such as crocus and gladiolus.

CROWN: 1. The highest portion of a tree. 2. The point on a herbaceous plant where stem and root meet.

CULTIVAR: A variety or strain of a plant that has originated and persisted under cultivation. Cultivars are given a specific name, usually distinguished by single quotation marks, as in *Acer rubrum* 'Autumn Blaze'.

CYME: A more or less flat-topped flower.

DEADHEADING: Removing dead or spent flower heads from flowering plants. Regular deadheading prevents seed formation, tidies the garden, and encourages prolonged blooming in many plants.

DECIDUOUS: A term used to describe plants that shed their leaves during the fall.

DIVISION: A method of propagation that involves cutting apart or separating root and crown clumps of perennials to create several new plants from the mother plant.

DORMANT: The resting period in a plant's life cycle when no growth occurs.

DRIP LINE: The imaginary line at ground level where water dripping from the outermost branches of a tree or shrub will fall.

ESTABLISHMENT: Refers to a plant's acclimation after transplanting. Often refers to the time before a plant reaches its drought-resistance potential. A typical establishment period takes a full growing season, but some plants take several years.

ESTABLISHMENT WATERING: Providing supplemental water during the stages of transplanting and establishing a plant before it can grow on its own with less frequent irrigation or natural precipitation.

FIREBLIGHT: A bacterial disease that infects the tips of the branches and progresses toward the trunk; infects some varieties of crabapples, apples, pears, and mountain ashes. Symptoms appear as if the foliage has been scorched.

FROG-EYE SPRINKLER: One of the oldest and best sprinklers that delivers water with coarse droplets and in a low arc so there is little waste from evaporation. Also known as the twin-eye sprinkler.

FROST CRACKS: The splits, fissures, or hairline cracks in the bark of a tree's trunk or branches caused from temperature fluctuations and winter desiccation.

GALL: A swollen growth caused by insects or fungus that can occur on the stems, branches, and foliage. Most are generally harmless and may be pruned out.

GERMINATE: The term used to describe a seed sprouting.

GRAFT UNION: The point on the stem of a woody plant where a stem from another desirable ornamental plant is grafted or inserted into the roots of a hardier plant. Hybrid tea roses are commonly grafted.

GROWING SEASON: The period between the last frost in spring and the first frost of autumn; the time when plants can grow without danger of frost.

GROUND COVER: A plant that grows by spreading or trailing to cover or carpet an expanse of soil. Although most ground covers are low growing, including lawn grasses and woolly thyme, taller plants of spreading habit, such as ornamental grasses and cotoneaster, can also be used for this purpose.

HARDENING OFF: A process by which transplants started indoors are gradually acclimatized to outdoor conditions before they are permanently transplanted to the outdoor garden.

HARDPAN: A layer of hard soil or ground that impedes the downward movement of water.

HARDY: The ability of a plant to grow in a specific area and survive low temperatures without protection.

HEAVING: The lifting or shifting of the plant crown caused by the repeated freezing and thawing of the soil.

HEELING IN: A technique of temporarily planting in a protected spot until the plants can be transplanted. The roots are protected from drying by covering with loose soil or a loose organic mulch.

HELLSTRIP: A term used to describe the area between the street and sidewalk that is traditionally planted with grass and trees.

HERBACEOUS: A plant whose aboveground parts are not hardy that will die back to the ground each winter.

HOLDFAST: A rootlike structure by which a plant clings to a wall or other structures.

HUMUS: The well-decomposed, fertile, and stable part of organic matter in the soil.

INORGANIC MULCH: Inert material used to cover the ground, including gravel, cobblestone, plastic, and synthetic fabrics.

ISLAND BED: A free-standing garden bed that can be viewed and maintained from all sides.

LAYERING: A method of starting plants by bending and securing a stem to the soil; roots and shoots then form along this stem to produce a new plant. Once the roots are established, the shoot is cut from the parent plant and transplanted.

LEAN SOIL: Soil lacking in organic matter and nutrients. Some plants, such as blue grama grass, saltbush, and mountain mahogany, do best in lean rather than rich soils.

LIMBING UP: A type of pruning in which the lower limbs are removed from a tree. Often referred to as "skirting," specifically, for evergreen trees.

LOAM: Medium-textured soil that contains a balanced mix of sand, silt, clay, and organic matter; also known as the "ideal soil."

MICROCLIMATE: The environmental conditions of a localized area that differ from the overall climate of the area, such as near a building, between large boulders, under a tree, or at the top of a hill.

MULCH: Any of the various organic and inorganic materials used to cover the soil to prevent moisture loss, discourage weed growth, maintain soil temperature, and reduce soil cultivation. Verb: To spread mulch around the root zone of plants or over the soil.

MYCORRHIZAE: Special fungi that live in and around plant roots and perform in symbiosis with plants to help extract water and nutrients from the soil.

NATIVE PLANTS: Species indigenous to the region or of local origin. They have adapted to specific environments and geographic regions and are best equipped to tolerate the regional climate and local weather conditions.

NATURALIZE: A technique of establishing plants in the landscape so that they adapt, grow, and spread unaided as though they were native, such as naturalizing daffodils.

PINCHING BACK: Removing the growing tips of plants using the thumb and forefinger. This stimulates plants to grow bushier and more compact.

PERENNIAL: A plant that continues to live from year to year. A short-lived perennial refers to a plant that may live three to five years; a long-lived perennial is likely to live indefinitely.

PH: The measure of the soil's acidity or alkalinity on a scale with a value of 7.0 representing neutral; the lower numbers indicate increasing acidity and the higher numbers increasing alkalinity.

PLANT STRESS: A disruption in normal plant growth generally caused by poor physiological or environmental conditions or insect, disease, or wildlife invasion.

POLE PEELINGS: An organic mulch made when branches, stems, and other woody byproducts are run through a grinder or wood chipper. The thin wood slivers that result will knit together so as not to blow away.

RHIZOME: A thickened underground stem or root that produces shoots above and roots below. Examples include bearded iris and bluegrass.

SALINE SOIL: A soil that contains a high level of soluble salts and can be injurious for plant growth.

SLOW-RELEASE FERTILIZER: Natural or synthetic materials that require microbial, chemical, or physical breakdown to become available to plants.

ROOT ZONE: The area in which the plant's roots are growing and expanding.

SCARIFICATION: Breaking the seed coat, such as by filing, to hasten seed germination.

SIDE DRESS: To work fertilizer into the soil around the root zone of a plant. Also, to spread mulch around the bases of plants.

SOIL DRAINAGE: The rate at which water can move through the soil profile.

STOLON: A horizontal stem that grows along the ground or just below the surface and roots along its nodes or tip, giving rise to new plants; an example is the strawberry.

SUCKER: A soft, fast-growing shoot that originates from the base of a tree trunk, on limbs, or from roots.

TRANSLOCATION: The movement of water, minerals, and nutrients within a plant.

TUBER: A short, thickened underground organ, usually, but not always, a stem. Tubers bear buds, or eyes, from which new shoots and roots develop. Dahlia is an example.

WATERLOGGED: A soil so saturated with water that it has poor aeration and is not conducive to healthy root growth.

WATERING IN: The technique of watering plants after planting to ensure soil and root contact for the plant's establishment.

WHORL: The arrangement of several leaves, flowers, or other organs around a common growth point or node.

XERISCAPE™: A term used to describe a dry or desertlike (xeric) view or scene (scape); coined in 1981 by the Associated Landscape Contractors of Colorado to promote water conservation through water-efficient landscaping.

ZONE: An area used to describe a plant's hardiness restricted by a range of annual average minimum temperatures.

GARDEN VEGETABLE PLANTING GUIDE

Crop	Days to maturity (range)	Seeds/plants per 100 ft. row	Planting depth (inches)	Spacing in row (inches)
VERY HARDY TO HARDY[1]				
Asparagus	Perennial	65 plants	plants, 10	18
Beet	60–65	1 oz.	1	2–3
Cabbage	60–70	50 plants		20–24
Carrot	65–70	½ oz.	½	2–3
Chard, Swiss	50	½ oz.	1	12
Chives	Perennial			12–18
Endive	65	½ oz.	½	8
Horseradish	Perennial			18
Jerusalem Artichoke	Perennial	65 plants	2–3	18
Kale	50–55	¼ oz.	½	18
Lettuce, Leaf	40–45	¼ oz.	½	3–6
Lettuce, Head	70–80	¼ oz.	½	12
Onion, Bulb	100	300 transplants		4
Onion, Bunching	60–80	½ oz.		1
Parsnip	85–120	½ oz.	½	3–4
Peas (fresh)	50–65	½ oz.	1½	2
Rhubarb	Perennial	30 plants		30
Rutabaga	90	¼ oz.	½	6
Turnip	50–60	½ oz.	½	3
HALF HARDY[2]				
Broccoli	70	50 plants		18
Brussels Sprouts	90–100	50 plants		18–24
Cauliflower	50–55	50 plants		18
Celery	85–100	200 plants		4–8
Chinese Cabbage	70	¼ oz.	¾	10–12
Kohlrabi	55	½ oz.	1	4–6
Parsley	70	½ oz.	¾	6
Potato	80–120	12 lbs.	4	10–20
Radish	20–30	1 oz.	½	1

Spacing between rows (inches)	Average yield per 10 ft. row*	Germination temperature	
		Minimum °F	Optimum °F
40–48	6 plants		
18	4 lb. greens 10 lb. roots	40	50–85
30	8 lb.	Transplants	
18	10 lb.	40	45–85
24–30	10 plants	40	50–85
8–10	10 plants	Plant division	
18	8 heads	35	40–80
18	varies	Plant division	
24	varies	Plant tubers	
24	7 lbs.	40	45–85
12–18	5 lbs.	35	40–80
18	10 heads	45	40–80
18	10 lbs.	Sets or plants	
12	10 lbs.	Plants	
18	7 lbs.	35	50–70
18–30	2 lbs.	40	40–75
40–48	4 plants	Crown division	
18	15 lbs.	40	55–80
18	5 lb. roots	40	60–105
30	7 lbs.	Transplants	
24–30	5 lbs.	Transplants	
30	8 lbs.	Transplants	
30–36	10 plants	Transplants	
24–36	6 heads	Transplants	
18	5 lbs.	40	45–85
18	varies	40	50–84
36–40	varies	Seed pieces from tubers	
12–18	10 bunches	40	45–90

GARDEN VEGETABLE PLANTING GUIDE

Crop	Days to maturity (range)	Seeds/plants per 100 ft. row	Planting depth (inches)	Spacing in row (inches)
WARM SEASON[3]				
Beans, Bush	45–50	½ lb.	2	4
Beans, Pole	60–65	½ lb.	2	4
Corn, Sweet	65–80	¼ lb.	2	12–36
Cucumber	50–00	½ oz.	¾	36–48
Eggplant	60–80	65 plants	½	18
Muskmelon or Cantaloupe	85–120	½ oz.	1–2	3–6
Okra	55–65	¼ oz.	½	12–15
Pepper	70–80	80 plants		15
Pumpkin	100	1 oz.	½	48
Squash, Summer	55–65	1 oz.	1	40–50
Squash, Winter	55–105	1 oz.	1	40–50
Tomato	60–85	40 plants	1	30
Watermelon	100–130	¾ oz.	1–2	72–96

[1] These vegetables survive hard frosts and can be planted 2–3 weeks before the average date of the last 32-degree temperature in spring.

[2] These vegetables withstand light frosts and their seeds germinate at low soil temperatures. Plant them 2 weeks before the average date of the last 32-degree temperature in spring.

[3] These vegetables do not withstand frost and their seeds will not germinate in cold soil. Plant them at about the average date of the last 32-degree temperature.

* Yields will vary with local conditions.

Spacing between rows (inches)	Average yield per 10 ft. row*	Germination temperature	
		Minimum °F	Optimum °F
18–24	8 lbs.	60	60–85
18–24	15 lbs.	60	60–85
36	10 ears	50	50–95
40–48	12 lbs.	60	60–95
25	7 lbs.	Transplants	
48–84	10 fruits	60	75–95
38	varies	60	70–95
24	5 lbs.	Transplants	
48–60	25 lbs.	60	70–95
48–60	20 lbs.	60	70–95
48–72	15 lbs.	60	70–95
36–40	15 lbs.	Transplants	
72–96	7 fruits.	60	70–95

PHOTOGRAPHY CREDITS

Cool Springs Press would like to thank the following contributors to *Rocky Mountain Gardener's Handbook*.

André Viette: 92, 102, 104c, 113c, 147b, 162, 189b, 204

Charles Mann: 6, 33c, 38c, 77b, 96c, 120c, 145b, 149a, 150b, 154c, 155c, 176b, 200, 215, 217

Cathy Barash: 45

David Cavagnaro: 42 and 233

David Winger: 169a and 179a

Ed Rode: 47, 48, 70

Fairegarden: 37b

Flower Fields: 196 and 202

iStockphoto.com/Marek Mierzejewski: 220

John Cretti: 111a and 113c

Jerry Pavia: 15b, 16ac, 17b, 19a, 20a, 21b, 22ab, 23a, 25b, 28, 31, 34c, 35b, 76c, 77a, 95b, 96b, 90, 123, 103c, 106c, 107c, 111b,c, 113a, 114c, 115a, 118a, 119c, 126, 127, 129, 133b, 135b, 136a, 137ab, 130, 146ab, 147c, 148b, 154a, 157a, 171c, 173a, 174ab, 177c, 178a, 187, 188, 189c, 190b, 192b, 222

John Pohly: 176b

Judy Mielke: 93b, 94a, and 169b

Lorenzo Gunn: 52b

Liz Ball: 21c, 34a, 66a, 76a, 78b, 80b, 148c, 152a, 156bc, 166, 170a, 172c, 173c, 178c, 192c

Dr. Michael Dirr: 176a, and 191c

Mary Ann Newcomer: 7, 10, 11, 17a, 20b, 24ac, 35ac, 36c, 38a, 50c, 52a, 53ac, 65b, 81, 75ab, 77c, 78a, 79ab, 94bc, 100, 125, 104a, 105ac, 107b, 109a, 110c, 112ac, 113a, 114c, 115b, 116abc, 117ab, 120b,145ac, 147a, 149bc, 151b, 152c, 153b, 154b, 155b, 170b, 171a, 174c, 180ab, 188, 190a, 191b, 198, 199, 205, 206, 207, 208, 209, 210, 211, 212, 213, 214, 218, 240, 244, 245

Neil Soderstrom: 134 and 225

Katie Elzer-Peters: 15c, 24b, and 155a

Pegi Ballister-Howells: 33b

Pam Harper: 96a, 117c, 171b, 173b, 181, and 190c

Peter Loewer: 86, 89, and 106c

Ralph Snodsmith: 150c, 152b, and 224

Scott Millard: 122a

Tom Eltzroth: 15a, 16b, 17c, 18abc, 19c, 20c, 21a, 22c, 23bc, 25a, 32, 33c, 36a, 37ac, 39ab, 49ac, 50ab, 51bc, 52c, 53b, 54abc, 55abc, 56abc, 57abc, 58abc, 59abc, 60abc, 61abc, 62abc, 63abc, 64abc, 65ac, 66bc, 67abc, 68abc, 69ab, 72, 74, 75c, 76b, 78b, 80a, 84, 92, 93c, 95ac, 97ab, 103ab, 104c, 105b, 106a, 107a, 108abc, 109bc, 110b, 112b, 115c, 118bc, 119b, 120a, 121abc, 122bc, 132, 132a, 135b, 136a, 140, 143, 144, 146c, 148a, 150a, 151ac, 154a, 156a, 157b, 160, 168, 169c, 170c, 172b, 175abc, 177ab, 178c, 179b, 191a, 192a, 211

© Lou-Foto/Alamy: 51a

Danian Palus/Shutterstock.com: 33a

Kirschner/Shutterstock.com: 36b

Martin Fowler/Shutterstock.com: 38b

Sixinepixels/Shutterstock.com: 228

Imageegami/Shutterstock.com: 230

Alta Oosthuizen/Shutterstock.com: 237

INDEX

LATIN INDEX

MEET JOHN CRETTI

John Cretti is known regionally and nationally as the Rocky Mountain and High Plain's horticulturist who is the long time host of the award-winning "Gardening with an ALTITUDE" radio and television programs. As a former home horticulture specialist for Colorado State University, John is an author, lecturer, award-winning garden communicator, and, above all, down-to-earth gardener. John is the regional editor for the Rocky Mountain region at www.garden.org (National Gardening Association) and contributes to various other websites.

John has spent his life growing plants, beginning as a child under the tutelage of his Italian grandmother, aunts and uncle. This inspired his interest and passion for gardening while growing up in Western Colorado.

John takes gardening to a different level, where there's an active relationship between man, environment, and plants: "To grow plants successfully, you have to think like a plant."

He has published hundreds of articles and features for garden magazines including *Flower and Garden*, *Horticulture*, *Colorado and Boulder County Home & Garden*, *Green Thumb Extra*, *Garden Talk*, and the *Rocky Mountain News*.

Gardeners who live in the unique and challenging climate of the Rocky Mountain region, where fluctuations of temperatures, wind, hail, lousy soil conditions, cunning critters, and unpredictable storms are the norm, will benefit from the practical wit and wisdom that John serves up. Many tricks and remedies that John recommends come from his degree in the horticultural sciences from Colorado State University and from his Italian grandmother who taught him old-fashioned remedies for pests and diseases that are still effective today.

John's passion for home horticulture has not gone unnoticed. He has received numerous awards, including the prestigious Award of Excellence and Quill and Trowel Awards from the Garden Writers' Association, the Scotts' Horticultural Professional Improvement Award for lawn and garden communications, and the National Association of County Agricultural Agents Award of Excellence in Horticulture Communications. He also was recognized for outstanding community service for garden and education programs by Xeriscape Colorado.

MEET MARY ANN NEWCOMER

Mary Ann Newcomer, scribe-scout-and-speaker blogs at www.gardensofthewildwildwest.com. Named one of the top garden blogs in the country by Horticulture Magazine, it's where she shares her wit, wisdom and garden adventures in the American West. She appears regularly as the Dirt Diva on the River Radio, 94.9 in Boise, ID. Her articles on gardening have been published in *MaryJane's Farm, Fine Gardening,* and *The American Gardener.* An accomplished horticulturalist, garden designer and former President of the Idaho Botanical Garden, she has wielded her creative and design talents on public, private and commercial gardens, and landscapes. She is always tweaking her wild and colorful garden in Boise, where she resides with her husband, Delos, and their Springer spaniel, Cash. She is a member of the Garden Writers Association.

GARDEN NOTES

GARDEN NOTES

GARDEN NOTES